JOHN MERROW

Below C Level

How American Education Encourages Mediocrity - and What We Can Do about It

ISBN: 1-4505-0353-5
ISBN-13: 9781450503532
LCCN: 2010902318

This book is dedicated to the memory of
Theodore R. Sizer and William E. McAnulty Jr.,
whose lives represent what is best in America.
Their vision, strength and belief in justice continue to contribute.

CONTENTS

ALSO BY JOHN MERROW

Choosing Excellence: "Good Enough" Schools Are Not Good Enough (2001)

Declining by Degrees: Higher Education at Risk (edited with Richard Hersh, 2005)

Preface

i

Shortly after I went to work for "The MacNeil/Lehrer News-Hour" in 1985, Robin MacNeil took me to lunch. While I don't remember where we ate, I've never forgotten a piece of advice Robin offered. Good ideas are rare, he said. Whenever you have one, use it in as many ways as you can. Produce a piece for us, write an op-ed or an article, and put it in a book.

The book you are holding indicates that I took Robin's good counsel to heart. Most of its chapters began as stories for the News-Hour or as opinion pieces for a newspaper. A few chapters grew out of events in my life, most notably a reunion of students I taught in high school in the late 1960s. A few others started as NewsHour stories, became op-ed pieces, morphed into posts for my weekly blog, Taking Note, and subsequently were deepened and improved by readers' comments. Welcome to the brave new world of interactive book writing!

I wish I'd received Robin's advice earlier (or had figured it out on my own) because I might have written something worthwhile about the reporting I was doing along the way. In 1977 I became the first National Public Radio reporter to get into China when I snuck in as a tourist with a group of Canadians, but I never wrote about it. In 1981 I spent three months in juvenile prisons but didn't write about it.[1] In 1980 I spent several months in mental hospitals for children and juveniles[2] but didn't think to write about it. I bonded with book burners in West Virginia in 1975 and reported on the plight of gay kids and gay teachers in 1976, but, again, wrote nothing. I probably should have written about getting the two presidents of the warring teachers unions[3] into the same studio for a radio debate in the mid-1970s, but I didn't do that either.

ii

In "Choosing Excellence," I argued that change was possible, even probable, as long as enough educators, politicians and parents believed in excellence and opportunities and were willing to work smart and hard to improve our country's education system. Further, I believed that this group could, with determination, overcome the system's inertia and its enemies.

I was wrong. I now understand that improving education in our country is a more complicated challenge. I realize that we must also confront and defeat those who benefit from the failure, inefficiency, waste, selfishness and corruption that seem endemic to our education system. Thus the title of this book, which represents a journey[4] through the landscape of education, over time and through the eyes of a veteran reporter.

"Choosing Excellence" had what is known as a TV tie-in—a program we called "School Sleuth: The Case of an Excellent School."[5] That program won the George Foster Peabody Award, broadcasting's highest honor, and was seen by about 10,000,000 people. My book sold fewer than 10,000 copies.

This new book has an Internet tie-in. Many of the essays link directly to my reporting, and if you're interested, you can watch those pieces (including "School Sleuth") online at www.belowClevel. org and www.learningmatters.tv. You'll also be able to access our NewsHour reports at www.pbs.org/newshour.

The title "Below C Level" intentionally echoes a phrase from "A Nation at Risk,"[6] the 1983 report that galvanized our nation. That seminal publication warned of "a rising tide of mediocrity" in our schools, one that continues to threaten our nation's future.[7] The solution, however, does not lie in another common expression—"a rising tide lifts all boats"—because the tide itself is the problem. Nor can we survive and prosper by manning the lifeboats; that approach saves only a few.

Schools are at the proverbial crossroads. Think of it this way: Just a few years ago, children went to schools (and libraries) to gain access to knowledge, but today knowledge is everywhere, thanks to technology and the Internet. So why should kids go to school?

Just a few years ago, children went to school to socialize and be socialized, but today there's an app for that. Kids have Facebook, FarmVille, MySpace, Twitter and other powerful social media, so why should they go to school?

I am asking the question, "Is school obsolete?" And my answer is, essentially, "No, but..."

As I will argue, many adults want schools to keep an eye on their children, and keep them safe. Those are not good enough reasons from a kid's perspective. I believe that effective schools must teach kids how to evaluate knowledge, how to separate the wheat from the chaff—and how to choose the wheat.

Yes, schools must teach values. Effective schools must slow the world down and enable students to dig deeply into issues while learning basic skills and truths, so that they will be able to function easily in the fast-changing world outside.

Good teachers will be like music conductors, but the music won't be classical. It will be jazz, full of riffs and tangents, and changing from performance to performance. Teaching will be tougher but infinitely more rewarding in these schools—if we are smart enough to build them.

American education cannot thrive without the participation and support of the larger public, beyond the 20 to 30 percent of households with school-age children. What's essential is a campaign that will remind us of the *crucial* role of our schools, and of their importance in a functioning democracy. To be sure, our schools exist to provide educational opportunities[8] for individual students, but they also help to unify us as a nation. The best American schools remind us of our common purposes while teaching the value of differences.

John Merrow

iii

I have been reporting about education for NPR and PBS since 1974. I've visited every state and a dozen countries. I've gone beyond the boundaries of the schoolyard to report on prenatal care, re-education for jobless adults, the "learning" that occurs in prisons, and other issues involving young people.

While much of my reporting has focused on uncovering malfeasance and other misbehaviors—such as corruption in charter and alternative schools, the creation of a man-made "epidemic" of attention deficit disorder, influence-buying by educational publishers, and misdiagnoses in special education—my reporting has also illuminated the accomplishments of dedicated educators and community leaders.

Please keep reading to discover why I believe we suffer from *affection* deficit disorder when it comes to caring for other people's children, why I believe educators who complain about "the lack of parental involvement" are copping out, how community colleges are the country's unsung heroes, and why our failure to enable all first-graders to read with comprehension is both financially crippling and morally offensive. And that's just for starters.

I will be disappointed if some of what follows does *not* make you angry. However, you will also encounter recipes for improvement and stories of success that I believe can and should be replicated.

Acknowledgments

The list of those who have helped me professionally includes Sam Halperin, my boss at the Institute for Educational Leadership who encouraged me to take a shot at radio back in 1974; Mike Usdan, George Kaplan and Betty Hale, also of IEL; "Doc" Howe, Ed Meade and Alison Bernstein of the Ford Foundation; Jim Russell, Midge Hart, Barney Quinn, Marcia Witten, Wendy Blair and Barbara Schelstrate at National Public Radio; Fred Rogers of "Mister Rogers' Neighborhood"; Marian Wright Edelman of the Children's Defense Fund; Albert Shanker of the American Federation of Teachers; Frank Newman of the Education Commission of the States; Doug Bodwell of the Corporation for Public Broadcasting; Linda Winslow, Robin MacNeil, Jim Lehrer, Joe Quinlan, Mike Joseloff, Tim Smith, Murrey Jacobson and Les Crystal of "PBS NewsHour"; Ted Sizer, Paul Ylvisaker, Mike Smith, Jay Featherstone, Larry Aaronson and David Cohen at the Harvard Graduate School of Education; Tony Cipollone of the Annie E. Casey Foundation; Vartan Gregorian, Avery Russell, Michael Levine, Dan Fallon and Susan King of Carnegie Corporation of New York; Anne Petersen of the W. K. Kellogg Foundation; Joan Lipsitz of the Lilly Endowment; Patricia Albjerg Graham at the National Institute of Education; Angela Covert and Joel Fleishman at the Atlantic Philanthropies (back when it was still a secret); Sophie Sa of the Panasonic Foundation (who told me that there was a secret foundation); Arthur Levine, Susan Fuhrman, John Rosenwald and Joe Brosnan of Teachers College, Columbia University; William E. McAnulty Jr. of the Kentucky Supreme Court, who was the founding Board chair of Learning Matters; Rob Shuman of Maryland Public Television; Walter and Lenore Annenberg, Wallis Annenberg, Gail Levin and Scott Roberts of the Annenberg Foundation; Ray Bacchetti, Gay

Clyburn, Tom Ehrlich, Tony Bryk and Lee Shulman at the Carnegie Foundation for the Advancement of Teaching; Bill Pauley of Toyota, our corporate underwriter from 1997-2002; Arnold Packer, E. D. Hirsch Jr., Deborah Meier, Linda Darling-Hammond, David Tyack, Lisa Walker, David Hornbeck, Ted Kolderie, Joe Nathan, Bob Frye, Jim Kelly and Dick Beattie; and the Board of Directors of Learning Matters, including Josh Kaufman, Sandy Welch, Karen Hein, Jerry Murphy, Bobbi Kamil, Wendy Puriefoy, Ginnie Edwards, Tania Brief, Bill Kelly and BJ Fogg.

While I have had dozens of remarkable colleagues at Learning Matters, none has meant more to me than John Tulenko. JT and I began working together in 1992—before there was a Learning Matters—and have collaborated on many memorable productions.

Special thanks to the high school students at Castilleja School and Palo Alto High School, and their teachers, Helen Shanks and Esther Wojcicki, for participating in a contest to design the book's cover. They made my choice—a design by Castilleja sophomore Caitlin Colvin—an exceptionally difficult one. Kudos as well to the talented runners-up: Palo Alto High School junior Lillian Xie and Castilleja students Emily Hayflick, '11, and Camille Stroe, '12.

Ben Harrison created the wonderful line drawings on the section header pages.

Kristen Garabedian provided invaluable creativity, research and editorial assistance with this manuscript. Any errors and omissions, however, are my responsibility, not hers.

And, finally, Joan Lonergan is a constant source of inspiration, ideas, support and affection. As the African proverb has it, because she is, I am.

Introduction

In 1983, "A Nation at Risk" warned of "a rising tide of mediocrity" in public education. I believe the tide of mediocrity continues to rise and that, more than a quarter of a century later, our nation is at greater risk. This disaster is largely man-made. Like the destruction of much of New Orleans in 2005 after Hurricane Katrina and the flooding, it was preventable. We are doing this to ourselves.

It's not that some haven't been bailing. We have, often valiantly and sometimes with success. All levels of government, foundations and individuals have spent billions trying to plug leaks. But, to borrow an image from Lou Gerstner, not enough people have built arks; others have been predicting rain and even punching holes in the dike. Why? Because the status quo—despite the damage it is doing to millions of children and to our democracy—is to their advantage. They're comfortable with things as they are. Some may even be getting rich.

A bit of history: In 1965, President Lyndon B. Johnson signed the Elementary and Secondary Education Act into law. Title I of that act created a massive federal program to aid the education of disadvantaged children. Apparently, chicanery and deception began almost immediately. School districts were supposed to use the new money to *supplement* programs for poor kids, but many used it to *supplant*, that is, to replace their own dollars. Others used the money for selfish ends: a new swimming pool, perhaps, or programs for the already well-off.

In hindsight, that was the beginning of a pattern that continues today: Washington trying and failing to get local districts and states to behave as Washington believes they should, and schools and districts putting their own (adult and financial) interests ahead of learning opportunities for students. Defenders of the status quo talk about "local control," while others speak of the rights of minorities, the disadvantaged, and people with disabilities. I think at its core, however, it's about power.

Title I of ESEA[9] sent federal dollars to high-poverty districts, year after year, based on the number of poor kids doing poorly. Although everyone was aware that the receiving districts had minimal incentive to improve education, and in fact could actually lose money if they got better, no one had the stomach to cut off money to districts that did not improve, largely because they didn't want to be portrayed as hurting poor children.

In President Clinton's two terms, Education Secretary Richard Riley and Undersecretary Marshall Smith tried to persuade Congress to set opportunity-to-learn[10] standards. The goal was a level playing field in terms of facilities, books, teachers and other input measures, but the states would have none of that, probably because it would have set real and measurable standards that they could be held accountable for achieving.[11]

President George W. Bush and a bipartisan coalition in Congress decided on a radical step. No longer would federal rules apply only to disadvantaged students. A new law, the direct descendant of ESEA's Title I, would apply to *all* students. From here on, every student counted, every student would be tested, and therefore no child would be left behind. And the law, called No Child Left Behind,[12] demanded that every child be at grade level by 2014.

Moreover, test scores could no longer be aggregated and presented as a single unit. The law required that scores of subgroups (Latinos, children with disabilities, etc.) be reported separately.

Failure to make what NCLB called "Adequate Yearly Progress"[13] would result in sanctions, which could include closing schools and firing all the adults.[14] In a stroke of the pen, the federal government became the primary rule-maker for public education, despite providing less than 9 percent of the money. No more free money, but real accountability.

That was the stated purpose. However, this dramatic action produced a host of unintended—but probably inevitable—consequences, given the pattern of evasion and deception established since ESEA. States and districts immediately began searching for loopholes in NCLB. There were almost too many to count.[15]

The ensuing years of NCLB's intense federal involvement in public education have shown that Washington's solutions are just as ineffective as all the other magic bullets that education is drawn to.

The argument of several essays in this book is straightforward: A web of "convenient lies" keeps public education from the dramatic changes that our times call for. The deceptions, untruths, half-truths and inertia are stifling promising reforms and misleading the public about the true nature of our situation. Moreover, many people and organizations actually *benefit* from the status quo. That is, mediocrity pays.

Because the damage is man-made, the situation can change. Regrettably, only *some* of the damage can be undone. Much human potential has been, and is being, wasted.

The solutions are neither simple nor easy, because radical steps are needed to save public education. "School improvement," "turnaround specialists," "weighted student formulas" and other silver bullets will not be enough. The solutions require hard work, commitment, money and time—but not patience. I think it's time to be impatient, to be mad as hell and not willing to take it anymore.

We also need to make sure we are asking the right questions.[16] As I will argue later in this book, our narrow focus on test scores and the "achievement gap" is a result of our not asking essential questions about the purposes of school and the fundamental difference between education and schooling. It's worth recalling Einstein's observation: "The formulation of the problem is often more important than the solution."[17]

John Merrow

We've been in denial for too long. Now, with the economy in tatters, education needs retooling.[18] It's past time for education at all levels to embrace the revolution in productivity and find ways to use technology and new teaching techniques to improve learning (and perhaps lower costs).

Three big steps to start:

1. Deal with a persistent contradiction in American society: The public consistently denigrates public education generally (a grade of C- or D on Gallup polls, for example) but then gives its own local public schools grades of B+ or A-.[19] This logical fallacy stands in the way of innovation, because in education, change occurs at the local level. As long as the general public believes that its own local schools are fine—despite evidence to the contrary—little will change.

2. Abandon our fantasy that a magic solution exists just around the corner. Our fixation on instant cures is actually part of the problem.

3. Be part of the truth telling. It's time to name those who are benefiting from the convenient lies about education.

No Child Left Behind strikes me in some ways as the biggest lie of all. While it has helped by requiring that all children be taught and tested and by shining the spotlight on teacher quality, this under-funded and overly prescriptive legislation has debased the curriculum and reduced the school experience for many poor children to incessant drilling. The combination of unreachable goals (all children at grade level by 2014) and obvious loopholes has invited deception, which in turn has bred cynicism. That, I believe, has led to a loss of faith in public education. The Obama administration raised some hopes when it turned its back on the law very publicly in January and introduced its own proposal in March 2010.[20]

However, until Congress writes a new version of No Child Left Behind, it remains the law of the land,[21] and cynicism abounds.

ii

This volume consists of five sections, organized in what I hope is a useful manner.

"Follow the Money" presents the basic argument of this book in eight chapters.

"Follow the Leader" introduces (or reintroduces) some of the education leaders I've been privileged to spend time—often years—with.

The chapters that make up "Follow the Teacher" are generally optimistic in tone and content. They are largely concerned with what goes on inside classrooms and schools.

The chapters in "Wheat from Chaff" are, I believe, full of common sense and hope for the future.

"After High School" jumps the pre-K-12 fence to focus on higher education and includes "My College Education" and "Unsung Heroes."

The Obama administration has signaled its intentions to change business as usual. What remains to be seen is whether the Washington Democrats will give the states back their power, which the Bush administration took for itself under No Child Left Behind. Does anyone ever give up power willingly? Will states attempt to assert themselves?

Other questions will be answered in the immediate future: What will happen to the emerging movement to create national or common standards[22] and tests? Will the early education community (think *pre*-preschool) clash with supporters of preschool, or will there be enough money to support programs for 4-year-olds *and* programs for children under 4? Will colleges and universities con-

John Merrow

tinue with business as usual and spend their share of the stimulus package(s) in the same old ways, or will they seek to innovate and cut costs? What will be done about student debt, now threatening to cripple a generation of graduates?

My hopes and suggestions are set forth in a final chapter: "A '12-Step Program' to Fix American Education."

Section One
FOLLOW THE MONEY

Chapter 1
CONVENIENT LIES

Example 1. "I'd rate our school five out of five," the eighth-grader said. "I think it's probably the best middle school in the city," another added, "or maybe second-best."

In fact, it's one of the worst, with substandard facilities and a dismal academic performance. We were sitting in the school's library, which was really not much more than a large classroom. The few shelves along one wall contained perhaps 200 books, and five of the six computers did not have keyboards. Moreover, no one had told these students (all African-American), that barely 10 percent of them had scored at a proficient level in reading and only 15 percent at a proficient level in math.

Example 2. The first-graders (all African-American) were eager to learn to read, and their first-year teacher was trying to teach them. Using the method known as "whole language," she taught the children to recognize words. Using the same book for months at a time, she convinced the children—and perhaps herself—that they were reading.

However, at the end of the year when we asked the children to read from a book they had never seen, they could not.

Example 3. The young teacher was giving his high school English students in rural Georgia their spelling words, writing them on the board for the ninth-graders (all African-American and Latino) to copy. One of the words was "strenuous," which he spelled "strenous." The students dutifully copied his mistake.

His high school principal had assigned him to teach math and history, despite his certification as a junior high physical education teacher and coach. Neither his students nor their parents were told of his "out-of-field" status.

John Merrow

Example 4. The federal No Child Left Behind law purports to hold states and school districts accountable for the education of all children, but it also allows each state to set passing scores and even to change them. When Illinois lowered the "proficient" score on its eighth-grade math test, its pass rate jumped from 54.2 percent (2005) to 80.4 percent (2007). This accomplishment was reported to the public, of course. [23]

All of the above are what I think of as "convenient lies"[24]—just a few of the hundreds of similar examples of evasion of responsibility, inadequate training and supervision, fundamental unfairness, half-truths, outright deception, lies and fraud found in our current education system.

We are a nation at greater risk today because these practices allow us to stay on a path of modest reform and minimal change, even though strong evidence points us in a clearer direction. In other words, these convenient lies allow us to stay within our comfort zone and ignore the serious damage being inflicted upon millions of young people, our economy and our democracy.

Change is possible, but time is running out.

American public education is failing our children, but not because we are aiming too high and falling short. On the contrary, we're aiming *too low*—and unfortunately, we're *succeeding*.

How ironic that public school students in Washington, D.C., California, Ohio and across much of the nation spent one week in April 2008—the 25th anniversary of "A Nation at Risk"—filling in standardized test bubbles.

That report, which memorably warned that our educational foundations were "being eroded by a rising tide of mediocrity," also includes a sentence painful to read today: "We should expect schools to have genuinely high standards rather than minimum ones."[25] We still *say* that, but actually doing that seems to be impossible under current realities.

Where are we now, more than a quarter of a century later? Sadly, it appears that we have given back the hard-won progress, and that politicians are largely to blame. What's more, it seems unlikely that most current reforms are powerful enough to reverse the still-rising tide.

According to that 1983 national commission, the United States was "committing an act of unthinking, unilateral educational disarmament."[26] "A Nation at Risk" called for higher standards; more demanding courses; tougher graduation requirements; and renewed emphasis on science, social studies and computer technology.

America responded with waves of education reform. A decade later, the United States entered an era of unparalleled economic prosperity; even today American workers are the world's most productive. While these improvements were fueled by the education reforms of the late 1980s, rarely is credit given to schools or teachers.

Reading "A Nation at Risk" today is eerie and disturbing, because so much of what it said then still applies. It cites our declining performance on international tests—something we read about every year. Then, as now, teachers were drawn from the lowest quartile; then, as now, schools could not find enough math and science teachers, and so on.

And we are at greater risk today.

Not even four in 10 fourth- and eighth-graders in America score at a "proficient" level in mathematics, according to the 2009 NAEP test. The 2009 NAEP also revealed that fourth-graders' math proficiency scores have stagnated since 2007 (previous NAEP math tests all the way back through 1990 showed increased learning scores in that group), and that only 39 percent of our students score "proficient" in math, while low-income students fare even worse: 22 percent on average, with Latinos at 21 percent and African-Americans at just 15 percent.[27] Recent ACT and SAT reports on high school graduates' preparedness for college math are disheartening. And, according to the National Center for Public Policy and Higher Education, "The racial and ethnic disparities that exist in preparation for and access to college are also found in college completion rates," with 59 percent of white students, 47 percent of Hispanic students, 40 percent of African-American students, and just 39 percent of Native American students earning their bachelor's degrees "within six years of enrolling in college."[28]

We may also be becoming "a nation of dropouts." The U.S. averaged freshman graduation rate was just 73.9 percent in 2006-2007—that's more than one out of every four American students not making it—ranging from 52 percent in Nevada to 88.6 percent in Vermont, according to the National Center for Education Statistics.[29] And in some urban areas, including sections of Milwaukee, Baltimore and Cleveland, the graduation rates are 35 percentage points (or more) lower than those in nearby suburbs, according to Editorial Projects in Education.[30]

"The crisis we're seeing in our nation's high schools is real, it's urgent, and it must be fixed," said Congressman George Miller, chair of the Committee on Education and Labor. "It's become increasingly clear that addressing this dropout crisis is one of the most important things we can do to turn our economy around and regain our competitive footing for good. We have a moral and economic obligation to ensure that, at a minimum, every student in this country can graduate high school prepared to succeed in college or the workforce. Our intent is to address this problem in this Congress in the most comprehensive way possible."[31]

High schools with particularly low graduation rates—commonly known as "dropout factories"—"are concentrated in a subset of 17 states that produce approximately 70 percent of the nation's dropouts,"[32] according to the Lumina Foundation.

Teens who do not graduate are more likely to be unemployed or underemployed, unhealthy, single parents, living in poverty, receiving public assistance or in prison, according to countless studies. And they are more likely to have children and grandchildren who will perpetuate this woeful cycle.

International comparisons are downright embarrassing. Just 1.5 percent of our 15-year-olds scored at the highest proficiency in science (Level 6), compared to 16.8 percent at the most basic (Level 1) and 7.6 percent below Level 1, on the 2006 Programme for International Student Assessment (PISA); not until Level 2, says PISA, do "students start to demonstrate the science competencies that will enable them to participate actively in life situations related to science and technology." About one in four U.S. students scored at or below Level 1 in mathematics, with just 9 percent at Level 6, ranking us below 24 other OECD countries, including the Czech Republic, Japan, Australia, Korea and Canada.[33] By contrast, Korea (27 percent) and Chinese Taipei (32 percent) had the highest percentages of students at the top two levels of math proficiency.

America's disadvantaged and minority children do poorly on international comparisons, but so do the rest of our kids. Basically, we are not getting much for our money. It reminds me of John Connally's failed presidential campaign. Many years ago, the Texas governor spent millions in a campaign for president but ended up winning only one delegate at the Republican convention.

Go back to those PISA scores referenced above, where our 15-year-olds were outscored by kids from Korea, the Czech Republic and 24 other OECD nations. The accounting firm of McKinsey & Company looked at test scores and spending to determine how much it cost each nation per point. In 2003, we spent more money to get fewer points, by a wide margin. Korea spent $77 per point, the Czechs $50 per point, but each math point cost the United States $165![34]

At least three forces washed away the hard-won gains that "A Nation at Risk" produced, and they have created the perilous situation we now find ourselves in:

- An ambitious but misguided federal law.
- An MBA-like "bottom-line" mentality.
- Parsimonious behavior.

The No Child Left Behind Act of 2001 began with bipartisan optimism. In language that resonates today, the new president from Texas decried "the soft bigotry of low expectations" and declared that unless *all* groups of students at a school made progress, the entire school would be found deficient.

Unfortunately, for the most part NCLB has not worked. I have spent hundreds of days in schools since the law's passage and have witnessed principals and teachers focusing on getting as many students as possible over the NCLB "basic" bar: a laughably low standard in most states. The kids "on the bubble" get the attention, while brighter ones must fend for themselves.

Did NCLB produce genuinely high standards? From what I've seen and reported, NCLB has driven down standards, dumbed down the curriculum, suffocated programs for talented students and driven away many of our best teachers. Moreover, it has actually led to an *increase* in school dropouts, as some educators "encourage" low-performing students to try their luck elsewhere.[35]

The MBA mentality is also at fault here. Schools seem to have abandoned their mission of preparing skilled and competent individuals to face a complex world with confidence. Instead, many schools focus on bubble test scores. "Drill often" replaces teaching and learning. As the "Challenge Based Learning" project notes, "Students today have instant access to information through technology and the web, manage their own acquisition of knowledge through informal learning, and have progressed beyond consumers of content to become producers and publishers. As a result, traditional teaching and learning methods are becoming less effective at engaging students and motivating them to achieve." That's a polite way of saying that many of our brightest kids are bored to tears.[36]

Money is the third cause of failure. The conventional wisdom, that education spending has been going up for years, is wrong. While the dollar amount increased from $100 billion in 1985 to about $500 billion in 2001, and is continuing to rise with President Obama's latest additions to the education budget, our *effort*—as a portion of our Gross Domestic Product and overall government spending—has declined significantly. According to the Office of Management and Budget, in 1980 we devoted 9 percent of GDP to education; in 2001, it was less than 5 percent. And according to the OECD, after five years it was just 5.5 percent in 2006.[37]

We are *not* trying harder![38]

I am not arguing that education dollars are well spent, because often they are not. We clearly have to do more with what we have now, in these difficult times.

And in case you are interested, teachers are actually worse off today.

In 1991, the average teacher made slightly more than the average college graduate; in 2008, the median annual wage for K-12 teachers was between $47,100 and $51,180, with the lowest 10 percent earning between $30,970 and $34,280, and the top 10 percent earning $75,190 to $80,970, according to the Bureau of Labor Statistics. The average starting salary for a 2010 graduate with a bachelor's degree, estimated to be down this year due to the economy, is $48,351, according to the National Association of Colleges and Employers.

Compared with their international counterparts, U.S. teachers fare worse. A 2007 OECD study found that a primary school teacher in America with 15 years of experience earned a ratio of about 96 percent of the country's GDP per capita; primary teachers with similar experience in other OECD countries typically earned 117 percent of their country's GDP per capita, with teachers in Korea earning the highest (221 percent).[39]

But nothing illustrates our parsimony as powerfully as our spending on testing. According to policy analysts at Education Sector, in 2006 we spent just 15 *cents* of every $100 on NCLB tests. Cheap tests, the tail wagging the dog, are the principal cause of education's decline into rote tedium.

(Just how cheap are we? In the same year, Hartz spent at least 10 times more testing its bird seed, flea powder and kitty litter than we devoted to assessing our students.[40])

Those cheap tests actually mask the severity of the problem, because young children can be drilled to pass them. They are drilled, and they do pass. That is, fourth-grade scores generally seem to suggest improvements in competency in reading and, up through 2007, math, but those gains are illusory; they begin to disappear as early as fifth and sixth grades and are often gone by eighth grade. By their sophomore and junior years in high school, many of our students have actually regressed.

I believe that most of the early gains are a mirage, created by teaching a narrow curriculum[41] and by teaching students how to pass the tests. In the name of getting enough passing test scores to meet NCLB's requirements, many schools are stifling student creativity and curiosity and drowning children's desire to learn.

The implications for our economy are frightening. "Over the past thirty years, the modern workplace has radically changed, and the demands on those making the transition from the classroom to the workforce continue to rise," notes the Alliance for Excellent Education. "Students from Birmingham and Boston no longer compete against each other for jobs; instead, their rivals are well-educated students from Sydney and Singapore. But as globalization has progressed, American educational progress has stagnated. Today, the United States' high school graduation rate ranks near the bottom among developed nations belonging to the Organization for Economic Co-operation and Development (OECD). And on virtually every international assessment of academic proficiency, American secondary school students' performance varies from mediocre to poor. Given that human capital is a prerequisite for success in the global economy, U.S. economic competitiveness is unsustainable with poorly prepared students feeding into the workforce."[42]

And we are failing those most in need. The gaps in opportunity, expectations and outcomes between rich and poor, and white and non-white, are increasing.

Strong measures are needed to save public education. NCLB (under a new name) will eventually[43] be reauthorized by Congress, which, unfortunately, shows few signs of having learned that *Washington cannot run public education.*

The Congress and President Obama are attempting to enable excellence by providing money to allow consortia of states to develop common standards and tests. (And yes, I do agree that we need accountability and good tests.)

But Congress must also provide more funds and tax breaks to encourage our best and brightest to become teachers. It could provide additional tax breaks for those willing to teach math and science or in economically impacted areas. Economists suggest that while these changes would not have strong effects, the symbolic significance—showing that the United States values teaching—would be powerful.

I hope the president will lead a national conversation about the goals of education in a democracy.[44] That conversation certainly did not take place in the last presidential campaign; by one count, only *21 minutes* of 30 hours of the presidential debates concerned education.

America needs more than a presidential conversation. It needs a wake-up call—because right now, in terms of convenient lies, we're telling ourselves some real whoppers.

The first truth we must face is that *we are a ticking time bomb.* As noted earlier, more than one in four American high school students will leave school without a diploma. About 1.2 million students drop out each year (that's between 6,000 and 7,000 American children every school day or one every 26 seconds), and close to 50 percent of Hispanic and African-American students do not finish high school on time.[45]

These dropout rates significantly impact the health of our economy. Observing that our country's "achievement gap" is similar to sustaining "a permanent national recession," McKinsey & Company estimated that if academic performance by minorities had equaled that of white students in 1998, America's 2009 GDP would have been between 2 to 4 percent higher (a difference of $310 billion to $525 billion, according to their calculations).[46]

"In a global economy where the most valuable skill you can sell is your knowledge, a good education is no longer just a pathway to opportunity—it is a prerequisite," said President Obama in February 2009, addressing the House and Senate. Citing the high dropout rate in our country and adding that only about half of American students have a college diploma, the president said this is a "prescription for economic decline because we know the countries that out-teach us today will out-compete us tomorrow." He added: "And dropping out of high school is no longer an option. It's not just quitting on yourself, it's quitting on your country—and this country needs and values the talents of every American."[47]

Just 20 years ago, the United States was home to the most college graduates on the planet; today we rank 15th out of 29 countries compared in "Measuring Up 2008," in which Pat Callan notes that "the U.S. adult population ages 35 and older still ranks among the world leaders in the percentage who have college degrees—reflecting the educational progress of earlier times. Among 25- to 34-year-olds, however, the U.S. population has slipped to 10th in the percentage who have an associate degree or higher.[48]

Compared with other countries, our students' performance in math and science is falling behind; one study even showed American eighth-graders tied with students in third-world Zimbabwe in mathematics.

Our economy will lose billions over the life of our "dropout nation," and as America moves from a manufacturing-based economy to a globalized service- and technology-based economy, our schools are not producing a well-enough educated work force to handle jobs that will keep the country clicking.

Educationally, we are the equivalent of a vinyl LP in an iPod world.

"Simply put, the world has changed and there is no work for high school dropouts," said Robert Balfanz of Johns Hopkins University. "To meet its graduation challenge, the nation must find a solution for its dropout factories."[49]

America has a history of surviving crises, of course. Think of the Morrill Act after the Civil War; the GI Bill after World War II; the National Defense Education Act after Sputnik; the Elementary and Secondary Education Act, the Voting Rights Act and the Civil Rights Act during Lyndon Johnson's presidency; and the waves of education reform that followed "A Nation at Risk" in 1983.

Today the stakes are higher, and our response has to be faster and stronger. If the $100-plus billion stimulus package (and any subsequent bailout packages that Congress might provide) turn out to have allowed schools to just keep on doing what they've been doing, then we will have merely postponed the day of reckoning.

Chapter 2
TESTING FLEA POWDER

Here's a question I've been pondering. What matters more to us in America, our pets or our children? We have many more pets: 62 percent of U.S. households (that's 71.4 million homes) have at least one pet. That's over 228 million cats, dogs, gerbils, etc., plus another 180 million fish. We have only about 75 million children under the age of 18 in our country.

But how do you measure caring? I'm a big fan of trying to compare effort, not just numbers, so here's what I came up with. I decided to compare the percent of revenue that a leading pet product company spent testing its goldfish food, puppy toys and flea powder to the percentage of education spending devoted to testing and measuring our children's performance in school.

A few years ago I decided to call Hartz, a well-known company whose products my family has used with our dogs and cats. I got a Hartz PR guy on the phone. My strategy was to soften him up before asking how Hartz spends its money. I told him about the cats in our office and our Labrador retriever at home. Then I said I knew that reliable companies like his invested heavily in testing and evaluating. Here I cited Bristol-Myers Squibb, which I discovered was spending $16 out of every $100 of revenue at the time, testing products like Enfamil and the cancer drug Erbitux and developing new ones. That's a whopping 16 percent!

It was time to pop my question. Did Hartz spend a lot testing Spectramax goldfish food, Advanced Care 3-in-1 Flea & Tick Drops and other stuff? If so, how much?

The PR guy buttoned up completely. "We're a privately held company," he said, "and we don't release that kind of information."

"How about a ballpark figure?"

"We're a privately held company," he repeated, a little more slowly this time.

"What I'm curious about," I said, putting my cards on the table, "is whether Hartz spends more testing pet products than education spends testing students."

When he told me his wife was an educator, I figured we were bonding. "I'll tell you how much education spends on testing, and then you tell me whether Hartz spends more than that," I said. "You don't have to give me the amount, just whether it's more or less than education."

I took his silence as a tacit agreement and told him the percentage that education spends.

"Is that true?" he blurted out. "You've got to be kidding!"

"Your reaction suggests to me that Hartz spends a larger percentage," I said eagerly. "Am I right?"

"We're a privately held company," he said, "and we don't release financial information."

Truth is, it would be hard for Hartz to spend less, because public education does its testing on the cheap. In "Margins of Error: The Testing Industry in the No Child Left Behind Era," Thomas Toch estimated that state spending on NCLB-related testing was less than $750 million, out of total K-12 spending of more than $500 billion in the 2005-2006 school year.[50] In other words, for every $100 we spent on K-12 education that year, we were devoting 15 cents to testing and measuring. That's 15/100ths of one percent! Even Massachusetts, which takes its responsibility at least as seriously as any state in the union, was devoting less than 1 percent of its education dollars to testing.

Chemical engineering companies spend at least 3 or 4 percent on research and evaluation, M. Blouke Carus told me at the time. Mr. Carus is a chemical engineer known to educators for developing the Open Court reading program and, with his wife Marianne, creating the Cricket, Ladybug and Spider magazines for children. As noted earlier, Bristol-Myers Squibb was spending 16 percent.

Educators are under constant pressure to raise test scores, and "teaching to the test" is common. That wouldn't be a bad thing if the curriculum and the tests were sufficiently challenging, so that passing the tests demanded a convincing demonstration of clear thinking, creativity and mastery. The exams that students in International Baccalaureate programs have to pass are all of these things, for example, and so IB faculty quite properly teach to the test.

When I posted a version of this on my blog, Taking Note, Steve Peha wrote to tell me that I was asking the wrong question. "It's not 'How much do we spend testing our students?'" he wrote. "The question is, 'How much do we spend testing our system?' For example, why are so many educational methods in use today never tested? Why are principals never tested? Why are districts themselves never tested? We do no true diagnostic work on the people doing the work. Only the children who get worked on. And that's what's dangerous about testing."

To me, that is a false dilemma. We have to assess students, and we should be measuring school and teacher effectiveness. Would you endorse a public system of choice, so that parents and kids could move from one school to another—a reasonable measure of perceived effectiveness? My quarrel is not with testing but with testing that is too frequent and with tests that are too cheap.

This won't be the last time that this book refers to Campbell's Law, a warning about the dangers inherent in over-reliance on narrow standardized tests. It holds that: "The more any quantitative social indicator is used for social decision-making, the more subject it will be to corruption pressures and the more apt it will be to distort and corrupt the social processes it is intended to monitor."

We are moving in the direction of national or common standards, which promises to be an adventure.[51] But setting higher standards won't be enough to solve our problems. Challenging curriculum is available, but that won't solve the problem, either. Let's be honest and acknowledge that testing drives curriculum, which means that more money must be spent developing sophisticated testing instruments. If we ask the questions in the right order, we finish with, "How do we measure learning?" Nowadays, it seems that we start with a question that goes something like, "What's the cheapest and easiest way to test?"

Good tests actually teach while they challenge and stimulate the brain. Good tests cost money. Having students demonstrate what they already know is time-consuming (and therefore expensive). Of course, we're not merely cheap here; we're also reluctant to trust teachers' evaluations, unfortunately.

Creating really good tests is going to be a problem even with federal money being available as part of the president's education stimulus package, because education doesn't have enough sophisticated test-makers.[52] However, I can tell you where to find more first-rate evaluators. They're working for Hartz, Bristol-Myers Squibb, Gerber and other organizations that take evaluation seriously.

Chapter 3
WHO BENEFITS?

Barack Obama's victory may have brought our nation closer to the vision of "a more perfect union," but at a time of severe stress on the country's economic system. Although the president has spoken eloquently about public education, it cannot be his highest priority in these tough times. At least 41 states cut back on their 2009-2010 education spending in response to declining revenues, and deeper cuts are being predicted for the year ahead. This disinvestment may help their bottom line, but it is certain to dramatically impact classrooms and schools across the nation.

However, every crisis also offers an opportunity. In the face of a deep recession, public education can opt for innovation. While some retrenchment may be inevitable, its extent can be controlled—*if* the system seizes upon this occasion as an opportunity to reimagine itself from the ground up. In the words of Clay Christensen, author of "Disrupting Class":

> This will not happen easily or quietly. Innovation must be encouraged and supported, wherever it is found. Moreover, those who heretofore have benefited from the mediocrity of the status quo must be given the opportunity to change— or be rooted out....The way young people learn has already changed. The disconnect between the dominant school strategy and the real world of our young people grows more apparent every day.
> But there is an entire industry wrapped around keeping things the way they are, even if it means perpetuating the persistent failure rates of another generation of young people.[53]

I believe Christensen is correct. There is "an entire industry" dedicated to maintaining the status quo. Of course, that would not be a bad thing if the status quo were producing quality.

But it's not. In fact, America is a ticking time bomb. More than one million young people drop out of high school each year, more than 6,000 every day. I ask you to imagine a graduation ceremony at almost any urban high school with a chair set out for each student who had entered four years earlier as a ninth-grader. At that ceremony, three out of every four chairs would be empty![54]

Unfortunately, this falls into the category of "Old News."

Think back to "A Nation at Risk" and its clear warning: "If an unfriendly foreign power had attempted to impose on America the mediocre educational performance that exists today, we might well have viewed it as an act of war."[55]

And while that report warned of our "unthinking, unilateral educational disarmament," it did *not* dig deeper. Unfortunately, it did not ask the logical (but potentially uncomfortable) follow-up questions, including "Who?" and "Why?" These unasked and unanswered questions can be summed up as *"Cui bono?"*—"Who benefits?"

That is, who was responsible for our educational disarmament, and why? Did these forces benefit from educational failure and inefficiency? Were they aware of the consequences?

More than 25 years later, the United States is spending more than $500 billion a year on public education, yet numerous reports indicate that our schools and our children are no better off, and are in some respects worse.

"A Nation at Risk" also warned that our educational foundations were "being eroded by a rising tide of mediocrity." And it imagined a brighter future: "We should expect schools to have genuinely high standards rather than minimum ones."[56]

What went wrong?

Education and its "savage inequalities" have been at or near the top of the public's agenda much of the time. We've spent billions, and the challenge has occupied some of the best minds of our society. Dozens of successful reforms have emerged, prospered for a time and then disappeared. We seem to have found the keys to improvement but, for some reason, the doors keep slamming shut.

Why is our education system so resistant to change? Who is benefiting from its mediocrity?

Consider Detroit, which has announced plans to close about 25 percent of its schools—41 of 172. Why? Because of a deficit of over $300 million and the specter of imminent financial bankruptcy. However, the system has been *educationally* bankrupt for *years* without anyone taking action. Right now just 4 percent of its fourth-graders are proficient on the NAEP math test, a situation that has existed for a long time.

Why is it that financial bankruptcy matters and educational bankruptcy doesn't? Here's my answer: When there's no money, adults don't get paid—and something must be done about that. However, when children don't learn, it's only children who lose out—so who cares!

But this is just one example. And the "benefits" of maintaining mediocrity in our education system are not necessarily financial. Rarely are people getting rich by ripping off the education system. Rather, they comfortably tread water, merely meeting the system's low expectations. Unfortunately, giving children maximum opportunities to learn and grow is rarely *anyone's* highest priority.

A teacher union president made the point perfectly. George Parker, while negotiating a new teachers' contract in Washington, D.C., with Chancellor Michelle Rhee, explained why teachers now—*for the first time*—have to be concerned about student achievement. Here's part of what he said:

> Certainly the union cannot survive if we don't have teachers. And we can't have teachers unless we have students. And so we have to stop the movement of students right now from our public schools to our public charter schools, because we're losing too many annually. So it becomes very important for us as a union, as a part of our agenda, to take on educational

success along with bread and butter issues, which is more of a progressive agenda. Because normally unions have not had to contend with any sense of accountability or responsibility for student achievement, because our existence and survival has not depended upon that.[57]

"Educational success" was not a bread and butter issue for teachers! There in black and white (and on videotape) is one answer to our question, "Who benefits?"

But many school boards have also stood in the way of positive change. Consider the saga of charter schools.[58] Any fair history of this experiment has to acknowledge that school boards have often impeded reform. We reported in detail for the NewsHour in 2007 about the prolonged battle in San Diego, where the board fought long and hard against the efforts of two schools (in "restructuring" under NCLB) to achieve charter status. The board changed the rules during the game but eventually was forced to allow the schools to proceed. In retaliation, the board removed Superintendent Alan Bersin, who had sided with the two schools.[59]

Paradoxically, most people in education (including teachers) would like nothing better than to put children first. But they work in organizations whose primary purpose has become self-perpetuation, organizational efficiency, job security or political influence—and not educating children. And so the solution to our educational problems is *not* to bring in "better" people. It is to understand what is being rewarded and decide, in the clear light of day, whether those rewards benefit the greater good, or merely reward the status quo. If the reward structure is perverse, it must be changed; this in turn will lead to fundamental structural change.

But the essential step, the road rarely taken, is to show how established interests are blocking change. If we show how these interests are blocking and resisting proposals that would produce a fairer or better-performing system, the argument for change should become impossible to resist.

Are there forces that resist change because the status quo is to their clear advantage? Does an organization, once established, devote most of its energy to perpetuating itself—and perhaps lose sight of its original reason for being? As an example, consider dropout prevention programs. Nationally we continue to spend millions on people and programs that are supposed to keep young people in school. But look at the results: The dropout rate has gone up, but has a single "dropout prevention specialist" lost his job as a result? I doubt it very much.

Other examples exist of people and organizations benefiting from the status quo (and that's a status quo in which more than a quarter of our children fail). The sheer numbers, I suspect, prevent change for the better.

Who is rewarded, and for what?

What can explain this persistent and seemingly irrational behavior? It's a generally accepted principle of organizational behavior that organizations behave in ways they are structured to behave and are rewarded for doing so. It follows then that, to change their behavior, *how* rewards are distributed must be addressed. For example, if teachers and administrators are rewarded for showing up on time, keeping order, following rules, taking attendance, giving tests and getting through the curriculum, but *not* for student achievement or graduation rates, should anyone expect educators to fall on their swords if children fail to learn or fail to graduate?

In the well-known "parable of the dangerous cliff," the town leaders face a dilemma. Every day, children fall off the cliff at the edge of their playground and suffer severe injuries. Some adults argue for a fence to keep children from falling; others advocate for building a hospital at the base of the cliff, because that would provide a much-needed boost to the economy. In the parable, of course, money rules, and the community leaders start drawing up plans for a new hospital.

Does this parable apply to American education? Who in public education benefits from mediocrity? Unfortunately, just about everyone. A partial list:

First, education has a sizable "failure industry," including the numerous for-profit tutoring companies that proliferated after the passage of No Child Left Behind. Do these "industries" have a vested interest in an ineffective education system? Consider these:

Dropout prevention: As pointed out above, in spite of failing to prevent a rising dropout rate, no "dropout specialists" seem to have been fired. When Time magazine devoted a cover story to this (April 2006), it revealed that most students dropping out of high school had passing grades at the time and may have been leaving school out of boredom and frustration. How does a "dropout prevention specialist" address that? Our Emmy-nominated reporting on practices in Florida[60] in 2006 uncovered ways in which school administrators were actually encouraging hundreds of students to drop out and transfer to GED programs. The endgame there was to increase graduation rates and scores, because a loophole in the law meant schools did not have to count these students as dropouts, even though very few of them actually enrolled in GED programs. Is a "dropout prevention specialist" expected to blow the whistle on his bosses? And who was benefiting from this practice?

Early in my career at NPR, I spent several months investigating juvenile institutions around the country. I learned that even when juvenile crime rates fell, the number of youths locked up remained constant. Minnesota accomplished this by redefining what sort of crime led to incarceration; when crime was high, a serious offense was required, but as juvenile crime fell, the state imprisoned kids for seemingly minor offenses like running away. The lesson was clear: The need of the institution—to have youth in custody—came first. The men and women working in the institutions did not set this policy, but they clearly were among its beneficiaries.[61]

Our national obsession with what is popularly called the "achievement gap" has created a virtual industry of beneficiaries, beginning with the companies that produce tests.[62] American children are by far the most tested in the world, and public education spends billions on testing[63] each year. While that's a small fraction of total education spending, companies like McGraw-Hill and Harcourt reap significant profits from this ongoing activity. Also benefiting are companies that process tests or create test-specific materials, such as Princeton Review and Kaplan.

And what are the economic interests of the hundreds of education associations populating Washington, D.C.? Who are their constituencies? Do these organizations exist primarily to improve educational opportunities for children, or do they have another, more important mission: the care and feeding of their adult constituency?

In the interview referenced earlier, Washington Teachers' Union president Parker spread the blame, saying that school boards were not overly concerned about student learning, either.

> It isn't just unions. School districts haven't had to worry about student achievement, other than from a humanitarian standpoint. I think that No Child Left Behind has some very glaring weaknesses, but probably one of the things that it did was put all school districts on notice that you're not going to let schools continue to fail without some type of repercussion. So I think it has made all school districts a little more accountable...I think that those who make decisions have had somewhat of a relaxed attitude inasmuch as "what are the consequences if the school district isn't successful?" There are consequences now.

Alan Bersin, the former superintendent of schools in San Diego, agrees that it's not just unions, but with this emphasis:

> I agree fully with your observation that unions are not alone in resisting change on behalf of self-interest. They should attract more attention from you only because they compose by far the most powerful (legislative/political) element in the so-called Education Coalition at the local/state/federal levels. The other conservative parties capitalize on this power and regularly ride union shirttails to and on the status quo, feigning complaint about unions much of the time. It is a tango of a particular beat now well practiced in the sector.[64]

John Merrow

The education of teachers demands scrutiny. Do university presidents who treat their schools of education as "cash cows" by failing to spend proportionate resources on teacher training, and accrediting agencies that rarely withdraw accreditation, serve the interests of our children's education? Or are they obstacles to improvement?

Several years ago, the dean of one of the nation's leading graduate schools of education told me that half of the institutions that train teachers should be closed down. And, the dean added, "With a few exceptions, it really doesn't make much difference which half."

Richard Elmore, a professor at the Harvard Graduate School of Education, once described the business as a three-part cartel. I am paraphrasing here from our conversation, but he said that in his view schools of education hold their collective noses and accept and graduate applicants from the bottom of the pool, while accrediting agencies cover their eyes and grant approval to these institutions. Finally, school boards hire the products of this flawed process. Someone, he said, has to say "no"—but no one does.

Although there are models of outstanding teacher preparation like the Stanford Teacher Education Program, most programs seem to more closely resemble one I visited at Texas A&M University several years ago. The young women, who wanted to teach early elementary grades, had been instructed by their professor to pretend to be 5-year-olds, while two other students conducted a mock lesson. The spectacle of college students trying to talk the way they imagined 5-year-olds would talk is captured in our documentary about the teacher shortage,[65] but most striking was that less than one-quarter of a mile away was a school full of real 5-year-olds that the class could easily have observed. Was the professor too lazy to be bothered, or did she feel that the faux experience was perfectly acceptable? Who was benefiting in that instance? Certainly not the young women perhaps destined to lead kindergarten classrooms in the future!

Interviewed later, most of these women said they would become teachers only if they could get jobs in their hometown. Otherwise, they confessed, majoring in education was an easy way to get through college.

When Arne Duncan went to Teachers College, Columbia University, in October 2009 to criticize teacher education, he got the profession's attention. He predicted that teacher training would be "a booming profession" because of the impending retirements of perhaps one million teachers over the next few years. But, he said, the profession needs an upgrade, big time. He cited the historical lack of respect for teacher training, calling it "the Rodney Dangerfield of the university world," historically dismissed "from the Oval Office to the provost's office." He also blamed universities for treating teacher education programs as a "cash cow," diverting tuition revenue to other programs. And he blamed accrediting agencies for approving teacher education programs without any evidence of their value.

The National Council for Accreditation of Teacher Education, the chief accrediting agency, announced the formation of a commission to raise standards and improve accountability. My hunch is that it's too little, too late.

I'd cheer loudly if NCATE adopted the British Soccer League approach: Identify the lowest-performing institutions each year and drop them into a B League, allowing those at the top of the B League to move up to the A League. That would get the right people's attention.[66]

State governance is also part of the story. For example, California's legislature has seen fit to create hundreds of very specific education programs (anti-smoking education, for example) and restrict the use of funds for those programs alone, thus tying the hands of local school leaders. Again—who benefits?[67]

Benefits are not always financial. Consider the organization of schools. Invariably they are organized by age, with 5-year-olds in kindergarten, 10-year-olds in fifth grade, and so on. But every neurologist, and every parent with more than one child, knows that learning occurs in spurts and at different times for different children. Age segregation, which exists only in schools, is largely for the convenience of the adults in charge. Adults have it easier when all the 6-year-olds can be viewed as a group, taught as a group, and their records kept as a group. But it makes little pedagogical sense, and it slows down those at the upper and lower ends of the bell-shaped curve. That is, a clear by-product of this practice is a mediocre educational experience for some children.

As Clay Christensen argues in "Disrupting Class," "most of education's problems have their roots in structure."

Special education is a burgeoning industry that absorbs an ever-larger share of school budgets. About 6.7 million students are receiving special education services, which generally cost about twice as much as is spent on students who do not receive special education.[68] However, special education students who are receiving services outside the public system (perhaps in a private school) now cost the system close to $30,000 per year per student.

As many have observed, special education operates on a medical model; it analyzes student weaknesses and then prescribes specific and expensive treatment. Lawyers often become involved in the development of Individualized Education Plans and the specific "treatment" of a disability. Certainly no one would return to the dark days before the passage of the Education for All Handicapped Children Act of 1975, now the Individuals with Disabilities Education Act. But one must ask who the primary beneficiaries of special education are, when very few of those labeled "special ed" ever lose that classification.

When I referred to special education's "cottage industry" of lawyers in a conversation with Miriam Freedman, she interrupted. "You're wrong," she said. "It's a *mansion* industry."[69]

Sometimes politics trumps everything else, including the best interests of children. An obvious case is Reading First, part of No Child Left Behind in George W. Bush's department of education. It insisted that only "scientifically validated" programs could receive federal funds, but most of those that qualified also had strong links to Republican supporters. Reading First allegedly tried to put programs that did not have ties to big publishers (such as Success for All and Reading Recovery) out of business. The government's inspector general has since identified these behaviors as "scandalous" and has found that some DOE decision-makers had financial interests in the companies they were endorsing. One comprehensive study found that Reading First has not helped children learn to read, and some suspect that it is largely responsible for the decline in reading scores on the National Assessment of Educational Progress.[70]

With so many beneficiaries of the status quo—textbook publishers, schools of education, unions, professional associations, school boards, testing companies, lobbyists, foundations, state and federal agencies, the news media, policy analysts, researchers and consultants—there's no need for an active and deliberate conspiracy. Instead, the momentum is on the side of standing still, a marvelous paradox.

It would be easier to bring about change if all those who benefit from the status quo were malevolent profiteers who could be exposed and condemned in the court of public opinion, and perhaps in courts of law. However, most of those who benefit are not bad people. In fact, many are admirable and well-meaning, but happen to work in systems in which failure and ineffectiveness are beneficial or perhaps essential. Put good people into a bad system, and systems win nearly every time.

In reformer Ted Kolderie's memorable phrasing, much talk today is about "getting better people for the job, not about getting a better job for the people." That is, reform[71] is generally centralized and top-down and not about changing systems—just people.

But if these institutions are behaving normally and their normal behavior is enough to derail change, then what will be required to create good schools for all?

Remember, the successes of many reform programs over the years demonstrate that we know what needs to be done. And yet inequities persist.

While we may be "beyond reform," we are not lost. Change is both necessary and inevitable, and it must be supported. A necessary first step is to identify those whose main interest is in maintaining the status quo. Perhaps they should be rooted out and humiliated. Perhaps they should be offered incentives to change as a precondition to staying. But change must come, and soon, if the United States is to reclaim its place on the international stage— and move closer to the vision of our founders.

Chapter 4
WASTING TALENT

Full many a flower is born to blush unseen,
And waste its sweetness on the desert air.
Thomas Gray, "Elegy Written in a Country Churchyard"

In Thomas Gray's "Elegy Written in a Country Churchyard," those flowers are a metaphor for talents and gifts. I have always loved the poem, and those lines, but I fear they may accurately describe what is likely to happen to talented youth today. What happens to gifts that are not nurtured?

I recall the late Daniel Patrick Moynihan, the gifted son of hardscrabble Irish immigrants, telling me, "Cream rises to the top." That was his experience, but my experience as a teacher in a federal penitentiary suggests otherwise. More importantly, so does hard data from solid research.

Let's put one important fact on the table to start: Talent is randomly distributed. It is not a function of social class, race, income or even education.[72] For more information see "Achievement Trap: How America Is Failing Millions of High-Achieving Students from Lower-Income Families," a report by the Jack Kent Cooke Foundation. It notes that upon entering elementary school, high-achieving, lower-income students mirror America both demographically and geographically. They exist proportionately to the overall first-grade population among males and females and within urban, suburban and rural communities, and are similar to the general first-grade population in terms of race and ethnicity (African-American, Hispanic, white and Asian-American).

Not only that, "More than one million K-12 children who qualify for free or reduced-price lunches rank in the top quartile academically. Overall, about 3.4 million K-12 children residing in households with incomes below the national median rank in the top quartile academically." This demographic is larger than the individual populations of 21 states, the report notes.

But then what happens? Here the news is not good, starting as early as first grade. Because ability is randomly distributed, kids from different income groups ought to appear in equal numbers in the four academic quartiles. Unfortunately, as the Jack Kent Cooke Foundation reported in late 2007, among first-grade students performing in the top academic quartile, only 28 percent were from lower-income families, while 72 percent were from higher-income families. As the report notes, "In elementary and high school, lower-income students neither maintain their status as high achievers nor rise into the ranks of high achievers as frequently as higher-income students. Only 56 percent of lower-income students maintain their status as high achievers in reading by fifth grade, versus 69 percent of higher-income students."

If programs for gifted and talented students[73] were adequately funded, things might be different. But as we and others have reported, these programs have been cut, victims of No Child Left Behind's frenzied pressure for higher test scores among kids who were just a point or two away from getting over the "adequate" bar.

Does "cream rise to the top" on its own? Not likely. However, talented kids born into upper-income families are likely to rise. Again quoting from the Jack Kent Cooke Foundation report:

> While 25 percent of high-achieving lower-income students fall out of the top academic quartile in math in high school, only 16 percent of high-achieving upper income students do so. Among those not in the top academic quartile in first grade, children from families in the upper income half are more than twice as likely as those from lower income families to rise into the top academic quartile by fifth grade. The same is true between eighth and twelfth grades.

They are also at least twice as likely to drop out of high school without graduating.

Renée Moore, a distinguished teacher and proponent of change, calls this a poignant truth, adding, "Not only have we educators allowed our expectations to limit the progress of too many students, but we have also allowed our silent complicity with bad policy to destroy the dreams of many more."

Researcher William Sanders sounded the alarm early in the reign of NCLB. He told me in 2003 that he was seeing indications that talented poor children, no longer getting their stimulation in schools, were "regressing toward the mean," a fancy term meaning that they were no longer excelling. Well-off children, he explained, don't suffer as much when gifted programs are cut because their parents take them to museums and the like. Children of the poor rely on schools for that special stimulation.

In 2004, producer Tira Gray and I did some reporting on this issue for the NewsHour and found that schools in downstate Illinois had cut or eliminated programs for gifted and talented children and were using the resources on children who were very close to passing the state tests. Why? Because the schools needed to get more kids over the bar. There was no pressure to see that high-performing kids continued to have opportunities to grow.

A mother (and blog reader) wrote to say that she has been living with this situation:

> I have two gifted boys who have been motivated and well behaved and even in fairly affluent school districts and private schools these two children have been ignored enough to make them cry. I can tend their wounds and give them the resources necessary to keep them emotionally healthy and intellectually challenged because I have been blessed by a comfortable standard of living, a good education and a work ethic. I worry every day, however, about the gifted children whose parents may not be themselves educated, may be working more than one job, and may not claim English as their first language. These children have the potential to raise their families out of poverty if they are given the tools to graduate high school and college and bring their gifts to

fruition. My relatives and my husband, immigrants themselves, were given these opportunities, and I am saddened that our society has stopped prioritizing such educational opportunities today. This lack of foresight will come back to haunt us.

She's stating a truth that many policymakers seem unaware of, one that is worth restating: Giftedness is randomly distributed.

Elizabeth Collins, a teacher and a parent, writes:

Nothing makes my blood pressure rise like the fallout from NCLB policies, and how so much opportunity and time are wasted teaching to dry tests which really don't give students the opportunity to learn much of real value, or to think creatively. I worry about how talent is being squandered both in the classroom—with its preoccupation with standardized testing, and because funding/time has been pulled away from programs that would allow students opportunities for further study in the areas which genuinely interest them. I am speaking not just of gifted programs, but also simple field trips and exposure to arts performances.... How late is too late, I wonder, before our students turn into people who neither read nor question anything?

Claus von Zastrow, executive director of the Learning First Alliance, is concerned about a resurgence in social Darwinism, noting, "Unfortunately, too many people seem willing to believe that the cream is already at the top, and that poverty is itself a mark of low ability."

And do these kids whose talent is not nurtured "waste their sweetness on the desert air," as Thomas Gray wrote? Here I have some direct experience. I taught in a federal penitentiary in Virginia for two years in the late 1960s. I had classes of approximately 20 young men who wanted to read literature and improve their writing. During my career I have also been a high school English teacher in New York, a summer school teacher at a junior high in Greenwich, Conn., and a teaching assistant at Harvard. The young men in that federal prison were easily the most focused, ambitious and responsive students I've ever taught. And while it's true that they were self-selected and that most prisoners have literacy issues, I still wonder, nearly 40 years later, where things went wrong for those guys. Why criminals instead of teachers or plumbers or business executives? What did not happen in their schools that might have set them on a productive path?

I stayed in touch with one of those former prisoners and later was best man at his wedding. Bobby worked hard, bought and fixed up a couple of two- and three-family homes, rented them out and before long became a very successful citizen. I hope the other guys did as well but, more than that, I hope that educators will address their own "expectations gap" when it comes to low-income kids. Kids from wealthy families are likely to get that extra stimulation at home, but poor kids need what schools can and should provide—field trips, challenging curriculum and the best teachers.

This country cannot afford to waste any talent. We've done that for too long.

Chapter 5
THE NEW A.D.D.

Although I'd suspected its existence for some time, I first came to understand what I call "the new A.D.D." in February 2007, while visiting an elementary school on Fort Bragg, N.C. My colleagues and I went because we were curious about the impact of the Iraq and Afghanistan wars on kids; I thought of them as "children of the surge." I expected to find a military atmosphere of "hop to" or "suck it up, kid." Instead I discovered what most of our schools could—and should—be.

I spent the day with Nancy Welsh, a veteran kindergarten teacher, and Gary Wieland, a military veteran who's been teaching for 16 years. Their demeanors couldn't be more different. Welsh is tender and loving, while Wieland is gruff. Welsh welcomed us (five adults and a big camera) into her classroom, while Wieland made it clear he was tolerating us only because his principal had ordered it. Both are, however, totally focused on their students and keenly attuned to their needs.

Early one morning, we observed Corey and Scarlette Keeling and their three children as Corey, a medic, boarded a military plane to leave for his third deployment. Scarlette later described the sudden emptiness: "Everything leaves, his clothes, you know, his shoes, the laundry's gone. It's like he was here and everything was great. And we argued and pinched and poked and drove each other crazy, you know, and it's like, 'Oh! If I could just have one more day of that.'"

Expecting that her kids would want to go home after this, Scarlette had rented movies and bought popcorn. But 5-year-old Austin insisted on going to school. When they arrived, Principal Tim Howle, a retired major in the Army's Special Forces, greeted them cheerfully with a high-five for each child. "My job is to take care of these kids, take care of the families, and take care of the teachers," he said. "We're the consistency in the lives of these kids." (Howle has since moved on to serve as principal at Irwin Intermediate School, also on Fort Bragg.)

McNair Elementary School is located in the middle of Fort Bragg. It's one of 191 schools run by the Department of Defense, with about 8,700 educators and a total enrollment of approximately 84,000 students. About 40 percent of the 372 students at McNair currently have a parent overseas in a war zone.

Most children we met at McNair had at least one parent serving in Iraq or Afghanistan. These kids were scared, sometimes angry, and often confused. The adults in that school—big, tough military men and women—understand the importance of *affection*, of a hug or a high-five. They don't lie and say, "Your dad (or mom) is going to be fine," because they don't know if it's true. But they've made school a *safe* place, a place where kids are allowed to be needy. Scarlette Keeling said it well: "Our children are already strong. They don't need somebody else to tell them to be strong. They need somebody to let them know that being sad is okay, being angry is okay, and being confused is okay."

Affection is the key. The old A.D.D is, of course, attention deficit disorder, but I've come to believe that this nation suffers from a tremendous "affection deficit," at least when it comes to other people's children. I reported on A.D.D in 1995, when PBS broadcast "A.D.D.: A Dubious Diagnosis?"[74] In that documentary, John Tulenko and I followed the money trail and discovered that, while the disorder was genuine, the A.D.D *epidemic* was man-made. We learned that the maker of Ritalin, the popular A.D.D drug, was quietly funneling money to a supposedly neutral parents' group called Children with Attention Deficit Disorder. CHADD had managed to infiltrate the U.S. Department of Education, which had underwritten a series of so-called "public service announcements" in which CHADD leaders passed themselves off as ordinary parents and praised Ritalin. And CHADD was lobbying Congress to change the drug regulations to make methylphenidate (Ritalin is a brand name of this) easier to come by. At the time, the United

States was consuming about 85 percent of the world's supply of the drug. When we made the film, several million kids were being medicated, the large majority of them white teenage boys. And today? I've heard estimates ranging from a low of 300,000 to a high of 4 million. And according to the Do It Now Foundation in 2007, "While use of Ritalin has declined in recent years, prescription patterns involving similar drugs have soared, primarily due to growing demand within the United States. In 2005, 1.9 million U.S. prescriptions were written for Ritalin, while prescriptions for Adderall-XR and Concerta totalled 8.7 million and 8.2 million, respectively. During that same year, use of methylphenidate and dextroamphetamine figured into 7,873 U.S. emergency-room visits."

A.D.D is a peculiar disorder. It says, *"You* are deficient because you aren't paying enough attention to what *we* (your teachers or parents) think is important. So *we* will medicate *you!*"

Medicating children with Ritalin[75] and other drugs is common, but it may not be very effective. In 2003 a review in the American Journal of Psychiatry found in six controlled trials of two-drug combinations, only one showed improvement that outweighed the side effects. "No one has been able to show that the benefits of these combinations outweigh the risks in children," said Daniel Safer, an author of the review.[76]

In mid-December 2009, The New York Times reported that poor children are four times more likely to be given powerful antipsychotic drugs than their middle-income counterparts.[77] One study cited indicates that poorer children also receive these strong drugs for less serious conditions. Why? Several explanations are offered: Medicaid pays less than private insurance for psychotherapy and counseling; fewer counselors are available to the poor; and drugs are frankly easier to dole out. As one co-author noted, "A lot of these kids are not getting other mental health services."

That's today's news, but for me it's déjà vu. I first reported on this issue in the 1970s and then again in the mid-'90s. Back in the late '70s when I was with NPR, I spent a couple of months investigating mental hospitals for poor and middle-class children in Maryland and Texas. It was horrifying to see how young children, whose major problem seemed to be poverty, were being drugged.[78] As I recall, their Medicaid coverage was limited to a small number of weeks, after which they were simply released to the streets. By contrast, the well-to-do children were less likely to be medicated, more likely to have one-on-one counseling with a psychiatrist, and so forth.

One teenage girl described how she was escorted out to the highway and told to hitchhike home. She said a group of young men picked her up, took her to an apartment, had sex with her despite her condition, and then let her go. Her language was far more graphic, but we ran the story as she told it, with an advance warning to stations. Despite the warning, "Children in Mental Institutions" got me kicked off the air in parts of Texas.[79]

Since the mid-'90s, we've been experiencing an A.D.D/ADHD epidemic almost exclusively among white middle-class boys.[80] John Tulenko and I spent months trying to figure out why this condition was suddenly so prevalent, and why Ritalin was becoming the treatment of choice. Gene Haislip of the U.S. Drug Enforcement Administration was responsible for determining annual production quotas for methylphenidate and Ritalin. Haislip said that, while there was a window of legitimate use for the drug, data suggested that "this has become a popular fad...especially when you realize that the United States is using five times as much as the entire rest of the planet."

As journalists are trained to do, we asked, "Who benefits?" We were shocked to discover in following the money trail, that Ciba-Geigy, then the primary producer of Ritalin,[81] was covertly funding the parents' group known as CHADD.[82] While not illegal for a pharmaceutical company to fund nonprofit organizations, the transactions (more than $800,000 over three years) were made public, if at all, in very small print. CHADD maintained that there was no quid pro quo, but its widely distributed materials recommended Ritalin by name to parents concerned about their children's behavior.

The exact cause of attention deficit disorder is unknown. There are no medical tests for it, no clear medical or physical evidence exists of its condition, and the identifying characteristics are blatantly subjective: They include fidgeting with hands and feet, squirming in a seat, getting out of a chair when expected to sit still, and running about and climbing excessively. That's a perfect description of millions of impatient children in crowded classrooms.

Clinching the case for me, though, was the first-hand testimony of many boys and their parents, all of whom noted that the condition seemed to disappear during summers, and even on weekends. In other words, whenever school was not a part of their lives!

CHADD, however, was telling concerned parents that A.D.D. was a neurobiological disorder stemming from a chemical imbalance in the brain. Ritalin, a psychostimulant, presumably corrects that imbalance by activating neurotransmitters (chemicals that carry messages in the brain).

We learned that teachers often recommend Ritalin for certain children. A father whose son had been recommended for the drug implicated school districts in the growth of A.D.D: "They're trying to cut their budgets and trying to keep big populations in the classes, and they can't have kids who are not under control. Teachers are more than happy to have kids on Ritalin, if it in fact will control their activities in the classrooms."

Some parents may accept an A.D.D diagnosis because it offers a more palatable explanation for their child's behavior. Helen Blackburn, an educational psychologist based at Greenwich High School in Connecticut, put it this way: "Parents want a school-based reason why a child isn't doing well. And to say that a child is not bright, that he may be a 'slow learner,' or that family issues are causing the problems in school, parents don't want to accept that. They want a diagnosis and a label that then makes the school responsible for solving the problem."

We learned that there are always doctors who will prescribe Ritalin for a child. Simon Epstein told me in 1995 that he prescribed Ritalin for about 150 children a year. He explained his dilemma: "If I tell them that I don't think it's clinically indicated, the parents will just go elsewhere. If that's what they want, they will go on until they find somebody who will prescribe it."

We discovered that some CHADD leaders had engaged in dubious behavior of their own, even going so far as to infiltrate parental information videos distributed by the U.S. Department of Education. On these videos, several ranking officials of state CHADD chapters present themselves as "typical parents" agonizing over their children's condition and then extolling the virtues of Ritalin. An embarrassed Department of Education hastily withdrew the videos after we reported the clear conflict of interest.[83]

At one point, I asked Mr. Parker if he felt compromised by accepting money from Ritalin's manufacturer and then recommending the drug. Did he feel "bought" by Ciba-Geigy? "I don't feel bought," he said. "I feel they owe us that as a matter of fact. I feel they owe it to the parents who are spending their money on medication. They owe it to these families to give them something back."

Gene Haislip of the DEA was incredulous. "You mean he really thinks there's nothing wrong in taking this money and keeping it a secret like they have? Well, I think it's an outlandish statement to make really, and I must say it surprises me."

A Ciba-Geigy spokesman expressed satisfaction with the arrangement at the time. "We're getting big information out there and I think that's the bottom line here…CHADD is essentially a conduit, providing this information directly to the patient population, and they do a pretty good job of it."

Subsequently, CHADD actively lobbied Congress—something nonprofit organizations are not allowed to do—to make it easier to get methylphenidate, the generic form of Ritalin. They did this, despite the gruesome fact that, at the time, the United States was consuming 85 percent of the world's supply of the drug. CHADD's lobbying effort was defeated, and for a time the consumption of methylphenidate actually fell. Since then, however, more studies have "proven" that methylphenidate works; today at least 5 percent of our children (mostly young middle-class boys) take Ritalin or a similar drug.[84]

Of course it works. It dulls a child's senses, making it easier for an adult to control the class. For the small number of children who really are hyperactive and whose condition does not respond to improved diet or more personal attention, the drug may be necessary.

But the message is pernicious: "You have something wrong with your brain, but this little pill will make everything better."[85]

Small wonder that some reports suggest a higher rate of *real* drug abuse among A.D.D "graduates." And since Ritalin is a black market favorite, known to provide a quick buzz when combined with alcohol, it's making yet another dubious contribution to our young.[86]

There's also the question of positive traits that may be sacrificed, when using ADHD drugs to control "problem behaviors." Some researchers question whether Ritalin and similar drugs may dampen creativity and innovative ways of thinking in children. In 2005, Jeff Zaslow of The Wall Street Journal wrote:

> In American schools these days, countless class clowns are sitting down and shutting up. In chemistry labs, students who used to mix chemicals haphazardly, out of an insatiable curiosity, now focus on their textbooks. In English classes, kids who once stared out the windows, concocting crazy life stories about passersby, now face the blackboard.
>
> Ritalin and other drugs for attention-deficit hyperactivity disorder have helped many children improve their focus and behavior—to the great relief of parents and teachers. But ADHD[87] support groups offer long lists of out-of-the-box thinkers who had classic ADHD traits such as impulsivity, a penchant for day-dreaming, and disorganized lives. Among those who are believed to have had the disorder: Thomas Edison, Albert Einstein, Salvador Dali, Winston Churchill....
>
> Some researchers now wonder if would-be Einsteins and Edisons will choose different career paths because their creativity and drive are dulled by ADHD drugs. They also worry that the stigma of being labeled with ADHD could lead some kids to lose confidence, and dream smaller dreams.[88]

For most children, the factors that often lead to an A.D.D di-agnosis are situational and can be changed: smaller classes, more personal attention, less sugar and caffeine, and a lot more hugs at home.

But that's the *old* A.D.D.[89] I now believe that what people commonly label as attention deficit disorder is more likely to be *affection* deficit disorder—we don't care enough about other people's children, and sometimes not enough about our own. All children crave affection, but a lot of the time that's not what they get. And all too often, *wealthy* kids get lots of "stuff" from their parents—their own credit cards, cell phones, computers, high definition TVs in their rooms, and a BMW at 16. From early on, they're scheduled to the max, with private lessons in ballet, skiing, piano, French and martial arts. That is, their parents hire private coaches to pay attention to them. But that sort of attention—private tutors and all the stuff you can charge—is no substitute for affection.

In public education, the United States is suffering from a kind of bipolar disorder. We have, increasingly, two worlds: the comfortable, seemingly smug world of wealthy (or "suburban" or "upper-middle-class") public schools, and the inefficient schools that the poor are isolated in. Schools for our country's disadvantaged students are most often dreary institutions with heavy emphasis on repetitive instruction and machine-scored bubble tests. Although some high-poverty schools are vibrant places of innovation and discovery, that is not necessarily a cause for celebration; what it can mean, is that reformers get to experiment on the poor, who don't have the political clout to control their own schools or reject the do-gooders.

Looking only at the best one-third of our public schools, a strong case could be made that this is The Golden Age of Public Education. These top schools may be better than they've ever been, but the overall trend lines in public education are depressing.

At the other end of the economic food chain, *poor* kids get the short end of the stick. *Poor* kids get plenty of the wrong kind of attention from their teachers, who run them through drill after drill in math and reading, in relentless pursuit of higher scores on standardized multiple-choice tests. These classrooms—particularly in grades four, five, six and seven—can be joyless places for children and adults alike. Plenty of attention, not enough *affection.*

Disadvantaged children are also likely to have inexperienced teachers. A few years ago, we followed two first-grade classes in Washington, D.C. Now, I happen to believe that most first-graders can learn to read. They want to because they know it's the currency of our culture. So we picked out two teachers, one a rookie fresh out of ed school who'd been trained to teach in the "whole language" method, and the other a veteran who used every tool and technique in his repertoire. They were right across the hall from each other, but the "close your classroom door and teach" rule was in effect, as it is in most schools. This meant that the young teacher was on her own, with little or no guidance. We watched as this young, well-meaning but poorly trained teacher told her children that they were learning to read—even though it was obvious to us that they were merely memorizing a book. Across the hall, veteran teacher Johnny Brinson used any method necessary, refusing to fall into either the "whole language" or "phonics" camp, and by year's end Mr. Brinson's first-graders were reading with fluency and comprehension. Never did we see the principal walk into the rookie's classroom, and no one offered her guidance or a critique. Does that happen in wealthy neighborhoods? I doubt it.

In November 2008, the Education Trust reported that "In high-poverty schools: More than one in every four core classes (27.1 percent) has an out-of-field teacher, compared with only about half as many classes (13.9 percent) in low-poverty schools." And "in grades 5-8, about four in ten (42 percent) core classes are assigned to out-of-field teachers." That is, they're teaching subjects they haven't studied.

Affection deficit disorder also manifests itself in class size. In many urban schools, teachers are likely to have too many students: 35 to 40 for elementary teachers and 150 or more for high school teachers. As Ted Sizer observed, when a teacher has that many students, it's not really teaching; it's crowd control.[90]

John Merrow

Outside evidence indicates that we have a serious problem.[91] In a UNICEF report ranking 21 nations in the overall well-being of their children and youth, the United States ranked 20th.

But at McNair Elementary School, we discovered children's well-being was a top priority. When Austin arrived at his kindergarten class that February day in 2007, teacher Nancy Welsh kept a close eye on him. "He's pretty agitated right now, his emotions bother him," she told me. "He's also tired, because it's been a big week for him." Welsh encouraged him to talk about his feelings; Austin told her he was sad. She responded by giving him a fun assignment: to draw a picture of a happy dream with his dad, which they worked on together as he talked about it.

"This is their security zone," Welsh said. "This is where they can be a kid. I let them be sad and I tell them it's okay to be sad. I say things like 'I would be sad too if my daddy was far away' or 'I'm sad that your mommy's not here.' So it's okay to be sad but I'll say 'Let's try to feel better now.'"

Austin was not the only kid in class with that situation; in fact, 14 out of 17 of Welsh's students had a parent on active duty overseas that day, and another was scheduled to leave in two days. While I was watching, a young boy came up and gave Welsh a hug. "Kenyon just came up to me and said, 'I miss Mommy,'" she explained later. "He just had a very sad look on his face, and I said, I'm sorry, I know you do' and I gave him a hug. He hugged me back and held on. I try to do for every single child whatever they need. And they don't always need the same thing, either."

But they all need to keep on learning, and Welsh never loses sight of that. Nor did her principal, Tim Howle. "I have made it a point to be personally involved with all the kids," he told me. "I know what caring and nurturing can do in education. I see it every day."

At that point, I asked him whether nurturing could get in the way of learning.[92] "No," he said, hitting it out of the park. "You can't separate education in relationships. If you want a great educational environment, you have to have a personal relationship with the kids. If we just comforted children all day, we would never

46

get to the standards that we have to teach. And it wouldn't help the parents to have a child who is not learning what they have to learn. No, we don't lose sight of the academics at all."

Nancy Welsh told me on that February day that nearly half of her students were beginning to read simple sentences. (Keep in mind that our national goal is to have children reading by the end of *third* grade.) When I checked back with her at the end of the year, she told me that nearly all of her kindergarteners were reading.

How does Welsh accomplish this? She makes learning fun, writing lyrics on big pieces of cardboard so the kids can read the words together before singing a song for the first time. "They get so excited partway through a song," she said. "One will shout out, 'There's *for!*' or 'There's *the!*' or 'Look, Mrs. Welsh, it has the word *he* and *said!*' They don't realize that I put the songs together and intentionally put all those words in there."

With the wars in Iraq and Afghanistan raging, I tried to find out her politics. She wouldn't tell me, no matter how hard I tried. "My position is to teach the children, to love the children," she said. "I'm not a politician, and I'm not someone who expresses opinions about whether we should be in Afghanistan or Iraq or Korea or anyplace else for that matter. I have such an influence on kindergarteners, and I am very, very careful about what I say."

"But do you have a position?"

"Sure," she said, with a small smile.

"Do you feel strongly?"

"I definitely do."

"Would you tell me?" I pressed.

"No," she laughed. "I will not."[93]

Across the hall in Gary Wieland's third-grade class, there was no ambiguity about the ongoing wars. "Our policy for being over there is right," he told me. "And these kids hear that from me."

Wieland has been teaching at McNair for 16 years; before that he served in the military for 30.[94] Wounded in Vietnam, he received a Silver Star and a Bronze Star. He clearly did not want us in his classroom and was only tolerating our presence because his principal told him to let us film there. A staunch conservative and self-identified "Fox News guy," he strongly mistrusts what he calls "the liberal media"—and he obviously put the NewsHour squarely in that group. Yet before the day was through, he and I had bonded (and are still in contact). But it wasn't a walk in the park, not by a long shot.

When we entered his classroom he was teaching about Iraq, asking his students for a working definition. "How do you like this so far—'a desert country in the Middle East'—does this cover what you been saying?" He looked at the definition written on the board, and then turned back to his students. "Now, why are your mom and dad there? Why did they go there? Why are they in Afghanistan? What are they bringing?" He waited. "Freedom," called out several children before long.

"Freedom?" Wieland asked, writing the word in large letters on the blackboard. "Yes!"

Later I asked him about what struck me as political indoctrination. "I didn't make that definition up," he bristled. "Students gave me that definition."

"But do you agree with it?"

"Yes, sure I do."

"Would it be okay if a teacher took the opposite position and defined Iraq as a country where America was wasting 2 billion dollars a week?" I asked.

Wieland glared at me. "I spent a career in the military on foreign soil so that those people could say that." His look indicated that I was one of "those people."

"It's not all about the ABC's," he continued. "They know I'm a safe haven for them when something is wrong. They know they can come to the old man and talk to me about it." (No affection deficit in *his* classroom!)

Principal Howle supported Wieland, saying (perhaps disingenuously): "I don't ask them their politics. I really don't care about their politics. As long as you love the kids and you do the right thing by the kids—what's more important?"

And Gary Wieland does love his kids, even as he pushes and teases some while hugging others. "It's about when a kid leaves here, what does he look like compared to when he walked in the door. Can he think independently? Can he solve problems? My kids blew the doors off the standardized tests that we took last year. I mean, I had reading scores; the entire class was in the 95th percentile on national norms, 93rd percentile for math," he told me.

On that day in February, seven of Wieland's 17 students had a parent in Iraq or Afghanistan. "I've become their surrogate dad," he said. "They really know that I have a relationship with them and that I'm going to stand in the gap."

He stands in, quite literally. In a very moving ceremony, which took place for years at McNair every time a parent was about to leave for a combat zone, Mr. Wieland would invite the parent to the classroom; in front of everyone, he would take a dollar from his wallet and give it to the parent. Here's what happened when a boy named Tedrick was about to see his father leave (we reported this on the NewsHour):

"His father came in the classroom and I said, 'Tedrick, stand up,'" said Wieland, "and I handed the dad a dollar and I said, 'When you get back you owe me that,' and I said to Tedrick, 'You know, you're now my kid, little boy.'"

Later I asked Tedrick's mother, Renee Philyaw, where the dollar was.

"Here in the wallet," she said. "He has it in his will that if something happens to him, Tedrick gets that dollar."

Wieland, the tough veteran, teared up when I related this. "I told Tedrick's dad, 'If you take care of my country, I'll take care of your kid,'" he said.

Wieland stays in touch with parents he's entered into "contracts" with. He started giving out the dollars during the Clinton era of Bosnia and other U.S. interventions. Although he hasn't kept a record, he guesses that he's given out about $100 to parents over the years. Tedrick's dad came home safely in 2008.[95]

I pressed both teachers and Principal Howle with questions about death and danger. Their answers differed, but their level of support for the kids was the same.

"If a kid asks the tough questions—'Is my dad going to die? Is Mom going to get killed?'—what do you say?" I asked.

Wieland answered: "I tell them, 'I didn't. Been there, done that. You know, they hurt me, but here I am to annoy you. Your dad is the best-trained soldier in the world. The folks around him are as good as he is. What's to worry about?"

"We had a child here," said Welsh, "not in my class, but another kindergarten class last year whose daddy did not come back, so I do not want to tell them your daddy's going to be fine or your mommy's going to be fine, because I don't know that."

Principal Howle added: "I can't tell you I'm going to be here tomorrow. I can't tell them Mom's going to be here tomorrow, but I'm going to tell you no matter what, there's someone here to take care of you. These kids are resilient. They come into this building every day doing what they have to, learning and going on with their life. They feel safe. They feel like someone cares."

And it wasn't just "someone" who cared. Everyone at that school cared about every child, as far as I could tell. And because there was no affection deficit at that school, the kids paid attention. Because there was no affection deficit, there was time and space to focus on learning, and much of it was joyful. And as noted earlier, the third- and fourth-graders at McNair excelled on standardized tests, with scores in the 80th and 90th percentile.

All children—rich, poor and in-between—crave affection. In education, affection is a necessary yet insufficient condition for learning. How can we change this? Parents are in the front lines in the fight against affection deficit disorder, but please—not with an American Express card or medication, but with hugs and thoughtful listening. Government can also be part of the solution. Government at all levels could act to end the affection deficit by restoring art, music, physical education, recess and field trips to our schools. And public school teachers could adopt the health model of schooling: Teach to strengths. Build on strengths.[96]

We need to change, because the new A.D.D is leaving kids behind. It's leaving them insufficiently skilled and without a sense of public purpose, and it's leaving them confused or angry. The new A.D.D is sowing seeds of social destruction. A split society of haves and have-nots will eventually pull us all down, and there's no wall high enough to protect us if we don't recommit to a decent opportunity for all.

Chapter 6
HYPOCRISY AND THE ACHIEVEMENT GAP

John F. Kennedy's promise to end "the missile gap" helped him win the presidency in 1960. Once the election was over, the public discovered that the missile gap was nonexistent, but one could argue that no harm was done, except perhaps to his opponent. For at least a dozen years now, politicians and educators have been currying favor by promising to close a different gap, this one in educational achievement.[97] While the "achievement gap" is more complicated than JFK's missile gap, the concept is equally misleading and, at the end of the day, more damaging. It helps win elections, too, which may be all that matters these days.

Our public education system actually has *four* gaps—in opportunity, expectations, affection and outcomes. The "opportunity gap" is obvious—rich schools typically have the most experienced teachers, the most up-to-date equipment and facilities, smaller classes and other advantages. What's more, children from upper-income families start school with distinct advantages. Some research indicates that as kindergarteners, these children have larger vocabularies than many *parents* of low-income children.

The "expectations gap" is more complicated. For one thing, some teachers simply do not expect their disadvantaged students to be excellent. And guess what—the kids often live down to those expectations. Janis Hiura, director of student leadership for Boyle Heights Learning Collaborative and a veteran teacher in East Los Angeles, calls this the "pobrecito" (poor little things) mentality of educators. When he was president, George W. Bush spoke often of "the soft bigotry of low expectations" in arguing for what became the No Child Left Behind law in 2001.

John Merrow

Many kids, their peers and their parents have a genuine expectations gap, perhaps because they have internalized the messages they receive from the outside world. Many disadvantaged children simply don't expect much of themselves. They may move in a peer culture that disdains intellectual achievement as "geeky" or "acting white," which might lead them to fear the isolation or attacks that academic success could bring. At home, their families may not have a tradition of academic success or ambition. While schools can re-educate teachers, overcoming peer and home attitudes is a tougher challenge.

Given those two gaps, a pronounced difference in outcomes is inevitable. And it's substantial. Low-income, non-white children score one, two or three grade levels below upper-income whites. Because life is unfair, poor children also face "gaps" in areas like housing, nutrition and health care.

The nutrition, housing and health care gaps can impact learning tremendously. It's tough to study and do homework when you share a studio apartment or an unheated garage with five or six family members. KIPP (Knowledge is Power Program) schools and others attack the housing gap by establishing a longer school day. Most public schools in disadvantaged areas provide breakfast, lunch and basic health care screening. That is, public schools work hard to address gaps that arguably ought to be of more concern to other agencies.

Schools are expected to close the gaps in opportunity, expectations and outcomes. Unfortunately, educators and politicians have focused almost exclusively on outcomes. Take the vocabulary gap that exists between children at different income levels. (I'll discuss this in "Failing at Preschool," later in the book.) Privileged children learn a significantly greater number of words in conversations with their parents, by having stories read to them and by asking questions than do their high-poverty peers. They certainly did not acquire their vocabulary through drill, but educators somehow seem to assume that vocabulary drill will work for the disadvantaged. "Drill them until they catch up" is akin to "whippings will continue until morale improves."

54

To focus only on outcomes is self-defeating. Even when schools do get those scores up, it's often the result of mind-numbing drill; classes in "reading readiness" instead of real reading; and cuts in physical education, art and music. Not long ago I overheard a successful principal explaining her secret of success to colleagues: In September, she replaced recess with test prep. Then, six weeks before the state tests, she eliminated art and music, again in favor of test drills. Not one of her colleagues objected, and why would they? Her approach worked on the only metric that mattered to the system, and she was recognized by her school district.

It's hard to fault principals for focusing, laser-like, on short-term gains, because they're ruled by an absurd bottom-line mentality that's worse than the stock market's pressure for improved quarterly profits. Test scores rule. It's as simple as that.

But that's not the case everywhere. In thousands of public schools, devoted educators do what's right, even if that means breaking rules and defying orders. Lincoln Elementary School in Mount Vernon, N.Y., doesn't have a performance gap, because its teachers simply refuse to allow children to fail.[98] Mount Vernon is urban America, and most of Lincoln's students are low-income, but nearly 100 percent of the students there succeed every year. At Lincoln (and at many other outstanding schools), art, music and physical education (along with chess and other "geeky" extracurricular activities) are integral, but subjects are often integrated. In art class, for example, students may design and create sneakers, using math in the process. Phys ed classes talk about velocity and might measure for accuracy and distance when throwing footballs. For years the principal at Lincoln refused to send report cards home, requiring instead that parents come to the school to get them. That's technically illegal, but it gave him an opportunity to meet every family and invite parents to be part of their children's education.

This will make some readers angry, but I believe that most of those who obsess about the "achievement gap" are cheap, intellectually lazy, ignorant or mendacious. The latter simply don't want public education to succeed, and they use every opportunity to call attention to failure.

People ignorant of the existence of opportunity and expectations gaps shouldn't hold office—political or educational. Those who shorthand the situation by blaming the "achievement gap" inadvertently contribute to public misunderstanding. Their intellectual laziness is inexcusable.

The cheapskates may be the largest group of offenders. What's cheap about the achievement gap? Testing turns out to be the least expensive educational "reform" of all. Testing is the educational equivalent of taking the temperature of a sick patient. A thermometer doesn't cost much, and it can be used again and again, and it doesn't help the patient get better. Equally useful in curing illness (this time, in our educational system), testing is on the rise, thanks largely to the well-intentioned No Child Left Behind law that since 2001 has mandated math and language arts testing in most grades.

Cheap, norm-referenced, multiple-choice, machine-scored tests invite the kind of skill-and-drill instruction that poor kids are subjected to. Because test prep works and scores can be improved, schools face irresistible pressures to focus heavily on the subject matter being tested, and to give short shrift to everything else. Cheap tests also drive out more nuanced assessment like teacher-made tests and individual assessments, which are much more expensive to implement.

However, being cheap can backfire. A few years ago Illinois spent well over $8 billion on public education—but only $45 million on tests to determine whether students were learning or schools succeeding. That's about half of 1 percent, which may have been cutting it a little too close. Harcourt Assessment, which received that $45 million contract in 2004 after hiring "a former top aide to Gov. Rod Blagojevich as its lobbyist," wasn't able to meet the contract deadlines, meaning that schools didn't give the Illinois Standards Achievement Test (I-SAT) as planned. State officials reported that Harcourt's materials not only failed to arrive on time to most districts, but that many test booklets and answer sheets contained misprints, that pages were out of order, and that sections of reading, math or science exams were either missing or duplicated. In 2006, Harcourt agreed to pay $1.6 million in damages, as well as reimbursing about $50,000 to school districts for "extra costs they incurred because of problems with test delivery," according to the Illinois State Board of Education's chair at the time, Jesse Ruiz.[99] In 2006 Pearson admitted that it had incorrectly scored thousands of the College Board's SAT tests; ETS agreed to pay $11.1 million to settle a class action suit brought on behalf of 4,100 people who had been informed that they had failed a teacher-licensing exam they had actually passed.

Cutting corners[100] creates other problems, too. Fairly recently, four questions on the New York State seventh- and eighth-grade mathematics exams also appeared, verbatim, on sample tests distributed to students earlier, embarrassing the State Department and the test-maker, CTB/McGraw-Hill. At the time, CTB/McGraw-Hill was being paid $4.5 million a year to publish the New York State exams, which means that the State Department was spending about .0005 percent of its annual budget to determine whether students were learning.

Finally, why is *white* the standard that blacks and Hispanics should aspire to? After all, Asian-American students outperform whites across the board in education. There's the best evidence of our foolishness and hypocrisy regarding the achievement gap: Why aren't educators and others wringing their hands over the widening achievement gap between Asian-American and white students? While it was "only" 30 points in 1981 (513-483), it rose to 44 points in math (580-536) in 2006, and Asian-Americans also outperformed whites by 18 points in English language arts in 2006.

Logically, that calls for more drill for *the white kids*, and no more art, music or recess either, until they get their scores up. Imagine the political storm that would ensue if someone in power analyzed the situation in *those* terms.

Chapter 7
THE "BUBBLE TEST" BUBBLE

The carpenter's wisdom—"Measure twice, cut once"—makes sense when building houses, but it's overly simplistic when applied to the business of learning. Unfortunately, it's being applied there, with terrible consequences.

When No Child Left Behind became the law of the land, high-stakes tests in reading and math for all students in grades 3-8 were mandatory. Many states require students to pass standardized tests for promotion and graduation. Under these circumstances, educators and politicians insist on "multiple opportunities" for students to take these critical tests. That is, they're demanding that schools "measure twice."

In truth, "twice" is an understatement. Ohio, for example, does not limit the number of times its high school students can take any and all sections of the mandatory Ohio Graduation Test; in fact, students who do not pass the OGT by the time the rest of their class graduates can continue taking any needed section areas of the test "for as long as the state continues to offer the test."[101] The Toledo Public Schools website encourages its high school students who have not passed all five areas of the mandatory Ohio Graduation Test to "retake the appropriate area test(s) at every opportunity," as it is a graduation requirement.[102] Many other states also say they don't plan to limit the number of times students can retake graduation tests. When he was secretary of education, Rod Paige endorsed multiple opportunities. "It's not a once-in-a-lifetime chance and then you're dead after that," he told the NewsHour. "We would encourage multiple opportunities to take the test."

This multiple approach continues to be favored by educators, because they know that even the best tests are flawed by nature;

they are well aware that error is built into every score. Because of what's called the "error range," a passing score (called a "cut score") of 200 might actually be 10 points higher or lower than reported. Thus, when 3,000 Massachusetts 10th-graders, who probably should have passed, were told they had failed the state reading test in 2001, state officials were not upset. As Jeff Nellhaus, director of testing, explained at the time, "It's fine with me as long as we have multiple re-testing opportunities for students who are under the cut, but who truly may be over-the-cut students."

Unfortunately, Nellhaus' "measure twice" approach is thrice-flawed logic, in terms of time, precision and diagnosis.

Time: A carpenter has only to read the ruler to see measurement results, but education's measurement results aren't available for weeks or months. Somehow "measure once, wait for months, and measure again" isn't particularly persuasive.

Precision: The carpenter knows precisely how long the two-by-four has to be. That's verifiable. But the "cut scores" that determine graduation and promotion are not based on observable fact or hard science. Instead, some committee decides what a passing score (the cut score) will be, and that's that. Or it is until someone else decides to change the score—which has happened in Illinois, Arizona, California, New Jersey and other states, as politicians try to avoid the embarrassment of high failure rates.

Diagnosis: Measuring lumber doesn't require diagnosis; the wood is too long, too short or just right. But scores on standardized tests only describe how a student performed on the test that day; they don't reveal what steps might improve student performance. That requires a trained adult, a teacher.

A more appropriate adage for education would be one borrowed from the medical profession: "First do no harm." Skilled doctors know that the instruments they use are imperfect. For example, the error range on a simple blood pressure test can be 10 percent or more, which means that a reading of 120 over 70 could actually be 130 over 80.

No responsible doctor would rush a patient to the operating room or even prescribe medication after taking a patient's blood pressure once—or even after taking it twice. Instead, that doctor would ask more questions, perform more tests, and get as much information as possible before making an informed diagnosis. Doctors typically rely on multiple *measures,* including their own judgment.

The best doctors teach their patients to take responsibility for their own health, because the ultimate goal is just that: health. Likewise, a skilled teacher diagnoses a student's strengths and weaknesses, using test results, classroom performance, homework and other measures (thus "multiple measures"). The goal here is to have students take responsibility for their own learning, as they progress toward adulthood.

"Multiple opportunities" may sound like humane policy, but it's based on attitudes toward students and teachers that ought to make us uncomfortable. Those who put so much trust in test scores are telling us that they have more faith in the imprecise "science" of standardized testing than in teachers. And "multiple opportunities," education's version of "measure twice," is tantamount to seeing students as objects to be manipulated—as lumber for the schooling mill.

Of course, it's not just students who are being tested these days. In many places, teachers and administrators must prove their worth by passing exams. Most new teachers have to pass tests, and now Massachusetts and a few other states insist that principals and superintendents pass an exam, as well.

In short, conditions are ripe for the educational equivalent of a "perfect storm," which would be widespread failure at all three levels: students, teachers and administrators. When this happened in a small northeastern city a few years ago, the aftershocks were revealing, if not especially comforting.

And since the subject is testing, here's a multiple-choice question for you: What happens when the school superintendent, 21 certified teachers and more than 40 percent of the town's high school seniors fail tests they're required to pass? (In the superintendent's case, it's the third time he's failed the basic literacy test.)

A: No one is punished, and all receive extra support so they have a better chance of passing the retest.

B: Everyone suffers the consequences. The seniors don't graduate on time, and the adults are suspended without pay until they pass their tests.

C: The students don't graduate, but the educators keep their jobs.

D: The students and teachers are punished, but the superintendent is praised by his state's governor and receives a 3 percent raise to $156,560.

"A" is an unlikely choice in the current "get tough" educational environment, which calls for real consequences.

If you chose "B," you deserve praise for consistency, but you're also naïve. Maybe hopelessly so.

If you selected "C," you have a better grasp of how the system works. You know that the world often operates on a double standard, with one set of rules for kids and another for adults. It's perfectly logical to assume the system would blame kids for failing to learn but not find fault with adults who failed to teach them, or the adult who failed to lead his teachers. But "C" is also a wrong answer because Lawrence, Mass., was operating on a different kind of double standard.

That's right, believe it or not: "D" is the correct answer. At a news conference in August 2003, then Massachusetts governor Mitt Romney praised Lawrence superintendent Wilfredo Laboy and indicated that, as long as teachers were literate, the superintendent apparently didn't need to be. "I'm not sure the superintendent of schools is in the same level of importance to me in terms of English skills as are the teachers in the classroom teaching our kids," said Romney.

Laboy liked the governor's reasoning. He told The Eagle-Tribune, which first reported the story, that the test had little relevance. "It bothers me because I'm trying to understand the congruence of what I do here every day and this stupid test," said Laboy. "I didn't meet the bar. But I think truly and honestly it has no relevancy to what I do every day. The fruits of my labor speak greater than not passing a test." Laboy did not comment about the apparent inconsistency of suspending employees without pay for failing to meet state requirements while he continued on salary. And if he had doubts about the relevance of the graduation test to the real world that students live in, he kept them quiet.

Other leaders pledged their support of Laboy, as well. "I judge him based on how well our kids are doing in the schools," Michael Sullivan, then the mayor and school committee chairman of Lawrence, told the Boston Herald. "I will stay the course with him because he's doing an incredible job for the kids." The mayor demonstrated a unique way of defining "incredible." The Massachusetts Department of Education reported that 254 out of 430 enrolled seniors in Lawrence passed the state exam, known as MCAS in 2003. That's a graduation rate of 59 percent or, put another way, a failure rate of 41 percent. Dig deeper, and Laboy's "incredible job" looks even less so. In ninth grade, the Lawrence Class of 2003 had 917 students, meaning that 480 students disappeared along the way. That's a pass rate of about 25 percent.

Any way you slice the data, Lawrence had the lowest pass rate in Massachusetts, although Laboy finally managed to pass the test—on his fourth try.

Testing teachers is also proving to be difficult. The Educational Testing Service was forced to admit that its mistakes in scoring led it to notify 4,100 teachers (10 percent of those taking it) that they had failed a 2004 licensing exam that they'd actually passed. ETS reimbursed the testing fees and cost of materials, but no one knows how many men and women lost out on teaching jobs due to their "failure." One who did was Paul Perrea, a 44-year-old electrical engineer from Cincinnati. He told The New York Times that he wanted to teach high school physics but couldn't get hired after receiving the (incorrect) failing score. "I wanted to teach in inner-city Cincinnati, where they really need good science teachers," he said.

The poignant issue—more important than our obsession with bubble tests for students, teachers or administrators—is disappearing students. Hundreds of thousands of ninth-graders disappear from school rolls in Houston, New York City and other urban districts every year. In Massachusetts alone, about 10,000 students disappear from school rolls each year. In Alexandria, Va., 11.1 percent of the Class of 2008 dropped out of high school (with 24.8 percent of the city's Hispanic students dropping out—that's about one in four). Some students transfer to other schools or enroll in GED programs, but many drop out rather than fail the high-stakes tests again. Still others are encouraged to drop out by educators, in the belief that "pushing out" these students will protect the school's pass rate and their own reputations. Whether these youngsters are called "dropouts" or "pushouts," school districts shouldn't be allowed to get away with hiding their failures.

By focusing so intensely on test scores,[103] we are missing the biggest accountability question of all: Are schools helping our *most vulnerable students* stay in school, especially in the face of policies that use tests to make important educational decisions?

If we were serious about educational accountability, we'd publicize the *disappearance* rate. We'd figure out why kids were leaving. And we'd figure out ways to keep them learning, in school and graduating.

To grasp the impact that high-stakes tests are having on school reform, imagine a 51st state. Let's say it's an island, the state of Atlantis. Imagine further that this island state is slowly sinking into the sea. To prepare for that eventuality, the schools in Atlantis teach only one subject: swimming.

Now imagine what happens when the standards movement lands on the doomed island.

When the pressure for higher standards reaches Atlantis, it sets off a frenzy of reform debate—a perfect mirror of what actually happened in most of our 50 states.

First Atlantis sets about creating *content* standards—what every student needs to know about swimming. This proves difficult, because some adults on Atlantis want a simple "survival swimming" curriculum that teaches children to tread water. Others want a rich curriculum in which all students learn the four competition strokes: butterfly, crawl, backstroke and breaststroke. Rather than make hard decisions, it proves easier to include just about everything, and soon Atlantis schools are teaching all swimming styles from the dogpaddle on up.

Establishing *performance* standards comes next. Performance standards set the levels of skill and knowledge a student must demonstrate to pass or to earn distinction. After prolonged debate, Atlantis adopts four performance levels: advanced, proficient, basic and below basic. "Advanced" swimmers must be able to swim four laps (one of each competition stroke) in less than nine minutes, while "proficient" swimmers need to complete the laps in less than 15 minutes.

Atlantis decides that "basic" swimmers can earn diplomas simply by finishing, no matter how long they take. This last decision angers educational conservatives, who accuse Atlantis education officials of watering down the curriculum.

Students who fail to complete the four laps are classified as "below basic." They either drown or drop out of school.

Like most of our real states, Atlantis simply ignores *opportunity-to-learn* standards. The idea behind this third type of standard is that it's unfair to hold students to performance standards unless conditions exist to give them a fair chance of meeting them. So, for example, for all Atlantis students to realistically master the four strokes, they would be taught in lap pools by trained swimming coaches. These coaches are hard to come by on Atlantis, though. While most schools have access to water (it's an island, after all), swimming instruction is generally left to adults who swim recreationally.

Measuring learning is the next hurdle. Teachers want classroom grades and their professional judgment to count, but Atlantis decides that students have to prove they can swim; then they can't agree on how to test them. Requiring each student to swim a lap of at least one of the four strokes is what educators call a *valid* test, just as testing writing skills by requiring students to write an essay is valid. Student flaws can be identified precisely and corrected immediately, and students can jump back in the pool and try again.

Unfortunately, direct demonstration of skill is costly and time-consuming, so Atlantis opts for a machine-scored, multiple-choice test—a test that students must pass in order to graduate.

This decision has an unintended effect on the curriculum at many Atlantis schools. Reporters find that students are spending less time in the water and more time on drill. Additionally, schools are found to have eliminated enrichment programs in water polo, diving and synchronized swimming in order to focus on the basics.

Responding to protests that a multiple-choice exam is not a valid test of swimming, Atlantis adds an essay question: "In 250 words, describe what it feels like to swim a lap of the butterfly, with particular attention to the turn."

Parents in some wealthy Atlantis communities threaten to boycott the high-stakes test. As one Atlantis parent puts it: "Our children learned to swim at home. We want our children playing water polo and learning to dive, not wasting time on drill."

A preliminary study suggests that low-performing students might benefit from taking multiple-choice exams, rather than an actual swimming test. "Since the adoption of the multiple-choice format, drowning as a reason for non-attendance has been virtually eliminated," the report asserts. School records confirm this; last year, only a handful of students stopped coming to school for that reason, all in the "below basic" classes. The dropout rate, however, remains high.

Every seemingly precise standardized test result has an error range, called the *standard error of measurement*. Thus, for example, a score of 72 means the student's so-called true score lies somewhere between 68 and 76. And so, reliance on machine-scored, multiple-choice tests always raises questions about the reliability of the results. Detailed analysis of last year's test results on Atlantis reveals that dozens of students passed at the "basic" swimmer level and earned diplomas, even though they couldn't keep their heads above water. Other students were denied diplomas because they scored at the "below basic" level, although they turned out to be capable swimmers (including a few certified lifeguards). Bad questions and mistakes by the testing company led to even more incorrect scores and denial of diplomas.

Atlantis may be imaginary, but everything I've described there is real in our world. Content standards are often bloated, and performance standards have been lowered in New York, New Jersey, New Mexico and other states in the face of high failure rates. A study released in October 2009 by the National Center for Educational Statistics reported, "In reading, 31 states set proficiency standards for grade 4 lower than NAEP's 'basic' level." For grade 8, "15 states set standards below...the NAEP basic point." One sentence gives the game away: "States with higher standards had fewer students achieving proficiency, while those with lower standards had more students reaching that level."[104]

States have ignored opportunity-to-learn standards, because it's too painful to confront the fact that, for example, more than one-third of classes in "high-poverty" public schools, and about 20 percent in "low-poverty" schools in the United States are taught by adults who neither studied nor trained to teach those subjects.[105]

No Atlantis educators were ever caught cheating (they're figments of my imagination, after all), but real ones have been fired or indicted in Maryland, Texas, Connecticut and other states.

Most of our states rely on machine-scored standardized tests, often resulting in cuts in "frills" like art, music and physical education, and the addition of more drill.

According to the Center on Education Policy, 26 states "currently have or plan to have mandatory exit exams for high school seniors," and test boycotts are a reality: Parents in well-to-do communities like Scarsdale, N.Y., and Berkeley, Calif., have kept their children home on test days.

Because standardized tests are not precise instruments, so-called "false negatives"' and "false positives" are also facts of life. By Massachusetts' own calculation, it's statistically likely that about

3,000 of the 10th-graders who were told they failed the state math test actually passed it. Errors by testing companies have penalized students in Arizona, Minnesota, Indiana, Massachusetts and New York.

On Atlantis and here in the United States, bad tests and over-reliance on test results are the enemies of good standards. On my fictional island *and in the real world,* it's the students who suffer most, not the politicians and other adults who make the policies. Of course, Atlantis is sinking slowly into the sea, meaning that its bitter arguments over educational standards and high-stakes tests will soon be over.

The rest of us should be so lucky.

Chapter 8
GUARANTEEING DISASTER

In the old joke about a farmer who wins the lottery, he's asked what he intends to do with the millions he's won. He replies laconically, "I'm just going to keep on farming until it's gone." The point of the joke is obvious: In farming, "business as usual" is a losing proposition for the farmer. But in public education, "business as usual" is a losing proposition for us all. It's the road we cannot continue to go down—not if we want our public schools and our democracy to survive. Because without an effective and efficient system of public education, our democracy will wither and die.

We may have already gone too far. Consider: Where are the people right now who, in 15 years, will be maintaining the planes we fly in, processing our tax returns, changing the IV-drips and dispensing our medications in hospitals, assembling the cars we buy, and teaching our children and grandchildren to make their way in the world?

In all probability, they're students in our public schools. Pretty soon these kids will be tuning up our cars, performing surgery on us and our loved ones, coming into our homes to install cable and phone connections, holding government jobs and running for office, fixing our plumbing, policing our communities, teaching[106] our children and grandchildren, caring (or not) for an aging population—guess who that will be—and performing other jobs that we will truly need them to do well, with intelligence, integrity, good judgment and often compassion. Pretty soon, these kids will be voting for the men and women who lead us.

I could write the following paragraphs about any of our states, but consider our most populous state—California (about 39 million people)—where one of every eight children goes to school. Californians should be seriously worried because the quality of their public school system has plummeted since the late 1950s and early 1960s. California hit bottom on the National Assessment of Educational Progress (NAEP) tests in 1994, and today, despite years of serious reform efforts, California students remain near the bottom in math, reading and science.

I'm writing this as a part-time Californian, but before that, in 2003-2004, I spent about 18 months in schools there making a documentary for PBS.[107] I was shocked by what I saw. Most California schools did not have regular art, music and physical education classes, foreign languages, counseling, or well-stocked school libraries with full-time librarians. Many California schools were deteriorating, overcrowded and understaffed. Some schools ran triple sessions, closing only on Christmas and New Year's Day.

About 9.4 million children live in California (that's about 13 percent of our country's children), and with 6.3 million students currently enrolled in public schools, California is responsible for teaching more students "in the K-12 public system than any other state in the nation."[108] The typical California pre-K-12 guidance counselor may be responsible for a mind-boggling 809 students; this number means that California ranks 50th in the nation in this regard, with the recommended ratio of guidance counselors per student being 250:1![109] As John Mockler, the veteran politician who once ran the State Board of Education, said, "It's like Calcutta."

For years the Golden State has been doing education on the cheap. California spends about $7,571 per child, about $2,400 below the national average, ranking the state 47th in the nation in terms of per-pupil spending, and earning it an "F" on student spending, in Education Week's "Quality Counts 2009." Responding to this ranking, and expressing deep concern for the effect of California's economic crisis and proposed budget cuts to education, State Schools Chief Jack O'Connell said: "This is a sad distinction considering the challenges we face to improve student achievement and close the achievement gap that exists between students who are white or Asian and their peers who are African American, Latino, or learning the English language. More than 1.5 million English learners attend school in California. It is critical to our entire state's economic future that these students succeed in school and are well-prepared for success in the competitive global economy."[110]

In the glory days, Californians spent 5.6 cents of every dollar on schools; today it's less than four cents.

"What would California parents do if they could see what's considered normal in public schools in Connecticut, Michigan and the rest of the country?" I asked John Deasy, who was the Santa Monica-Malibu superintendent at the time.

"They'd move! If they stayed here, they'd revolt," he said. Ironically it was Deasy, himself, who moved. Frustrated with the situation and seeing no possibility of change, he resigned in 2006 and became superintendent in Prince George's County, Md.[111]

For a hopeful moment, there seemed to be some good news. California governor Arnold Schwarzenegger initially seemed determined to fix the state's broken schools. Early in his administration he settled the ACLU's lawsuit against the state (his predecessor spent upwards of $16 million defending it) and forged an alliance with the state's powerful teachers union. He also "borrowed" $3.9 billion from the state's education fund, which some analysts said cost each classroom as much as $25,000.

Apparently seeking to make amends, he publicly declared on several occasions in 2007 that the next year, 2008, would be "the year of education."

That did not happen. Despite a comprehensive report, "Getting Down to Facts: A Research Project Examining California's School Governance and Finance Systems,"[112] which detailed how the system is overregulated, underfunded and "broken," Governor Schwarzenegger has not been able to keep state spending at previous levels.

Because more than 400 of California's 1,000-plus school districts have private non-profit foundations, well-to-do school districts will be able to make up any shortfall with private fundraising. That may minimize the political flak, but it shouldn't be allowed to obscure the fact that California has *two* public school systems— and the one for poor kids is taking yet another hit.

John Merrow

To see what's at stake, and also what's possible, I'd recommend that public officials visit Breed Street Elementary School in Boyle Heights, just east of downtown Los Angeles. This K-5 school is in a tough Mexican-American (and Mexican) neighborhood where about 40 gangs were operating in a 20-square-block radius at the time I visited. Of the 550 kids at Breed, 93.39 percent are on the "free and reduced" meal program, the normal marker for poverty.

I was at Breed Elementary in January 2005, filming a piece for the NewsHour about Breed's SOS program. SOS stands for "Society of Students," although the kids who participate say it also means "save our schools," "save our society" and "save our souls." Janis Hiura, the nearly 40-year veteran of public education who founded SOS, says it stands for all these things and more: "I tell the kids that first they have to save themselves, and once they do that, they can save schools, society and other souls."

In 2005, I described a number of things that Governor Schwarzenegger would see if he visited Breed. I wrote that he would find a clean, orderly building, and well-behaved kids in simple blue-and-white uniforms, and that upon entering any classroom, at least five students would walk up to him, introduce themselves, and thank him for coming to their school. They would do this whether or not they recognized him, because that's how they greet every visitor.

If the governor asked kids where they were from, though, they'd answer "nowhere." They would *not* give the name of their street, because they've learned that questioners sometimes shoot people who live on rival turf—and "nowhere" means they have no gang affiliation.

I also said that the governor would see "popcorn" when watching a class lesson (that's what SOS calls kids popping up to volunteer answers to a teacher's question), and that when more than one child pops up, whoever's spoken most recently defers. (SOS calls this "new blood.") And when a student answers correctly or in a particularly thoughtful manner, classmates often call out in unison, "You're the man (or woman)." That's because SOS members,

Hiura says, believe that "you never succeed alone and you never watch your buddies drown."

Well, guess what. Perhaps Governor Schwarzenegger watches the NewsHour, because on May 20, 2006, he did visit Breed Elementary School, along with Mayor Antonio Villaraigosa, Speaker of the Assembly Fabian Nunez, City of Los Angeles Councilman Jose Huizar, School Board President Marlene Canter, State Superintendent of Public Instruction Jack O'Connell and a group of legislators. You see, the governor's office requested Breed as "the location for the signing of SOS student leadership program" and, as the Boyle Heights Learning Collaborative website continues, "kindly congratulated our students for making great progress as leaders in their community and for promoting a positive culture of learning. Our SOS students were very excited as they met our elected officials."[113]

"Our children deserve to go to safe, modern and uncrowded schools," said Governor Schwarzenegger at Breed Street Elementary School during the bill signing ceremony. "The education bond will finance urgently needed infrastructure projects throughout California's education system."

Hiura started SOS in her fifth-grade class in the 2000-2001 school year, and, after one year, was encouraged by her principal at the time, Katty Iriarte, to expand across the school. SOS is now an integral part of Breed Street Elementary School, requiring students to commit to do their best in school, turn in all homework, participate in class and encourage others to be good citizens. Thanks to a grant from the Annenberg Foundation, Hiura (now director of student leadership for the Boyle Heights Learning Collaborative) was able to leave the classroom to focus on growing the SOS program. In 2005-2006, nearly 300 of Breed's 717 students were active SOS members.[114]

None of this has been easy. When I visited Breed in 2005, it was not considered cool to be a good student; in fact, it was an insult to be called a "schoolboy" or a "schoolgirl," Hiura noted at the time. "But we want our kids to be seen and heard," she said, "because if they don't speak up for themselves, no one will."

Hopefully, while visiting Breed the governor did not also have to join kids in practicing the "pancake drill": hitting the floor to make themselves as flat as possible. They are taught to do this whenever they hear gunshots. All the 9-year-olds I interviewed at Breed said they'd seen handguns up close.

While we were filming in 2005, this announcement came over the PA: "We are on lockdown. Everybody inside immediately." It was 3 p.m., and even the parents who had come to pick up their children were ordered inside, where they sat against the corridor walls and waited. Just four blocks away, two gang members had been gunned down—probably, we were told, by members of a rival gang. The kids' nonchalance during all of this was striking. Unfortunately, it's all too familiar to them.

I don't know if Governor Schwarzenegger went on to visit the middle and high schools that Breed students will be sent to after fifth grade. They'll go to Hollenbeck Middle School (enrollment varies from day to day, according to school staff, but is currently estimated at 1,750) and then on to Theodore Roosevelt Senior High School (enrollment just over 4,000 students, and expected to drop to about 3,500 in September 2010 when the new Esteban Torres Learning Complex opens), in the Los Angeles Unified School District—a district with a reported dropout rate of about 35 percent in 2008. But the Breed Street kids do have the Boyle Heights Learning Collaborative on their side, which is working to convene principals and teachers from these schools and others, to build capacity and make transitions easier for the students.

I hope the tremendous strides by SOS will be enough to ensure that the kids survive the harsh, impersonal environments of Hollenbeck and Roosevelt. In those schools, where students are numbers and it's dangerous to be a "schoolboy" or "schoolgirl," many adolescents find identity by joining gangs.

Seeing the Society of Students program in action might be just the SOS warning that California's governor needs. To stop California's slide toward third-world status, the state needs leadership that will fund education properly, whatever that takes. And California needs more adults who are ashamed to live in a state that treats its children so shabbily—and are angry enough to get rid of politicians who refuse to act.

In its defense, the Schwarzenegger administration has expressed interest in reforms that have been successful in Edmonton, Alberta, and Seattle. These are described in William Ouchi's book, "Making Schools Work." I've seen the Seattle reforms in action, and if California—or even some California cities and towns—could duplicate them, prospects for the future would look considerably brighter.[115]

Those reforms turn the power pyramid upside-down and make schools, principals, teachers and parents the center of the educational universe. It all begins where it should, with children. Once the cost of educating an "average" child is determined, the authorities figure out how much extra it costs to educate a child with special needs, a child whose first language is not English, and so on. Then, figuratively speaking, a sticker with that dollar amount is put on the forehead of each child, and parents are encouraged to shop around for the public school that seems most appropriate. That's parental choice.

Schools have choices of their own, as well. Teachers don't have seniority rights, meaning that principals can hire candidates who best fit their needs, rather than having to take someone just because he or she has been teaching the longest.

In these reforms, principals control most of the money spent in their schools—a far cry from California's reality. What percentage of their schools' money do California principals actually control? The *highest* number, according to those I've asked, has been 4 percent. By comparison, Edmonton principals control 97 percent of their funds, according to Professor Ouchi.

When parents choose and when principals are free to hire (particularly with full involvement of teachers, as in the Seattle reform), a school can become "an intentional community" made up of adults and children who want to be there. Then, if the system is clear about educational goals and has reliable measurement instruments, each school can devise its own path to those goals.

There are, however, serious obstacles to statewide reform in California. For one thing, educational power resides in the capital, and the legislature is heavily influenced by the California Teachers Association (the union). Sacramento collects the money and then parcels it out with strings attached, in various "categorical" education programs. School districts must be careful to keep track of how they spend those categorical dollars. One superintendent said she spends a good chunk of the money, plus a lot of staff time, on accounting. Add to that the recent $18 billion in cuts to education over two years, in the wake of the state's severe budget crisis, and you've got a formula for serious obstacles to change. "It doesn't take much to realize what these cuts mean for education," said State Superintendent O'Connell in May 2009. "School leaders are going to be doing all they can just to keep the lights on and the doors open. I fear that the progress we've made for seven years is likely to be completely derailed and our efforts to close the achievement gap will be an afterthought."[116]

True reform requires flexibility in hiring. But seniority generally rules in California, meaning that teachers with the most seniority can lay claim to openings. Would California's teachers give up seniority rights? John Perez, former president of United Teachers Los Angeles, told me at the time that his members *might consider* waiving seniority *if* they got something significant in return—such as a real role in hiring.[117]

There are local impediments, as well. California law makes it very difficult to raise money for schools. The easiest way, believe it or not, is through a highly regressive tax known as a "parcel tax": a fixed amount, no matter the value of the property. To gain approval, two-thirds of the voters must approve. Regarding the recent $18 billion in budget cuts for education, O'Connell said: "And even if we somehow manage to come up with a workable budget, it will take major budget reforms to get us moving again in the right direction. I have called for passage of a constitutional amendment to help local districts more easily pass parcel taxes and I have called for a majority vote budget to end gridlock and increase budget accountability. But we all must be open to new ideas and reforms that will help us get California back on track."[118]

I followed a parcel tax election in the wealthy community of Santa Monica in 2003, interviewing dozens of voters. I asked one young woman who had just emerged from the voting booth if she'd voted for the special measure to give the schools more money. Her answer did not surprise me. "Education is very important, but I don't know why I, as a single person who doesn't have kids, should have to bear so much of it," she said.

Many adults feel the same way. And since the majority of U.S. households do not have school-age children and because senior citizens are reliable voters, schools face an uphill battle when it comes to raising money because in California it takes a 55 percent approval to pass local school facility bonds and a two-thirds supermajority to approve extra funds through parcel taxes. This is spelled out in Proposition 39, which in 2000 amended the 1978 California law known as Proposition 13.[119]

That woman (and every voter without school-age children) should care very much indeed about our public schools. *Who* on earth, I wanted to ask her, do you think will take care of you when you grow old? Who do you think will maintain the commercial jets you fly on, manage your investments and retirement accounts, inspect your medications and food products for safety, and repair your electricity and plumbing? When you're older, who do you think will be working in hospitals and in retirement homes, perhaps deciding if you'll be allowed to keep the pet you love like a child if you need to move into an assisted-care facility? Who do you think will be breaking difficult medical news to you or someone you love, and making decisions that will directly impact your physical and emotional welfare at every level?

Will they be thoughtful, empathetic and broad-minded people? Or will they be products of a mediocre public school education, who never learned to appreciate art, music or physical fitness, and who never learned to develop their imaginations enough to put themselves in another person's shoes?

John Merrow

Finding more money is the biggest challenge of all, given the state's tremendous budget deficit. Closely following that challenge is figuring out how to spend it much more effectively.

California cannot afford to tinker around the margins; radical change is needed.[120] Too many children are being lost, and too many of those lost are children of color. California *cannot afford* to have its future majority grow up undereducated.

What's happening in California schools should concern Americans everywhere. One of every eight children in the United States goes to a California public school, and there are no walls or moats to keep our most populous state's undereducated graduates from spreading out to Illinois and Connecticut and Florida. What kids learn, or don't learn, in California's public schools will ultimately affect us all.

And if California's problems are a harbinger of what's ahead for the rest of us, the future is, shall we say, challenging.

Section Two
FOLLOW THE LEADER

Chapter 9
FOLLOWING LEADERS[121]

<u>Michelle Rhee:</u> "I'm going to fire somebody in a little while," the young superintendent said. "Do you want to see that?"

In our world, "see" means "videotape." Washington, D.C., schools chancellor Michelle Rhee was actually inviting us to film her as she fired one of her employees.

My colleagues Jane Renaud and Cat McGrath had spent the morning in Chancellor Rhee's office, filming her meeting with parents, community groups and principals. A dynamo, Rhee moved easily from meeting to meeting, seemingly unaware of the presence of our camera.

Jane and Cat were stunned by her invitation, but not so much that they didn't accept on the spot. As Jane recalls, "She told us to come back at a specific time, and so we got a sandwich, returned to her office, set up the equipment and shot the meeting."

That event, shown on national television on the NewsHour, helped create the media persona of Michelle Rhee: the fearless and determined reformer who puts the interests of children first.

How we ended up in her office in the first place is a somewhat complicated tale.

Rhee was unknown to those outside the world of education reform when Washington's newly elected mayor, Adrian Fenty, asked her to become chancellor of the public schools that he had just taken control of and had promised to turn into a world-class system. No small challenge, since D.C.'s students scored at the very bottom of the pile on the National Assessment of Educational Progress.

When I read about the appointment of a 37-year-old Korean-American who had never even been a school principal, let alone a superintendent, I talked with my colleagues about chronicling her efforts on the NewsHour. All agreed that it could be history in the making and she sounded like an appealing character for television. I determined to call her, introduce myself and make the pitch.

However, another strong leader—this one a proven commodity—had just accepted the challenge of leading another dreadful school system. That story also intrigued us.

Paul Vallas: I met Paul Vallas in 1996 when he was CEO of the Chicago Public Schools, which had just recently been put under the mayor's control. Not an educator by training, Vallas stepped down from his post as Mayor Daley's budget director to accept the challenge. Tall and gangly, the 43-year-old Vallas struck me as the Energizer Bunny incarnate: moving fast and talking even faster. He also seemed remarkably thin-skinned for a public figure, prone to over-reacting to criticism of any sort.

I subsequently saw him a few times during his controversial tenure in Philadelphia, where he pushed hard for change, privatized about 40 schools, raised test scores—and spent more dollars than the city or the state wanted to.

When this proven leader accepted the challenge in 2007 to spearhead what Louisiana named the "Recovery School District" (basically the worst-performing schools in the state, most of which were in New Orleans), I was intrigued. I was already invested in the story because we'd reported from that zone three times since Hurricane Katrina and the subsequent flooding that had ravaged the schools (and everything else). Perhaps Vallas would be interested in having us follow him around, documenting his efforts.

The NewsHour was also excited about the possibility of a strong serial that would draw in viewers.[122]

Since Rhee and Vallas were new to their jobs, I decided to hedge my bets and call both, figuring there was no way both would agree. To have one, I believed I needed to ask two, so I called them both.

Rhee's response was, I came to understand, typically direct and forceful. "I have to figure out whether this would help me do what I have to do, which is make things better for kids. If I think it will, I will say yes. If not, I won't do it." We agreed to meet for dinner the next evening.

Then I called Paul Vallas. "Sure, come on down," he said immediately.

"We'll want complete access," I said.

"No problem."

"Do you know what you're getting yourself into?"

He replied that he did. "Two-thirds of the kids are at least one year older than grade level, and a large number of the kids are two years or older than grade level," he said. "I'm talking about 17-year-old eighth-graders and 18-year-old ninth-graders who are two, three, four years below grade level academically." But, he added, he also had unprecedented authority: the power to hire and fire, to change the school day and the school year, to bring in new curriculum, and so forth. Most superintendents work for a school board, but Vallas reports directly to the state superintendent, a pragmatic, brainy lawyer named Paul Pastorek.

The next night Murrey Jacobsen of the NewsHour and I took Michelle Rhee out for dinner. She asked good questions, weighed our answers and—to my great surprise—agreed to open her professional life to our cameras.

Bingo! We had access to two major school reform efforts, a coup for us. But with that elation came grim realization: We couldn't afford to cover both stories. In fact, we barely had enough to guarantee full coverage for just one year, and we knew we'd have to stick around for at least two to see any significant educational change.

What to do? Should we choose between Rhee and Vallas? If so, whom should we follow? Both were compelling stories, both leaders had promised access, both had big plans.

It was my call, and, rather than flip a coin, I decided to gamble on a better future. We'd follow both of them, with two production teams,[123] and I'd have to find the money somewhere.

To their credit, three foundations stepped up to the plate and allowed us to follow both stories.[124] The Wallace Foundation, the

Bill & Melinda Gates Foundation and the Eli and Edythe Broad Foundation[125] all made grants. Not only that, they did it with a minimum of fuss, freeing us to concentrate on the work at hand.

And I can't exactly call it work—it's been more of an adventure.

Michelle Rhee: Before becoming D.C.'s chancellor, Rhee was president and chief executive of the New Teacher Project, a nonprofit she founded to recruit and train teachers for hard-to-staff schools and help school districts reform their operations. She'd be moving from a 120-employee organization managing—and radically changing—a school system with 55,000 students and 11,500 employees. Rhee, a Cornell grad with a master's from Harvard's Kennedy School, had taught for three years at Harlem Park Elementary School in Baltimore through Teach For America. She's told many audiences about her early failures and her eventual success in dramatically raising test scores.[126]

Mayor Fenty wanted a catalyst and had asked New York City school chancellor Joel Klein for advice. Klein didn't hesitate. "There's a culture of mediocrity, typically, in a lot of school systems," he said. "A lot of school systems make excuses for nonperformance. And someone like Michelle, I think, can come in and, with her vision and her commitment, lead them in a different direction."

Clearly, D.C. needed a change: 88 percent of eighth-graders had recently scored below proficient in reading on the national report card, with 93 percent below proficient in math.

Mayor Fenty persuaded Rhee to fly out from Denver, but he had one major problem: She wasn't looking for a job.

"I told him, 'You don't want me for this job,'" said Rhee. "'You are a politician. Your job is to keep the noise to a minimum level and to keep your constituents happy.' I said, 'I am a change agent, and change doesn't come without significant pushback and opposition, which is absolutely counter to what you want.'"

The mayor persisted. Finally Rhee asked, "What would you risk just for the chance to turn this school district around, to truly transform it?"

Fenty did not hesitate: "I said 'Everything,' that one word. And it's true."

In June 2007, Mayor Fenty introduced his new chancellor, who minced no words about her intentions: "I am going to run this district in a way that is constantly looking out for the best interests of the children and of the schools."

The mayor made it clear that he had her back.[127] "We have a once-in-a-lifetime opportunity to make this school system excellent," he said. "And to the extent we can allow her to do that, as free from outside obstacles as humanly possible, the faster she will move." He told his Cabinet that he was the only person who could say "no" to her, warning them that interfering with her efforts could be a firing offense.

Rhee hit the ground running and made headlines when she toured the District's supply building. "By the time I got onto the second floor, I thought I was going to throw up," she said. "I actually felt nauseous because of what I was seeing. It was boxes and boxes of glue and scissors and composition books, binders, boxes of unopened trade books, class sets of novels, things that teachers not only are dying for but spend their own money on."

She straightened that mess out, got her 146 schools open and running on time, and then set her sights on her own central office. "You know, as I walk around, and I listen to how people operate, and I listen to the way that they answer the phone or the way they're dealing with people as they're coming to the central office, it sounds like they're very annoyed. This is not a nuisance; this is your job. So if you consider answering their questions or giving them information a nuisance, then this is not the place for you to work."

According to Joel Klein, there was only one path for Rhee to follow. "You have to get rid of people," he said. "I mean, the real fact is—she knows it, anybody who studies it knows it—there are people who are put there for patronage and other reasons and who don't really have a vital role to play. And we don't have dollars to spend on people who don't have a vital role to play."

Rhee and Fenty asked the City Council to rewrite the law to give the chancellor more leeway when it came to removing her own staff. "I need this authority for the long term to make sure that, any time there's any employee who's not producing results and who's not doing the right thing for kids, that we're able to move them out of the system," Rhee said at the time.

This made the Washington Teachers' Union and its president, George Parker, very nervous. They feared that Rhee would want more power over teachers. "The chancellor already has more than enough authority to remove from the system any teachers that are deemed ineffective or incompetent," Parker told us. "I cannot at this point imagine what additional authority the chancellor would need in order to remove ineffective teachers."

And the union had reason to be nervous. Its contract had expired, and many feared that Rhee would try to make big changes in the process used to remove ineffective teachers, the so-called "90-day plan." (This requires numerous precise steps on the administration's part, and failure to follow the letter of the law can abort the process completely, requiring the administration to start all over again.)

Rhee made no secret of the value she places on teacher quality: "I cannot risk children's education for very long while they are sitting, languishing in an ineffective teacher's classroom."

And she seemed to embrace the attention, the national spotlight.[128] "All the eyes of the country are now on D.C.," she told us. "I believe that what we are embarking upon is a fight for the lives of children." On another occasion she said, "I hope that everything that we do in some ways will have reverberations across the country."

She was also impatient. "I think what I am, is somebody who is focused on the end result that I think needs to happen," she said. "So if the rule is standing in the way of that, I will question those rules. I will bend those rules."

Rule-bending wasn't required to remove school principals, so she put them on notice: Improve or else. She also gave each school leader a specific target: better test scores.

Rhee had her critics, including some veteran superintendents who felt that her emphasis on people ignored structural problems. Union president George Parker sent a message: Help teachers improve; don't just make threats. He told the NewsHour, "We have to move the discussion away from hiring and firing of ineffective employees and begin to move the discussion to what kind of supports are we going to put in place in our district to support teachers and children."

But Rhee believed the general public was on her side: "On the weekends I'm in the grocery store. I am like in my flip-flops, and people come up to me, and they say, 'Thank goodness you're doing this. You can't do it quick enough. Don't give up.'"

Paul Vallas: Vallas hit the ground running, full of confidence. He had, after all, managed two large districts and was now just in charge of about 13,000 students, only 60 schools[129]—and no tough teachers union to deal with. Given the size of the district, Vallas predicted improvements: "I think the institutional framework can be laid here within the next two years, and I think we can start seeing results within the next year or so."

How confident was he? "If within two years[130] this district has not significantly improved," he said, "if I have not achieved 90 percent of what I've promised then, you, they should put me on the Amtrak and send me back home to Chicago."[131]

Like Michelle Rhee in Washington, Vallas seems to have boundless energy. "My day will usually begin about 7:30 in the morning, particularly if I'm doing a school visit," he said. "An early day for me is 6:30, a late day for me is 9:30, 10 o'clock."

Educationally, New Orleans schools were terrible even before Katrina. On one state test, for instance, 80 percent of students were below basic on math, 88 percent below basic in English. Many schools not badly damaged by Katrina and the flooding were already falling apart. Parents who could afford private or parochial school took their children out of the public system, and most of Vallas' new students were living in poverty or near-poverty.

Vallas had a plan. He gave parents a laundry list of physical improvements he wanted to see in the still-devastated city: air-conditioned classrooms with proper lighting, modern furniture, up-to-date textbooks, a benchmarked instructional program, regular testing and modern technology—including laptops for all high school students.

Veteran teachers were skeptical. "He is bright-eyed. I know he's been successful elsewhere, but New Orleans is different," one high school teacher told us. "He doesn't understand the reality. He doesn't have to deal with the logistics of the laptop when it gets stolen."

Vallas dismissed her criticism as negativity. "I suggest that teacher look for another school district because that's the exact low expectations that we set for inner-city kids, and that's the same attitude that resulted in many inner-city districts deciding that children shouldn't take textbooks home, because they'll lose the textbooks," he said.

In Vallas' view, low expectations all but guarantee low performance. "A lot of time when you raise expectations, people say you're being naïve, but it's like what comes first, the chicken or the egg? What comes first, the low performance or the low expectations?" For him, the question is rhetorical. Low expectations produce poor results.

Like Michelle Rhee, Vallas believes that good teachers are the foundation. "There's no substitute for that enthusiastic teacher who's willing to work like there's no tomorrow," he said.

That's why he invested heavily in Teach For America, recruiting as many corps members as he could. "What they bring to the classroom are content mastery, enthusiasm and unbelievable work ethic, very high expectations for kids, high expectations for success and a sense of optimism," he said. Vallas also loved their willingness to work. "They don't punch a clock. They're not 9 to 4, they're not five days a week. They really commit themselves and throw themselves into the job."

But Vallas didn't dictate to his principals about their hiring practices, meaning that Cheryllyn Branche was free to hire the teachers she wanted at Benjamin Banneker Elementary School. "I prefer people who know what they're doing. I prefer people who have a proven track record. I prefer people who are going to stay here and work with our children for the long haul," Ms. Branche said. In other words, no one from Teach For America need apply.

Vallas wanted dedication above all. And what sort of teachers ought to be worried about their jobs, I asked him. "If you have poor attendance, if you have low expectations for children, if you're showing up at school five minutes before the school day begins and you're leaving school five minutes after the school day ends, I think you should probably be a little nervous," he said.

Vallas has had to deal with different perceptions on the part of some of his teachers, who seem to expect little from their students. "You have kids who don't think education is important. You have kids who come from families who don't push the issue about getting to school on time or even getting to school at all," one teacher told us. From her perspective, the problem was "the apathy in the home/community environment."

Even if Vallas held that view, his response would be to attack the problem. "The challenge for us is to try to compensate for what's missing at home. And that means you keep the schools open longer. You provide the children with three meals a day. You expand the number of social services that you can provide," he said.

At faculty convocation just before school opened, Vallas rallied his troops, telling them that, by dedicating themselves to the education of young people, they were part of "the greatest chapter in the American civil rights movement."

"You will set that bar, you will raise that bar," he exhorted. "You will set those high expectations."

The teachers cheered, but, unfortunately, the students didn't get the message. On opening day, about 40 percent stayed home.

Michelle Rhee: Early in her first year, Rhee had to confront a deficit of $100 million. Her response? "We spend more per pupil than almost any other urban jurisdiction does, and that's partially because we have a lot of our resources and money going into facilities that are a quarter-full or a half-full." She was right. Enrollment in D.C. had dropped by 27 percent in the previous 10 years, and two dozen or more schools were significantly under-enrolled. Her solution: to immediately close 15 percent of the buildings. When that news leaked, the City Council was furious.

Rhee held community meetings to hear complaints and explain her thinking, but she refused to consider group decision-making or consensus-building. "If the leader of the school district went about closing schools by saying, 'What does everyone think about this? How do you think we should do it?' I would lose faith immediately in that person," she said. Mayor Fenty agreed: "By definition, if she had done that, it would no longer have been the plan to make the schools excellent. Before you even started, it would have already been compromised."

Rhee showed her willingness—some say her eagerness—to embrace confrontation. "Bottom line is, I'm not going to get to a point where everybody agrees on one decision. No matter what decision we make in the end, some group of people is going to be unhappy. I can guarantee you that."

As opposition grew, Rhee had the support of the only person who really mattered: Mayor Adrian Fenty. And he made his wishes perfectly clear: "People say, 'You're moving too fast; you're trying to push too much right now.'…But when you're out in the neighborhoods of the District of Columbia talking to regular people, they're saying, 'Go faster. Fix things. Do more.'"

In the end, Rhee announced that six of the 23 schools she'd intended to close would be spared, but added four new ones to the list.

Paul Vallas: He may have inherited a small district compared to his previous Chicago and Philadelphia posts, but New Orleans had, and has, major problems—and Vallas knows it. "There's drug deals going on, drive-by shootings. The violence that we face in our communities is tied to poverty and tied to educational failure and things of this nature," he said.

Educational failure was rampant. At one point, 85 percent of New Orleans students were scoring below basic on state tests. "This is a very tough job," he said. "This is a very tough environment. We're educating kids that are way behind. All the kids are at least one, two, three years below grade level. That's really a challenge."

My impression of Paul Vallas is that he is willing to try just about anything—and everything—if there's even the slightest chance it will make a difference. And if something isn't working, he'll pull the plug, even though he may not be willing to admit that he made a mistake.

For students who were farthest behind, Vallas created alternative schools. "If you have a 17-year-old reading at the fourth-grade reading level, it would make sense to ability group them rather than keep 16- and 17-year-olds in a fifth- or sixth- or seventh-grade class," he said.

He hired a private company, Camelot, to run them. At Booker T. Washington, students and teachers complained vociferously. As one teacher told us, "Most of the students say this is just a prison, a detention center."

That same teacher, Luke Strattner, said he didn't have the proper textbooks for his math classes. "I teach math for kids who are first- through third-grade level, but I only have eighth-grade books. These kids are not anywhere close to eighth-grade. If I had fifth-grade books or fourth-grade books, I might be able to handle it a lot better."

But the content of books appropriate to their skill level often reminds students how far behind they are, according to teacher Jeffrey Berman. "It's hard to get this age group interested in material that is traditionally intended for a younger audience," he said. "That's probably the biggest challenge—getting them interested in stuff that normally they might give the response, 'This is baby stuff, why am I doing this?'"

He went on. "If you experience failure long enough, you're not going to want to even try anymore because you are going to expect to fail every time." He told us that many of his students say,

"I'm sick of being in the eighth grade. I'm sick of not being able to pass this."

Vallas' early efforts at Booker T. Washington failed. Camelot tried to run a tight ship in terms of behavior, but, according to Strattner, "There was so much chaos that the Camelot guys were all trying to control, but it wasn't really working." Moreover, few students made significant academic progress.

On Camelot's watch, only a small handful passed the state test, known as LEAP, but most were allowed to move to high school anyway. Vallas defended the decision. "A number of the students may have not passed all of the subjects on the eighth-grade exit exam, but they've gotten good grades, good behavior, good attendance. For all practical purposes they can manage ninth-grade work."

But in what seemed like sleight of hand, he added that they weren't really ninth-graders, more like eighth-and-a-half-graders, if such a thing is possible.

Strattner was critical, calling this just more social promotion. "We're doing the same thing that's the problem in the first place," he said. "They're too old to be in eighth grade so let's move them to ninth grade. That's basically just putting the problem on somebody else."

At the end of his second year, Vallas changed course. He did not renew Camelot's contract. He turned his four alternative schools over to Deputy Superintendent Michael Haggen, who opted for a very different approach, one that empowered students. At Booker T. Washington Accelerated Academy, students now meet daily in what's called Circle of Courage. They're encouraged to talk about whatever's on their mind, guided by several non-traditional teachers: men who have been incarcerated.

Haggen believes Circle of Courage will teach these young men and women how to make better decisions. "They're learning how to de-escalate on their own," he said. "They're learning how to do peer mediation. They're learning that there are opportunities where you are going to be on the outside, where you're going to have to make a choice. Do you want to do something that's a poor decision? Or do you want to make the best decision?"

And that, says Principal Rosemary Martin, will lead to academic success. "A lot of them put up walls," she said. "And we've had to chisel away at those walls, so that we can get into their minds, so that they have a mindset of wanting to be taught, wanting to achieve and wanting to learn, even though they may be three or four grades below or behind their age level."

What's most surprising is that Martin is willing to acknowledge that adults screwed up, passing along the students from grade to grade. So if a student asks why no one taught him to read, she says, "I tell the students that some way, somewhere along the road someone dropped the ball."

Does she tell students they're not to blame? "It's not their fault," she said. "That's the first step, is acknowledgment."

At another alternative school—this one for students who've had run-ins with the law—Vallas is taking another chance. He's encouraging them to enroll in college-level courses at a nearby technical institute. Students with good attendance and a strong academic record spend afternoons studying nursing and other subjects.

"I like taking young people out of the traditional high school environment, and putting them in an environment where they are surrounded with individuals who are focused on their careers," said Vallas. "Those are the type of role models that these young people should be exposed to."

Vallas has also embraced so-called "smart boards," which allow a teacher to project material from a laptop computer. Early on, he promised laptop computers for all high school students, and, when they were distributed, he described the plan to a group of local clergy.[132] "That simple act, putting that computer in the hands of that child and allowing that child to take that computer home was our statement of confidence and optimism about the potential of that child," he said. "That's what it's about."

Still, he couldn't help boasting to the clergy about his students. The computer experts had told him that the laptops were set up so students couldn't access the Internet, but "it took the kids 20 minutes to hack into the computers," he said. "Just 20 minutes. Don't tell me that our inner-city kids are not the brightest kids on the block, because they are."

With nearly unlimited power to change schedules, Vallas has instituted an extended day program and an extended year. This year many schools run past 5 p.m., and the school year, which began in August, may continue into July.

"The game plan is to get the elementary school kids up to grade level. And to get them up to grade level at an accelerated pace," Vallas said, adding that children will spend four hours a day on reading, language arts, comprehension and vocabulary, and two hours a day on mathematics. He nearly jumped out of his chair to make the next point. "There is an absolute direct correlation between the amount of instructional time on task and student progress."

Another of Vallas' ideas is to combine school with paid work, which he thinks could keep kids coming to school. With great enthusiasm, he delineated the plan, modeled after a parochial school program he first saw in Chicago. "If I can give them a paid work-study opportunity, if they come to high school, have regular attendance and get passing grades, I think that might change the culture. It may change the dynamic. It might change their attitudes. It might give them a reason, an incentive, to come to school and to stay in school."

Paul Vallas seems to grasp that his greatest challenge is an ugly tradition of school failure: a deep belief that public schools just don't work. If a young person grows up knowing that going to school didn't do much for either his parents or his grandparents, how much faith should he have in schools? Outside of Vallas' enthusiasm, we saw, again and again, a pattern of indifference. The following conversation with some high school students captures it well:

Me: *A lot of students don't show up on a Friday? Why is that?*

Young man: It's kind of like Friday doesn't matter because most teachers don't really give a lot of work that day. It's kind of like a half day to relax.

Young woman: Because it's just a half a day, some people want to get their weekend early.

Another young woman: They want an early weekend.

Me: *Sounds like you're saying Friday is part of the weekend.*

Young man: Most likely.

Me: *But a lot of kids also skip school on Monday. Why is that?*

Young woman: They don't come on Monday because Sunday they didn't get any rest, so they rest on Monday.

When Paul Vallas arrived in New Orleans, he set about the task of rebuilding a broken school system. He tore down ruined buildings and spent millions refurbishing damaged ones. He truly believed in that cliché from the movie "Field of Dreams": If you build it, they will come.[133]

So far that has not been true, but Vallas isn't giving up. "It is a serious problem but I'm not going to change to accommodate the culture. I want the culture to change to accommodate me," he said.

Michelle Rhee: Trouble was brewing on the labor relations front, especially after the City Council gave Rhee authority to fire central office staff at will—which she used to fire 98 employees (over 10 percent of the staff).[134]

The teachers union, whose contract had expired, was nervous. "There are many who feel that they can transform education by simply focusing on children and supporting children. You have to support those who interact daily with children, our teachers, if you're going to get the results." That was George Parker's hopeful comment to us, even as the chancellor and her staff were taking hard-line positions about D.C.'s teaching force.

Michelle Rhee has a comic's timing and a politician's gift for phrase-making, a combination that has occasionally gotten her into trouble. For example, she didn't help her cause when she said this to us: "People now are beginning to cast me as heartless— 'Fire everybody, get rid of everybody.' That is not, in and of itself, the answer in isolation." (And here she paused.) "But it's a good start."

Was the chancellor anti-union?

"Let me say this," replied Parker. "Her statements in the past have not been very favorable to unions."

When the chancellor first met her teachers in August 2007, she was supportive. "There is no one that I would rather have on my team leading this, as the people in this room," she told them. But six months later her tune had changed. "There will be some schools where a significant amount of the teaching force will turn over," she told us. "I think that we are going to need a different breed of educators."

We asked what a "significant amount" meant. Rhee's director of professional development, Cheryl Krehbiel, was candid. "Fifty percent don't have the right mindset," she told us. "And there's the possibility that more of them don't have the content knowledge to do the job."[135]

Some school principals agreed. L. Nelson Burton, principal of Coolidge High School, said: "It's a terrible thing to say, but half of the staff here ought not be. They just don't fit into what we're doing here. And I dare say many of them won't fit into any program where we're trying to raise student achievement."

Did it surprise the chancellor to hear one of her principals say: "I wish I could fire half my teachers. They're not on board. They're not effective."?

Her response was typically blunt: "Does it surprise me? No. I've heard things like that from lots of principals."

But principals like Burton have the means to remove ineffective teachers: the "90-day plan." They can give teachers notice, provide help over a 90-day period, and then remove them if they don't show improvement. At the time, Burton had only four of his teachers on the 90-day plan. The union's Parker was quick to criticize: "If you're telling me half of your staff is not living up to par, the next question I want to ask you, as a leader, talk to me about what you've done to try to develop that staff."

Rhee made no secret of her desire for a new breed of teacher: men and women who thought the way she had when she was in the classroom.[136] "We have to have people who are willing to take personal responsibility and to say, despite all of the obstacles that are currently in the way of our kids—because there are tremendous obstacles—if you're not willing to say, 'But despite all those things, I'm going to make sure that my kids are going to succeed at the highest levels,' then this might not be the district for you."

And she was confident that her kind of teachers were out there. "I get e-mails from people across the country who want to come and work for us. There are a lot of people who are very excited about what we're doing."

She also wanted to revolutionize the way teachers are paid, tying wages to student performance. Under most contracts, pay is based on years served and graduate credits earned, a system Rhee finds absurd.

She had a distinct advantage in the negotiations, because the union was losing members to charter schools.[137] At the time, more than 25 percent of D.C. students were attending charters. To stop the loss, Parker said, the union had to pay attention to student learning. "Normally, unions have not had to contend with any sense of accountability or responsibility for student achievement, and our existence and survival has not depended upon that," he told us. Now it was, he said, a "bread and butter issue" for teachers.

Rhee put a bold two-tiered proposal on the table, offering teachers the chance to earn six-figure salaries if their students did well. But there was a catch: Tenured teachers would have to give up job security for a year. Then, if their students did well, they got the money and got their tenure back. But if not, they could lose their jobs.

In D.C., a 10-year veteran with a master's degree was earning just over $64,000. Under Rhee's two-tiered proposal, teachers could stick with that approach, the so-called "red path," and get step raises.

But if teachers chose what's known as a "pay for performance" model ("the green path") and if their students performed well, that 10-year veteran could earn as much as $122,000 in salary and bonuses.[138]

Parker said that most of his members opposed Rhee's plan, and Rhee said she would push back hard. Then she issued what sounded like a take-it-or-leave-it offer: "And the bottom line is that the union is going to have to decide whether they're going to accept my final offer and we're going to roll this out in a tentative agreement or not." And, she added, whether the plan passed or not, she would find ways to remove ineffective teachers.

Negotiations stalled, and the chancellor's prominence became an issue, particularly when she appeared on the cover of Time magazine, posed in an empty classroom with a broom in her hand.[139]

George Parker did not mince words: "It created a culture of low morale, one that was the lowest that I've seen since I've been in D.C. public schools, and I've been here for 25 years."

Some teachers agreed, saying that students were now openly disrespecting them. "There will be students who will start your day off saying, 'Oh, yeah, I've read the article. You all are getting fired anyway,'" said Randy Brown, a ninth-grade English teacher. "And they absolutely believe it. You can't really be accountable when you're undermined. They don't believe in you. They've lost their confidence in their teachers."

Had Rhee's criticism of some teachers alienated others to such a degree that a contract was beyond reach? Parker felt it had. "The morale is so low it would be very difficult to have folks truly buy into where you want to go and ride the train, because if folks are feeling that, 'Look, they're just waiting to throw me off the train,' that it's going to be very difficult for me to ride it."

In response, Rhee said she wants to help her teachers succeed. She increased the budget for professional development to almost $20 million, about five times greater than before. She also provided most schools with new staff whose job it was to help teachers improve.

She told us that more support for teachers and better teamwork were among her priorities for the District, and then—not for the first time—she blamed the press. "A lot of the things that were coming out in the press were sort of saying, you know, 'Rhee wants to fire people. It's all about firing people.' And I don't think that it was a comprehensive sort of view of what I actually believe," she said.

At one point during her second year, Rhee launched an effort to speak directly to teachers, holding meetings after school where teachers could ask her anything. She called them "listening sessions." We were not allowed to watch these, but the reviews were, at best, mixed. Most of the teachers we spoke with said Rhee did most of the talking.

Negotiations came to a halt during the summer of 2009, when Rhee's principals dismissed 239 teachers, even though the system had hired over 900 for the coming year. This situation required a "reduction in force," or RIF. Because Rhee tied the layoffs to budget pressures, she was not bound by the existing teachers' contract. To make the reduction in force, principals used a formula devised by Rhee, in which seniority counted for just 5 percent.

Some charged that Rhee had deliberately over-hired so she could then fire teachers she deemed ineffective. The national union, the American Federation of Teachers, stepped up its involvement, tempers blazed and the matter went to court. Rhee was adamant when she appeared before the City Council. "My understanding is that I do have the authority, as the agency head, to make the decisions about moving budget from one place to another," she testified.

The courts agreed, and the firings were not reversed. How much damage that has done to the chancellor's standing with her teachers is impossible to calculate.

During the session, Councilmember Michael Brown asked Rhee: "You clearly don't trust a lot of the stakeholders. It's obvious the stakeholders don't trust your office. So, how do we repair this?"

John Merrow

"I will fully do my part, to the extent that people have suggestions about how we move forward," she responded. "Some of the difficult decisions that we make will indeed cause some people to be unhappy. But we know we have to push forward on those decisions because they are right for schools and kids."

Paul Vallas: Whatever else he may accomplish in New Orleans, Paul Vallas is likely to be remembered—and mostly celebrated—for his enthusiastic embrace of charter schools. On his watch, the Recovery School District has become the most heavily chartered district in the nation, and Vallas predicts that before he leaves every school will either have a charter or be what he calls "charter-like," meaning that most of the authority rests at the school level.

His support is philosophical. "I'm a believer in schools having the freedom and autonomy to make decisions that are in the best interest of the children. And so I support charter schools, because charter schools are a vehicle for achieving that type of freedom," he said.

Vallas' support of charters is also political. While he can recommend that failing schools become charters, the final decision is up to State Superintendent Paul Pastorek. Here the two Pauls share a goal: Keep the old New Orleans School Board, infamous for its corruption, patronage and academic failure, from returning to power. Here's how Paul Vallas explains it: "My goal is to make sure that within the next two to three years we will have a system of schools that are independent of the old damaging covenants that existed prior to the hurricane. And that is a top-down management control structure that limits your ability to hire the best people and fire the worst people, that limits your ability to have a longer school day and longer school year, that keeps you from doing things in the best interests of the kids."

He likes the idea of decentralized authority. So do his principals, including Sharon Clark. "As principal of a charter school you are responsible for everything," she said. "I make sure instruction is in place and it's effective and aligned with the state standards. I make sure that the budget is balanced and that we have money for

100

payroll. I make sure that we continue to register kids and that our attendance works." Her school, Sophie B. Wright Middle School, was failing until Vallas made it into a charter. Now it's wildly successful, with parents petitioning Vallas to let the school add another grade—so their children won't have to leave to go to a regular high school.

Not everyone is enthusiastic about Vallas' grand design. Cheryllyn Branche, principal of Benjamin Banneker Elementary (one of the most improved schools in the district), says she spurned Vallas' invitation to become a charter school. "I think there are good charters and bad charters," she told us. "I really do feel that there's room at the table, but I don't think to designate that the entire city be 'charterized' makes any sense. Good schools make sense for every child."

What troubles Branche is how some charter schools treat children with special needs. She believes some schools are pushing these children away—which is illegal—and are doing it in subtle ways. "Parents are seeking places for their children who may have physical handicaps, mental or emotional handicapping conditions and they're not being accepted by charters," she said. Instead, she said, parents report that charter school principals recommend enrolling the child at Banneker: "Go to Banneker, tell Miss Branche I sent you. Go to Banneker."

Vallas denies that "dumping"—the common term—is going on, but he's sharpened his eye nonetheless. Here's how he explains it: "Charters are generally much smaller than regular traditionally run schools, so charters may not have the capacity to have the various specialties like the speech therapists, etc. A parent's going to ask, 'Do you have these services?' And if the charter doesn't have those services, the parent's going to look for another school."

At best, Vallas is splitting hairs here, because a parent is entitled by law to enroll a child at the school of his or her choice, and the school is then obligated to provide the necessary services. Is that blatant discrimination? Parent advocate Karran Harper Royal doesn't mince words: "That's discrimination. That's discrimination. You can dress it up however you'd like to, but it's really discrimination."

While Vallas denies the charge, he hopes to create ways for charter schools to share the cost of expensive services, like special education. He recognizes that decentralization can provide opportunities for misbehavior and worse, and so he's promised to be on guard. "As more of our schools are granted charter-like independence, we're going to be doing more policing," he said. "We're going to focus more on accountability. And if a school is deliberately discouraging people or turning people away, that would be breach of contract, and it could lose its charter."

Vallas continues to encourage and create charter schools. He expects that, at the start of school year 2010-2011, at least 60 percent of his schools will be operating under their own charters.

Michelle Rhee: She is a wonderful interview, smart and engaging and honest, perhaps to a fault. At one point I asked her if she had any regrets about any of her actions. She paused for a moment and then said, "You know, I'm a very unusual person in that, in my entire life, I don't have any regrets."

And, she noted, she couldn't be happier. "I'm living what I think education reformers and parents throughout this country have long hoped for, which is somebody who will just come in, and do the things that they felt were right, and everything else be damned."

On another occasion, I asked her about her leadership style: specifically, if she saw herself as a benevolent dictator.

"Maybe," she said with a smile.

"'Dictator' is OK?"

"If by 'dictator,' you mean somebody who, at the end of the day, is fully comfortable being held accountable for, you know, the results and is going to be incredibly decisive about the direction that we're heading in," she replied, "then yes."

The Washington schools have shown some improvement on her watch. In fall 2009, math scores on the prestigious NAEP test, known as "The Nation's Report Card," were released. Although

Washington's scores remain lowest in the nation, only D.C. and four states saw gains at both levels tested: fourth and eighth grades.

As for Rhee, she says she intends to stay as long as the mayor wants her to, which could be eight years if Mayor Fenty is re-elected. Rumors continue to swirl around Rhee, of course, the latest being that she might resign to move to California to be with her fiancé, Sacramento mayor Kevin Johnson.

And after D.C., what then? Rhee has never wavered from her initial position: "This is my first and only superintendent's job."

My takeaway from spending this time with Michelle Rhee is that she is very comfortable in her own skin, secure in her belief in accountability and measurement. She's a "bottom-line" leader who believes in what can be measured, and she's willing to use any carrots and sticks necessary to get results.

She has said it herself on many occasions: "The bottom line is that, yes, everybody who works for me has to feel comfortable and know that at the end of the day we're going to look at the results. And if the results are not there, if they are not producing significant gains for kids, then there is a chance that they won't be here in the long term."

"So it is really 'Produce or you're out?'" I asked.

"Shouldn't it be?" she asked back.

Shouldn't it be? Her question is a potent reminder that, whatever happens next, Michelle Rhee has won a major victory. Simply put, she has reframed the debate about how teachers are paid. Largely because of her, it's no longer possible to argue convincingly that teachers, whether effective or not, should be paid based on their years on the job and graduate credits earned. Largely because of her, it's impossible not to recognize the absurdity of the current system. Largely because of her, George Parker and the Washington Teachers' Union, Randi Weingarten of the American Federation of Teachers, and the Obama administration's Race to the Top program all acknowledge that, somehow, teacher evaluation must be based on student performance.[140]

What formulas will be used, how heavily test scores will count and how well the new approaches will work—all that is yet to be determined. But as for the name of this new system, why not call it "Rhee-pay"?

Paul Vallas: At times, Paul Vallas seemed to be trying to position himself as the opposite of Michelle Rhee, particularly when it came to the question of firing people. When I asked him if he thought he would be replacing many of his principals, he smiled. "Well, I don't know if I anticipate replacing a lot," he said. "We'll probably replace some, but I'm not going to parade out principals or teachers or give you a body count." He paused, then added, "You need to be careful that you're not grandstanding and that you're not alienating your rank and file."

Vallas seems congenitally unable to either slow down or dwell on negativity. Once while we were riding in his car to a school, he got into a phone conversation with his boss, Superintendent Paul Pastorek. I heard him say, more than once, that he must have been crazy to take this job. Later in an interview I asked him if he'd ever regretted coming to New Orleans.

"Never!"

I reminded him of what he'd said that morning on the phone to Pastorek. His response: "I was just commiserating, trying to cheer him up."

And when he's having a bad day? "It's usually for a good reason," he said. "And that just means I intensify my efforts. We've got a steep hill to climb."

Vallas has made progress. Scores on state tests have gone up every year, but he's not satisfied. As he puts it: "I say that we're just at base camp preparing to climb Mount Everest. But last year we weren't even in the Himalayas."

When he signed on in New Orleans, Paul Vallas made it clear that he was staying for only two years, and no longer. He has, of course, re-upped for the third year, which he did with all sorts of political rumors swirling around his head. He may stay for a fourth year, now that one of his sons has enrolled in high school there. Admittedly ambitious and still youthful and energetic at 57, Vallas admits to thinking occasionally about what might have been. He lost the Democratic nomination for governor of Illinois by a tiny margin to the since-disgraced Rod Blagojevich, and, when he was in charge of the Chicago schools, he hired Arne Duncan, the man who is now secretary of education.

The pattern in school districts rarely varies. A new superintendent comes in, shakes things up and tries to build a strong system that will continue after he or she leaves: a monument, in effect. That rarely happens, precisely because the next man or woman follows the same path of dismantling and rebranding.

New Orleans might be a different story. Whether he leaves now or stays on, Paul Vallas has created a new model for running schools. His Recovery School District is very close to being "a system of schools," and not "a school system," which is his avowed goal. Challenges remain. If he can create a strong oversight mechanism to keep charter schools on track, if he can develop economies of scale for costly services like special education, if he can identify and train his successor[141] and if he can convince the downtrodden half of New Orleans that this new public education system exists for their benefit, then Paul Vallas' legacy in New Orleans will be secure—and the "system of schools" will be working so well that his successors will work to improve it, not reinvent things.

Chapter 10
TURNING AROUND
TROUBLED SCHOOLS

In its never-ending search for quick, preferably inexpensive cures,[142] public education has latched onto the notion of "The Turnaround Specialist." It was the hot idea in education in 2004, the brainchild of then Virginia governor (now senator) Mark Warner, who was a venture capitalist and successful businessman before he entered politics. Former governor Warner wanted to create a training program that would turn successful principals into the equivalent of the turnaround managers he had seen work wonders in the business arena.

Turning around schools, and the specialists who make it happen, are hot ideas again. In fact, "turning around" troubled schools is one of the four so-called pillars of the Department of Education's Race to the Top competition for $4.35 billion in federal discretionary funds.[143] Education Secretary Arne Duncan embraced the turnaround concept when he led Chicago's public schools, and today he's calling for a cadre of "warrior principals" to fix failing schools.

Back in 2004 Virginia was the leader, with a program based at the University of Virginia involving both the school of education and the business school.[144] What began as a summer institute has grown into a two-year program that is developing a jargon all its own. For instance, educators in participating districts who work with those training to become turnaround specialists are known as "shepherds." Virginia's turnaround program is unabashedly pro-business, emphasizing the techniques of good management and the bottom line of test scores over pedagogy.[145] As its website notes, those chosen for the program receive "the type of executive education typically received only by top-level business leaders."[146]

Today other states[147] and districts are on the bandwagon, with the federal government leading the band.

However, I suggest you hold your applause. We spent a year with one of Virginia's turnaround specialists at a school in Richmond, Va., and what we saw makes me wary of this approach. Parker Land, a successful principal for nine years at a high school in suburban Virginia, just outside of Washington, was chosen for the second cadre of turnaround specialists. We followed him throughout his training and his first year as principal of a troubled urban middle school in Richmond, the state capital. We produced four segments[148] for the NewsHour, pieces that have relevance today.

Idealistic and restless, Land, then in his mid-50s, took a pay cut to join the program. After the training, he was put in charge of Thomas C. Boushall Middle School and its 735 students. Boushall was on a state warning list, put there by a nearly 50 percent failure rate in reading. It had gone through three principals in seven years, and the year before Land arrived, the staff had issued some 2,500 infractions for student misconduct.

Warm and engaging, Land was open about his reason for taking on this challenge. "I truly believe that if we don't solve the problems of inner-city schools, our democracy is going to suffer," he said.

His new boss, Richmond superintendent Deborah Jewell-Sherman, was confident Land would be successful. "I believe he is tough enough. I believe he has the commitment. I think he'll be able to inspire his staff with a 'can do' spirit."

Land was equally confident. "It's not a huge mystery as to how to turn schools around. It's leadership, establishing a basic understanding of respect among all parties, and that includes students." Land saw the school passing the state test for the first time. And by the end of the year, he predicted, Boushall itself would be transformed. "I see a school that sparkles. I see student work everywhere, everywhere. I see smiles. I hear joy."

"Are you a missionary?" I asked.

"One of the things I really don't want to sound like is a missionary," he replied. "I do not want to sound like a missionary. But I have a mission."

"He may not like that word," his superintendent said, "but the one thing I can't teach anyone is to love the kids and believe in them and move any mountain to get the best for those students. Some call it fire in the belly, some call it passion, but whatever you call it, he has it."

Land brought the best of intentions and 31 years of experience in public education to his new school, where three out of four students were living in poverty and nearly all were African-American. The new environment didn't scare him. "I have been able to create a kind of an expectation in the schools I've worked in that improvement is the norm. Change is the norm."

But that was in the comfortable suburbs. We walked through Boushall with Land a few days before it officially opened, and he pointed to many of its physical deficiencies—broken clocks, dirty windows, and shades that didn't work—but what upset him most was the way students were greeted. "I don't like the fact that the first thing a kid does when he walks in the building is have to go through a metal detector. One of my personal goals is that we won't have to do that for very much longer," he told us. "What I want to get across to kids is that this is a real caring environment and it's a helping environment."

Maybe so, but to get into that caring environment, kids had to take off their outer clothing and pass through metal detectors. Some were frisked by a cadre of security officers immediately after shaking the hand of their new principal.

On the first morning, Land was taken aback. "I was not prepared for the pandemonium at that entry area," he said. "It's all due to the fact that we have to get all those kids through the metal detector. I just wasn't used to that. I wasn't prepared for that."

His approach was to get to know as many students as possible and to engage them at their level. One day they asked him about his new role.

"What is a turnover teacher?" a student asked.

"Actually, my title is a turnaround specialist, but all I am is a principal," Land said.

"What kind of training did you have to go through to become a turnaround specialist?" a different student asked.

"I had to go to about two weeks of classes on all kinds of different things, like how to set goals and objectives for staff, how to work through problems, those kinds of things."

"How long do you plan on working as a principal?"

"I plan on working as a principal for at least three more years and I hope to be here longer than that."

The turnaround specialist program required a three-year commitment from all participants. "My commitment is three years," said Land. "I tell everybody that."

We learned Land's management philosophy pretty early on the first day, when he saw how many kids were roaming the halls. This, he told us, was the responsibility of teachers. In fact, we learned that in his worldview, most school problems traced back to the same source. "So much of misbehavior is a result of teachers just being poorly planned," he said.

Clearly he intended to take a hard line: "I am trying to get across in everything I do that the teacher is accountable. The teacher is accountable for every kid who is out in the hall and for every kid that's asleep in their class—all those things."

Did he really believe that bad behavior was a consequence of bad teaching? His response was firm: "You can preclude a lot of student misbehavior with a good lesson plan."

A seventh-grader agreed. "A lot of students don't pay attention in class because I don't think the teachers are putting forth effort to make us feel interested in class. If they had more activities and more fun things to do in class, 90 percent of us would be doing our work."

Was that analysis—it's essentially all on the teachers—overly simplistic? A veteran teacher suspected Land was not aware of Boushall's reality. "He's walking into a school that, for one thing, is not fully accredited," English teacher Madieth Malone told us.

"He's walking into a school that is predominantly black. He's walking into a situation that, unfortunately, is surrounded by very low-income housing. He's walking into a typical inner-city school."

Malone had her own analysis of the challenge: "In order for him to be a turnaround specialist the way I understand turnaround specialists, he has to turn around the attitudes that teachers have, he has to turn around parents' attitudes, and he has to turn the attitudes of the community as they perceive our school family. He has a lot of turning around to do."

Soon Land's idealism was put to the test, the first of many tests, as it turned out. Kids were fighting, pushing and shoving, and Land himself had to grapple with a seventh-grader, who nearly pushed him to the ground.

Just a month into the year, he was candid about the lack of progress. "I can't stand failure. And it feels like failure, is what it feels like." But he continued to believe that teachers were the key to a successful turnaround. "I see the bigger picture. I'm working on discipline. You cannot separate classroom management, behavior management and good instruction," he told us.

Teachers were skeptical. "To me, that is the utopia-type situation you want to have," math teacher Lois Smith said, "but come on. We need some reality here."

Reality turned out to be a string of daily fights and a wakeup call for Land. "One I had to actually break up myself with a security guard," he acknowledged. "I was on the floor, trying to get kids apart, and it was pretty ugly."

Reluctantly Land dropped the strategy he'd announced to teachers at the beginning of the school year, that good instruction was *the* solution to bad behavior. Now he had a new plan, he told his teachers: "Solid rules, solid consequences, solid rewards. That's a program."

Lois Smith was not persuaded. "I'm not sure if he really knew what he was getting into," she told us. "I don't know if he realized what the inner-city student was like."

Land didn't entirely disagree. "I have lots of experience with kids who have real tough environments and abusive environments, and those emotional issues, and those kind of needs that prevent them from learning. But it's the sheer number that's here; that was something I wasn't prepared for."

But when Land asked teachers to buy into his new plan, which included having them monitor the halls and stay after school to run detention hall as ways of bringing control to Boushall, he hit a wall. Teachers who had been told that their teaching was the problem were now unwilling to become the solution.

It was a compelling scene: the principal asking plaintively, "What do you all think? I need to know. What's the commitment?" and getting nothing but blank stares in return.

A teacher told us later that Land should show them the money. "They feel fine, as long as they can get paid," said Thaddeus Smith. In fact, Boushall teachers were earning on average $11,000 a year less than teachers in the suburbs.

"We have a lot of teachers that have other responsibilities, other jobs and things like that," Mr. Smith continued. "If we have to stay after school, can we get some funds for it? Unfortunately, we didn't have that. You know, even though it's for the benefit or the betterment of the school, money talks and everything else walks."

Land became a disciplinarian. He moved disruptive students to split up cliques, and suspended others, sending them to a trailer (called "Choices") used by previous principals to keep troublemakers out of the way.

One of his supervisors was not impressed. She told him: "We're going to need to look at your plan for remediation recovery because if you look at your writing scores, they were not good. We're going to have to be on it, and we're going to have to be very vigilant; we see things that are not going in the direction we want them to go." She seemed to be telling him that spending so much time on discipline was taking away from instructional time.

Seventh-graders had a better grasp of reality. "There was basically a fight every single day; it was fight after fight after fight," one student told us.

Another echoed her complaint: "I was heading to my locker, and I heard somebody say, "Hit him!" And then I turned around, and they were getting them serious faces, and I knew I had to get out of there."

After we witnessed another day of constant fighting, Land suspended *us!* No more cameras to document his struggles for a national audience, although he promised he'd invite us back "once things settled down."

Boushall was noticeably quieter when he let us back in, four months later.

"We've reduced the fighting, but not to the point where anybody feels that we're successful. The tendencies are there, but I think what you're seeing is more of a calmness," Land said.

He had created a system of positive rewards, including after-school dances and ice cream socials for students with good attendance. "I believe that kids respond to positive rewards," he said. "We're going to stroke our kids who do their homework, who don't cut class and all the kinds of things that we know make kids successful in school."

Of course these are tried-and-true strategies used in schools everywhere, not discoveries from the world of business.

Land provided his own analysis: "In a sense, there's a turnaround going on here. There really is. But the term 'turnaround' kind of connotes something dramatic, you know? But I don't know if it's so dramatic. I don't think it's going to be that dramatic. I think it's little victories that you win on a daily basis."

"Are you, then, a gradual turnaround specialist?" I asked.

"Maybe so," he said. "We'll see."

His boss, Superintendent Deborah Jewell-Sherman, wasn't into gradualism. "I have serious 'come to the woodshed' conversations about my expectations," she said. "I want that school fully accredited."

And the key to accreditation was test scores.

Teachers changed their routine. "A lot of time is being spent on how to take tests, what kinds of questions are on tests, how to read test questions, the facts that are needed to answer questions on a test," English teacher Madieth Malone told us. "We usually spend time reading novels. I would love to do that, but now I need to spend my time focused on the bare necessities, those absolute things that I know will be tested."

In Lois Smith's math classes, test prep had taken over. "The goal is that they've got to pass the test. Some of the kids aren't going to learn all the concepts, but if they have some of the strategies, they still can pass."

And so she taught strategies, not mathematical concepts.

Malone was upset. "I can't go along with that, no. I can't support that. The goal for all of our schools—and I guess it's the goal for schools across the country—is to pass standardized tests, but the goal of educators is to prepare children to become responsible, contributing adults."

Land accepted the compromise. "There's so much more to these kids that needs to be developed, but the educational world says, 'Show me academic test scores.' That's life now. So that's the way it's going to be."

After the testing and a few days before school ended, Land had a surprise announcement. His promise of a three-year commitment was null and void. He was leaving Boushall.

"It was out of the blue," he told us. "I never, never thought that that would happen. I really did expect to be here for three years." He had been reassigned to a Richmond high school[149] by Superintendent Jewell-Sherman. It was, she said, a business decision. "There is a vacancy at a high school that Boushall feeds into. Parker's the best man for the job."

Boushall would have a new principal, its fourth in eight years. Madieth Malone was angry. "A lot of our kids are disappointed," she said. "Many of them have very inconsistent environments. The school is one place that they can come and be assured that things will be consistent. Instability, once again, is being created in a school where our kids are so fragile they don't need that instability."

The superintendent was unmoved. "He's not their father; he's their principal."

Land tried to rally the troops as he said goodbye. "I think we're right there on the doorstep, and I hope that when we get our scores back, you invite me back to celebrate, because it's going to be a nice celebration. It's going to be a really special, sweet celebration when we make those federal standards and those state standards."

All summer long, Land and Boushall waited for the results, but there would be no celebration. The scores dropped to a 55 percent pass rate in English and a 46 percent pass rate in math. No $8,000 bonus for Land. And no "turnaround" for Boushall, which remained on the warning list.

Superintendent Jewell-Sherman, soon to leave Richmond to teach at the Harvard Graduate School of Education, was matter-of-fact about Boushall's test scores. "We'll analyze it and move from there. That's part of public education in these United States."

Madieth Malone, soon to retire, was upset. She felt Boushall had begun to change for the better. "The bottom line, that's what everybody looks at," she said. "They don't see the small successes; that's what I look at. I have to look at kids who were not coming to school who are coming, kids who were not working who are working. Kids who are smiling more, who are enjoying school more."

Despite the scores, Land agreed. "I think the school year has improved. I'm not going to say I've seen a big change, a drastic change, 180-degree turnaround, you know, but I have seen improvement."

So had Parker Land failed as a turnaround specialist?

"I wouldn't feel personally that I've failed," he said. "I've learned an awful lot. I've learned that our kids, a significant number of those kids are in crisis. And there's a level of support that's needed that we just haven't realized yet."

Parker Land wasn't the only one of Virginia's turnaround specialists to struggle. Fourteen of the program's 21 principals at the time failed to meet federal standards for improvement. All made three-year commitments, but more than half either changed schools or left the program entirely after little more than one year.

Is the turnaround specialist approach flawed, superficial or inadequate? Maybe so. At least we can say that the concept has evolved. The newest wrinkle, borrowing the business concept of enterprise zones, calls for "partnership zones." The Massachusetts-based organization Mass Insight Education & Research Institute is leading the way.[150] To quote from its literature, the partnership zone project is designed to "use the leverage and urgency of school turnaround to transform urban education and help thousands—ultimately millions—of disadvantaged children develop the skills they need to be successful in 21st century America.... This is not incremental reform. The Partnership Zones will create and put in place new systems, new structures, and new approaches, but unlike most efforts to undertake real transformation in public education (e.g., the charter movement), it provides a plausible change management pathway to bring it about *at scale* and (at least partially) *from within the system.*"

While this sounds as if these new reformers may have learned lessons from the turnaround specialist approach, I again suggest we hold our applause.

Chapter 11
SERIOUS FUN?

The shrill whistle pierced the humid August air, and the 10 players—all African-American high school students—gathered around the referee. The ref pointed to a young man wearing a T-shirt.

"Malik, here's the word. 'Ambiguous.' Define it and use it in a sentence."

The young man did so in a strong voice, and the ref called over to the scorer's desk, "That's a point for the Shirts!"

Then he turned to the other team (the Skins), picked out a player, and gave him a word: "Optimism." When the player confused the noun with the adjective, the ref turned to a player on the Shirts, who gave the correct answer.

"Another point for the Shirts," the ref called. "Now let's play ball!"

At least a dozen times during that game the ref, a 30-something English teacher named David Felsen, stopped play for vocabulary. As I recall, the "vocabulary points" amassed by the Shirts provided the margin of victory.

I say "as I recall" because that game took place more than 25 years ago on a basketball court at a Friends School in Philadelphia. David Felsen, the man who created that program, went on to become headmaster of the school. When he left to lead another school, the summer games continued—as they do even now. The rules for Felsen's summer program were simple: Do the reading and other homework if you want to play basketball. Skip the homework, and you sit out the game. Define the words correctly, and your team gets points. Over the years the intervention worked: Dozens and dozens of young African-American boys from inner-city Philadelphia went on to college—perhaps with basketball scholarships, perhaps not.

That program's genius was that it met kids where they were. In this case, they were mad for basketball. It recognized that kids love to play and compete. They'll study in order to get on the court, and, once on the court, they'll do their best to "score" by knowing the words. Nobody wants to be embarrassed publicly or let the team down. Moreover, the rewards were immediate: no waiting around for the results of machine-scored tests.

Children learn valuable lessons—and not just vocabulary or math—by playing games.[151] A seventh-grader who was playing on an organized team for the first time told me about her team's success: "It's like our team did really good so far this season and we're just getting ready for the championship. Now, we want to win it, so we still know we have a lot of work to do and it's not been easy getting here, but it feels really good, and I think it feels really good because we know we have actually worked together to do this."

The best games teach teamwork and cooperation. Children like that seventh-grader learn that their chances of winning improve when they work together. Play is natural, but children also seem to know intuitively that play is serious fun.

When I posted a version of this on my blog in mid-2009, a teacher named Steve Peha[152] weighed in. School has to be fun, he said, but it can't be fake fun, like an occasional game. Fun can't be icing on the cake, he said. "It has to be baked in. What's not fun? Using a textbook. Doing test prep activities. Having no choices over what you study. Being told again and again that you're a bad student because you keep getting D's and F's, even though the problem is the material you're studying—it's way above your grade level and there's no differentiated instruction going on."

Systems seem to lose sight of a basic truth: Learning, a natural human experience, *is* inherently fun. We are a curious species. As the Nobel Prize-winning physicist Leon Lederman told us, all children are instinctive natural scientists, and schools and teachers have to learn to get out of the way. Nurture, don't kill, their desire to learn.

Mr. Peha elaborated on this idea: "It's the traditions of school that take the fun out of learning. It's the mindless focus on product over process and participation. It's discovering that school is not about you. It's teachers who have forgotten that teaching is fun who take the fun out of learning."

Sneaking education into summer games is one thing, but can games, and the spirit of games, be made essential to education in genuine system-changing ways? Can schools meet kids where they are and devise ways to take them to places that we, as adults, know they need to be?

Bringing games and competition into classes with spelling bees and math Olympiads works, but in my experience many teachers trivialize games and score-keeping by giving points for good behavior and taking away points for misdeeds. Texas pioneered "No Pass, No Play" rules, setting an academic bar for varsity sports, but that's working from the negative. And a lot of what happens now in schools is basically a "gotcha" game, in which deficiencies and shortcomings are identified.

Have we forgotten that kids are people, too? That they enjoy what we all enjoy: the thrill of independence coupled with meaningful, healthy social interaction with others, the opportunity to know they are learning, to be able to monitor their own progress, and meaningful work that is neither too easy nor impossibly hard?

Here's why I worry. I hear educators talking all the time about "getting kids *ready to learn*." Well, do'h! Kids are *born* ready to learn. We are a curious species by nature. Who are these educators who don't get that, and why are they still holding sway over our children? Either re-educate them, or get them out, and maybe we can move ahead.

Can school be serious fun? Should it be? If so, how? We need rules, a way to keep score, a referee, reasonably high stakes, genuine results, meaningful competition, teamwork—and *fun*.

I don't know the answers, but the questions are worth pondering.

Chapter 12
MUSICAL CHAIRS AT THE RECYCLING CENTER

When I began writing this chapter, nine large city school districts were looking for superintendents, including Tucson, St. Louis, Houston and Pittsburgh. Other smaller cities like East Baton Rouge, La., were also in the market for new superintendents. And whenever you happen to be reading this, it's a safe bet that at least as many cities are searching for leadership.

My old hometown, the District of Columbia, was then in the hunt, having gone through four superintendents in eight years and two acting chiefs in eight months. During that quest, the District suffered the public humiliation of being turned down by two well-respected educators: Rudy Crew and Carl Cohn. Then in 2007, Washington broke the mould (and the mold?) by hiring a young woman who had never even been a school principal, let alone a superintendent. Michelle Rhee, backed by a strong mayor, began turning the Washington schools on their ear from day one on the job.

However, most large districts, including pre-Rhee D.C., approach the process in pretty much the same way. They hire a search firm that specializes in education and pay it many thousands of dollars. The winning search firm goes out and interviews potential candidates, usually men who have left, or want to leave, other superintendencies. At some point, the search firm presents two, three, maybe four "finalists" (again, usually men), who supposedly represent the cream of the crop to the board of education, which makes the final decision. And it's usually some guy who's been around the track a few times.

At the risk of sounding unkind, I find this a bit like shopping at the recycling center—a bizarre game of musical chairs. It's fair to ask "Who benefits?" from this ritual.

Another flaw in the search approach limits chances for success. School districts hire just one person, not a team, and when that individual arrives, he has to spend a lot of time and energy figuring out which of his inherited colleagues are trustworthy and competent, who resents regime change and who welcomes it. That minefield has destroyed many a capable leader.

Typically, a new superintendent arrives in a city and is hailed as the answer to every problem: low test scores, poor attendance, embarrassing graduation rates. He creates some new (or new-sounding) programs. When change does not occur overnight, disappointment sets in. The superintendent departs for a new city, and the cycle begins anew.

Instead of producing candidates with the hard-eyed management skills and single-minded concentration needed to figure out how best to teach kids, the search process gives these school systems more of the same.

What's striking, at least to this observer, is how unimaginative and predictable this process is. Just as the National Football League, the National Basketball Association and Major League Baseball seem to play musical chairs with their coaches/managers, search firms recycle superintendents. No matter how long and hard these companies search, they inevitably seem to turn up the usual suspects: career educators, most of them white men.

In the fall of 2004, for example, only 16 of the superintendents in the 63 largest districts were women. Five years later, in 2009-2010, the needle had barely moved: Women were leading just 18 of the nation's 66 largest big-city school districts. According to Michael Casserly, executive director of the Council of the Great City Schools, "This percentage is actually way above national averages. While women are still a minority among urban superintendents, they are even more underrepresented in the suburbs, small towns and rural areas."

In addition to virtually ignoring the talent pool of women, the superintendent search process is faddish to a fault. For several years retired military leaders were all the rage, inspired by the remarkable success of Major General John Stanford in Seattle. That approach was not a panacea, as Washington discovered when it hired its own general. Nobody seemed to realize that it was what General Stanford *did* in Seattle that improved the schools, not where he had worked earlier. After that, districts turned to attorneys: Joel Klein in New York City, Alan Bersin in San Diego and, earlier, David Hornbeck in Philadelphia. (Hornbeck lasted six years, Bersin five, before being shown the door.)

As it happens, one of the men who turned Washington down, Carl Cohn, described in detail what needs to be done. Cohn, former superintendent in Long Beach, Calif., told The Washington Post: "It has to be made clear to everyone that this is about the kids. Then you bring in a take-no-prisoners company that addresses the fundamental issues of operation, of people not doing their jobs."

In that interview, Cohn specifically referenced St. Louis, an urban district that matches Washington, D.C., when it comes to underperformance. For example, 23 percent of K-5 students, 13 percent of middle school students and only 5 percent of St. Louis high school juniors tested at or above the "proficient" level in reading in 2002, despite the district's spending more than $11,000 per pupil.

In 2003, St. Louis took the bold step of hiring a bankruptcy firm to run the schools for a year. The New York firm, Alvarez & Marsal, prefers to call its work "restructuring and turnaround," but rescuing bankrupt companies is its goal, and its method is best described as "take-no-prisoners." Alvarez & Marsal sent Bill Roberti (now a managing director) and a team that had worked together on other projects to St. Louis. Roberti took charge early in June 2003 with a mandate to make the system financially and operationally efficient. Sensibly, "education reform" was not his mandate because Roberti, a businessman who once ran Brooks Brothers, had never worked in education.

The day after Roberti took charge, he and the school board learned from the departing superintendent that the projected budget surplus of $37 million was actually a deficit of at least $35 million and perhaps as much as $90 million.

Roberti and his team went to work.[153] They closed 16 schools and sold 40 properties. They outsourced some school services, including transportation, food services and custodial care. In his year in St. Louis, Roberti gave pink slips to more than 1,400 employees—without laying off a single teacher. When school opened in fall 2004, St. Louis had 5,000 employees, not 7,000, although many of those laid off were then hired by the private bus, food and janitorial vendors. Roberti was harshly criticized by elements in the community but remained unrepentant. "This is not a jobs program," said Roberti, nearly jumping out of his chair to make the point. "This is a school system that is supposed to teach kids, not to provide jobs to the community. It is a business enterprise. Its outcome is student achievement, not providing jobs to the community."

He added, "I think that the public has a right to the same level of expertise in management, whether it's a school business or any kind of business that's public and trades stock. People should be held accountable."

"Financially, the school system was flying blind," Vincent Schoemehl, a school board member at the time and former mayor of St. Louis, told Education Week.[154] "The transparency is infinitely improved. We know to the nickel where we are. We've demonstrated that there is a way to connect the cultures of the private sector with the culture of urban education. I would recommend the model to any public entity that needs to refresh itself."

I asked Roberti whether educators could be trusted to fix their own systems. "No, I don't think so," he replied without hesitation. "Educators are an absolutely important component here but only one piece of the equation. St. Louis schools are a $500 million enterprise. Miami's a $4.2 billion enterprise. New York is probably

$11 billion. These are big enterprises with lots of complex issues and problems, not just a bunch of classrooms with kids."

Roberti was not hired to fix the city's education problems, but he did not ignore them. He asked the Council of the Great City Schools to come in to assess the system, an act that CGCS's Casserly said was "a bit like the battalion commander calling in an air strike on his own position."

Casserly and his team did not mince words. "St. Louis' instructional program was among the worst that we had seen in any major city across the country," they reported. "The school district has no instructional focus; it lacks a plan for raising student achievement; its instructional staff is poorly organized; and its sense of direction has splintered. The district is also marked by little sense of urgency for improving achievement, no accountability for results, and very low expectations for children.

"To make matters worse," the private report continued, "the district has piled one program on top of another for so many years that one cannot tell what the system is trying to do academically and why."

The report also noted that middle management demonstrated a strong reluctance to change what it was doing, as well as an exceptionally high tolerance for mediocrity. During the year, school attendance improved, but Casserly and Roberti agreed that it would take several years to see significant academic improvement.

William Tate, education department chair at Washington University in St. Louis, criticized Alvarez & Marsal for failing to build public support for the drastic cuts and for ignoring academics. "If you're running a restaurant, you need to have your accounting in order, but you don't stop serving food," Mr. Tate told Education Week.[155] "It's important to have your financial place in order, but it's mandatory, when as an organization your mission is teaching and learning, to pay attention to education. They don't talk about academics."

Although Roberti did not claim that he and his team solved all of St. Louis' financial and operational problems, he has no patience with those who wish he'd never been hired. "Some people still believe that they don't have a problem. Those people are saying, 'Give us our system back.' Well, where do you want to go back to? The 23, the 13, and the 5 percent of kids reading at a proficient level? Is that what you want back?"

Fortunately, there is help for urban districts. The Eli and Edythe Broad Foundation has established a training academy to prepare business leaders and other talented individuals from outside the world of education to run urban districts.[156]

Other cities might want to heed Roberti's recipe for fixing urban education. "It's a little bit like alcoholism," he said. "First, you've got to admit you have a problem, and then you have to move to solve it. And you cannot fix the education problems until the operating and financial systems are in order." That, then, is the question cities must ask about their public schools: Is the system broken? Is it educationally bankrupt? As the lawyers say, "Asked and answered."

When Michelle Rhee was hired in Washington in 2007, only 25 percent of ninth-graders in D.C. were reading at grade level, and only about half of those entering high school managed to graduate. In its analysis of the D.C. schools, the same group that analyzed St. Louis declared that they were falling woefully short, with "no plan for improving student performance, low expectations for children, no accountability for results, haphazard instruction, incoherent programming and dismal outcomes."

St. Louis paid Alvarez & Marsal just over $4.4 million for its one year of work, during which time Roberti claimed that he and his team "took $65 million worth of cost out of the system." The $90 million budget deficit was reported to be down to about $20 million when Roberti left, but it almost immediately ballooned to $38 million.

Did Alvarez & Marsal leave St. Louis schools better off than it found them? That seems to depend on whom you ask. "The general morale in the St. Louis public schools is lower than I have ever seen it," the Rev. B.T. Rice, a member of a local civic group called the St. Louis Black Leadership Roundtable, told Education Week.

School board meetings were marked by yelling and other disruptions, including chair throwing. On the other hand, Robbyn Wahby, an education aide to the mayor at the time, said she believed the district to be steadily moving in the right direction and praised the management firm for building a strong foundation.[157]

As for Alvarez & Marsal, it moved on to New Orleans, where it signed two multi-million dollar contracts[158] to bring order to the school district there. What precipitated this contract was the discovery that roughly $70 million in federal funds could not be properly accounted for. That led state education officials to compel the Orleans Parish School Board to hire Alvarez & Marsal.[159]

I caught up with Roberti and his colleagues in New Orleans a few weeks after Hurricane Katrina and the subsequent flooding that devastated the city—and destroyed many of the school system's financial records. Katrina kept some school people out of prison, Roberti told me one afternoon, because a lot of people had been stealing the system blind. He said one employee had been on paid administrative leave for more than a dozen years![160]

Alvarez & Marsal also received mixed reviews for its work in New Orleans. Its most strident critic may be the man who became superintendent after Alvarez & Marsal's contract expired and the state created the Recovery School District after the hurricane.

"That was a waste of money," said Paul Vallas, the veteran leader from Chicago and Philadelphia. "I'd love to have those millions now, to pay for instructional programs."

Hiring a bankruptcy firm is obviously not a magic bullet. In fact, it's more an act of desperation. And it will fail if the school board and the mayor continue their micromanaging. It will fail if the mayor and the board continue to treat the school system as a jobs program for adults. But even with the odds stacked against it, a bankruptcy firm could be a viable option, if only because it has the freedom to do what others cannot: take drastic steps and then ride out of town. Roberti and the St. Louis school board knew that going in. As Roberti told me, "The board brought a firm in from outside to do this difficult work because they believed no one inside the city limits could do this and live here when it was over. No one inside the city of St. Louis could get away with doing some of the things that had to be done and live here later without suffering the consequences of it."

That sounds a lot better than a never-ending game of musical chairs.

Chapter 13
A MODEST PROPOSAL FOR NEW SCHOOL LEADERSHIP

Two questions are running through my mind: Who's running the enterprise known as public education, and can we do better? I think we can.

In the beginning, local citizens ran their public schools, an arrangement that continued for more than 50 years. By the early years of the 20th century, though, more than 100,000 school districts had sprung up, and many of the amateurs in charge were hiring their friends as teachers, principals, custodians and every other job. In response, a class of professional educators emerged, and it ran schools for the next 70 or 80 years.

By the 1980s, dissatisfaction with education and the professionals in charge was palpable. Districts began reaching outside the guild to hire retired military generals, prosecuting attorneys, politicians and business leaders to run school districts. This achieved only occasional success, most notably in Seattle under retired Army Major General John Stanford.

In the 1990s, states took more interest in managing schooling. Some set standards and mandated exams for adults and children. Many passed laws allowing a new form of school management called "charter schools": institutions that were allowed to manage themselves. But significant improvement continued to elude the system.

The search for a better way to run schools took a new turn when President George W. Bush proposed, and Congress passed, No Child Left Behind. That law meant that Washington told schools how to run things: more testing, new requirements for teachers and free tutoring. How poorly that turned out is evidenced by the fact that almost no one in Washington even refers to NCLB any longer;

instead everyone except for hard-core Bush defenders calls it by its original name, the one that dates back to Lyndon Johnson.[161]

The Obama administration says it's all about ends and outcomes. It talks about "loose" controls of the process, but close or "tight" attention to the results. We'll see.

With all due respect to educators and politicians, I think the situation calls for a new and radically different philosophy. I have a modest proposal for new leadership: Put the fire chief, the swimming coach, the band director or the highway engineer in charge of public education.

A competent fire chief manages resources responsibly. He can't put the best equipment and most of the firefighters in one neighborhood. In fact, rather than distributing firefighting resources equally, a competent chief puts them where and when they are needed. Put a fire chief in charge of education, and the best teachers would be in the neediest schools—at least until the "educational fires" were extinguished.

Today's educators often rationalize student failure by saying, "We taught them the material, but they didn't learn it." That's why I suggest putting a swimming coach in charge of schools. A swimming coach would never dream of patting herself on the back if even *one* of her students were found floating face down or lying at the bottom of the pool. With a swimming coach calling the shots, teachers would have to show results, which would force them to develop methods that worked.

When a high school has a dozen National Merit Semifinalists, nobody pays much attention to how everyone else is doing. That's why it makes sense to put a band director in charge. No capable band director would boast about the band's performance if only the trumpets played well, but the percussion and woodwind sections were out of tune or off the beat. Band directors pay attention to everything: music selection, individual training of musicians and teamwork. They encourage individual talent but at the same time acknowledge that the whole *is* greater than the sum of the parts.

A competent highway engineer would also be a distinct improvement. After all, highway engineers design highways with one major goal: to get travelers to their destination. Thus, they make lanes about one-third wider than the cars, to allow for occasional inattention and wandering. They anticipate mistakes, and they design systems to prevent accidents. By contrast, schools play "gotcha" in classrooms, penalizing students for mistakes and, increasingly, telling them to go back and start the trip over. They are designed to sort students, not to see that all succeed.

If these proposals seem fanciful, I ask you to imagine educators, with their operating philosophies, working as fire chiefs, highway engineers, band directors or swimming coaches. Make a school administrator your fire chief, and the nicest neighborhoods would have all the fire engines. Put an educator in charge of highway design, and interstate highway lanes would be one inch wider than cars, perfectly designed to punish any and all driving errors. If the school superintendent is directing the band, cover your ears! As for letting someone who says "I taught it, but they didn't learn it" become a swimming instructor, let's not even go there.

Let's be honest about this. No fire chief, highway engineer, band leader or swimming coach would take the job, because running a school system is just about the toughest task imaginable. So we'll have to push for a change in attitudes by the people now in charge. They need to learn to think, and act, like the fire chief, etc. Then we'll have the public schools our democracy needs.

Chapter 14
INNOVATION AND TECHNOLOGY

Is technology an essential component of innovation? I find myself wondering what produces innovation in education—in teaching, actually. And it occurs to me that unless one happens to be sadistic or off-the-charts antisocial, all of us are on occasion innovative teachers. At those moments, we become wonderful role models of what our education system ought to be striving to emulate. And our motivation is a combination of self-interest and basic human decency.

You're not a teacher, you say? Okay, neither am I by profession, but sometimes we're put in that role. Imagine you're walking in your neighborhood when a stranger stops her car, rolls down the window and asks for directions to a local restaurant. You know the place she's asking about, so you immediately start figuring out how to explain it to her.

For the moment, you're her teacher and she's your pupil. You'll explain it as clearly as you can. ("Continue for three blocks, turn right on Maple Street and go for two more blocks. The restaurant is on your right.") As her teacher, you'll be watching to see if she understands your directions.

Innovation occurs when you realize you're not getting through. At that point, like a good teacher, you'll scrap the "lesson plan" and devise a new one. That is, you'll find another way to teach her how to get where she needs to be. ("See that church steeple? Go one block past that and turn right. Then when you see the two gas stations…")

Suppose she still doesn't get it. At that point, more creativity: You might draw a map—anything, just to get her where she's going.

Why is that innovation? Maps aren't new and neither is re-phrasing. But being innovative doesn't require complete invention, only finding different approaches to a problem. Putting new wine into old bottles qualifies as an innovation because it solves the problem of what to do with the wine.

So what conditions are necessary for innovation in education? I find several, and all exist in my example of the lost driver: a relevant task, a measurable outcome, a willing student and instructional flexibility.

You (the teacher) and the driver (your student) have a clear goal: getting her to understand how to reach her destination. Because the challenge is relevant (she wants to get to her destination), she's a willing student. You, the teacher, have instructional flexibility, the room to be innovative, precisely because the goal is clear. And because the goal is clear (and you are not sadistic or antisocial), you want to be successful. It's odd, because you've never even seen the lost driver before and most likely will never see her again once she heads down the road following your directions, but at that moment you're measuring your own worth by how well she learns from you. In effect, you believe that you haven't taught effectively if she doesn't learn it.

The parallel works in another way, in that most of the work—ultimate success—is up to the student, not the teacher. The driver still has to follow those directions in order to get to her destination, and that's as it should be. Teachers should not be expected to do it all.

But don't you wish all teachers worked that way? Many, perhaps most, would like to but cannot because schooling's goals and outcomes are murky or trivial. Without clear, relevant goals, process inevitably becomes the focus. Because process rules, many teachers today are given detailed lesson plans describing what they should be doing in class every day. Innovation is neither expected nor encouraged. That in turn leads to a "cover the material" philosophy, as in "I taught it, but they didn't learn it." What they really are doing is covering a certain part of their anatomy.

Transfer that situation—unclear goals and outcomes and a consequent focus on process—to my analogy of the lost driver. What might happen if you asked a stranger for directions and then didn't grasp what he told you? Rather than find an innovative way to communicate, he'd just say the same thing again, but loudly, or maybe more slowly. And if you still didn't get it, he'd raise his voice again. Before long, he'd be SHOUTING slowly.

It wouldn't take you long to realize that, with this guy as your teacher, you'd never get where you needed to go. So you'd step on the gas and peel out of there to seek help somewhere else.

And he would write you off as a dense student who failed to grasp the material.

Some teachers, schools and systems take that approach to learning. Just as that guy would blame you for not grasping his shouted directions, schools and teachers often blame students for not understanding. When students don't get it, they fail and have to repeat the grade, which is the equivalent of just shouting the same words at someone.

Many of those failing students—well over one million a year—do the equivalent of "driving away." They drop out of school.

My question is, who is failing? If school systems consistently fail at teaching and then at remediation (and that's often what happens), how can we just blame it on students? In fact, most remediation programs are echoes of what's already failed.

When I raised these issues on my blog, Taking Note, a few people took issue with my reasoning, apparently assuming that I was endorsing "command and control" teaching.

Marcelo Lage wrote:

Comparing education and innovation within education with giving directions has implicit in it that you see education as the teacher giving the student the answer to her problem. And that's not innovative at all. That follows the same "instructionism" model that has ruled our schools for over a century and that doesn't fit the needs of our society anymore. Education is hardly as simple as "getting students to where they want to go." Particularly these days where information is overflowing and learning can take place virtually every-where, assessing if she has the skills and knows whom to ask to find out how to get to the restaurant is ever more impor-tant. Otherwise the next time the student needs to get some-where, she'll just ask the teacher. Where is the proactivity and entrepreneurship in that behavior?

The recipe for good schools calls for three ingredients, which must be blended:

1. Figure out where we want to go and how we will measure our achievement.
2. Hire capable, trained people and let them figure out how to get there.
3. Hold them accountable for results.

Those three steps—plus one condition: Provide compensa-tion and reward structures that encourage good results. That will mean not paying for seniority only (which just motivates someone to live a long time). Instead there should be pay and promotions for teachers who work harder, are more innovative, produce mea-surable gains and take on leadership roles.[162] And then we have to get out of the way of teachers who have proven themselves.

Innovation per se isn't a goal and shouldn't be, but we can encourage it by replicating the conditions described above: clear and measurable goals, relevant tasks, instructional flexibility and the freedom to innovate.

So, then, what ultimately produces innovation? Why does there seem to be such an abundance of it in serious fields like medicine and computer technology and trivial ones like online dating, but so little in education, arguably the most important of human activities?

First, let me support my premise that schooling is largely be-reft of innovation. A doctor or an auto mechanic from the 1950s, if dropped into today's hospital or garage, would be baffled. A teacher from the '50s, however, would feel pretty darn comfortable in today's classrooms. Maybe the desks wouldn't be attached to the floor, and perhaps the blackboards would have been replaced by whiteboards, but there'd be bells every 50 minutes or so, attendance to be taken and interruptions by the principal. I rest my case.

Back to why: The thirst for money, prestige and fame are reliable spurs of innovation. Living in Silicon Valley, I've seen plenty of evidence of that. Unfortunately, public education is not the road to travel if your goals are money, prestige and fame.

Another spur to innovate is a supportive but challenging environment, one in which failure is seen as an opportunity to learn, not as a stain. Does that describe most schools? I don't think so. The New Schools Venture Fund, co-founded by John Doerr, is working to recreate in education some of the conditions that spurred Silicon Valley's growth. That's an uphill battle with a number of hurdles, including a "one size fits all" mentality and a glut of "experts."

Education's "one size fits all" approach to evaluating and paying teachers has to dampen enthusiasm for trying new approaches. Why bother if you aren't going to be rewarded? As "The Widget Effect," a report from the New Teacher Project, makes clear, administrators don't pay much attention to teacher effectiveness. "Evaluation systems fail to differentiate performance among teachers. As a result, teacher effectiveness is largely ignored. Excellent teachers cannot be recognized or rewarded, chronically low-performing teachers languish, and the wide majority of teachers performing at moderate levels do not get the differentiated support and development they need to improve as professionals."

Steve Peha, a reader of my blog, believes he knows why innovation is in short supply in public education. He writes:

It's simply the result of the people who enter the profession. Most teachers and administrators are not innovators. That's precisely why they fit into education. Can you think of a profession that is more predictable from year to year? If I'm a person who is risk-averse and who likes being told what to do all the time, education is the place for me. Many teachers work an entire career and never change schools, grades, or classes. Few teachers even innovate their own practice, relying instead on textbooks,

137

worksheets, and other publisher-supplied materials. The lack of innovation in education is a purely cultural phenomenon. Innovative people tend to innovate wherever they are regardless of external circumstances like money and recognition. Educators tend not to innovate because, for the vast majority, that's just not who they are.

Is he right? Or does a reactive system "train" people to be cautious? In either case, his diatribe prompted this response from Claus von Zastrow:

> Many people in education are real innovators. They think long and hard about new ways of making materials fresh and inspiring for students. They create new curriculum, consider new teaching strategies. They teach because they believe in the power of new ideas. In fact, education requires more day-to-day innovation than many other jobs do. Many of those teachers lose their innovative spirit over time, because it is ground out of them. How many people labor under so many new mandates, often contradictory or incomplete models of "best practice," or inconsistent expectations from their various "customers?" In fact, it's often the "innovations" that come down from on high that smother teachers' innovative spirit by robbing them of autonomy.

Debbie Meier believes that many early teachers probably did innovate, given their natures and relative lack of supervision of the one- and two-room schoolhouses. She added wryly, "The great innovation of the 21st century is our capacity to use technology to get into every classroom and insure compliance."

Is the problem the shortage of courses in "technology education," as some have suggested? For me, the issue is not technology education per se but school's unwillingness to embrace modern technology's possibilities. As noted earlier, too many students have to "power down" when they get to school, because public education is stuck in a rut. Schools should be using the various technologies to break down the physical walls of school to connect students around the country and the world; instead they use technology to control.

Here's an example: Every high school and middle school that's close to a major river like the Ohio or the Sacramento ought to be participating in a science project wherein students go to the river, take and analyze water samples, measure the speed of the current, and capture detritus during specified time periods. The students could then share the data and independently develop hypotheses as to why, for instance, the water is more alkaline at one point. Their findings might lead to class investigations to discover the sources of the differences, which could lead to identification of the sources of pollutants. Other students could be using video technology to record these activities and then produce short documentary reports, which could be posted on YouTube for widespread viewing.

But if one looks deeper, it's not simply the failure of public schools to embrace modern technology's potential; it's also the institutional failure to embrace project-based learning (and challenge-based learning). We adults work together because it's effective and efficient and far more rewarding. That's called collaboration. In schools, however, collaboration is called cheating!

In a sense, one can also trace this unfortunate situation to one word, noun and adjective: rigor and rigorous. Good education is challenging—it invites and dares and challenges kids—but much of what goes on in school is instead designed to be "rigorous." Look that word up! "Harsh and unyielding" are central to the definition, as in rigor mortis. Why on earth should learning be construed so negatively?

While I believe that children need education in what's called "media literacy," adults need ways to grow comfortable with the power and potential of technology, and they need an attitude shift. Today's kids—those with economic advantages, anyway—swim in a sea of technology. Most kids today are inclined to be collaborative and to be risk-takers. For them, technology is play, and we ought to take full advantage of that.

Another barrier to innovation in education is the glut of "experts," meaning that all of us went to school and therefore "know" what school should be like. It's tough to argue for new and different approaches when everyone's an expert. Imagine, for example, trying to create an ungraded classroom for children in the K-2 range. It makes sense, because children learn in spurts and at different times. We segregate by age largely because it's administratively convenient, not for pedagogical reasons. Now suppose an enlightened principal wanted to put all the kindergarten, first-grade and second-grade students into one group, empowering teachers to work with them in skill-appropriate groups. She'd say, in effect, "Your job is to get them all to a certain level by the end of what we used to call second grade."

That's innovation at its best, in my view, because it empowers teachers, sets standards and encourages responsibility.

What would happen if we did try to innovate? Imagine the conversations at the hairdresser's or the hardware store:

"How's little Charlie doing this year? He's in first grade, right?"

"Well, no. There's no such thing as first grade any more. Now they call it 'K-2.' Charlie's 6, but they've got him in with a bunch of 4-, 5- and 7-year-olds."

"That's crazy. We didn't do stuff like that when I went to school. Have they lost their minds down there? Wait till I tell people about this!"

How long would *that* innovation last?

Perhaps bad times will spur innovation. A theory going around is that today's desperate circumstances are likely to produce educational breakthroughs.

Certainly desperation can be a source of innovation, as in Apollo 13 ("Houston, we've got a problem") or in countless big-game situations when time is running out. The Apollo 13 astronauts solved a life-threatening crisis with stuff like duct tape, baling wire and paper clips, just as quarterbacks like Peyton Manning and Drew Brees manage to find ways to overcome long odds and

140

win the game. But those are not innovations with a long shelf life, just ways to get past a challenge.

I'm hearing that recession conditions—45 students in a class, and so on—do not have a silver lining, at least not one that teachers themselves have been able to discern. Teachers are too stressed trying to survive to have time to innovate.

And that brings me back to the issue of technology.

I hope it's clear that I am a huge fan of technology and a believer in its potential to fundamentally change how schools are run. Emerging technologies, often called "social media," are changing how many young people communicate and learn, how they approach learning and how they process information.

But I think there are three reasons to worry. Reason one, the technology will be unevenly distributed, meaning that the gap between rich and poor will actually widen. Two, schools won't respond to the creative potential of technology in positive ways. And three, they will respond uncritically.

First, the technology gap is major, because in most of history the rich have gotten richer, and there's no reason to expect things to be different this time around. Creating special programs to put technology into schools with poor children won't work unless those programs are accompanied by serious professional development, because most teachers I know are uncomfortable with computers and even more uncomfortable with the notion that kids know more than they do.

What do poor kids get when schools are their main source of advanced technology? Not much! As teacher Esther Wojcicki of Palo Alto High School notes, kids in school are forced into what she calls "the airplane mode."

"They're told to sit down, strap in and face straight ahead for the duration of the flight," she said.

Right now, well-off children have access to technology at home, meaning that they will find it easier to cope with the "powering down" that happens when they walk into their schools. Not so for poor kids, who end up suffering through a lot of drill.

My second fear is that schools will resist innovation and become irrelevant. A tsunami—a huge wave of technology in the hands of young people—is approaching, but many educators seem unaware that their students swim in a sea of technology outside the school. They want to keep using computers and other tools to control students[163] and to manage information, and that's about it.

Because they fear technology in the hands of kids, they look for ways to keep it out of schools. When a couple of students were found looking at "inappropriate" videos on YouTube in one school, the administration decided on the spot that no students would have access to the site. Another school banned Facebook because some kids were using it to communicate with friends. That's over-reaction[164] based on ignorance, and a valuable teachable moment thrown away. Of course kids are going to go to places we don't want them to, but what that requires is vigilance on the part of adults as well as scads of interesting and challenging work. Even in a high-tech world, idle hands (and minds) do the devil's work. As Matt Montagne, director of technology at an independent school, notes, "The real digital divide is proving to have little to do with hardware/connectivity and everything to do with a mindset and willingness to use the free and open platform of the Internet in creative ways that allow for the deep customization of learning."[165]

Imagine the response of the rest of the kids when they learned that YouTube couldn't be accessed at school. Guess what site they were sure to visit at home?

My third fear involves what happens when schools do embrace technology.[166] That is, I worry about the enthusiasm of technology's supporters. In October 2009, I participated in a two-day event held at Google headquarters in Mountain View and organized by Sesame Workshop, Common Sense Media and the John D. and Catherine T. MacArthur Foundation. At one point we watched a short homemade video of a young man purporting to teach how to solve a quadratic equation. With great energy, the boy lunged at the camera lens and enthused about how easy it is. He wrote on a whiteboard, enthused more about changing minus signs to plus signs, and concluded by nearly shouting again that it was easy. The audience applauded, but for what? He hadn't explained why he was changing signs, or anything else for that matter. It was terrible teaching, pure and simple, but technology was being used, so most of the adults loved it!

But ignoring technology is the greater danger. We saw another video in which a high school student told us that he never read books, hadn't read one in years. Why bother, he asked rhetorically, when you can read plot summaries online in 30 seconds? He confessed (rather, he boasted) that he'd aced a test on "Romeo and Juliet" without reading a word of Shakespeare.

I think technology is potentially a huge threat to a decent education precisely because it allows shortcuts like that. We know that students everywhere are downloading term papers written by others and submitting them as their own, and now they don't even have to read the material. We're producing students with no deep understanding of our culture and a fundamental contempt for education.

There is a solution, of course. It's not anti-technology, but it does require slowing things down. Take "Macbeth." I'll wager it was one of three or four plays the students were assigned to read and the teacher was required to "cover" in a few weeks. Under those circumstances, SparkNotes may be appropriate.

But suppose three or four weeks could be devoted to one play? Then the odds would be that no student could get by without reading. And if students don't give a rip about Shakespeare, change the assignment: Put Macbeth and Lady Macbeth on trial for first-degree murder, with kids playing the roles of Macbeth, his wife, Duncan, Banquo, etc. Now they'll have to prepare to give testimony, while the students who are the defense and prosecutors will have to prep for cross-examination. That is, they'll have to read what Shakespeare wrote, think about the meaning, perhaps even watch Olivier or Orson Welles in film versions, and more.

There's a marvelous role for technology[167] in this. Assign students to videotape the proceedings and prepare nightly news reports "from the courtroom," to be posted on the Web and aired on the school's broadcast or narrowcast system. To be able to interview intelligently, these students also would have to dig deep into the play itself. So long, SparkNotes!

In a perfect world, this kind of curriculum would be found in our poorest schools, giving those kids the opportunity for deep learning and powerful intellectual challenges, not the "drill and kill" routine they are more likely to encounter.

Today's path—a breakneck pace through a required curriculum aimed at enabling students to pass cheap bubble tests—is antithetical to the effective use of technology. Instead, students in East Palo Alto, Greenwich, Mumbai, Shanghai and London should be connected, working together on projects to analyze election results, for example, or traffic patterns or acidity in rainfall. (Often kids are already connected outside of school, through Facebook, MySpace and Twitter.)

Much has been made about the loss of art and music in the schools as a result of emphasis on "the basics." Another basic course of study is also being neglected: civic education. Our kids still say the Pledge of Allegiance and may even sing "The Star-Spangled Banner" or "America the Beautiful." Our flag flies over every school. But that may be the extent of what kids "study" about what it means to be an American. Just a few decades ago students took courses in government, civics and democracy. Today the norm is a one-semester class on government.[168]

The choice is ours. We can use technology in schools to support students who dig deeply and create knowledge, or we can continue with business as usual—an environment that invites kids to use technology's power in ways that ultimately hurt us all.

And so we have circled back to innovation. Could it be that the issue of using technology surfaces the many problems that schools have around the issue of innovation in general? Why is it that schools of 2010 look so much like the schools of 1910, despite thousands of different attempts to make significant, lasting change? Why are schools so resistant to change?

We have to make sure we are on the right side of history and progress. One happy thought: We are not likely to leave children behind—because so many of them are already ahead of us.

Chapter 15
CHARTER SCHOOLS

When two roads diverge in a yellow wood, in poetry and in life, one must choose. After picking a path to follow, inevitably you ask the unanswerable question: What *would have happened* if you had chosen the other path?

Now we know what happens, at least in education, thanks to a remarkable study of charter schools in New York City. And that study, released in September 2009, suggests that it's time to widen *one* of the roads.[169]

Because New York City doesn't have enough room in its charter schools, admission is by lottery. Over the past seven years, only about half of the 80,000 students who have applied have been accepted. Most of the others ended up going to traditional public schools in their neighborhoods.

Not only were the applicants similar in observable characteristics of race, gender, poverty, disability and English proficiency, but, because all had made the effort to enroll in a charter school, researchers could infer similarity in motivation and family interest in education. Such an opportunity is what the study's principal investigator, Caroline Hoxby of Stanford University, calls "the gold standard" in research: the opportunity to compare apples to apples.

The announced results were dramatic. The lottery winners went to 48 public charter schools, and those who finished eighth grade performed nearly as well as students in affluent suburban school districts in math, and about two-thirds as well in English. Every year in a charter school mattered, the study found, and by the end of eighth grade, what the researchers call the "Harlem-Scarsdale achievement gap" had been narrowed by 86 percent.

Overall, each year in a charter added about 5 points to math and English language arts scores on state exams, compared with those who lost the lottery. Every year in a charter increased a student's likelihood of earning a state Regents diploma by 7 percent.

The study's results can be generalized, Professor Hoxby maintains, because most charters are in cities, most urban districts use a lottery system and New York's students resemble urban students everywhere.

But, as with all education research, *caveat emptor* is a good rule to adhere to. For one thing, nowhere in the published study does Hoxby reveal how many children actually went through eight years in charter schools. She does, however, acknowledge that she did a fair amount of extrapolating.

Just what does that mean? Think of an 8-mile road race in which only *some* runners go the entire distance. Most, however, run only a portion of the distance—miles 1 through 3, say, or miles 5 through 7. And then the race officials compile the final standings by assuming that those partial race times would have been replicated over the full distance. If someone who ran only 3 or 4 miles of the course got a trophy, there'd be an uproar, of course, but statisticians like Hoxby are comfortable drawing inferences about academic performance.

But did she extrapolate beyond what the data support? Some in the field[170] are skeptical of the study's conclusions. They note that the research hasn't yet been peer-reviewed, and that the study's scope, confined to New York City charters, limits its usefulness on a national scale. A few also point out that Hoxby's studies of charters tend to be consistently positive. But Hoxby stands behind her results and their meaning. What's particularly relevant to her, she says, is whether someone can articulate an actual problem with the methodology.

Meanwhile, her research shows that not all charter schools are the same. That is, there are clear performance differences among New York City's charter schools. While Hoxby will not name the best and worst, she is willing to identify the characteristics of the high-performing charters: a longer school day and year, more time devoted to studying English, pay based on performance and not simply on seniority and credentials, a clear academic mission, and a moderate disciplinary policy of both small rewards and small punishments (meaning that behavior issues, good and bad, are attended to on the spot). Every student of this movement immediately recognized that she was referring to KIPP schools.

Not all the charters were successful, though. Fourteen percent of students in the study attended charter schools that had an overall *negative* effect on math performance, compared with students who did not win the lottery.

So what does all this mean for choosing education's road to the future? What will happen now? Hoxby sees these results as a clear call to create more charter opportunities, something President Obama, Secretary of Education Duncan and many others have been urging. The federal government, in fact, is doing more than talking. It has made it clear that states with limits on charters will not fare well in the competition for $4.35 billion in Race to the Top stimulus funds that it's awarding. At this writing, at least eight states had removed their charter caps, and more will do so.

The general public clearly wants more charter schools—64 percent in the 2009 PDK/Gallup poll on education are in favor of charters. And a 2009 survey conducted by Education Next reports that 52 percent of public school *teachers* support charters, a number that jumps to 60 percent when respondents are told of President Obama's support.[171]

Parents want charter schools, too. In Washington, D.C., one-third of school-age children attend charter schools, the result of parents voting with their feet. In Los Angeles, only 10 percent attend charters, but enrollment jumped by one-fifth in 2009 alone. In other cities, parents are demanding more choices, more charters.

But, that support notwithstanding, charter schools are not home free. To understand why requires some history.

Although the notion of chartering schools had been around for a few years by 1988, it was in October of that year that the movement to legalize charter schools was born, at a small meeting by the headwaters of the Mississippi River in Itasca, Minn. Among those in attendance were two New York educators, Albert Shanker and Seymour Fliegel; Ember Reichgott Junge, a visionary Minnesota state senator at the time; and Minnesota educators Joe Nathan and Ted Kolderie. The concept of a charter—a renewable license to innovate, free of most school district rules—was built on a simple idea: Educators would be free to carry out their dreams, but would be held responsible for results.[172]

I ran that meeting and remember well the overriding spirit of optimism. Chartering would be embraced by school districts, which would use them to "incubate" best practices. That has rarely happened, unfortunately. Most districts have resisted the idea of weakening their central control. And because charter teachers would no longer be obliged to belong to a union, Shanker came to see them as a threat to union power.

Still, the idea had legs, in part because people could read into the term "charter" what they wished. Some on the political right supported charter schools as a wedge to break up the public school monopoly, while others on the left thought charters would be the equivalent of their own private schools. Allowing profit-making firms to create charter schools, encouraged by state laws, produced more support.

The first charter school opened in Minnesota in 1992, with fewer than 100 students; today, 4,000 charter schools in 40 states and the District of Columbia enroll over 1.3 million students—and counting. Many of the charters have been granted by entities other than the local school district (the State University of New York grants charters in New York state, for example), effectively ending district monopolies.

Leading the way have been nontraditional educators like New York City schools chancellor Joel Klein, Superintendent Paul Vallas of the Recovery School District in New Orleans, and Chancellor Michelle Rhee in Washington. In the latter city, about 30 percent of students are in charters, and well over half of Vallas' schools are charters. These three leaders encourage charters not as "incubators" but as challenges to the rest of their schools.

Still, as Nathan, a founder of the movement, says, "Some terrific charters are doing great things for kids, but charlatans have entered the field and have ripped off kids and taxpayers." He says charter school organizations must develop better ways of screening out crooks and incompetents *before* they get to start schools. He adds: "I see the charter movement, at its best, as an expansion of the civil rights movement, in which some of us participated. It's worth noting that Rosa Parks spent part of the last decade of her life trying to help create charters in Detroit. Some African-American and white families have asked for help in creating a charter in Topeka, Kansas, in the same school building that Linda Brown was not allowed to attend in 1954....Sadly, the local school board in Topeka turned down this request. The hostility of some professional educators towards charters today echoes the hostility we faced 30 years ago when we began trying to offer other options within public education."

Kolderie, another founder, believes unions are coming to terms with the idea. He cites a United Federation of Teachers initiative in New York City, teacher cooperative schools in Milwaukee, and the charter organization Green Dot Public Schools in Los Angeles as evidence that "when teachers play significant professional roles, the massive contracts generated by a boss-worker model are no longer required."

A trend that disturbs some is the propensity of wealthy individuals to adopt and support charter schools. To cite the best-known case, wealthy hedge fund managers like Julian Robertson Jr. and Whitney Tilson have made large contributions to charter schools in New York City. The Robin Hood Foundation, which raises many millions for worthy causes from Wall Street, lists charter schools as one of its top priorities. Are they supporting these schools to spur the system to improve, or to undermine it? critics ask. UFT president Michael Mulgrew told The New York Times that their support was "all well and good," adding, "I would wish they would do it in a more foundational way, a way that would help all children instead of just a small group."[173]

The ground keeps shifting under this movement, but two issues remain: quality control and persistent opposition.

For one thing, the Obama administration is embracing charter schools with great enthusiasm. Now, it's true that Secretary Duncan adds a qualification, saying that they support "good charter schools," but that strikes me as, for the moment anyway, an empty distinction, largely because of an absence of ways of measuring quality.

It's true that egregiously bad charters get shut down, but mediocre ones keep plugging along, doing just as much damage to kids as mediocre public schools. But what the charter school proponents don't seem to realize is that these mediocre institutions are also damaging "the movement." I've heard them (and you know who you are) say that mediocre public schools aren't punished, as if that justifies not closing mediocre charter schools. But it's no justification precisely *because* charter school advocates are claiming to be different.[174] They cannot claim to be different and then act like the systems they are so critical of.

I think that charter schools risk becoming like schools of education if they aren't careful. How many of the 1,400 or so institutions that train teachers are excellent? I'd say 50 but, if you want to argue for 100, I'll go along with that. But are the 100 excellent ones doing anything to get rid of the dreadful 500 to 700 schools? If they are, it hasn't made my radar screen.

I think for the charter movement to succeed, it must take the lead on setting high standards and then enforcing them. Is that realistic? Is it happening somewhere?

Then there's the issue of opposition to charter schools. Everyone knows that unions have fought against charter schools because they've seen it in their self-interest (teachers in charter schools don't have to belong to unions). But guess what—local school boards have been as great a roadblock, and in some cases, even fiercer opponents. They go to court to keep charter schools from opening or expanding. Why? It's about money and control, as far as I can tell. But if the demand exists for charter schools, why wouldn't elected officials whose mandate is education be supportive?

Often they are not. For example, in fall 2009 in Los Altos, Calif., a county judge ruled against a charter school and for the local school board. The charter school had sued because it wanted to expand to include seventh grade and needed space to do so. Forget for a minute the particulars of that case and ask yourselves why it wanted a seventh grade. Could it be that parents of sixth graders wanted to keep their children in the charter school? And why are school boards so hostile to success?[175] Shouldn't they be trying to figure out what that successful school was doing, so they could copy it? That was the hope of charter schools, that they'd be incubators.

If you and I both operated restaurants,[176] and mine was drawing a crowd and yours wasn't, wouldn't you want to know why? Wouldn't you think seriously about changing some aspect of what you were doing?

Or would you behave like many in the education establishment and sue me or try to shut me down? In other words, what can be done to change school board behavior? Is it all about money and power?

Just as the waters of Lake Itasca flow into the Mississippi and down to the Gulf of Mexico, expect the movement that began there to continue to grow. However, just as the Mississippi is a dangerous and sometimes unpredictable river, the charter movement should not expect smooth sailing.

Because the New York City study will—quite properly—produce more enthusiasm for charters, it's important to remember that 14-percent negative effect on math cited above. A buyer-beware attitude is more important than ever. Never forget that the name "charter" on a schoolhouse door reveals no more about a school's quality than the word "restaurant" on a sign tells you about the food inside. There's no substitute for transparency, high standards and direct observation of the sort reported in this remarkable study.

Chapter 16
PICTURING SUPERMAN

Picture Superman in your mind's eye. Red cape? Blue tights? Nope, you've got it wrong. The Superman I know is five feet seven inches; he's on the pudgy side and walks with a limp. But I know he's Superman, because this 60+-year-old elementary school principal has done what few in education seem able to do: He's closing the academic performance gaps between white and Asian-American kids and their black and Hispanic peers—what educators and politicians call the "achievement gap." This gap is everywhere and at every grade level. Take fourth-graders in New York State, where the gap is about 35 percentage points in math, English and science. But focusing on outcomes alone is a fool's exercise. My Superman understands this.

Incidentally, if you happened to Google my Superman by his real name, George C. Albano, not that many entries appear. Maybe that's why the gap persists, because nobody's paying attention to Superman, even though he's been fighting educational crime for 30[177] years at Lincoln Elementary School in Mount Vernon, N.Y. This inner-city K-6 school has 800 students, (63 percent black and Hispanic, 35 percent white and 2 percent Asian-American). More than half the kids receive free or reduced-price lunches, and 9 percent are in special education. It could be the poster child for an achievement gap school.

Except there *is* no achievement gap at Lincoln. In 2008, for example, 99 percent of Lincoln's fourth-graders made it over the achievement bar that New York State sets in English, math, social studies and science. By the numbers, that means that a total of three kids did not make it, and the teachers at Lincoln are now giving those children extra attention so they get over the bar next time.

George Albano has figured it out. But if you're hoping for a solution that's faster than a speeding bullet, or want a shortcut for deflecting kryptonite, forget it. The recipe calls for hard work; great and dedicated teachers; a thoughtful approach to testing; an integrated curriculum; lots of art, music and physical education; the willingness to bend and break rules on occasion; and the complete refusal to let any child fail to learn. As Albano says: "When your child comes to school, he or she comes to an oasis. I think we have an obligation that, no matter what's happening outside, we have to push that aside and make this youngster succeed."

"No matter what's happening outside" is George Albano's recognition that many of his children live with economic hardship and don't have book-lined libraries or a private place to study in their homes. Albano does his best to close these and any other "opportunity gaps" by bringing in teachers with special expertise, by raising outside funds and by keeping classes as small as possible. He knows that if a teacher is responsible for 35 to 40 students, she's almost forced to triage, thus lowering expectations for some kids, and presto—you've got an "expectations gap" that's understandable, if not acceptable.

"No matter what's happening outside" means a school-wide "no excuses" attitude. If a Lincoln teacher said, "I covered the material, but the kids didn't learn it," George Albano would educate that teacher or move her out.

Albano may be genetically wired to care about children. His parents, Carmen and Eleanor, were a loved and respected doctor/ nurse team known across Westchester County. Four of Carmen and Eleanor's five children chose careers in education, and currently George has 23 family members working in public education, including all three of his children.

Let's go through Lincoln's "recipe," beginning with a crucial ingredient: teachers. As former Mount Vernon superintendent Ron Ross notes: "When we talk about student achievement and an achievement gap, we generally focus on the students. That's wrong. You're never going to close it by that. Focus on the teachers."

That's where George Albano focuses. Most of his 70 teachers have been at the school for at least 15 years, even though teachers in neighboring districts earn as much as 20 percent more money. Albano finds teachers by tapping into business connections, combing through hundreds of résumés and getting recommendations from his 23 family members who work in education. "When I interview a teacher, obviously a person has to be certified, qualified, but to me, it's equally important that the person brings something else to the table," he said. And so Lincoln's faculty has included a former NASA administrator and a former executive of a Fortune 500 company, not to mention a professional opera singer and a chess master.[178]

One day I watched several teachers working with second-graders, who were designing sneakers and ad campaigns to "sell" their products. The next day their cardboard and papier-mâché sneakers were hanging in the halls. Dana Bhatnagar has performed numerous times at Carnegie Hall—she's that good—but when I visited Lincoln, the young opera singer was spending her days teaching music at the school. And she didn't coast through her days. "I'm actually more tired than I am after performing a three-hour opera," she told me at the time. "Not because it's hard work, but because I'm giving them everything I've got." George Albano recruited Ms. Bhatnager when she was 27 years old; she worked with him for several years and taught Lincoln's students the beauty and value of all kinds of music, including classical.

"Before Ms. Bhatnager came to Lincoln School, I only liked Hip-Hop music," said third-grader Aurora Hudson at the time, "but after having her for music class I now also love classical music."[179]

Of course academic standards matter, but instead of the "drill, baby, drill" approach that many inner-city schools adopt, academic content is built into just about every aspect of school. Dana was well aware that her kids were learning math in her music classes. Math also finds its way into gym; in a phys ed class I watched, the teacher combined exercise with a lesson about velocity and force.

John Merrow

Lincoln doesn't shy away from practicing or teaching values. As Ron Ross notes: "Good schools teach character. We teach values. We have to teach the next generation how to get along with each other. If we don't do that, then we ought to close the schools, because I don't care how good you are on a test, if you can't live with your neighbor, then I don't think you've been taught."

"Is that risky business?" I asked him.

"There is a line that one doesn't cross," he replied. "I'm not telling students, 'You must be a Baptist' or 'You must be a Roman Catholic.' But we are saying, 'You must not fight, you must not cheat, you must not steal.' The schools are supposed to transmit the values of society, not just give multiple-choice tests. We wonder why so many kids are cheating, it's because they came from schools where they concentrated on a test."

But tests do matter, and I wondered how much time and attention Lincoln's teachers devoted to passing them. I asked a group of fifth- and sixth-graders whether they got nervous before the big state exams in math, reading and science. One boy almost laughed.

"I know they taught me everything I'm supposed to know," he said, "and I know I know it, so I just go and I take the test like it's a regular test."

"The teachers are more nervous than us," a girl chimed in, "because they want to make sure that they taught us everything. We're the ones taking a test, and they're like, 'Oh, my gosh, what is she going to do? Did I teach her that?'"

When I asked what teachers did when a student wasn't getting it, one kid cut to the chase: "They'll say, 'You want to stay after school with me and I'll help you?' Or they'll say, 'Can you stay in at recess?' or 'Can I tutor you?' They just try their best to give you special attention so that you can learn."

Lincoln teachers were specific about strategies—and eager to explain them. What they said struck me as a primer for successful teaching and learning. Their comments included:

156

"First of all, you don't give up. You try a number of strategies to develop a rapport with the child, which could be just sitting down after school and having a conversation."

"A lot of times being punitive with a child isn't going to be successful.

You have to have rules, but punishment is not necessarily the thing you want to go to the first time, and perhaps even the second time, to get your point across."

"Always capitalize on the parts children do well. All children do something well, and if you praise them and capitalize on just that little bit, I think you can get some growth from them."

"Let them know that you really care about what they're doing correctly."

"If I am not getting through, the teacher that had the child last year is the one I go to and ask, 'What was successful with this child? What did you do that really worked?'"

"As a younger teacher, I'm always looking to the other teachers for advice, and everybody always has ideas to help me out."

"The most important thing is to not to make the child who's not getting it feel embarrassed. You have to do it privately. Go over it again at lunchtime. You do things with them by themselves. Treat them with the respect that you want back."

That word, "respect," came up again and again. Teachers told me that three words define Lincoln: respect, enjoyment and success. One put it this way: "The culture of Lincoln is success. Whatever it takes to help them succeed. To get higher than they were. To bring them up, so that they enjoy life, because they can read better, so they can do math, so they get along with each other."

At Lincoln, there is none of the "soft bigotry of low expectations." Sadly, many schools do have an expectations gap, but racism and stupidity are not sufficient to explain why there are reduced expectations for some kids, but not for all. Often schools expect less because no one has made the goals clear. Once we know what the goals are and how they're going to be measured, it's easier to make it clear where the bar is being set. The purpose of schooling then becomes to get everyone over the bar—and it doesn't matter by how much any particular kid clears the bar, as long as the bar is meaningfully high, and as long as the adults are committed to getting everyone over it.

The kids I met at Lincoln seemed to have an intuitive understanding of the expectations gap. As one noted, "I think in the other schools, it's the teachers' fault that the students don't do well, because the teachers sometimes expect good scores from the white kids, but from the black kids they just say, 'Nah, he's not going to learn as well as the white kids.'"

Ah, race, our American dilemma. I asked a mixed group of kids to tell me what percentage of the Lincoln students were African-American and Hispanic. The correct answer is 63 percent, but none of them came close; their estimates ranged from a low of 10 percent to a high of "more than 70 percent." Curiously, the teachers' estimates were just as far off. Albano's explanation for this apparent color-blindness is simple: When all children are succeeding, there's no reason to focus on anyone's race.

Social class doesn't seem to be an issue at Lincoln, perhaps because, while the school has a "range of children whose parents are at both ends of the educational and socio-economic scale," according to Albano, most families are working class. That fact, however, was not at all apparent, at least not to me. I spent about an hour chatting with six kids, all fifth- and sixth-graders. Three came to Lincoln from other countries and arrived not speaking any English. I was impressed with their intelligence, curiosity and eloquence, and when I asked what their parents did for a living, I was expecting to hear "lawyer," "doctor" and "banker." I was bowled over by their answers: Two fathers were garage mechanics, three mothers cleaned houses, one father worked at a Blimpy's, and so forth.

Part of Lincoln's recipe for success may shock traditionalists: The kids enjoy school! As one boy said, "Some people say school is so boring, like 'I can't wait until I get out of high school or college,' but I don't really think that. I like school. It's fun, but we deserve a little fun here, because that's where we spend most of our time."

158

They told me stories about their friends who weren't lucky enough to go to Lincoln. "I have friends in other schools who say, 'Oh, my teacher's stupid, I hate her,'" said one student.

Another chimed in, "Sometimes they like kick the wall of the school, saying, 'Oh, you suck, I hate you!'" Amid laughter he explained further: "As soon as school gets out, they go, 'Freedom!' And then they start kicking it and everything like that. And then they just leave."

It's a curious comment on the profession that Lincoln's teachers get scant recognition from their peers—and even from their families. As Lucille DiRoucco, who has since retired, told me at the time: "When I socialize with my friends they say, 'Where do you teach?' And when I say 'Mount Vernon,' you can see the expressions; they won't say anything, but you can see the expression in their faces that say, 'Oh good Lord, you teach down there?'"

"They look down on us," Mary Anderson added. "I live in Eastchester where there are Scarsdale teachers who don't understand how I could work in Mount Vernon and why would I go in as early as I do and stay as late as I do. They think that's foolish." Anderson is an interesting case. She's well past retirement age and was actually losing money by continuing to teach, but she loves her job, loves the success that she, her colleagues and her kids enjoy. And watching her second-graders take apart words and sentences with energy and skill made me hope she'd never retire! (Anderson is now teaching fourth grade at Lincoln.)

Veteran Jim LeRay, who teaches fifth grade at Lincoln, has felt his own family's disappointment. "Some are kind of uneasy with the fact that I'm still teaching and I'm teaching in Mount Vernon. It's almost as if I didn't make it professionally."

Given George Albano's family history, it comes as no surprise that he believes in parent involvement, another ingredient in the recipe for success. As he says, "If children grow up in an environment where they see their parents involved…they will follow suit." But he faced a dilemma when he took over at Lincoln, because not many Mount Vernon parents were coming to school for parents' night or other activities. He decided to *make* them show up. Report cards are supposed to go home with the kids, but he sent a note instead: If you want to see your child's report card, come to school to pick it up.

What happened? "People complained, the board told me to change and I was even threatened with lawsuits," Albano said. "My answer to the critics was to say that I would accommodate parents from six in the morning to any time at night, but they had to come."

In the beginning, he recalls, 25 to 30 percent of parents did not come. But now? "Now if we have one, two or three parents, out of 800-plus children, it's a lot," he said. "If parents do not come, as far as I'm concerned, they should be in court for educational neglect."

What George Albano did was in flagrant defiance of the rules but, as Ron Ross said with a laugh: "You show me a principal who follows the book on everything and I'll show you a lousy principal. You can't make a good school by following the rules."

Lincoln's success turns on leadership, but what kind of leader is my Superman? The adjective I heard most often was "strong," as in, "Mr. Albano is a very strong principal." But strength has a special meaning at Lincoln.

"When I say 'strong,' I don't mean he's just telling you what to do and making sure you're getting it done," said one Lincoln teacher. "'Strong' means he's getting things done for you....Any help that you need, any assistance that you need, he will provide it for you. We have the materials and support. So that kind of strong leadership allows us to do the things that we're doing in the classroom."

Another teacher described Albano's strength in a different way: "He's a master at capitalizing on the talents and expertise of others. He loves to admit that we know more than he does, and he's not afraid to say that. And so he empowers us, and he delegates. He makes us feel important, and he gives us a lot of respect. And that's what keeps us going."

Albano calls what he provides *situational leadership*. "I can be very direct when it comes to the well-being of children, their best interests and their health, but I also can work collaboratively," he said. I asked him just how much effective leadership has to do with getting out of the way of people who know what they're doing. "Some people," he said, "have a problem doing that, but I'm comfortable with who I am, I love that so many of my teachers have special expertise and I don't mind giving them whatever they need to be successful with children. That's the bottom line, not who gets the credit."

So that's the recipe: strong leadership, parental involvement, teachers who do whatever it takes, respect, the arts and physical education, a curriculum that matches the tests and a genuine belief that all children can learn. Ron Ross told me that if he could clone George Albano, the achievement gap would disappear, but on this point I don't agree.

Although thousands of George Albanos would be a good start, schools need more. We must begin by acknowledging that our main problem is not the "achievement gap." What we have is more complex: It's also an *opportunity gap*, an *expectations gap* and an *outcomes gap*. Until we distribute resources more fairly *and* staff our schools with adults who expect the best from every child, we will continue to have big gaps in performance. George Albano works hard to dig up extra resources to close the opportunity gap, and he only hires teachers who expect the best from every child, which eliminates any expectations gap. Then, magically, the outcomes gap disappears.

Right now states and school districts, politicians and educators, focus almost entirely on the achievement gap and create compensatory programs, etc., with all the best intentions in the world. That exercise is doomed to failure. The gap won't disappear if one day poor and minority kids score at the same level as whites and well-to-do kids. And isn't it fundamentally racist to assume that white is the measuring stick against which to judge all others?

It's like judging Head Start by comparing Head Start kids to preschoolers of middle- and upper-middle-class families. The latter are going to keep moving up, because those families know about the importance of early stimulation. Then, because the well-off keep moving up, it's easy to conclude that Head Start has failed. That's wrong. If, instead, we had some rational set of expectations for Head Start, we could judge its success or failure against that set of standards (are kids healthier, do they know the alphabet and the sounds of letters, and other questions).

White performance on standardized tests shouldn't be the standard against which others are judged. Instead, we need to do the hard work of setting standards, which requires even more hard work from us in advance. And we need to debate deep questions, including, "What does it mean to be educated?" and "What skills and knowledge does one need in order to be productive, lead a satisfying life and contribute to the greater good?"

A cautionary note: Albano's message, which has attracted attention from as far away as New Zealand, has been largely ignored in his own district. At the time I visited the school, not one member of the Mount Vernon School Board had been to Lincoln.[180] When his students leave Lincoln Elementary School, they are likely to attend "real world" public schools of differential expectations: drill and boredom. Both Albano and former superintendent Ron Ross concede that many will likely be lost, because middle schools and high schools in Mount Vernon—and everywhere else—do business in the same old way.

There's no silver bullet. The recipe for success includes some mix of strong leadership, committed teachers, an integrated curriculum, a willingness to challenge conventional wisdom and accepted practices, and the moral imperative to care for and about all of our children. *Real change requires real change.* You cannot snip off one loose end and expect genuine improvement; nor can you change one faulty policy and expect a new world. This is tough work, as George Albano's story demonstrates.

The policy of "closing the achievement gap" between racial groups is doomed to failure, because school performance is closely linked to socio-economic status. As a group, children of the poor—whatever their color—don't do as well in school as children who grow up eating well; living in warm, clean homes; and being cared for by parents who read to them, limit their television time and take them to museums.

The latter are born ahead and, individual success stories to the contrary notwithstanding, schools by themselves aren't going to close the gap. Nor will they ever catch up—after following a cohort of 4 million American children from birth to preschool enrollment at age 4, the National Center for Education Statistics notes that: "The percentage of children who were in a center-based setting increased as parents' highest level of education increased. For example, 43 percent of children about 4 years old whose parents' highest level of education was less than high school were enrolled in a center-based setting, compared with 71 percent of their peers whose parents' highest level of education was any graduate or professional school."[181]

Stressing a racial achievement gap allows educators to rationalize their own performance, as in "I taught it, but they—*those* children—didn't learn it." A healthier approach involves setting clear, measurable standards and then providing whatever resources are needed to ensure that all measure up. For example, to graduate from my college, Dartmouth, students had to pass a physical education test, including swimming 100 yards. We didn't have to swim it faster than someone else; we just had to swim it, and instruction was available for those who needed it. It was a realistic, clearly defined standard, for both students and coaches. And no coach could have said, "I taught them swimming; it's not *my* fault that they're at the bottom of the pool."

So let's stop talking about the achievement gap and focus for a moment on the leadership gap.

How else can we explain why we have islands of excellence of at least one classroom in virtually every school, some excellent schools in the poorest neighborhoods in every district, and several smaller school districts in our country that have closed the achievement gap, and yet the lessons from these examples of excellence have not been scaled up in the school, in the district and across the nation?

Too often educational leadership does not know that diffusing successful innovations is what they should be laser-focused on doing. Or, if they do know what to do, they don't know how to do it.

Why is it that most teachers don't have opportunities to visit each other's classrooms in their own building, let alone visit outstanding schools in their district that have been profiled in the local and national media? The leadership at every level in school districts does not encourage teachers and principals to take the time to learn from the best. It rarely rewards or recognizes those who are learning from others.

The leadership gap is defined not by words, but by inaction. It is leaders who do not have or do not implement strategies for identifying and learning from best practice, regardless of how much they talk about the importance of best practice.

School boards contribute to the leadership gap by not demanding more. Why are their expectations for their own results, including those of their superintendents, so low, when they are surrounded by examples of best practice in the schools and districts all around?

Ninety percent of the Fortune 1000 corporations wouldn't exist today if their leadership had thought and led as most of America's education leaders have over the past 30 years. The diffusion of innovation, and the daily effort to accelerate the pace of diffusion, is the lifeblood of these companies.[182]

And so we end where we began, with Superman and the perplexing question: Does it take a Superman (or Superwoman) to create excellent schools? If it does, we are in big trouble because they're in short supply. I took that question to Ron Ross, the former superintendent of Mount Vernon, who told me that our worst schools need outstanding leaders who will be on the job 24/7, until the schools can climb out of the hole.

Ross added a cautionary note: "Even when schools are performing, they require strong leadership. Anyone who wants to excel shouldn't expect to go home at three o'clock. I tell anyone who gets into teaching, 'If you're coming in here because you think it's a 5- or 6-hour job with summers off, do me a favor. Find something else to do with your life.'"

So how many George Albanos are out there? And why aren't there more? My Superman's success relies on being subversive, on being a strong swimmer, because he's working his way through a very strong and dangerous current. And how can we do our part? Should we be hiring more strong swimmers, or should we be trying to change the current?

Section Three
FOLLOW THE TEACHER

Chapter 17
ONE FIRST-GRADER AT A TIME

"The purple pancake went swimming in the lake and ate a fish."

When the first-graders in Elizabeth Holloway's class at Benjamin Banneker Elementary School in New Orleans read that sentence on the blackboard, they almost jumped out of their chairs, waving their hands excitedly.

"Is something wrong with that story?" I asked.

"Lots!" they shouted, volunteering that pancakes weren't purple, can't swim and don't eat fish.

That silly story, or some variation of it, produced similar reactions in another first-grade class at Banneker and in first-grade classes at Fannie C. Williams Elementary School, also in New Orleans. That is, the children read what I wrote and understood what they were reading.

To be doubly certain, I then picked children at random and asked them to read from "Nate the Great," a book that's not used in New Orleans first-grade classes. All of the children read with comprehension.

Learning to read with understanding is the foundation for all learning, but most low-income children in the United States are below grade level in reading by fourth grade.[183] So *any* New Orleans first-grader who's learning to read in school is beating the odds.

In the years *before* Hurricane Katrina, most New Orleans public school first-graders were not learning to read. In 2008, only 26 percent of current eighth-graders read with proficiency, and 85 percent of all students were a year-and-a-half or more behind.

Long before Katrina, parents of school-age children had voted with their checkbooks; in 2005, more than half of New Orleans children were in private or parochial schools.

After Katrina, Louisiana created the Recovery School District to run 60 of the city's worst schools and in 2007 hired Paul Vallas, who had run the Chicago and Philadelphia school systems with some success. Vallas filled 30 percent of his classrooms with teachers from Teach For America, TeachNOLA and Troops for Teachers, programs that recruit eager but untrained people and give them summer training before they begin teaching.

New Orleans has made progress. On the spring 2008 state tests, students in grades 3-12 made gains at nearly every level in math and reading. However, most students remain below grade level. "I tell people that we're at base camp preparing to climb Mount Everest, but last year we weren't even in the Himalayas," Vallas said.

However, unless *first-graders* are learning to read, New Orleans will be playing catch-up forever.

Benjamin Banneker, where Elizabeth Holloway teaches, is one of a handful of schools not devastated by Katrina and the flooding. Banneker, which sits on a piece of high ground called "the sliver by the river," currently enrolls 464 students in grades pre-K-8, and 94 percent of its students receive free or reduced-price lunch, a generally accepted marker for poverty.

Fannie C. Williams Elementary School (489 students, 93 percent receiving free or reduced-price lunches) was nothing more than a collection of trailers, way out in east New Orleans, when I visited. Most of that part of the city was under water for weeks, rendering nearly all school buildings unusable. When I was there, Williams had no playground[184] to speak of—but I did meet the school's experienced principal, Kelly Batiste.

Banneker's principal, Cherylynn Branche, has staffed Banneker with veteran teachers. "I prefer people who know what they're doing," she said. "I prefer people who have a proven track record. I prefer people who are going to stay here and work with our children for the long haul." By contrast, 40 percent of Batiste's classroom teachers when I visited were new, many from Teach For America or a similar organization.

But experience may not be the key variable. Second-graders in Lindsay Enters' class were reading with excitement and comprehension. The University of Wisconsin graduate was part of Teach-NOLA. "There is really no way to prepare yourself for teaching and the challenges you face," she said in 2008. "It's the same for people coming out of regular education programs." The rookie teacher decided to make reading the core of her class, "to make them all phenomenal readers," she said. "When I came in not one of them was reading their chapter books and now I have 16 out of 19 doing it."

She said she understood that not everyone could teach a child to read and admitted that she approached the task with some trepidation. "Reading is something that always frightened me a little bit, because it is such a responsibility. I don't know that everyone could teach reading. To be a teacher you need to be able to assess where the children are, and know where you're headed."

Then she said what for me are the magic words: "If I'm teaching it, but they aren't getting it, then I have to change what I'm doing." In other words, if the kids aren't learning, the teacher has to do something different. Attitude matters!

Of course, not all New Orleans first-graders are reading. Sarah T. Reed Elementary (553 students, 94 percent receiving free or reduced-price lunches) was also a collection of trailers in east New Orleans when I visited. As at Banneker and Williams, the majority of Reed students live in poverty, but the similarities seemed to end there at the time of my visit. My nonsense story about the pancake produced a less enthusiastic response, and fewer hands went in the air when I asked what was wrong with the story.

Only one or two children were able to read from "Nate the Great" with comprehension. Most read without expression—clear evidence that they did not understand the meaning. One boy, already 8, could not even decode.

If there's a silver lining anywhere in these bleak results, it seems to have taken a "perfect storm" of inauspicious circumstances at Reed to create the disaster. When I visited Reed in 2008, the principal and 75 percent of her teachers were in their first year. The school expected 125 students, but 387 showed up. One first-grade class was taught by a substitute from January to June because the regular teacher was let go for reasons the principal wouldn't explain. How close to the bottom of the barrel was she scraping? Whenever I looked in on his class during the day, the sub was wearing a Bluetooth device; at least twice he appeared to be engaged in a telephone conversation.

Another first-grade teacher, a military veteran hired in November 2008, acknowledged her lack of preparation at the time. "I didn't think I could teach the children to read," said Nicole Tate. "I thought, 'Maybe if I let them read and they hear themselves read, they'll be better readers.' But I never had anybody say, 'Okay Miss Tate, you're doing this wrong, but let me show you how to do it.' Nobody never [sic] came, so I had to figure it out on my own."

Principal Daphyne Burnett said she'd asked for more help but was given only one "reading interventionist."

What might the future hold for Reed's many non-readers, or for other children who don't master reading in first grade? Research indicates that children who are behind in reading in first grade have only a 1-in-8 chance of catching up.[185] But if New Orleans devotes serious resources to the school next year, including well-trained veterans and more "interventionists," the grim prognosis could be reversed.

However, those children do *not* need more drill in decoding. Reading specialists often draw a false distinction between decoding and comprehending, and because most tests reward decoding, teachers in the early grades may be tempted to treat it as a goal rather than what it is: a means to an end.

It's also high time to stop fighting the Reading Wars. Children are the only casualties of this protracted stand-off between crusaders for phonics and defenders of whole language. That this battle continues to rage is a perfect example of systems putting adult interests—money and ego—ahead of those of children.

About 11 years ago I tracked the progress of a classroom of first-graders, as their first-year teacher tried to teach them to read. Employing the method known as whole language, she taught the children to recognize words. Using the same book for months at a time, she convinced the children—and perhaps herself—that they were learning to read. Only at the end of the year when I asked the children, all African-American and low-income, to read from a book they had never seen did they learn that they had not been taught to read.

The painful irony of that situation was that, on the first day of school, the teacher had asked the children what they wanted to achieve that year. While a few wanted to get to know their fathers or go see a grandparent, the majority told her that they wanted to learn to read!

Across the hall, the first-graders in veteran Johnny Brinson's class learned to read with comprehension. No ideologue, Brinson used a combination of techniques—"whatever works," he told me. He taught his kids that letters have sounds associated with them, and that the sounds change depending on the combinations of letters. He teased and cajoled, scolded and praised, but he never seemed to lower his expectations or standards in the 20 or more days that I spent in his class during the year. The rookie matched Mr. Brinson when it came to affection; her problem was that no one had taught her how to teach reading.[186]

The national goal, all children reading by the end of *third* grade, is a ludicrously low floor that I suspect has become a ceiling. Children don't learn to walk just so they can walk in place; they want to get somewhere more efficiently. So too with reading; children want to learn to read so they can make sense of the world around them. Good teachers capitalize on that intrinsic motivation and teach children the many strategies they need to read with understanding, of which decoding is only a part.[187]

What is happening in New Orleans should *not* stay in New Orleans. That is, principals everywhere should put their best teachers in first grade (and kindergarten) and then devote whatever addi-

John Merrow

tional resources are needed to ensure that children learn to read with comprehension. To do otherwise is to create candidates for remediation, special education and other expensive programs.

Chapter 18
THE INFLUENCE OF TEACHERS

After college in the mid-1960s, I spent two years as a high school English teacher at Paul D. Schreiber High School in Port Washington, N.Y. Although I've been around educators for most of my professional life and currently work as the education correspondent for "PBS NewsHour,"[188] these would be the only years I taught high school full time. So it was to my great surprise when, in 2006, some former Schreiber students invited me to their 40th high school reunion. How could they possibly remember me? And how could I turn down such an opportunity? I accepted the invitation and prepared for a sentimental stroll down memory lane. What the day ended up offering, though, was altogether different: a powerful reminder of the lasting influence that teachers have on the lives of their students, as well as some insights into where education in this democratic nation has missed the mark in recent years.

Like most high schools in the 1960s, Paul D. Schreiber High School was rigidly tracked. As a new teacher fresh out of college, I wasn't allowed near the top two tracks of college-bound students, the "ones" and "twos." Instead, I was assigned to what the administration called "threes" and "fours"—students we weren't supposed to expect much from. Fortunately, I didn't have a philosophy of education or any real plan at the time. I didn't know how I was supposed to approach "those kids." So I did with my students what William Sullivan, my English teacher at Taft School (in Connecticut) during my junior and senior years, had done for me: I made my kids rewrite and rewrite again, as often as necessary, until their themes and essays were well-written and persuasive.

I hadn't learned how to be a teacher while I was in college. I'd majored in English at Dartmouth, not education. But I had an image of Mr. Sullivan in my head and, because I thought he was an effective teacher, I adopted some of his techniques. Mr. Sullivan demanded our best and didn't cut anyone any slack. He wasn't mean, but he could be caustic even as he was encouraging us. He would give what he called the "2-8-2" writing test almost daily. He'd write a phrase on the board, tell us we had two minutes to think about it, eight minutes to write, and then the final two minutes to proofread what we had written. The top grade was a 10, but any significant error in spelling or punctuation meant a zero. If we were writing dialogue and wanted a character to speak in incomplete sentences, we had to mark these "sentence errors" with asterisks to let him know we knew the difference. At the end of the grading period, he threw out our lowest five or 10 scores, but that didn't lessen the pressure of each 2-8-2.

I still remember some of the phrases Mr. Sullivan used as writing prompts, like "Turn out the lights. I don't want to go home in the dark." These, he said, were the dying words[189] of someone named William Sydney Porter. What could they mean? Was he delusional or somehow insightful? (Later he told us that Porter was better known as O. Henry.) And there was an enigmatic line—"Put out the light, and then put out the light"—that we had to wrestle with, long before we actually read Shakespeare's "Othello."

So there I was in 1966 at Paul D. Schreiber High School, teaching "threes" and "fours": kids who, for the most part, didn't read poetry, didn't care about Shakespeare, and didn't want to be in English class. Truth is, I didn't want to be there either. I'd been accepted into the Peace Corps earlier that year and was heading for Kenya or Tanganyika or Zanzibar, but when I couldn't pass the physical, I had to find a new direction. (I'd had a spinal fusion operation right after graduation and wore an elaborate back brace for my first semester at Schreiber.) But I was lucky. At Schreiber, I found some very supportive colleagues, a department chair who wanted us to be successful teachers, and a treasure trove of back issues of the magazine put out by the National Council of Teachers of English, chock full of techniques and lesson plans.

So I was a Sullivan imitator for two wonderful years and then left for graduate school at Indiana University. After Indiana, I taught again, this time at a black college in the South and in a federal prison at night. Perhaps, by this time, there was a little bit of Merrow in my teaching, but most of it was still Sullivan, along with whatever I'd learned from my Schreiber colleagues.

I offer this as prologue to the Class of 1966's 40th reunion. That night, I learned that the teachers who had influenced me also influenced my students, often in very specific ways.

Throughout the evening, I met former students, found their pictures in the yearbook and asked after a while, "What's your story?" Wow, the things they told me, and the valleys and hills they described. But even the sad stories were bathed in survivor's light. As I listened, I learned a lot about myself as a teacher, as well.

The first person to come up to me, calling me Mr. Merrow even though we were both in our 60s, thanked me for helping him become a writer. "You made us rewrite everything," he said, "and later on, when I realized that I had something to say, I knew that I would be able to say it clearly, as long as I rewrote it." I asked what sort of things he wrote about. Transgender issues mostly, he said. When I started leafing through the yearbook to find his picture, he added, "I was a girl then." Sure enough, "Dana" had become "Steve."

That development would certainly have shocked Mr. Sullivan, but he would have been happy about the rewriting.

A woman came up to me and began reciting the lyrics to "Fun, Fun, Fun" by the Beach Boys. ("She's got her daddy's car, she can cruise to the hamburger stand now; she forgot all about the library, like she told her old man now.") She told me I'd taught her class poetry by starting with popular songs, and then got them to read "Renascence" by Edna St. Vincent Millay and the war poetry of Wilfred Owen. Details I didn't recall.[190]

Another former student, who described himself as a "classic underachiever," said he'd been so angry about being forced to rewrite his term paper that he swore he'd show me by making something of himself. He's now a lawyer. Mr. Sullivan would be proud.

Did I remember, one student wanted to know, my campaign to elevate the level of bathroom graffiti? I didn't, but learned that

I'd done something Mr. Sullivan might have tried under the same circumstances. My classroom was next to the boys' room (which I used, because the faculty bathroom was two corridors away), and the walls were scrawled with the usual profanities. One day in class, my former student told me, I had semi-seriously encouraged the students to "upgrade the graffiti" with lines from Shakespeare, T.S. Eliot, Edna St. Vincent Millay and others. It caught on, and "To be or not to be" replaced "Schreiber Sucks." "This is the way the world ends" took the place of "Susie does it with dogs," and so on. Before long, we had bathroom walls that would have been the envy of any university town coffeehouse.

But it wasn't just the fact that, as a teacher, I'd been obsessed with rewriting that came to light at the reunion. That night, I discovered that I'd unconsciously absorbed from Mr. Sullivan another crucial lesson about teaching: the importance of empathizing without lowering standards.

Here's what happened. Before the reunion, I'd gone through the 1966 yearbook to see how many faces and names I could remember. One face jumped out at me: a young man named Sandy whose life, I knew, had been awful beyond belief. His divorced parents had been alcoholics. One day his mother had drowned while intoxicated, and Sandy had been ordered by a court to live with his father on a boat in the harbor. I knew that his dad, a mean drunk, regularly beat and otherwise abused him. A guidance counselor and I used to talk about how powerless we felt. I can remember looking at Sandy in class and wondering how he held his life together. Now I was hoping to find out that he had made it.

Late in the evening, as I was leaving to go home, a man standing outside said, "Mr. Merrow?" It was Sandy. He told me he'd left home immediately after graduating, had gone into the service, and was now retired and living in Arizona. He said he was driving a school bus, just to keep busy. Had I known about his family? he asked. I told him how hard it had been not to act sympathetic and understanding and cut him some slack on assignments. But he thanked me profusely for not letting him slide, for treating him like a regular student. I know now that that's exactly how Mr. Sullivan would have treated Sandy, but it was a pleasant shock to discover that I had, unknowingly, done the right thing.

Sandy recalled how, one Sunday, I'd seen him tooling around on his motorcycle and had called out to remind him of the huge English assignment due on Monday. He told me he'd actually been working on it all that morning and was just taking a quick break, but that he went back immediately after seeing me and finished it! Once again, a reminder of the influence of teachers. And once again, an incident that I have no memory of.

He also told me that, just a few months earlier on his school bus, a 15-year-old girl he'd gotten to know pretty well (well enough to know that her 16th birthday was approaching) told him that she didn't really expect to celebrate that birthday. He read her tone, correctly as it turned out, as a warning sign and went to the high school and spoke to a counselor. The girl not only made it to her 16th birthday, but also got counseling and straightened out. Sandy rightly felt that he'd made his contribution. It struck me that Sandy had been able to do for that troubled girl what his guidance counselor and English teacher hadn't been able to do for him 40 years earlier. The girl Sandy helped may never know what he did for her, but hearing the story reminded me, for the hundredth time that night, that we are a part of all we touch, and what seems a small and forgettable gesture or action to us may have a deep and lasting impact on another's life. In that sense, we are all teachers.

The night of the reunion I came to understand that, more than 40 years earlier, I had not accepted the administration's label ("threes" and "fours") for these kids, but had expected them to become competent writers who could be moved, and move others, by the power of words. That is what my teachers expected of me, and I could hardly do less for my own students. In truth, I didn't really know another way.

Of course, I also know from my current work in education that I had a great deal of latitude to shape my classes as I saw fit. Most teachers today don't have the freedom to do what I did. While my job was to prepare students to pass the New York State Regents Exams, we did not have a step-by-step curriculum or regular bubble tests, and I was free to innovate. Our curriculum had enough slack in it to allow me to insist upon rewriting, and more rewriting.

In my work for the NewsHour, I spend a lot of time with teachers, some of whom have stayed in touch over the years. I remember an e-mail message from a veteran special education teacher in Maryland, a woman I know to be dedicated and competent. She wrote that her school had failed to make what No Child Left Behind calls "Adequate Yearly Progress" for the second year in a row and, because of that, they were going to teach to the test—because if they didn't make AYP that year, the school might be shut down. She was clearly distraught by this Sophie's Choice. She wrote: "In teaching to the test, I am afraid that we are raising a nation of idiots who may be able to pass standardized assessments without being able to think. I am trying to keep focused on the fact that we are educating the citizens of our nation's future, which is not necessarily compatible with the vision of No Child Left Behind." My heart goes out to that teacher, and I am angry that we continue to put her, and many thousands like her, in that position.

The teaching mission is complex and difficult, and yet oh so vital. Teachers can never declare "Mission Accomplished," because they are a bridge, not an endpoint, for all the boys and girls (and men and women) who come into their lives. Their involvement doesn't begin or end at the classroom door; or once they've covered Newton and Galileo, the Hundred Years' War or the past perfect tense; or even when the semester ends. Good teachers do a lot of counseling on the run in casual interactions and they do a lot of listening, often in fits and starts. Good teachers let kids talk about their feelings without saying, "I know how you feel," because they know it's always about their students' experiences, not their own. They work with kids who are a mixture of self-absorption, insecurity, raging hormones and ambition. They may have to face parents who want their offspring to get into the Ivy League and have jobs they can boast about, but the teacher's job is to help students build a self, create the entity that will be constant company for life. That's why the best teachers listen to students and draw out their thinking, but don't try to solve every problem. That's why the best teachers empathize and care deeply about students as individuals, but never lower standards or expectations.

Some teachers believe, incorrectly, that they can improve a student's self-esteem with words and other easy expressions of praise (like high grades) even though the student isn't doing the best work that he or she can. The wisest know that accomplishment is the foundation of self-esteem. Students know when they're doing their best, and they know when they're being allowed to cut corners. They may grumble that their teachers are expecting too much, but good teachers know enough not to listen to that particular complaint.

But today it's not enough for outstanding teachers to teach and listen well. Their real challenge is to consciously push students out of their comfort zones. In a way, it's a "value added" issue. Let me put it this way: In America, unless a teacher works with the poor—in urban areas, Appalachia or wherever—most of his or her students are sufficiently well-off children of the richest society the world has ever known. What can and should teachers do to ensure that the talents and gifts they work to maximize in their already privileged students are put to use in the service of others?

It's not enough to equip these students to do well. These students need to learn to do *good*: to contribute to society, to serve. H. G. Wells observed that civilization is a race between education and catastrophe. Right now, catastrophe seems to be in the lead—and perhaps pulling away. In our current education system, the United States is suffering from a kind of bipolar disorder. We have, increasingly, two worlds: the comfortable, often smug world of wealthy (or "suburban" or "upper-middle-class") schools, and the underfunded and inefficient schools in which the poor are isolated. Schools for the poor are most often dreary institutions with heavy emphasis on repetitive instruction and machine-scored bubble tests. Although some underprivileged schools are vibrant places of innovation and discovery, that is not necessarily a cause for celebration; what it often means is that reformers get to experiment on the poor, who don't have the political clout to control their own schools or reject the do-gooders. In terms of our public education system, while we do have some wonderful schools, the trend lines in public education are depressing.

Why expect teachers to do this work? First, because they can. Teachers are uniquely positioned, as I learned at the reunion, to make a lasting impression on hundreds of children. All they need is enough professional support and guidance on the one hand, and enough leeway on the other, to make lasting connections. And second, because no one else seems willing to accept the challenge today.

In truth, I fear for our country—something I never expected to happen. I see a nation that remains fragmented. I lived through the divisiveness of the Vietnam War era and the selfishness of the Reagan years, but the George W. Bush years were in some ways worse. Cynicism ("All politicians are crooked"), indifference ("I don't care who wins the election") and a frightening willingness to accept authority blindly (religious fundamentalism) are on the rise, along with a growing gap between rich and poor. In Washington today, bipartisanship is nowhere to be found, and the strident voices on the right (the tea party movement, for example) grow louder.

When that bleak mood strikes, I turn in one of two directions. If it's three o'clock in the morning—the time it always is in "the dark night of the soul," according to F. Scott Fitzgerald—I turn to the "self" that my teachers and parents helped me build. Living in my heart and mind, as part of that self, are the likes of John Keats, Alfred, Lord Tennyson and E.E. Cummings; Bach and Mozart; Ella Fitzgerald, Frank Sinatra and Dave Brubeck; Shakespeare, Mark Twain and F. Scott Fitzgerald; Picasso and Renoir. That's good company. They help get me through the moment, and I get up to try again.

Or, if it's daytime, I go to a school and feed off the energy and youthful optimism of students[191] and the dedication of the best teachers. I regain my balance and optimism and leave rejuvenated.

I left that 40th high school reunion reminded of the special place that teachers occupy in the lives of children and young people—especially those who haven't had many advantages in life. Society needs to acknowledge this truth and trust teachers to do more of the character-building work that is an unspoken but vital part of their mission.

Chapter 19
NURSE FOR AMERICA?

Florence Nightingale once observed, "Were there none who were discontented with what they have, the world would never reach anything better." With 2010 marking the 100th anniversary of Ms. Nightingale's passing, this seems like a good time to consider teaching—particularly the highly successful Teach For America—in relation to her important and life-giving profession.

To what extent is classroom teaching a skill? How long does it take to learn those skills, and is there a best way to learn them? These are important questions at any time, but I submit they are of particular importance today, with Teach For America (and other alternative routes into the classroom) in ascendance.

No doubt about Teach For America's ascendancy; it has become the country's largest provider of teachers for low-income communities. What began in 1990 with 500 men and women working in six communities currently has about 7,300 Teach For America corps members working in 35 high-poverty urban and rural areas, and will be expanding to additional regions in 2010 (including a cohort of 30 TFA teachers going to public schools and a charter school in Rhode Island in the fall). Currently, nearly half a million children are being taught by TFA teachers.

During the 2008 presidential campaign, both candidates spoke favorably about the program. President Obama continues to speak highly of it. For example, when he signed the Edward M. Kennedy Serve America Act in April 2009, he cited the growing popularity of TFA as evidence of young America's commitment to public service, saying in part: "I've seen a rising generation of young people work and volunteer and turn out in record numbers...they have become a generation of activists possessed with that most American of ideas—that people who love their country can change it…they are why 35,000 young people applied for only 4,000 slots in Teach For America."

That's a 42 percent increase over the previous year, and many of those young people come straight out of our finest colleges and universities.

And when I linked President Obama and TFA in a Google search, it produced nearly 9 million citations.

At his Senate confirmation hearing in January 2009, Obama's choice for secretary of education, Arne Duncan, had high praise for Teach For America and for Wendy Kopp herself.

Teach For America has become a household word in its short history. I suspect everyone knows that Kopp developed the idea as her senior thesis at Princeton in 1989 and then founded the program in 1990. As TFA celebrates its 20th anniversary, it has put more than 14,000 teachers into hard-to-staff classrooms, usually for two-year stints. Although only about a quarter remain in the classroom beyond two years, over 60 percent of TFA "graduates" stay connected to public education. Prominent alumni include KIPP founders Mike Feinberg and Dave Levin and Washington schools chancellor Michelle Rhee.

In a funny way, I was *in* Teach For America long before Wendy Kopp came up with the idea. I had been accepted into the Peace Corps and was scheduled to teach English in East Africa, but then I failed the physical just a few months before graduation from Dartmouth in 1964. Even though I'd taken only one education course in college, I was determined to teach. And so, two months after my spinal fusion and still in a brace, I began teaching at a high school just outside New York City.

I worked long hours, spent most weekends grading papers, made a lot of mistakes and tried to bring imagination and creativity into my lessons. There were four other rookies on the staff that year. We supported each other, and, to be truthful, we shared a certain smug attitude toward many of the veteran teachers, who we felt were just putting in the hours and didn't care as much about the kids as we did.

By the end of my second year, I hit my stride and was doing a pretty good job. That's when I left to go to graduate school.

As a reporter, I've been in a fair number of classrooms with TFA corps members. On our website[192] you'll find a series of video portraits of Teach For America teachers at work, with scenes from their classrooms in New Orleans high schools. I think you will end up liking all of these young men and women. We certainly did. And you would be thrilled to have some of them teaching your children, but probably not all of them.

A careful viewer of our "Teaching for America" series detected a thread running through many of the TFA teacher profiles. "Most of these teachers seem to be overly concerned about control," he told me. "I get the feeling that they've been taught some simple rule like 'Control first, teaching next.'"

"What about Lindsay or Colleston?" I asked him.

"They're the exception," he said. "They seem to understand that control is a by-product of stimulating education."

I told the man about a Teach For America rookie whose class we visited in early February 2010. Matt Taylor teaches English at an alternative school, a middle school for kids who are four, five or six years below grade level. Just imagine trying to teach 16-year-olds whose literacy level is not much above "See Spot Run," but who are acutely sensitive to their age/skill level discrepancy. In the 90-minute class I observed, Matt engaged his students in eight or nine different activities, using a Promethean Board to make everything interactive. He peppered students with questions, rewarding correct answers without calling attention to incorrect ones. At one point he displayed a long paragraph on the board—a passage that contained at least a dozen errors in grammar, spelling and punctuation. What ensued was a game in which all but one student engaged (one slept most of the class). If I remember correctly, Matt told the students that he had found only 12 errors. They found two or three more and enjoyed the triumph of outdoing their teacher, a damn good strategy on the teacher's part.

Control was not an issue, ever. It never is when kids are engaged.

John Merrow

In my experience, Teach For America corps members are almost always fun to be around, because they are bright, energetic and outgoing. Their idealism and goodness virtually ooze out of every pore. What's not to like?

Well, to be honest, sometimes their *teaching* is not to like. After all, they are first-year teachers who have had just five or six weeks of summer training and a short orientation in their assigned city. They make all sorts of rookie mistakes. Occasionally I recognized in them that smug attitude I once exhibited toward veterans.

It's a curious paradox that teaching, the profession that is *easiest* to get into, can be among the most difficult to enter. Most schools of education accept just about everyone who applies, but Teach For America, which puts all those capable, smart, idealistic young men and women into some of the country's toughest public schools, rejects an astonishing number (88 percent last year) of its applicants; in the 2008-2009 school year, it received an unprecedented 35,000 applications for about 1,400 available teaching positions. At more than 20 colleges and universities, Teach For America was the top recruiter. At Harvard, 13 percent of graduating seniors applied. At Spelman College in Atlanta, 25 percent did. If they don't make the cut at TFA, many will then fall back to their *second* choices, often a top law or business school.

Nearly all—78 percent—of those accepted will enter TFA. By contrast, only about 70 percent of those accepted into Yale chose to enroll.

What I find most impressive about Teach For America is how it continues to work to improve the model. It recently released the results of an intensive study of its most successful teachers. What was it about them, TFA hoped to find out, that made them successful? And could TFA fine-tune its own admission process to make sure it accepted more who had those qualities?[193] In a highly readable and thoughtful article in The Atlantic Monthly, Steven Farr, Teach For America's chief knowledge officer, told writer Amanda Ripley, "Great teachers constantly reevaluate what they are doing." He added: "Superstar teachers had four other tendencies in common: they avidly recruited students and their families into the process;

188

they maintained focus, ensuring that everything they did contributed to student learning; they planned exhaustively and purposefully—for the next day or the year ahead—by working backward from the desired outcome; and they worked relentlessly, refusing to surrender to the combined menaces of poverty, bureaucracy, and budgetary shortfalls."[194]

It may well be that Teach For America's greatest contribution to education will not be the kids who are helped or the talented young men and women who develop a connection with and affection for public education, but its relentless self-examination—a process that quite simply puts the rest of teacher education to shame. If Teach For America can work hard to figure out why some of its trainees become better teachers than others, why can't regular schools of education?[195]

One reason they don't is that many schools of education accept just about everyone who applies. The implication of being able to predict the likelihood of an applicant's becoming a successful teacher based on his or her application is that some applicants would be denied admission. TFA wants to be in that position, but do most schools of education? "Asked and answered," as the lawyers say.

The success of TFA inspired the Jack Kent Cooke Foundation to create an equivalent program that provides guidance and counseling to encourage low-income high school and community college students to earn their bachelor's degrees; it's awarded 11 $1 million grants to date. The program recruits and trains recent college graduates from top colleges and universities to work as full-time advisors for a year or two after graduation. "It will be the next Teach For America," Vance Lancaster, formerly of the Foundation, wrote in an e-mail in 2008, although they're not calling it "Advise For America." Instead it's the "College Advising Corps."

But I believe that the success of Teach For America[196] reveals an unpleasant truth about how *little* we value education and children. Consider nursing—another helping profession that's often compared with teaching. Just as there's a teaching shortage, the United States desperately needs nurses. Hospitals today have more than 135,000 empty nursing slots, according to the American Association of Colleges of Nursing.

But there is no "Nurse For America" program, because it's *inconceivable* that someone could step in and provide nursing care after just five weeks of summer training.

Just imagine: "Hi, Mrs. Lingering. I'm John Merrow, your new nurse. I just graduated from Dartmouth. Now let's see...it says you get two cc's of this medicine. That's about the same as a tablespoon, isn't it? And I'm supposed to examine you. I'm pretty sure I remember which orifice this instrument goes in."

No, we will never have a "Nurse For America" program, because that profession's standards[197] are higher than those of teaching. Nobody says, "Those who can, do. Those who can't, *nurse.*" That slur is reserved for teaching, an occupation that's ridiculously easy to join.

So, two-and-a-half cheers[198] for Teach For America, but wouldn't it be wonderful if "Nurse For America" and TFA were *equally* inconceivable? If teaching could become not merely an honorable calling but also a well-paid, highly respected profession that's difficult to get into?

Chapter 20
EVALUATING TEACHERS

How should teachers be evaluated? And who should do the job? These questions are central to one of education's hot buttons, the notion that judgments about a teacher—and perhaps her salary—should be based on how much her students learn. It's been called "merit pay" and "pay for performance" and a lot of other things, too. In the current system, a teacher's pay is almost entirely determined by years on the job and number of graduate credits. The reactions to this system, as well as to the idea of disrupting it, are often visceral.

School leaders like Michelle Rhee are determined to create a system that rewards superior teachers with more money, and by "superior" she means teachers whose students perform well academically. (Rhee's effort is described in some detail in Chapter 9, "Following Leaders.")

Why would you want to change, others ask, including National Education Association president Dennis Van Roekel. "Right now, in fifty states, in over the last fifty years, they've pretty much all kind of moved to the same place," he declared. "Why is that? Why are they using what they use now? Nobody's telling them to. There's no law, or regulation, or requirement. Yet at over fifty years, with over 15,000 school districts, they've moved to the same compensation system. There must be a reason. I believe it's because it works."[199]

For some this is a Pandora's box, because if we begin paying more to teachers whose students do well academically, sooner or later the flip side of the issue comes into play: *What do we do with teachers whose students aren't learning (again, based on tests)?* Should those teachers lose their jobs if reasonable efforts to help them improve don't work?

President Obama weighed in on this issue when he supported a Rhode Island school district's decision to dismiss the faculty and staff at a persistently failing high school. "Our kids get only one chance at an education, and we need to get it right," he told the U.S. Chamber of Commerce in March 2010.

What do the unions say? Should failing teachers get sacked? Van Roekel's answer is clear: "In any system, if someone is given the opportunity to improve and they can't, or won't, they shouldn't be in the system. Absolutely not!" he said in March 2010.

I also interviewed American Federation of Teachers president Randi Weingarten for the NewsHour in March 2010. "Suppose I'm an ineffective teacher," I said. "They intervene, try to help me, but I'm ineffective three years in a row. Should I be fired? It's a yes or no question."

"Of course," Weingarten said, but then qualified her answer somewhat. "If someone is not effective by whatever fair measure we come up with, and you help them, and it doesn't work, of course. The real issue becomes, for us, making sure there is a fair and humane process."

Of course, these issues defy black-and-white analysis. If a simple solution existed, we'd probably have come upon it by now. Teacher unions, and quite a few teachers,[200] have consistently rejected the idea of connecting scores and salaries,[201] fearing that administrators will use cheap bubble-test scores to the exclusion of all else.

Then there's the student turnover issue. In cities, it's endemic. When a niece of mine was teaching in Orlando, she told me that half her class typically turned over by mid-January. That's pretty common. And when student turnover reaches 75 to 100 percent in the course of a year, as it does in some urban classrooms, is it possible to know *which* teacher is responsible for *particular* student gains? Who gets the credit: the teacher at the beginning of the year, the one who taught most of the material mid-year or the teacher who administered the test at year's-end?

Complications aside, the tide seems to be moving inexorably toward connecting the dots between teachers and student performance.[202] What we don't know yet is what form this will take.[203]

This is faddishness and would not be happening if people knew their history, Richard Rothstein suggests. The highly respected research associate of the Economic Policy Institute and former New York Times education columnist says, "There has never been any research that shows this works, although it's fashionable to think that it should work."[204] Rothstein fears that, since only math and reading lend themselves to easy testing, the curriculum will be further narrowed, an eventuality he believes would be "disastrous."

The NEA's Van Roekel opposes merit pay because, he says, it's expensive. Do the math, he challenges. If there's a set pot of money and the best teachers make a lot more, then others have to have their pay cut, unless the public is willing to pay more. "It will cost more money. I guarantee it. It will cost more money. And so if your plan doesn't build in a sustainable revenue source to manage that program, it won't work."

More than pay is involved here—a lot more. "Tenure should be a significant and consequential milestone in a teacher's career," notes the National Council on Teacher Quality.[205] "Unfortunately, the awarding of tenure occurs virtually automatically in just about all states, with little deliberation or consideration of evidence of teacher performance. Teacher effectiveness in the classroom, rather than years of experience, should be the preponderant criterion in tenure decisions."

In the current system, most teachers gain tenure, a lifetime job, after just three years of teaching. In eight states, including California and Maryland, tenure is granted after two years. Hawaii and Mississippi offer tenure after just one year, and our nation's capital requires no set amount of teaching performance before granting tenure.[206] In other words, many school administrators are forced to make this critical and lasting decision halfway through a teacher's first or second year in the classroom.

To me, that's absurd—and the deeper you dig, the more dysfunctional the system looks. Equally disturbing is the fact that, no matter how dumb or counterproductive these policies are, somewhere, some school boards and unions agreed to them, and some state legislators may have approved them.

Unions and boards have negotiated some other dumb rules, as well. In certain districts a principal may not enter a classroom to observe a teacher without providing "adequate" advance notice, perhaps in writing, perhaps days before the visit. No drop-in visits—not if they're going to "count" in the teacher's personnel file.

The only observations allowed to count must be scheduled in advance, so the teacher can carefully choreograph the day's activities. Will this orchestrated day resemble her regular teaching style? Of course not. But that's the way it works, to everyone's comfort and no one's advantage.

The emptiness of teacher evaluation was brought into the spotlight in 2009 with the publication of "The Widget Effect," a report by the New Teacher Project. Researchers studied evaluation in 12 districts in four states, surveying 15,000 teachers and 1,300 administrators. What they learned is that *virtually every teacher is outstanding*, at least according to their evaluations. "In districts that use binary evaluation ratings (generally "satisfactory" or "unsatisfactory"), more than 99 percent of teachers receive the satisfactory rating. Districts that use a broader range of rating options do little better; in these districts, 94 percent of teachers receive one of the top two ratings and less than 1 percent are rated unsatisfactory."[207]

Obviously administrators and teachers know the evaluation system is a fraud, because 81 percent of administrators and 58 percent of teachers acknowledged that their schools employed tenured teachers who weren't performing adequately.

And when virtually every teacher is good or great, how is a truly outstanding teacher recognized? Not!

So how does classroom evaluation work, according to the study? It's not pretty.

194

"Evaluations are short and infrequent (most are based on two or fewer classroom observations totaling 60 minutes or less), conducted by untrained administrators, and influenced by powerful cultural forces—in particular, an expectation among teachers that they will be among the vast majority rated as top performers."[208]

I've sat in on evaluations during my reporting for the NewsHour and have to agree. In fact, we once produced a piece comparing a teacher's evaluation to a figure skating exhibition: carefully choreographed and well-rehearsed, with the judges sitting there knowing exactly what to expect. That metaphor nailed the artifice of teacher evaluation but missed the emptiness. In skating, the contestant can get low scores, something "The Widget Effect" suggests almost never happens in classroom evaluations.

Was classroom evaluation ever a useful process? Has the method of evaluating teachers (administrators in the back of the room watching and taking notes) ever felt collegial and professional? I decided to ask some teachers, some from "the good old days" and some who are teaching today, how frequent, and how useful, their evaluations have been.

Stanford professor Linda Darling-Hammond, who taught high school English in 1973-1974, was left completely alone. "I was never observed at all during my first year, not once," she told me. My own situation was eerily similar. In my first year teaching high school English in the mid-'60s, I taught 900 classes—five classes a day for 180 days—and remember being observed only three times.

Other veterans have similar memories. Anthony Cody, now a science content coach for Oakland Unified School District, began teaching in 1987 in Oakland, Calif. Trained to teach science, Mr. Cody was assigned to teach Spanish, English and Earth science. "I do not believe I was observed that first year at all," he said. He remembers just one administrator coming in to watch him during his second year, after which he gained tenure.

David Cohen, who teaches in Palo Alto, said: "In my first California public school job, over in Fremont, I was observed once or twice a year by principals with science backgrounds (I'm an Eng-

195

lish teacher)....They saw that I controlled the classroom, but did little to engage me in questions/reflections about my instructional choices or goals for improvement."

Curtis Johnson, a co-author of "Disrupting Class," remembers President Lyndon B. Johnson, himself a former teacher, visiting his school to sign the Elementary and Secondary Education Act. But, he adds: "No administrators ever visited my classroom. They assumed that if we weren't doing what we should, they would hear about it."

That's how the system worked in "the good old days." You closed your door and ran things your way, and as long as your class wasn't noisy enough to bother anyone else, you were assumed to be doing your job. Administrators rarely opened classroom doors to see what was going on, and teachers watched each other at work even less frequently. (That's changing now: In some schools, teachers get to watch their peers teach, after which they share their analysis. In other schools, though, principals armed with lists sit in the back of the class checking off "behaviors" and later give the teachers "scorecards" with their "batting average.")

As for me, I remember being observed by my high school principal in Port Washington, N.Y. After sitting in on a lively discussion of "Macbeth," he took me aside and suggested that if I would just remember to use the bathroom before class, I wouldn't have to move around so much![209]

Not everyone had a low opinion of evaluations, of course. Kathleen Sullivan Alioto, a former teacher and now dean of development at City College of San Francisco, recalled an excellent evaluator who observed her class: "She asked me about several of the students by name, congratulated me on some interchanges and made suggestions on others. Her assistance helped me to think about students and their strengths individually, a practice that became a positive characteristic of my teaching."

And what about today? Most districts still require observations, with the numbers and procedures often spelled out in union contracts. These rules may be honored in the breach, of course, as in the past. But most important is whether observations are actually useful. The recent Scholastic/Gates Foundation survey of 40,000 teachers sheds some light on this. Here's part of that report's summary:

> Teachers are skeptical of current measures of teacher performance, with only 22% indicating that principal observation is a very accurate measure. At the same time, more than half of teachers indicate that student academic growth (60%) and student engagement (55%) are very accurate measures of teacher performance—much more so than teacher tenure, which a significant number of teachers said is not at all accurate. When asked about teacher retention, nearly all teachers say that non-monetary rewards like supportive leadership and collaborative working environments are the most important factors to retaining good teachers. Fewer than half of teachers say higher salaries are absolutely essential for retaining good teachers and only 8% say pay for performance is absolutely essential.[210]

My own non-scientific sample suggests that, although the process may be changing for the better in some places, it is, unfortunately, still mostly useless.

Chris Krook-Magnuson, who began teaching math at Coolidge High School in Washington, D.C., in 2005 said: "I was observed two times by an administrator my first year and did not receive useful feedback, just a checklist of what I was supposed to have posted in the room and on the board. I was supposed to be observed by my American University Mentor (as part of my M.A.T.), but I never saw her that entire year."

Certainly, the subject of evaluation does get teachers thinking. Sue Davis, an educator who reads my blog, wrote: "I have mixed feelings on this. I have received very helpful feedback when colleagues sat in on my classes...I might feel differently if this observation was 'forced' and if I did not have a trusting relationship with the observer—that would add a 'threat' element to the experience."

John Merrow

Kenneth Bernstein, a veteran teacher at Eleanor Roosevelt High School in Maryland who changed careers to become a teacher, wrote on my blog, in part:

> If the purpose of the observation is merely to fulfill a legal requirement, it is a waste of time. If the purpose is to provide some feedback to the teacher, and thus help improve instruction, it is often best done by those with no authority over the one being observed. And if all teachers were trained how to observe and give feedback, the mere act of observing another teacher would help improve one's own teaching practice.

That doesn't happen very often, according to the 2009 MetLife Survey of the American Teacher. It reports: "The least frequent type of collaborative activity is teachers observing each other in the classroom and providing feedback. Less than one-third of teachers or principals report that this frequently occurs at their school."[211]

The MetLife survey divides teachers into two groups: those who teach in schools with high and low levels of collaboration. The results suggest that the answer to that age-old question "What do teachers want?" is *collaboration*. Forty-five percent of teachers in "high-collaboration" schools get to observe each other teach, versus 10 percent in the "low-collaboration" schools. Similar results run though the survey. In the "high" schools, 95 percent of new teachers get to work with experienced colleagues, versus 59 percent in "low" schools. In the "high" schools, 95 percent of teachers say their principal pays attention to their views about school improvement strategies, versus 48 percent in "low" schools. And 94 percent of "high-collaboration" schools have structured time for teachers to meet, versus only 47 percent of "low-collaboration" schools.

"That's the crime," said Sue Quetin, a veteran first-grade teacher at Roosevelt Elementary School in Salinas, California.

> I think we have to approach education as a team. They're all our kids. Not just this one classroom of kids is mine, all

the kids are mine. Teachers need to work together. The first-grade teachers need to be in touch with the kindergarten teachers, letting them know what we need—like, I need kids to come to my class knowing how to cut paper. Simple things, but the kids who start a new grade without those skills are immediately behind. And as a first-grade teacher, I'm also in touch with the second-grade teachers, to see what they need from me. I think the movement toward professional learning communities is wonderful. Children don't learn in a vacuum, and teachers shouldn't be working in a vacuum either, because you do not learn.

Kimberly Domangue—a former consumer credit counselor, mortgage default counselor and foster care caseworker who changed careers in her late 30s to become a teacher—said she ran into rigidity and even more stress than her previous jobs had caused:

There is no room for student-directed discovery learning; everything is required to be cookie-cutter perfect. I'm criticized if my students' notebooks do not get on their desks soon enough, if I take lesson time to praise a student with the entire class, or if I take too much time reissuing directions because some students have that "lost" look. I'm about fed up. Working in other fields did not take excessive time from my family or give me ulcers from criticism.

Deena Bar Lev, a Maryland veteran teacher, wrote in part:

I am not disturbed by how frequent observations are, only how useless they have become. Our school system requires administrators to undergo a rigorous training program called Observing and Analyzing Teaching, part of the Studying Skillful Teaching franchise. Sadly, this process has virtually homogenized and sterilized the entire observation experience by requiring that the observer transcribe word for word what the teacher SAYS ("scripting"), leaving them little opportunity to even look up from their paper, and all but prohibiting them from noting all the REAL magic that

goes on while teaching—the savvy proximal cues, subtle fa-
cial expressions, and animated gestures of the teacher—not
to mention everything that is going on with the kids! The
resulting "transcript" reads like Weber Gas Grill assembly
instructions.

The most positive report came from Liz Wisniewski, a third-
grade teacher in Massachusetts:

My principal pops in at least once a week informally. At these
informal viewings he always leaves a note of what he saw and
questions for me to think about. I really like it. I also find the
formal observations helpful—mainly because the feedback
is useful and pointed. My principal was once an excellent
teacher himself, and his opinions and insights are excellent.
So, if the observer is good, the information is good, and isn't
that the way it should be?

Because much learning—including when teachers are doing
the learning—is social, Ann Lieberman told me, "teacher evaluation shouldn't be about finding fault but about helping teachers
learn by building on what they already know, what can help them
move forward, and what can help them become more thoughtful
about the complexities of their classrooms." In other words, be-
ware of simple, simplistic approaches to evaluating teachers.

Lack of evaluation, excessively rigid evaluation and ineffective evaluation—we have three simultaneous (and very serious)
problems, but what's the solution for our education system? Given
that Arne Duncan's Race to the Top program required states to
promise to connect the dots between student and teacher performance (just to qualify to apply), the thoughtful evaluation of
teachers matters more than ever. Someone has to decide not only
what the criteria are but also *who* does the evaluating—and make
sure those evaluators are prepared for the job.

No Child Left Behind was supposed to force schools to pay
attention to all children, but the biggest change resulting from
NCLB may have been in teaching itself. What teachers used to

do behind closed doors is now scrutinized because of NCLB's pressures to raise test scores. Unless it's a violation of the union contract, principals drop in regularly to watch teachers at work. Whether these observations are diagnostic in nature and designed to help teachers improve, an empty ritual that leads to inflated ratings, or a "gotcha" game is the essential question.

In my experience, most teachers are not afraid of being evaluated. But what do they want? My conversations with teachers over the years suggest that, above all, they want to work in an environment that respects their professionalism and allows and encourages them to improve. The new MetLife survey, discussed above, bears this out. I think of teachers I've watched in Chattanooga, Baltimore and a small town near Seattle, all of whom were expected to plan together and were encouraged to watch each other teach on occasion. Every week they gathered for the school equivalent of a hospital's "grand rounds," where they shared insights about students they had in common.

Teachers shouldn't have a problem with student performance scores being part of the evaluation equation, as long as the results allow them to examine and improve their own skills. If Mrs. Smith's students show a good grasp of multiplying fractions and her colleagues' scores do not, then her colleagues would like to know what she's doing. But if those scores are simply used in a "gotcha" game to reward Mrs. Smith and punish everyone else, expect continued hostility.

Chapter 21

THE CRUELEST MONTH

April is the cruellest month, breeding
Lilacs out of the dead land, mixing
Memory and desire, stirring
Dull roots with spring rain.
T. S. Eliot, "The Waste Land"

As far as most children are concerned, T.S. Eliot got it wrong. It's the start of a new school year that arouses hope and desire in the hearts of young children.

Visit *any* elementary school on a morning of the first week of school, and you'll see joyful youngsters cavorting, laughing and shouting with glee. Their giddy anticipation will be palpable and infectious, because they are actually eager to go back to school. "This year will be different," their behavior screams. "This year I will be a great student, I will learn everything and teachers will help me whenever I need help!"

However, this celebration represents a child's version of the triumph of hope over experience, and unfortunately it's generally short-lived. In most schools and in many classrooms, pretty soon it gets down to business as usual. Schools resume their sorting function, assigning children—in ways blunt or subtle—their status as "A children," "B children" and so on down the scale.

The happiness will last longer in classrooms with particularly gifted teachers or in affluent neighborhoods, but schools have been set up to identify winners and losers, which they do with efficiency.

The best teachers are both "sage on the stage" and "guide on the side," depending on circumstance. But in schools filled with poor children, many teachers are neither. Instead they are expected to be ringmasters, training the "animals" with whips and treats.

Under great pressure to close the "achievement gap," these teachers drill students in test-taking. That may include instruction in filling in bubbles or writing short responses. ("In your first sentence, use key words from the paragraph you have just read.")

Sad to say, that approach actually *can* work, because most children in elementary schools can be whipped and cajoled into performing. Evidence can be found in test scores from the National Assessment of Educational Progress, often called "The Nation's Report Card." American third- and fourth-graders outperform their counterparts in most industrialized countries.

However, those gains begin to disappear in seventh and eighth grades. Before long our children lag far behind, probably because, in my considered opinion, those early scores do not reflect genuine learning but are largely illusory, the results of the ringmaster's efforts.

When students become older and wise to the ways of the ringmaster, things change. In spring 2009 a dynamic school principal in Washington, D.C., resorted to every trick in the book to get his test scores up. Brian Betts[212] of Shaw Middle School offered $100 to every student who, as the tests drew near, came to school every day on time and answered every test question, right or wrong. What's more, Betts promised he would get a tattoo if scores went up.

Ringmaster Betts' approach failed. Reading scores declined 9 percent, to 29 percent proficiency, and math scores fell 4 percent to 29 percent.

A classic cartoon from Gary Larson's "The Far Side" shows a lion tamer snapping his whip and shooting his pistol, seemingly in complete control. However, one lion seated docilely on a chair is whispering to another, "Pass it on, he's using blanks."

Older students generally don't turn on their ringmasters, of course. Instead more than one million drop out every year. They pay a price—and cost the rest of us. As Chris Swanson of Education Week's "Quality Counts"[213] report has said, "It's not a not-in-my-backyard problem any more when you have 3 out of 10 high school students not finishing. When you start looking especially at African-American and Latino males, it raises to the level of a civil rights problem, a problem of equity." A new Texas A&M study projects that the dropouts from just one class (2012) alone will cost the state and its economy between $6 billion and $10.7 billion over their lifetimes.

Students who put in the seat time earn a diploma, but have they been educated[214] to be responsible participants in a democracy? The persistent decline in voting would suggest not.

It doesn't have to be this way.

While parents may not be able to easily articulate it, they send their children to school for intellectual, social, civic, aesthetic and even ethical reasons—because they know that education is a lot more than test scores. Evidence of public awareness, and dissatisfaction, can be seen in polls showing that families prefer private and charter schools over regular public schools by wide margins.[215]

Educators need to respect this and tear down the artificial wall between schools and parents, which educators have built up over the years. Every child's first and most important educators are his parents, even if they are indifferent to learning. Schools should acknowledge this and work to involve families at the most basic levels in the early grades. And not with high-falutin' pedagogical concepts and lectures or with "parent involvement committees," but with classroom work.

Here are a few simple examples: Have kindergarteners and first-graders work with their parents to find triangles, circles and rectangles in everyday things around their home and neighborhood, such as window panes, floor patterns and street signs. Second-grade teachers could assign the kids to report on their mom's favorite foods, flowers and animals. The next week's assignment: Interview a grandparent about her favorites. Find out why. What are your own favorite colors? Why? And so on, every week.

Make it a bit more complex in third grade by assigning homework that requires the child to write about his/her parents or grandparents: the first movie they remember seeing, their secret dream growing up and so on.

Math must be part of this. Assign fourth- and fifth-graders to go shopping with an adult and compare the prices of several products in different stores. Do the math to figure out unit costs. For another assignment, ask a family member how much a movie cost back when she was a kid. What's the difference between that price and the cost of a ticket today? Compare other items. Do the math and then report to the class.

You can bet that parents and grandparents would want to see the homework before it's turned in, and certainly afterwards to read what the teacher wrote about it.

Thus encouraged, many parents would be open for conversations about what it is we want our schools to achieve, and how that might be measured. That in turn might well lead to a re-examination of our over-reliance on machine-scored multiple-choice tests. While scores matter, they cannot be the be-all and end-all of education. Glorious and exciting curriculum (such as the National Writing Project, the JASON Project, and Our History, Our Selves) that are proven to engage the brains and hearts of students often get pushed aside simply because school leaders fear that these stimulating materials won't produce higher test scores.

Neither of these changes—close connections with families and deeper, more thoughtful education that relies less on bubble tests—will be easy to pull off. But if we don't try, public education will continue to wither.

Schools can be places that nurture hope in all of our children, where students study "The Waste Land," rather than occupy it.

Chapter 22
TEACHERS AND THEIR UNIONS

Teacher unions are necessary. Some are progressive, but it seems to me that some unions have for many years done more harm than good for the clientele of the public schools, our children. Ask "Who benefits?" and the answer is obvious: Teachers come first, union leaders second and kids third. (And in a few cases, the union leaders have put their interests ahead of those of teachers!) While a fair amount of the blame must be laid at the door of school boards that have caved in to union demands, unions have been, for the most part, protectionist and regressive (and, on a few regrettable occasions, criminal).

Take seniority. Seniority privileges are important in systems that devalue teachers and discourage challenges and experimentation. That probably describes most school systems, which is why teachers value the privileges of seniority: They cannot be moved around on management whim. Reform requires dramatic changes in how teachers are valued; when that happens, seniority won't be an issue.

But the first step must, I believe, be taken by teachers and their unions. It may take a hard slap upside the head, but unions are going to have to acknowledge what we all know—that there's a relationship between teaching and learning.

Suppose a swimming instructor told the 10-year-olds in his class to swim the length of the pool to demonstrate what he'd taught them, and half of them nearly drowned in the process? Would it be reasonable to make a judgment about his effectiveness as a swimming teacher?

Or suppose that nearly all the 10-year-olds studying clarinet for the first time learned to play five or six pieces well in a semester?

Would it be reasonable to consider that when deciding whether to rehire the music teacher?

Those questions answer themselves. Only an idiot would overlook student performance, be it dismal or outstanding.

However, suppose test results indicate that most students in a particular class do not have a clue about multiplying with fractions or other material in the curriculum? Should that be considered when the math teacher comes up for tenure?

Whoops, the obvious answer is wrong, because public education lives in an upside-down, irrational universe in which student outcomes are not allowed to be connected to teaching.

Here's an excerpt from my interview with Jack Steinberg, the vice president of the teachers union in Philadelphia:

Union VP: You're asking can you evaluate a teacher on the performance of the students?
Me: *Yes or no?*
Union VP: No, you cannot.
Me (incredulously): *You cannot evaluate a teacher on the performance of his or her students?*
Union VP: Right.

That was one man's *opinion* about 12 years ago, but in New York that opinion became the *law*, because of the power of the teachers union. In 2007, the law allowed Chancellor Joel Klein to consider, among other things, "the extent to which the teacher successfully utilized analysis of available student performance data" when reviewing candidates for tenure, a lifetime appointment.

Of course, that's *not* the same as judging a teacher based on student performance, but the mere possibility of connecting student performance with teacher effectiveness was enough to cause fits at union headquarters. Both the state and city teacher unions lobbied hard for a change, and in April 2008 the legislature went along.

It changed the law to read, "The teacher shall not be granted or denied tenure based on student performance data."

That's what Richard Iannuzzi, the president of the New York State United Teachers, said in so many words: "Student assessments are designed to assess students, not teachers."

Klein called the legislature's action "unconscionable." Celebrating the victory, then UFT president Randi Weingarten said, "There is no independent or conclusive research that shows you can accurately measure the impact of an individual teacher on a student's academic achievement."

Independent analysts disagree. Eric Hanushek, who specializes in the economics of education at Stanford University, wrote in an e-mail: "It is very clear from the research into variations in teacher quality that such information would be useful. This NYS action says it cannot even be looked at. The implication is that tenure decisions cannot be made on performance."

Calling this "very bad public policy," Professor Hanushek added dryly, "I guess only friendships and politics count—just what the unions have always railed against."

Weingarten denied that her members are afraid of accountability, but this action may put unions into a hole they'll have trouble digging out of, because school administrators have reams of data about student performance, thanks largely to the federal No Child Left Behind law.

Unions are correct to worry about oversimplification. Urged to "drill down" to find out who is learning and who is not, administrators believe they can pinpoint which teachers are effective at teaching certain skills. I've sat with superintendents, principals and department chairs and heard them name teachers who, they said, were either outstanding or deficient at teaching specific skills. "X doesn't seem to be able to teach his students how to multiply with fractions," one educator said, showing me student performance data and contrasting it with data from another teacher's class.

Unfortunately, these administrators did not bring up the make-up of the classes being tested—whether they were new immigrants or students with disabilities or gifted children—even though *who* is being taught clearly affects scores. That's what makes teachers worry, and rightly so.

Test data invites oversimplification because it ignores the fact that students *bring* value (and baggage) to school, just as good teachers *add* value. Unions and administrators have an interest in figuring out how to measure both, if only to ensure that teachers are not penalized for working with difficult-to-teach children.

Because test data is not going to go away, progressive union leadership ought to be lobbying hard for *creative* uses of it, not punitive ones. Forward-looking leadership would be demanding immediate help for teachers, so that they could improve in those areas where the evidence suggests deficiency. It would be helping to create solutions, instead of wielding political power to protect every union member's job. It would be looking for ways to use evidence of student learning in sophisticated ways and in conjunction with other evidence.[216]

Denying that there's any connection between teaching and learning contradicts what experience teaches us, and flies in the face of common sense. If unions are telling us that there's *no* connection between teaching and learning, why support teachers, or public education for that matter?

And Washington's Race to the Top has, in effect, thrown down the gauntlet to unions, challenging them to participate in a competition for billions of dollars, money that states qualify for only if they agree to develop plans to base teacher evaluation in part on student performance. Stay tuned for this one!

Seniority

Where seniority rules, new teachers are likely to suffer. They are often assigned to the least desirable schools, given the "worst" classes, the most preparations and the additional assignments nobody else wants. But here's a radical thought: Seniority, at least in its most rigid forms, hurts veteran teachers, too.

It's not difficult to find administrators who dislike the rigidities of seniority. When I asked an assistant principal how his elementary school went about hiring teachers, he answered wryly: "You want to know how we fill vacancies? *We* don't. A day or two before school opens, someone shows up with some paperwork and says, 'I'm your new fourth-grade teacher. Where's my classroom?' And we take the paperwork and point to the empty room."

His distaste was palpable. "What other profession doesn't allow the professionals to select their colleagues?" he wanted to know. "How can we create a genuine learning environment when we can't control who teaches here?"

When teachers have seniority, "Who benefits?" That's a question I've been pondering ever since I happened to meet Marlene, a middle-aged veteran of more than 20 years in the classroom.

"This is the worst school I've ever taught in," the teacher muttered to herself, just loud enough for me to hear. We were watching several hundred high school students streaming into school on a fall morning a few years ago. I asked how long she'd been teaching there. "It's my first year," she said bitterly.

Because her union was fiercely protective of teachers' seniority rights, I assumed she'd made the decision to teach there, and I asked her why. Her answer stunned me: "It's the closest school to my home, and I wanted a short commute."

We introduced ourselves and talked for a while. I don't know what sort of teacher Marlene is, but it's easy to hypothesize that she's a burned-out, bored worker counting the hours until she can go home for the day. I can imagine her contempt for the school playing itself out with her students.

Is Marlene "Exhibit A," proving the evils of the seniority system, or could there be more to the story? I'm assuming that 20 or 25 years ago she was a typical new teacher: idealistic, energetic and determined to contribute to the growth and learning of her students. What happened to make her view her profession through such a narrow prism? Have the rewards of teaching been so slight that *commuting time*, not her colleagues, the curriculum or the work environment, has become her highest priority?

Unions fought for seniority to protect their members from what they perceived as arbitrary decisions of administrators, and any veteran teacher can tell horror stories of being treated contemptuously or indifferently. Does that still happen? Do administrators still treat trained teachers as if they were "interchangeable parts?" Sadly, in many places they do.

A few years ago I watched a first-year teacher showing high school sophomores how to determine the area of a rectangle. She gave her students the formula and did three sample problems on the board. Each time she gave the answer in meters. No one in the class, including the teacher, knew that the answers had to be in *square* meters.

What she was experiencing in her first year on the job helps explain why unions fight so hard for teachers' rights. As a new teacher, she had no rights at all, and she was treated disrespectfully. The school district had hired her to teach *physical education*, the subject she'd trained to teach, but on the first day of school her principal assigned her to teach two sections of algebra, a subject she herself had not studied since high school. Could she have refused? "Yes," she said, smiling ruefully, "but I wouldn't have had a job."

"Teachers as Interchangeable Parts" seemed to be the operating principle of that school principal. Elsewhere in the school, an art teacher was teaching basic math and a middle school basketball coach was teaching high school English.[217]

That fundamental attitude of anti-professionalism goes beyond individual administrators. It's built into laws and regulations. For example, Georgia (where that young woman was teaching) said at the time that it was fine for teachers to spend 40 percent of their time teaching subjects out of their field without being categorized as "out-of-field."

A persuasive analogy, perhaps, has to do with automobiles. Consider this: A BMW mechanic could not spend 40 percent of his time repairing Volvos or Fords, but a phys ed teacher can be told to teach two physics classes! So cars are more important than children (or other people's children, anyway).

The world of teachers is one of small victories, and dozens of routine indignities: constant interruptions from the main office ("Please send Joey Brown to the office"), hall patrol, lunch room duty and the difficulty of taking a bathroom break when nature calls.

Over the years this treatment takes its toll. Many teachers simply leave. In fact, the data show that over 40 percent of new teachers quit the profession in the first five years, according to Richard Ingersoll, professor of education and sociology at the University of Pennsylvania;[218] that's an exit rate far higher than in law, medicine, nursing or the ministry—professions that teaching is often compared to. In many districts, the numbers are even worse. The University of Chicago's Urban Education Institute reported in June 2009 that in Chicago: "Teacher mobility rates at schools with low teacher commitment are abysmal—67 percent in elementary schools leave within five years, and 76 percent turn over in the high schools. These are schools where teachers do not feel loyal to their schools, would not recommend their school to parents, and do not look forward to teaching every day."[219]

What happens to those who stay? While thousands continue to do wonderful work, despite it all many become, in the current lingo, "burned out." That is, they're on the job, but they've lost sight of why they became teachers in the first place. Perhaps that's what happened to Marlene.

Seniority gives veterans—finally—the opportunity to thumb their noses at these indignities, and that's how I explain Marlene's way of choosing her school.

There are alternatives, ways to allow teachers to be professionals. In Seattle, for instance, progressive union leadership and a visionary superintendent, the late John Stanford, pushed through an agreement allowing teachers to be part of the hiring process at individual schools, while at the same time allowing schools to hire without regard to seniority. That meant teachers were able, for the first time in their professional lives, to participate in choosing their colleagues, in building a professional team at their workplace.

Improving the system, however, cannot *start* with doing away with seniority. Most teachers I've known want to be good at their jobs, but they're working in systems that don't let that happen. Seniority is a desperate protection, but if I were a teacher I'd fight to hold onto it, unless and until management demonstrated its commitment to teaching as a profession.

Chapter 23
A TEACHER SHORTAGE?

On a warm spring afternoon in Texas, about 25 education majors, all young white women, are waving plastic toys in the air, giggling and singing "Row, Row, Row Your Boat." They're pretending to be 5-year-olds as part of their teacher training.

In rural Georgia, 1,200 miles to the east, a young man is leading his ninth-grade English class through the day's vocabulary. One of the words is "strenuous," which he has written on the board as "strenous." During the lesson he reviews the definition, the spelling and the syllabification, never catching his mistake. His students dutifully copy his spelling mistake into their workbooks.

And in Oakland, Calif., an 11th-grade biology class is having its 167th consecutive class without a certified science teacher; they've had a parade of substitute teachers for an entire year.

Taken together, these anecdotes would seem to indicate that we are facing a major crisis in teaching—that we need more teachers and we need better-trained teachers.

However, the plural of anecdote is not data, and so I would make a different argument. I believe these vignettes, and the circumstances behind them, demonstrate that our education system has an unacceptably high tolerance for mediocrity, and that national, state and local policies merely reinforce the status quo.[220]

Some regions of the country will always have difficulty recruiting teachers, and shortages exist in science, math and special education, but we now produce more teachers than we need. Where there are shortages, these are generally self-inflicted wounds. These fall into three categories: Schools underpay and mistreat teachers and eventually drive them from the profession;

inept school districts cannot find the qualified teachers living under their noses; and substandard training ill-prepares young men and women for the realities of classroom life.

Imagine a swimming pool with a serious leak. You wouldn't expect that pouring more and more water into the pool would, in time, fix the leak—but that's precisely the approach we are taking toward the so-called teacher shortage. Everyone's noticed that the teaching "pool" is low, and getting lower. The response has been to recruit more people into teaching, using a variety of strategies including PSA campaigns, millions of federal dollars, hiring bonuses, help with mortgages and recruitment trips to Spain and other distant lands.

Most of this is not new. Almost every U.S. president since Harry Truman has warned of teacher shortages, and large-scale recruitment efforts have followed.

Yet the pool keeps losing water because no one is paying attention to the leak. That is, we're misdiagnosing the problem as "recruitment" when it's really "retention." Simply put, we train teachers poorly[221] and then treat them badly—and so they leave in droves.

This is not a trivial issue. The well-respected National Commission on Teaching and America's Future has put the cost of what ought to be called a "teacher dropout problem" at more than $7 billion a year.[222]

As it happens, new evidence indicates increased interest in teaching among our nation's university students. Survey after survey of entering college freshmen reveals that more than 10 percent say they want to teach after graduation. Probably because of a failing economy, the recent results are the best showing for the teaching profession since the early 1970s and almost twice what they were in 1982, the lowest point of interest in teaching.

On the surface, this news is encouraging. But just because more undergraduates want to teach, and Teach For America is flooded with applications, no one should assume we're out of the woods. We aren't.

The fact remains that our nation's schools and colleges of education[223] already produce more than enough teachers. But about 30 percent of newly minted teachers don't go into classrooms. Some never intended to; they majored in education because it's an easy way to get a degree or so they could have a "fall back" option. Others found they couldn't get teaching jobs in their hometown, so they found other work; in other words, *staying home* was the goal, not being a teacher.

Those who avoid teaching may be making a wise career move, because teaching is often hard and unrewarding work, particularly for rookies, and particularly in cities.

While shortages exist in some regions of the country and in some subjects (math, science and special education), the harsh truth is that our persistent teacher shortage is a self-inflicted wound.

The real problems lie within the system that is already in place, and no influx of idealistic men and women will change that. In our reporting for PBS in 1999, we found that school administrators in Georgia frequently assigned teachers to teach subjects regardless of whether they had majored, or even minored, in those subjects in college. For example, the young man who couldn't spell "strenuous" is actually a junior high school physical education teacher and coach, but he'd been assigned to teach English, history and math at the local high school instead. He knew he was in over his head, but he had no choice. In that particular high school, at least 20 percent of faculty members were teaching classes in subjects they hadn't themselves studied.

This is standard operating procedure in many school districts, not just in Georgia, because lax state accreditation rules metaphorically look the other way. At the time, Georgia's particular loophole allowed a teacher to teach two of five classes "out-of-field" without being counted "out-of-field." Imagine the uproar if a podiatrist were to spend 40 percent of his time performing brain surgery!

In other places we found qualified, certified teachers who simply couldn't penetrate incompetent school bureaucracies.

John Merrow

Katherine Scheuermann, who earned a California license to teach science, applied for a teaching position in Oakland in June of 1997 and again in June of 1998. She finally got a response, in March 1999, in the form of a letter inviting her to apply for a position in bilingual education. Without much difficulty we found two other certified teachers who told essentially the same story: Oakland's bureaucracy was impenetrable, so they looked elsewhere.

Those who do get hired to teach in cities aren't likely to stay long. American cities lose teachers at an alarming rate. For example, Oakland has been losing up to 30 percent of its teachers every year, even though it pays well for a school district. Why do science teachers leave? Ask veteran Nancy Caruso:

> I had no water, and I was supposed to teach science. I was toting water from a decaying toilet, basically little gallon containers, one at a time, and it was just very frustrating for me. And if you look around, I'm in a decaying building. It's graffiti ridden, trash everywhere, and it seems like nothing that could get done gets done.

New teachers seem to be treated even worse. As Caruso, who left after 10 years at Oakland High School, wryly observed:

> Administrators give new teachers the hardest, most challenging classes and the most preparations, so they have maybe four different classes to prepare for every day, and then administrators expect that that's going to make them excited about teaching. It's just not conducive to retaining young, enthusiastic people. They get burnt out and so they go to the suburbs or they leave teaching completely.

But mediocrity and incompetence begin earlier at many of the institutions that train teachers. They tend to treat their education programs more as "cash cows" for their overall needs, diverting tuition paid by education majors into law, medicine, engineering and nursing programs, for example. As Linda Darling-Hammond of Stanford University notes, "If you are preparing to be a teacher,

218

you can expect about half of the tuition money you put into the till to come back to support your preparation."

Training teachers on the cheap means large classes on campus, rather than intensive (and more expensive) work in real schools with real children. So, for example, we found those would-be teachers at Texas A&M earnestly pretending to be 5-year-olds for 50 minutes at a stretch. "It's as close as we can get to the real thing," one student told us, apparently unaware of the existence of a dozen elementary schools within a few miles of campus.

Training on the cheap means more part-time faculty and lower salaries for those with full-time jobs. It's no secret that schools of education are at the bottom of the university pecking order and that the lowest *within* the ed school itself are those who actually train teachers.

It's likely that unimaginative training has an unintended consequence: breeding contempt for the profession these students are supposed to be getting ready for. We asked a class of seniors, on the verge of graduating and moving into classrooms, whether they were having doubts about their career choice. Virtually every hand went up.

At least some of the faculty at Texas A&M and every other school of education actually know how to train teachers well, but that requires more time and money. That year about 30 percent of A&M's education students were enrolled in a separate and much more demanding program that required them to spend 40 hours a week working with a mentor teacher in a public school. Throughout the year, these students took most of their university classes in the public school, often taught by experienced public school teachers.

Where were the university's education professors? Most were back on campus, lecturing, writing and doing research, and for good reason: They won't get tenure for doing a good job of training teachers, but they might if they do enough research and publish enough articles.

Competition from alternative certification programs is forcing ed schools to shape up. These programs, designed to attract and train older professionals looking to change careers, generally provide an intensive summer of training and a year of weekend meetings, a far cry from the four- or five-year ed school programs. Some alternative certification programs are suspect,[224] but others seem to be effective. For example, graduates of a state-run alternative program in Austin that same year were routinely outperforming graduates of nearly every education school in Texas on the state test for teachers.

Recruiting teachers is an appealingly simple solution to a complex problem. It's also the wrong approach. It not only lets education schools and public school systems off the hook, it actually rewards them; after all, those federal training dollars are going to be spent at ed schools. It also treats them as part of the solution, which seems akin to asking the polluters to clean up the river.

Most of all, however, current national policy seems to be a waste of money and a strategy that's destined to fail. As Richard Ingersoll of the University of Pennsylvania told us:

> We can recruit all kinds of qualified people and persuade them to go into teaching, but if they get into jobs that aren't well paid and don't have particularly good working conditions in which they're given little say in the way schools operate, it's not going to really solve the problem because a lot of these people will leave.

Professor Ingersoll is correct. *If* teacher training were challenging, and *if* teaching were a well-paid occupation—in which expertise was respected and teachers were given opportunities to collaborate and improve—and *if* out-of-field teaching were simply unacceptable, there would be no teacher shortage. Attending to those conditions would fix the leak.

Section Four
WHEAT FROM CHAFF

Chapter 24
UNLEARNING BAD SCIENCE

The news of the so-so performance in science by American students on the Trends in International Mathematics and Science Study did cause more hand-wringing, but I hope it does not lead to more testing, because that may actually make matters worse. It could lead to more rote teaching of material that's easy to test on multiple-choice exams. It also could lead to dumbing down of the science curriculum, which will drive competent teachers either to distraction or to other occupations.

The larger picture isn't much brighter. Congress has slashed funds that the National Science Foundation uses to improve science teaching, and ever larger numbers of school districts are embracing "creation science." All of this is obscuring what may be a greater challenge—*unlearning* bad science.

A few years ago, I watched a science teacher at Cary Academy in North Carolina ask his students which organism had the most chromosomes per cell: mosquitoes, corn, broad beans, cats or humans? The kids always pick humans, and they are correct, because we have 46 chromosomes, while cats have 38 and mosquitoes only 6. Then he expanded the list to include horses, chickens, goldfish and potatoes. Once again, his students confidently chose their own species. At that point he revealed that even potatoes, with 48 chromosomes, beat us humans, and goldfish weigh in with a whopping 104 chromosomes, more than twice as many as humans.

Invariably the students are stunned. How can they be less evolved than a potato? Or a goldfish? What the teacher wanted them to do was confront their assumptions, because he knew that, in order for students to learn science, they first have to *unlearn* what they have assumed (in this case, the more chromosomes the better).

John Merrow

As kids, we make all sorts of "common sense" assumptions about how the world works, which is a loose definition of science. "We have more brains than goldfish or potatoes do, so we must have more chromosomes" or "The sun makes us warm, it's warm in summer, so the sun must be closer." All too often, we never unlearn our assumptions; instead, "book learning" gets layered on top, just long enough for us to pass exams. Then we revert.

Filmmakers at Harvard's graduation provided powerful evidence of this when they asked new graduates why it's colder in New England in the winter and warmer in the summer. In the 1988 video "A Private Universe," each young man and woman explains with perfect confidence that the sun is closer to Earth in the summer and farther away in winter.

Of course, the opposite is true; Earth's orbit is elliptical, and New Englanders are actually *closer* to the sun in winter. Our planet is tilted away, though, and it's the tilt of Earth's axis that determines climate.

We can assume that nobody taught those Harvard seniors bad science. Instead, they probably intuited that "fact" when they were young and never *unlearned* it. Since they were admitted to Harvard, they must have learned enough classroom science to get high grades on tests, but without dislodging or unlearning what they thought they knew from observation. As Lee Shulman, former president of the Carnegie Foundation for the Advancement of Teaching, has noted, "The first influence on learning is not what teachers do pedagogically, but the learning that's already inside the learner."

How do teachers help their students unlearn? That science teacher forced Cary Academy students to confront their assumptions (we have more chromosomes than potatoes) because he knew that mere rote learning of scientific facts doesn't do the trick.

Melanie Krieger, author and former director of research at Plainview-Old Bethpage JFK High School on Long Island, N.Y., believes that hands-on, project-based science helps students unlearn. Her students in grades 9-12 would develop and carry out research projects, usually with the help of real scientists working at nearby labs, hospitals and technology companies. I watched Samuel John and Omar Ghani catch carpenter ants for their project several years ago, developing ways to kill the ants using only biological controls and natural enemies (i.e., no pesticides).

Projects like these take months, often including summer vacations, and demand intense work; but the kids don't mind the work (although the ants probably do). As Samuel John described it: "Science is hands-on stuff: You learn it, and then you apply it, and the applying part is where the fun comes in." John's and Ghani's carpenter ant project did not win any awards, but the following year Samuel John scored a "clean sweep," winning Siemens Westinghouse,[225] Intel Science Talent Search, and Intel International Science and Engineering Fair. He went on to Rensselaer Polytechnic Institute.

Although Krieger's students entered their projects in prestigious science fairs like ISEF (and sometimes won!), her class was always open to all interested students, not merely honor students. Krieger noted in 2004 that while about 60 percent of the 100 school districts in her region used the project-based approach, only two or three were open to all interested students. "All the other programs have strict entry criteria and quite often seem to look for ways to 'weed out' kids," she said.

If just the elite enjoy the liveliest approaches to science teaching, scientific illiteracy will only increase. That worries Leon Lederman, the Nobel Prize-winning physicist, who said: "Our populations have never been more ignorant of science, and yet their lives are being influenced ever more by the technological developments: cell phones, implants, and revolutions in molecular biology, genetics and surgery. There's so much fake science, junk science, out there, and people have to be able to recognize it."

Lederman says science teaching can't be elitist because: "All kids are born scientists. A scientist is someone who asks questions, and kids ask questions. They have those embers of curiosity. You blow on the embers, they get hotter and hotter, until finally they erupt into a flame of passionate interest in the world."

But too often science class for "regular" students is rote memorization, particularly with today's emphasis on multiple-choice testing. For example, the Maryland State Department of Education was replacing bubble tests with performance-based tests that required students to show how they arrived at their answers. With No Child Left Behind[226] requiring testing in all grades every year, Maryland scrapped its Maryland School Performance Assessment Program in 2002 and returned to cheaper, more traditional methods of testing. High-stakes tests and multiple-choice testing often determine how science is taught, says Lederman, who deplores what he calls a "winner takes all" mentality. "Too many kids are having their curiosity stomped out by insensitive teaching in the schools," he said.

Ray Bacchetti, the education veteran now retired from the Carnegie Foundation for the Advancement of Teaching, shares Lederman's concern: "I've been in too many elementary schools where the reading and math emphasis was sucking the oxygen out of just about everything else. Teachers would try to work on bits of science…but seldom with strong curricular strategies and hardly ever with useful support from their districts."

Textbooks are another problem. Jonathan Cole of Columbia University found that many textbooks contained more references to Madonna, the singer, than to Watson and Crick and DNA. He noted, "College students who don't major in science probably conclude that scientific developments and accomplishments sprang from whole cloth, because they're not covered in the books they read."

Lederman believes a crisis is upon us. "If we don't fix our science and math educational system," he warns, "the nation is really in deep trouble. Our economy has been surviving on immigration, but that's not going to last, because country after country is getting wise and is keeping their scientists at home."

But despite superficial textbooks, rote teaching and a shortage of project-based learning, there is hope for science education. Robert Ballard, the scientist and underwater explorer who discovered the Titanic, is one source of inspiration. First Ballard realized that all of his graduate students were foreign-born. Where, he wondered, were the young American scientists? Then, spurred by the outpouring of letters (16,000 in two weeks) from children after he found the Titanic, he created the JASON Project,[227] which has allowed more than 12 million students and teachers around the world to participate in virtual explorations and scientific research over the last 20 years. Like Leon Lederman, Ballard believes most children are "natural" scientists. "Any parent can tell you kids are fired up with curiosity," he said. "The first question they ask is 'why?' Our job is to capture that natural curiosity and turn it into a lifelong passion for learning."

Because of the JASON Project and the power of technology, millions of kids have explored the ocean floor, mapped wetlands and discovered sunken ships and treasures since the project's founding in 1989. Some of these students have grown up and become scientists in their own right, but that's not Ballard's goal. Like Leon Lederman, Ballard wants *all* American citizens, regardless of their occupations, to be scientifically literate.

Another ray of hope, albeit a faint one, emerged when high school seniors were asked pretty much the same question that the Harvard graduates got wrong in 1988. The question was on the National Assessment of Educational Progress (often called "The Nation's Report Card') science test in 2007, and 40 percent got it right. That's not good enough, but at least it's better than those Harvard graduates did.

Chapter 25
SAFETY FIRST[228]

One spring day, our friend Kathleen[229] stopped by on her way home from retrieving her 12-year-old son's backpack, which he'd accidentally left in his classroom at school. Her son Joey, a bright, thoughtful, somewhat quiet boy, is the target of relentless bullying by the jock majority on campus. Why are the jocks picking on him? Because he loves to read, and is often seen carrying a book.

That's too bad, you might say, but isn't bullying a normal but unfortunate part of growing up? Isn't it something that kids work through, and maybe even manage to build some character in the process? Well, I've got a lot to say about that, but I'm not done with the story yet.

As I said, Kathleen went to her son's classroom to pick up his backpack. While she was there, she ran into the mother of one of Joey's classmates, who observed that Kathleen had only her younger child with her. "So where's Joey?" quipped the woman. "Home reading 'War and Peace,' or something?"

We talk of "the natural cruelty of children" as a kind of given: a rite of passage of sorts that's unfortunate but normal, and that we expect kids to either work through or grow out of in time. But what of this adult response—this tacit approval of, even participation in, the kind of "deliberate cruelty"[230] that's been damaging and scarring millions of children in schools across our country for centuries, and now seems to be getting worse with new technologies available and the advent of "cyberbullying"? This kind of heartless adult response is all too common. And when adults don't step in and actively work to stop bullying, they become a serious and sometimes deadly part of the problem. At the very least, their absence and willingness to ignore the situation creates a vacuum, in which a vulnerable child stands alone, and into which a bully (or a gang of them) easily steps and begins to fill the void with cruelty.

Did you read "Lord of the Flies," by William Golding, back in high school as I did? In the opening scene, Ralph (the protagonist) and a heavyset boy (later called "Piggy") are picking their way through a jungle after their school group's plane has crashed. Ralph observes that there may not be any grownups on the island, and (Golding writes): "The fat boy looked startled."[231]

"The fat boy" has good reason to look startled. As a victim of bullying before meeting Ralph, and with increasingly hostile cruelties inflicted by the other boys on the island, "Piggy" is a walking target, and he knows what happens when adults are not there to intervene. As the story unfolds and nearly all the stranded boys turn savage, they torment "Piggy" to his death. When the tribe turns on Ralph and chases him down to the beach—hunting him in earnest, and ready to kill—only the appearance of an adult (a British naval officer who saw smoke rising from the island and sailed over to investigate) saves the boy's life.

But what happens then?

"Are there any adults—any grownups with you?" the officer asks. Ralph shakes his head, turning dazedly back to see a "semicircle of little boys, their bodies streaked with colored clay, sharp sticks in their hands...standing on the beach making no noise at all."

"Fun and games,"[232] the officer says.

Fun and games. Kids being kids. A normal but unfortunate part of growing up. How many times have we heard words like these applied to the subject of bullying? And even in "Lord of the Flies," though the officer has unwittingly stepped in and prevented a murder, does he really comprehend the emotional and intellectual violence that's led to the physically dangerous scene he's just interrupted? And when the boys start to cry, does he, the adult, try to deal with them on an emotional level or does he feel uncomfortable and turn away until the boys can pull themselves together?[233]

Schools are spending hundreds of millions of dollars trying to ensure the physical safety of their students. They install metal detectors, hire security guards, pay for administrator and teacher training programs, and implement all kinds of other measures to create physically safe learning environments. This effort and commitment is laudable, and physical safety is important, but the real issue—the underlying one that paves the way for physical violence and for some victimized children to take their own lives to escape bullying—is *emotional* and *intellectual* safety. That's what adults need to pay attention to. And that's where adults are really failing.

Did you know that between 60 and 90 percent of school children have been bullied, and at least 20 percent of students are bullies, according to some studies?[234] Or that "chronic victims of bullying, bullied once a week or more, generally constitute between 8 and 20 percent of the student population," according to a 2009 U.S. Department of Justice publication for police officers?[235]

Or that, in a major study called "Bullying and the Gifted," researchers reported that by eighth grade more than two-thirds of gifted students surveyed had been victimized?[236] Or that in a recent study of California third- to sixth-graders, about 90 percent said they'd experienced bullying, and 59 percent admitted to bullying others?[237]

Or that every day about 160,000 children miss school because they're afraid of being bullied, according to the National Association of School Psychologists?[238]

And because most incidents of bullying go unnoticed by adults and unreported by the victims, the numbers I've just given you are probably pretty low compared to reality.

Ted Sizer, the late school reformer, once told me: "What you should worry about are the kids who seem to take pleasure in harassing and insulting other kids. The bullies, the ones who see school as a game and are constantly pushing the limits...Those kids need to be dealt with."

That's true. And besides all the obvious reasons we should worry about bullies (the children who suffer at their hands, the "bystander" children who observe abuse and are affected by it, etc.), there's a flip side regarding the bullies themselves. Sizer said what he most worried about were students who took pleasure in tormenting others—and their actions and influence move out from the schoolyard into the community at large. According to "Bullying in Schools,"[239] a 2009 U.S. Department of Justice publication created to educate police officers about bullying:

> It is not only victims who are at risk for short- and long-term problems; bullies also are at increased risk for negative outcomes. One researcher found that those elementary students who were bullies attended school less frequently and were more likely to drop out than other students. Several studies suggest that bullying in early childhood may be a critical risk factor for the development of future problems with violence and delinquency. For example, Olweus' research found that in addition to threatening other children, bullies were several times more likely than their nonbullying peers to commit antisocial acts, including vandalism, fighting, theft, drunkenness and truancy, and to have an arrest by young adulthood. Another study of more than 500 children found that aggressive behavior at the age of 8 was a powerful predictor of criminality and violent behavior at the age of 30.

According to "Bullying in Schools," bullies tend to grow up and have children who also become bullies. In other words, bullying engenders bullying, which engenders bullying, which engenders bullying. It's like that image of the snake with its tail in its mouth, forming a perfect circle; there's no end without first breaking the circle and then sending the snake on its way. And that leads to the question of whether bullies actually enjoy seeing others suffer, and what that means for our society. A 2008 University of Chicago study[240] used functional MRI technology to compare brain activity in a group of teenage boys with aggressive conduct disorder, compared to a non-aggressive control group, as they watched images of people in pain due to various circumstances. When the boys with a violent history saw video clips of people purposely inflicting pain on others, an area of their brain associated with reward and pleasure lit up significantly in the fMRI monitoring; this did not occur in the brain activity of their non-aggressive counterparts. "We think it means that they like seeing people in pain," said University of Chicago professor Benjamin Lahey, a co-author of the study, in a National Geographic article. "If that is true, they are getting positively reinforced every time they bully and are aggressive to other people."[241] Obviously, this is just one study and cannot be applied to the wide range of bullies in our society and classrooms, but it does give one pause and it makes one wonder.

The fact is, most bullying between students is verbal, rather than physical. It's the so-called "normal" teasing that kids inflict on each other. So how does bullying begin? Usually it starts in an atmosphere lacking in emotional and intellectual safety.

As a reporter, I meet students all the time who talk openly about being teased:

"I'm just sick of some people making fun of me because of the color of my skin, or because of what I wear," said Jessica, a young white girl in a nearly all-black middle school in New York City.

"Kids would make fun of my ears, because they're big, and I just hated it," said Charles, 17 years old and about six feet two inches, recalling painful years of merciless teasing by classmates.

"They call me stupid, stuff like that, because I get nervous and start stuttering," said Carlos, a Maryland high school student, describing how other students reacted when he tried to read aloud.

"They'd go 'Hahaha, A.D.D. boy, you can't do anything right. You're so stupid,'" said John, who'd been diagnosed with A.D.D. and was on Ritalin.

Students tell their stories to me, a reporter from outside. I often ask, "What happens if you complain to teachers or to your parents?" Usually, the kids tell me, the adults say: "Get tough. That's just normal, so get used to it."

I've heard that before. I remember one of my daughters coming home after being cruelly teased at school. I was concerned enough to visit the head of the school. When I related my daughter's experience, he nodded. "We're aware of it," he said, "and we're watching to see how it turns out."

His detached attitude and his unwillingness to stop the bullying infuriated me. "Why isn't it your job to intervene?" I demanded.

"This is a natural part of growing up," he said, unfazed, "and kids have to get tough." We took our child out of that school, because we could. Why keep a child in an institution whose leader believes in going with the flow, instead of taking responsibility?[242]

Add to that attitude the new "advances" in bullying, via social networking sites like Facebook and MySpace, cell phones, text messages, etc., and you've got an environment that sparks the same old cruelty to spread like wildfire.

Deborah Meier, founder of the world-renowned Central Park East Secondary School, believes that most teachers and adults tend to dismiss teasing as normal, something children just have to adapt to. "We turn our backs," she said, "because we don't know what to do about it."

Meier believes that non-violent teasing and other cruelties are directly connected to physical violence. She insists that adults have a duty to become involved, and to intervene on behalf of those being harassed. "A truly safe school is willing to tackle the tough issues," she said. "Teachers are confident enough and powerful enough to say: 'Stop everything! We're not going to move until we have made sure this isn't going to happen again.'"

Cruel words are weapons, which adults often underestimate. Cruel words don't just sting; they lodge in the heart and can fester for a lifetime. "The pen is mightier than the sword" isn't a popular expression for nothing: Words have the power to build up, and unfortunately they have the same (and sometimes even greater) power to devastate and destroy. Excellent schools know this, and they pay close attention to issues of emotional and intellectual safety: If children are teased, frightened, bothered or threatened (in person or in cyberspace), they must be able to feel confident taking their problems to teachers and other adult authority figures, who in turn will not dismiss them. Lisa Delpit, director of the Center for Urban Education and Innovation, gave me a positive example of one middle school teacher's technique for handling excessive teasing: "Whenever he sees a child being put down, he makes the 'putter downer' stand in front of the class and do 'put ups,'" she said. "That means the kid has to say good things about the child who's been teased until the rest of the class feels there have been a sufficient number and with enough sincerity to count as a 'put up.'"

But what happens when adults aren't available, or able, or—since children tend not to report bullying—even aware of a bullying situation, and therefore don't help those being victimized? Various outcomes are possible, depending on the child and the situation, but tragically they can include the worst imaginable.

Consider just one month, January 2010, and two apparent child suicides linked to incessant bullying. Phoebe Prince, 15, who transferred in fall 2009 from a small village in Ireland to South Hadley High School in Massachusetts (enrollment 700-plus), and was described as a smart, charming, popular girl who loved to read, was found dead by her 12-year-old sister in January, hanging from a stairwell outside her family's apartment. Phoebe had hanged herself with her new Christmas scarf (a gift from the young sister who found her) after three months of relentless taunting and physical threats by schoolmates, both in person and through her cell phone, on Facebook and by text messages. Did the bullying stop then? Amazingly, it continued after her death, with many cruel comments posted on Phoebe's Facebook memorial page.[243] Nine teens, three of them juveniles, were indicted in spring 2010 in connection with Phoebe's death. No adults were charged, despite the inexplicable and disgraceful inaction of an unknown number of teachers and administrators at the high school who were—according to the district attorney—aware of the harsh bullying and yet did nothing.

The teachers and administrators in South Hadley who did not act have changed lives, one permanently. The prosecutor said that the teenagers' taunting and physical threats were beyond the pale. Two boys and four girls, ages 16 to 18, face felony charges that include statutory rape, violation of civil rights with bodily injury, harassment, stalking and disturbing a school assembly. Three younger girls were charged in juvenile court.

As The New York Times reported, "It was particularly alarming, the district attorney said, that some teachers, administrators and other staff members at the school were aware of the harassment but did not stop it. 'The actions or inactions of some adults at the school were troublesome,' Ms. (Elizabeth) Scheibel said, but did not violate any laws."

No laws were broken? What about fundamental ethical principles? Moral laws? Common decency? What sort of moral vacuum exists at South Hadley High School? Does this happen at many other schools? The answer is, unfortunately, yes.

Days after Phoebe's death, a 9-year-old boy named Montana Lance was found hanged in a school bathroom at Stewart's Creek Elementary School in Lewisville, Texas, an apparent suicide. The school district said that bullying was not involved. CBS News reported that friends from school said the boy was frequently teased. "He was just bullied too much," Keeley Blackwell, who walked home with the boy on occasion, told CBS station KTVT-TV. "Some of the things that people would say were harsh."[244] Montana Lance's Facebook memorial page provides links to information about bullying prevention.

Two months later on March 28, Jon Carmichael, 13, hanged himself in his family's barn in Joshua, Texas. "Most of the school" bullied Jon, according to a classmate (who said that he'd also bullied Jon, but that they were both "just messing around"; the classmate added that he wished he could take back the things he'd done, but said he knew he couldn't).[245] And why were the other kids picking on him? Because he was small for his age, and was shorter than many of the other children. The bullying had been going on for years. Jon's mother said that students bullied him in physical education class and that schoolmates had put her son in a trash can.[246]

And who can forget the story of 13-year-old Megan Meier, who ended her life in 2006 after receiving cruel and taunting emails from a person she believed to be a 13-year-old boy named Josh Evans, who, in fact, turned out to be the 47-year-old mother of Megan's ex-best friend, who had helped created the phony persona of Josh and corresponded with Megan in Josh's "voice" with the specific intent to harass and emotionally hurt the girl?

Bullying impacts all kinds of children, from all walks of life. Some of the harshest bullying is directed at students who are gay, or even just perceived or rumored to be gay. These children's problems are often overlooked, and most teachers have not been prepared to cope with them. I asked Ramon Gonzalez, a brilliant young math teacher in a New York City middle school who was also studying to be a superintendent, about his awareness of students who might be gay. "Now I'm starting to be aware of the issue," he said. "It's hard for me to deal with because I grew up in a very traditional environment, so I'm trying to come to terms with that for myself. I've asked my counselor, 'What do I do?' And they don't know what to do either."

Somebody needs to figure it out, because the harassment continues. According to news reports, an 11-year-old Massachusetts boy, Carl Joseph Walker-Hoover (who, incidentally, was not identified as gay) went upstairs to his bedroom before dinner and hanged himself with an extension cord in April 2009 after enduring daily taunts of being gay and other forms of severe bullying at school. "I just want to help some other child," said his grieving mother, Sirdeaner Walker, who had repeatedly contacted the school for assistance.[247] "I know there are other kids being picked on," Walker continued, "and it's day in and day out....If anything can come of this, it's that another child doesn't have to suffer like this and there can be some justice for some other child. I don't want any other parent to go through this."[248]

Carl reportedly ate lunch every day with the school guidance counselor because he was so fearful of being in the lunch room. In March 2010, Ms. Walker said, "At some level, the school has to have responsibility for their level of inaction....The day Carl died, there was a fight at school and the school never called me." She added, "He was happy all the time, except when he was in school. He had so much promise."[249]

According to the activist group Gay, Lesbian and Straight Education Network (GLSEN), this was at least the fourth suicide of a middle-school-aged child linked to bullying in 2009. Three other known suicides among middle-schoolers took place in Chatham,

Evanston and Chicago, Ill., in the month of February. Two of the top three reasons students said their peers were most often bullied at school were actual or perceived sexual orientation and gender expression.[250]

According to GLSEN, nearly nine out of 10 lesbian, gay, bisexual or transgender youth (86.2 percent) reported verbal harassment at school due to their sexual orientation, 44.1 percent reported physical harassment and 22.1 percent reported being physically assaulted. Incidentally, the top reason for being bullied is neither a gay nor a straight issue. It's not gender or sexuality. It's physical appearance.

It's clear that bullying negatively impacts all children in one way or another. Even those who are not direct participants in a bullying situation (neither the bully nor the victim, but instead witnesses and bystanders) are affected; studies indicate that only 10 to 20 percent of children who witness an act of bullying step in to "provide any real kind of help."[251] Many of these students are probably afraid to get involved, but what kind of training for the future, and what feelings of intimidation, guilt or powerlessness, does that foster in kids who witness the abuse? Children and adolescents can be extremely cruel; bullies probe for soft spots and attack where they find vulnerability. Parents need to know how the adults in charge respond.

As I've said, a lot of trouble goes unnoticed—unless you know where to look and whom to ask. Talk to students. Ask them about the places in school where they feel unsafe, and check them out for yourself. Bathrooms are a good place to start, because if some kids are being bothered, there's a good chance you'll read about it there. Look for graffiti that singles out kids in a mean or threatening way.

Keep an eye out for stuff that smacks of sexual harassment, because schools now have a legal responsibility to protect students from this kind of treatment by their peers. When a federal court ordered a Wisconsin school district to pay $900,000 to a student for its failure to stop sexual harassment in 1998, you can be sure that system got the message.

Having lots of adults—and not just security guards—around can minimize violence and harassment, if the adults do their jobs. In safe schools, the teachers maintain a presence in the halls. They're around talking with students, not as policemen but as responsible adults. Unfortunately, some collective bargaining agreements place limits on the time teachers can be asked to spend in the halls. To my mind, this is a good example of what should not be negotiated—or what needs to be. In excellent schools, teachers know most students by name and want to be in contact with them because they genuinely like them, not just because they feel like they need to keep an eye on them.

As touched on earlier, in most cases harassment goes unreported. According to GLSEN, nearly two-thirds of LGBT students (60.8 percent) who experienced harassment or assault never reported the incident to the school. The most common reason was that they didn't believe anything would be done to address the problem. Of those who did report the incident, nearly a third (31.1 percent) said the school staff did nothing in response. While LGBT youth face extreme victimization, bullying in general continues its swath of destruction. Carl's suicide came about a year after 15-year-old Lawrence King was shot and killed by a fellow student in a California classroom, allegedly due to issues involving King's sexual orientation and gender expression.

Intellectual safety, like emotional safety, is a critical issue in schools; without it, children are left vulnerable to cruelty and torment in the very place that they're supposed to feel safe enough to open their minds and learn.

"There can't be a climate where the kids laugh at the wrong answer," said Ted Sizer. "When that happens, a kid will immediately shut down and refuse to participate. And that's when learning stops. For me, the ultimate test of a school is the willingness of any student to display his or her ignorance, because the riskiest thing you can do in a school, whatever your age, is to say, 'I don't know' or 'I don't understand.'"

Just how common is intellectual safety in schools? "It's not as common as it should be," says E.D. Hirsch Jr. "That's the kind of safety I'm most interested in, because it's the most closely connected to academic achievement, which is what I think schools should be focused on."

Think about what happens in most classrooms when a student admits he doesn't understand and asks for clarification. Other students snicker and begin teasing their bewildered classmate. In excellent schools, however, a display of ignorance, coupled with a desire to understand, is applauded. That sounds like a contradiction, but as Sizer noted: "Unless a kid can say, 'I don't get it, I don't understand,' secure in the knowledge that the adults will try to fill that void, genuinely excellent education is impossible. So in a really excellent school, the kids who are struggling know that their struggle is respected as legitimate, and so they're willing to expose themselves, to be vulnerable."

Parents should take note that they can (and often do) contribute to a climate of "intellectual danger" by putting intense pressure on their children to "get it right" and earn honor grades. Pressure to achieve those external rewards creates an atmosphere in which kids are afraid to explore, afraid to take intellectual risks and afraid to say, "I don't know."

The late Frank McCourt, author of "Angela's Ashes" and "'Tis," taught English at one of New York City's elite public high schools for 18 years, an experience that brought him into daily contact with parental pressure. In his entire career at Stuyvesant, he told me, only one parent asked, "Is my son enjoying school?" McCourt was shocked. "Only one. The rest would say things like, 'Oh God, is he doing his work?' and 'I'm worried about his PSAT's and his SAT's,' and 'She hasn't finished her application to Yale and Cornell.'"

McCourt said that forced him to question what he was doing with his own life. He began to doubt the direction public education was taking. "We test and test, because we want to make sure a kid fits, but we don't pursue wisdom in any Socratic way. We ought to want to have the kids think for themselves and not to be afraid to think for themselves, but they're discouraged from doing that because they're told all the time 'the test, the test, the test.'"

Intellectual safety means more than being able to say, "I don't know." It means that students feel free to think and question and doubt. It also means being free to take unpopular positions.[252] "Schools must encourage the idea of rational persuasion," Hirsch said. "A student might have some oddball idea like 'the Holocaust never happened.' That would then be discussible, although I would like to think that reason would prevail. It's the old Jeffersonian principle: 'We tolerate any error as long as reason is free to combat it.' I would like to feel that we encourage an atmosphere in which we didn't let a false idea go without at least an attempt at rational persuasion."

An intellectually safe school values ideas and exploration. As the educator Luyen Chou, who is also chief product officer for Schoolnet Inc., told me, "It's an environment where students do not feel restricted in their ability to admit what they don't know. And the teachers feel that they can admit that as well." In that environment, Chou says, there's a communal commitment to knowledge-building, instead of classrooms where teachers present a set of facts and ideas that students must learn and regurgitate.

Intellectual safety—freedom to make mistakes and raise questions—allows real teaching and real learning to happen. As writer Alfie Kohn notes, "In excellent classrooms, the teacher is always listening, always watching, to see what kind of mistakes are being made and what information that provides me about how this kid's mind is working."

I asked Kohn for an example. "Let's say the answer to a math problem is 17 but a kid says 18. A lot of caring teachers in 'good enough' classrooms might try to be supportive and sympathetic and say, 'Ooh, you're close.' But that's silly and counterproductive, because the teacher doesn't know why the kid missed. The kid might not understand the underlying principle and just by luck arrived one digit away from the correct answer."

In Kohn's view, the excellent teacher would push to find out how the student arrived at her answer—even when the answer is correct. "The teacher shouldn't just say it when the kid's wrong, because you want to know how the student is looking at this issue.

What has he gotten or failed to quite grasp that has led to his answer? When a teacher creates a climate of safety where mistakes are truly welcomed, you have a classroom where teachers understand where kids are falling short and why, and so they're in a much better position to help them."

Kohn believes that the more schools focus on competition and rewards, the less intellectually safe they become. That is, the kids who don't win the gold stars get the message, "I'm a loser." And Kohn believes that competition undermines a school's sense of community. "What competition teaches, above all, is that other people are potential obstacles to my own success. And that is a poisonous message, for winner and loser alike, because now we can't take advantage of the kind of collaboration that leads to genuine excellence for everyone."

Intellectual competition actually is both good and natural, in my view, but if students are simply competing for places on the honor roll, it can work against excellence, as Kohn observes. Competition for grades reduces student interest in knowledge for its own sake, because, as Kohn says: "If the point is to get an award, or to get a sticker, or to get an A, now I'm less interested in figuring out the problem. I'm not interested in science now; I'm interested in beating someone else."

In a highly competitive environment, Kohn maintains, students are likely to pick the easiest possible tasks, and that's counterproductive if we want kids to pick the most interesting or most challenging. "They figure, all right, the point here is not to try something a little beyond my competence; the point here is to do what I know I can succeed at, pick the shortest book or the easiest project because the point is not understanding and excellence, the point is getting an A."

Kohn would say that truly excellent schools minimize competition, or at least place community first. That's an oversimplification, in my view. I believe that the marketplace of ideas is competitive; the rewards, however, must be more complex and more thoughtful than simple letter grades or other external rewards.

242

Excellent schools and excellent teachers try to put that sense of purpose first, and teach to the purpose, so that students understand why they're learning something in the first place. That's a very different mentality from learning a skill or learning a piece of the curriculum in order to pass a test or receive an external reward like an A or get into college or not make your parents angry.

Cliques are often blamed for contributing to an intellectually and emotionally unsafe school environment. I asked Sizer if he felt this was the case. That all depends, he told me; in excellent high schools adults don't try to stamp out cliques, because they're part of everyday life. "All you have to do is go into a bar or a faculty room, and see the cliques of adults," he said. "There's nothing necessarily wrong with it. Every group of kids and adults will form cliques. The kids who like to play music together. The kids who like to fix cars. The thing is to make sure they're benign." That can be done by rewarding healthy, positive cliques with support and encouragement, he said. "An excellent school has cliques of kids who say, 'We don't do that here' when something bad comes up."

When there is such an alliance, kids know the school is theirs, and they take pride in it. In such a school, students will approach a teacher to express concern about another student, or will ask a teacher to intervene in support of a student who's being victimized. "The truly safe school really starts with this alliance, where, if there's going to be some kind of physical violence or violence to ideas (like cheating), a significant number of kids will feel their reputation will be tarnished if something happens, and they will speak out," he said.

Sizer also said he believed that schools, perhaps the most autocratic of our institutions, should be democratically run, and that high school kids should be part of the leadership. "Why shouldn't kids that age be?" he asked. He didn't argue for formal voting but instead for a collective commitment to the school. That entails conversations with students and families, asking them, "What is school for, what's good, and what isn't, and what should be done?"

"I think the kids and adults have to make the rules together," Sizer said. "Take the issue of drugs in school. Adults cannot keep drugs out of the school unless a significant percentage of kids say, 'We don't do that here.' You can't bring in enough cops and dogs. Kids are a lot smarter than dogs. You can have searches and you can only have transparent backpacks and all that, but those are desperate steps after the situation is out of control."

In excellent schools, the adults know the students in the building and approach them with respect. School is seen as a shared enterprise, with students as partners in that enterprise. Not equal partners of course, because roles and obligations are different, but students in excellent schools are not objects to be manipulated or watched.

Arnold Packer, the economist, agreed that involving kids makes schools safer on all levels. "People want to be part of the solution, and if you don't give them an opportunity to be part of the solution they're going to be part of the problem."

The more we understand about bullying, and the more accessible we are to help children who are being victimized, the safer we can make our schools and communities. The terrorist attacks of September 11, 2001, raised the stakes, making our children—and us—feel more vulnerable. Adults in schools[253] must now do more to make children feel emotionally secure. Here are some concrete steps:

1. Allow children and youth to express their feelings.
Many will want to talk. Others may need to express their fears through drawing, working with clay or other nonverbal mediums. Try not to make value judgments, or tell them it will go away, or let them believe that a tragedy will never happen again. Their fears may not be realistic, but they are real. Acknowledge their concerns and let them know that grief hurts. Also, assure them that adults will take care of them.

2. At the same time, model tolerance and understanding.
America is an increasingly diverse country, and many schools enroll students who "do not look like us." Now more than ever, adults must protect those who are different. They must not turn a blind eye toward teasing and harassment of any sort, but particularly not

the kind that involves a student's faith or ethnic background. Passions run high today, and ignorance must not be allowed to rule the classroom or the playground.

3. Listen and show children you care by providing extra attention and physical contact.

Touching and holding are comforting for very young children. If children experience great distress over a situation, now or later, seek support from appropriate counseling services.

4. Answer questions with simple, accurate information, and do not go into morbid detail.

Teachers may need to answer the same questions over and over as children seek reassurance. It is okay to say, "I don't know" and "I wonder about that, too." There are no magic "right" words, but there also should be no questions that are out of bounds.

In a way, terrorists seeking to do harm to America and Americans are similar to the new forms of bullying our students face at school. In the past, our country's enemies were relatively known quantities. Like the classic bully in the schoolyard, however aggressive and powerful they may have been, at least they seemed more tangible and more knowable; they were easier to find, identify and try to deal with in a physical or concrete manner. The bullying that travels today through technologies like social networking sites, cell phones, text messages, etc., feels more like stealth attacks. With their cloak of anonymity, their potential for rapid and large-scale destruction at the fingertips of one or a smattering of cowards who taunt and torment from the comfort of home and then quickly disappear without identification, these assaults seem to me more like terrorist strikes.

Consider the following from the U.S. Justice Department's "Bullying at School":[254]

The Internet creates opportunities for cyber-bullies, who can operate anonymously and harm a wide audience. For example, middle school, high school and college students from Los Angeles' San Fernando Valley area posted web site messages that were...full of sexual innuendo aimed at individual students and focusing on topics such as 'the weirdest people at your school.'

The online bulletin boards had been accessed more than 67,000 times [in a two-week period], prompting a sense of despair among scores of teenagers disparaged on the site, and frustration among parents and school administrators.... One crying student, whose address and phone number were published on the site, was barraged with calls from people calling her a slut and a prostitute.

A psychologist interviewed for the *Los Angeles Times* remarked on the harm of such Internet bullying: "It's not just a few of the kids at school; it's the whole world....Anybody could log on and see what they said about you....What's written remains, haunting, torturing these kids. The imbalance of power here was not in the bully's size or strength, but in the instrument the bully chose to use, bringing worldwide publication to vicious school gossip."

So how can we as adults—who often don't move in the same cyber-circles or have the same skills or understanding of new technologies as today's children—better understand cyberbullying? The National Crime Prevention Center[255] warns that this phenomenon is similar to classic forms of bullying in that it can lead to a loss of interest in school, a drop in grades and even depression. But cyberbullying is harder to run from and potentially more destructive, the site points out, because:

- It occurs in the child's home. Being bullied at home can take away the place children feel most safe.
- It can be harsher. Often kids say things online that they wouldn't say in person, mainly because they can't see the other person's reaction.
- It can be far reaching. Kids can send emails making fun of someone to their entire class or school with a few clicks, or post them on a website for the whole world to see.
- It can be anonymous. Cyberbullies often hide behind screen names and email addresses that don't identify

who they are. Not knowing who is responsible for bullying messages can add to a victim's insecurity.

- It may seem inescapable. It may seem easy to get away from a cyberbully by just getting offline, but for some kids not going online takes away one of the major places they socialize.

Elizabeth Englander, director of the Massachusetts Aggression Reduction Centers at Bridgewater State College, gives some good advice in Emily Bazelon's article, "Could Anyone Have Saved Phoebe Prince?": "The best thing parents can do, Englander says, is simply to start a conversation with their children." The article continues:

> Ask teens and 'tweens where they go and what they do online. Ask if they've seen hurtful postings or texts. Ask what they'd do if they did. Schools can jump start this process by giving parents advice about how to respond, so they don't feel like they're fumbling around in a brave new world they don't understand.
> If all of this sounds obvious, well, that's the upside. These efforts take awareness and effort and commitment on the part of schools and parents, but they're not technical or particularly difficult—you don't need to open [a] Twitter account to help your kid navigate the online world. That's a relief, because cyberbullying and traditional bullying are increasingly tangled up with each other."[256]

Cyberbullying ups the ante for parents, but it can be stopped. Adults have to set the right tone in a school. They have to intervene instead of standing on the sidelines. They have to empower children rather than simply shutting down computers, for example. Above all, they must pay attention. And in order to know what to watch for, parents must understand that in many ways the face of bullying is changing. According to an article by Rick Hampson in USA Today:

The perpetrators are attractive, athletic and academically accomplished—and comfortable enough around adults to know what they can and can't get away with, in school and online.

These bullies are so subtle and cunning it's hard for school staff to know if what looks like bullying really is, and what to do about it...Many are less overt than their predecessors a few generations ago. They try to dominate others with gossip and rumor, a rolled eyeball or long stare, a nasty text message or vicious Internet video...

If it's not low self-esteem, what causes the new bullying? "That's the $64,000 question," [Englander] says. "There are a lot of ideas":

- **Less play time in kindergarten and pre-school**. In the past, children spent much of their time in programs playing with, and learning to get along with, other children. Now they spend much more time on academics and tests.

- **More electronic communication**. If you can ask someone out and break up with them via text or instant messaging, you don't have to develop the social skills necessary for face-to-face encounters. This produces socially maladroit kids who are fodder for bullies.

- **TV and movies with the wrong message.** A study by one of Englander's graduate students found that kids' entertainment programs [are] so full of situations in which teenage meanness is rewarded that the project's parameters had to be adjusted.

- **Parental ignorance.** This takes two forms: obliviousness to what their kids do online—in a survey of Bridgewater State students, half said their parents never supervised their online activity in high school—and a denial about bullying.[257]

Schools are supposed to be safe havens, physically, intellectually and emotionally. We shouldn't need anti-bullying laws, although at least 40 other states have or are contemplating legislation, and Massachusetts is putting the finishing touches on its own law—after a year of debate and discussion. No doubt we will have federal action as well. One such bill is the Safe Schools Improvement Act, H.R. 2262, which would require schools that receive federal education funding to implement a comprehensive, enumerated anti-bullying policy that also requires schools to report bullying incidents.

These laws are largely aimed at youthful offenders. It seems to me that what's needed is adult training in how to intervene, as well as sanctions for failure to intervene. Just as adults are required by law to report suspected sexual abuse, so too should they be required to act in clear cases of bullying.

Let me end with a simple, common sense test of school safety, whether it's emotional, intellectual or physical: Listen to your children. They will tell you, perhaps not directly but by their behavior, whether they feel safe at school.

In other words, if a child often wants to stay in bed in the morning instead of going to school, or keeps having mysterious stomachaches or begins to rack up a lot of unexplained absences, the responsible adults must pay attention. These "illnesses" may be something that a visit to the doctor cannot cure, but a visit to the school just might.

Chapter 26
TELEVISION AND SCHOOL

Because I've worked in television for 28 years, I just couldn't let this book go by without a chapter on the subject, even if TV is falling out of favor in some circles.

"You can't just use traditional media like TV these days," Tina Wells, the vibrant CEO of Buzz Marketing, says. She recommends contests on Web sites and text messaging on cell phones.

That view may represent the newest thinking in how to reach and sell to youth, but in most schools television is the reality, perhaps still with videotapes played on a VCR. In fact, most schools have never figured out how to harness the power of television to the creative energies of students.

Television is a fact of young children's lives, and they're spending more time in front of the set than they have in years. Children between the ages of 2 and 5 watch more than 32 hours of television a week on average, according to a 2009 Nielsen report, and those between 6 and 11 watch about 28 hours a week. Put another way, TV viewing by younger children is currently at an eight-year high, and children are spending the equivalent of more than two months of the year watching television. Their TV viewing drops when they become teenagers, because they have "graduated" to cell phones and all sorts of social media.

Dry statistics about TV's ubiquity come to life in conversations with young people everywhere. One afternoon a few years ago in a high school in Peoria, Ill., I was allowed to take over a sophomore English class. "Let's talk about TV," I suggested. Most students told me that TV was "boring and repetitive," but what I remember most was not the shows they said they watched or the number of hours; it was the number of TV sets. Three-quarters of these young people had their own TV sets; every household had at least two, and a few had as many as five. The youngsters reported that at least one set was on "all the time."

I asked whether they watched TV with their parents, and, if so, who picked the program? One young girl's answer: "Nobody really chooses. We just watch whatever's on. Mom or Dad may be in the same room with us, watching the same shows, but they're not really with us, if you know what I mean." That conjures up images of television as a soporific, enervating experience that leaves viewers tired, frustrated and angry—without knowing why.

However, attacks on television watching are all too common, and all too easy. Politicians, educators and religious leaders call on students to "turn off that TV" and "buckle down and study." These lines always draw applause, but students, more than any other group in our society, have already turned their backs.[258]

For many youngsters, school is repetitive and unchallenging,[259] which, of course, is what they also say about television.

Not everyone attacks television, though. We've also had our share of constructive criticism. In the past four decades, researchers have produced more than 3,500 reports and commentaries about television and children, often calling for more children's programming, more public access channels or for "media literacy" training in schools. My experience as a journalist and a parent tells me that a more helpful step would be to let children be *around, in and on* television.

I am arguing for rethinking how we use TV in the schools. Children want desperately to "be on TV," as any reporter who's taken a camera crew into a school can attest. When I was a radio reporter covering schooling, children would flock around me, clamoring for attention and demanding to know "what channel" they would be on, even though I was carrying only a small cassette recorder. Post-game interviews with athletes are invariably conducted over, around and through a crowd, aping, waving or calling out, "Hi, Mom!"

What are children telling us when they mob camera operators, making faces and crying out, "Can I be on TV?" I don't think they're demanding the 15 minutes of celebrity that Andy Warhol

predicted we'd all get. I think that their mob-like behavior is, paradoxically, a search for individuality. We seem to have become polar
opposites of the aborigines who fear that cameras will steal their
essential beings. To children especially, "being on TV" proves they
exist. Why is posting homemade videos on YouTube so popular?
Sure, it's a real product, not another homework paper, but maybe
it's also tangible proof that the young person exists. Schools, on
the other hand, often send students the message that they're empty vessels into which teachers will pour knowledge. At best, these
young people see themselves as minor cogs in the vast machine of
schooling. They reject that message either by quitting school or by
tolerating it, putting in the "seat time" necessary to graduate.

But saying that children are "seeking individuality" when
they jump up and down in front of the camera doesn't help the
filmmaker, who, after all, only wants them to stop doing it.[260] At
first we tried letting them get it out of their systems by wasting 20
minutes or so of videotape, which is fairly cheap. But that didn't
work. Our entire tape supply would have been exhausted long before the children.[261]

What *does* work is making young people part of the production
process itself, sitting down with them and explaining everything,
answering every question. That gives them power (knowledge is
power, remember) and a stake in the outcome. Understanding
how television is made, and actually helping to make it, provides
young people with an even greater sense of self.

Because children learn quickly what they want to understand, only rarely do we have to explain something more than
once. That's because television is so much a part of their lives, their
"friend and neighbor." But it's more than that: Television is their
common language and the collector of their experiences. Even
children who rarely watch TV know what's on and what's happening to which characters on what series. My own children showed
me that. We restricted their TV watching to a couple of hours a
week at most, with special emphasis on "Sesame Street" and "Mister Rogers' Neighborhood" when they were small. Despite this re-

John Merrow

striction, they always seemed to know everything about "Charlie's Angels" or "M*A*S*H" or "Dallas."

More proof of TV's power with children can be gained by watching them watch the tube. My children always liked commercials best. At first the razzle-dazzle (what we call "production values") drew them in. Later, the seductive power of the ads did battle with their desire to understand the how and why of the message construction. We often talked about the ads—not about whether such-and-such a product really had more cleansing power, but about the intended audience for the ads.

I think there's a message for the schools in all of this, a message that excellent schools already understand. Most schools generally use television as a medium of instruction. Draw the shades, lower the lights and watch videotapes in science or social studies class. Teachers attuned to "media literacy" often acquire scripts of network series and build lessons around them, as a way of teaching writing and other skills. But these uses of TV do not tap children's creative energy and desire to learn in the way that actually *making* television can.

High schools (and a few middle schools) in prosperous districts are likely to have their own production facilities, perhaps even closed-circuit channels; a few cable systems even broadcast programs produced entirely by children, for children. Today, however, the advent of low-cost digital cameras and computer-based editing systems means that most schools can afford one or more complete systems.

Excellent schools have this equipment *and* use it creatively. I've been in elementary schools that produce their own news programs, complete with fake commercials. These programs were shown throughout the school, and copies of the master tape were distributed to local TV stations. Today, however, the gates are down, and school productions do not have to rely on traditional broadcasting. The Web is a more convenient outlet, and student programs could be webcast to (potentially larger) audiences everywhere in the world.

The possibilities are endless. For example, every junior high school social studies class could make a news program about a particular historical period, and a panel of judges could choose the best one. Or a chemistry experiment could be videotaped and tightly edited to teach both the new material and lab technique. Any competent music, art, physical education or dramatic arts teacher can think of dozens of creative ways to have students use the equipment.

Just as studying rhetoric and the tools of persuasion arms kids against the relentless flow of commercial messages, so does teaching production make children intolerant of shoddy work in media. Moreover, it brings schools into the 21st century in ways that engage learners.

Let me give an example from my own high school teaching. I decided to try bringing Shakespeare's "Macbeth" to life by putting Macbeth and his wife on trial for first-degree murder. Some students took roles of major characters in the play, which required them to know the play well enough to testify accurately. Other students served as attorneys, and the principal was the judge.

But this was a large class, and there weren't enough major parts to go around, which meant that some students had the less interesting job of juror.

Introduce a video system, however, and a whole new dimension emerges. Student "newscasters" could deliver regular reports on the trial (careful writing required here); a panel show could provide a forum for interviewing the defendants (more careful study of the play required); technicians would be needed to tape and edit the proceedings (I'd also have them prepare a written plan and a subsequent report); and so on. Some curious students would probably end up analyzing the plot, perhaps comparing it to one of the daytime soaps. Everyone would learn something about the cooperative nature of television production, not to mention a great deal about "Macbeth" and Shakespearean tragedy.

Before we left "Macbeth," we'd probably try our hands at acting and videotaping some scenes and speeches. I'd have the students watch different actors in TV dramas and ask them to figure

John Merrow

out where the camera was, and why. They'd be thinking, and writing and learning.

In the early 1980s, the Markle Foundation recommended five sensible objectives for realizing the educational potential of television:

Availability. Programs directed at children should be shown at the hours when children watch television.
Diversity. The range of content, style and subject matter should be as broad as a child's curiosity and needs.
Selectivity. Programs should use television for purposes that it meets better or more efficiently than other forces influencing children.
Focus. Different programs should be made for children of different ages.
Innovation. Programs should try concepts and tasks not yet extensively explored.

I strongly suggest a sixth objective: *access.* Children should be given access to information about how television is made and to the TV-making equipment itself. Access invites inquiry and encourages curiosity and creativity. So as not to scare anyone, I've labeled what I'm talking about as "access," but in fact I mean power—giving young people more control over their own learning. Actually, all I'm doing is recognizing in what ways television is important, even central, to the lives of young people. It's time to recognize that television, the most powerful medium of mass communication ever invented, is also a wonderfully effective way to acknowledge individuality, foster cooperation and encourage genuine citizenship.

Hands-on involvement with television makes school a place that young people want to be, and interested students make school a more satisfying place for everyone else. Hands-on experience with television makes children better-educated, better-informed consumers of television, which will lead them to demand better television, avoid inferior programming and hopefully recognize propaganda

256

when they see it. Some educators call this "media literacy," an insider's term for a level of understanding essential today.

To those who worry that TV and other media will replace the textbook, I think there is a real possibility that the text*book* may go out of fashion, but *text* itself will not disappear. Words will always matter. In my experience, students who become avidly media literate remain curious about the world around them. They read to learn. A furniture company used to hawk its wares with the slogan, "An educated consumer is our best customer." That should be adapted to education: "An educated citizen is our democracy's best hope."

Chapter 27
SOMETIMES IT'S BETTER TO GET CAUGHT

"Did you cheat in school when you were my age?" My 12-year-old niece looked at me as she asked the question, then turned to her father, my younger brother.

We were talking about her school, a *gymnasium* outside Munich. Because I knew about the intense pressure at these elite German schools, I wondered whether German students cheated as much as their American counterparts. (According to the Josephson Institute's 2008 Report Card on the Ethics of American Youth, which surveyed about 30,000 high school students across the country, 64 percent of the respondents admitted cheating on a test in the past year, with 38 percent saying they'd cheated on two or more tests. Thirty-six percent of the high school kids said they'd plagiarized from the Internet, up from 33 percent in 2006. Interestingly, 93 percent said they were satisfied with their personal ethics and character and 77 percent said that "when it comes to doing what is right, I am better than most people I know.")

My niece confessed that once she "helped some friends" on a test by giving them answers, and that other kids did the same thing.

And now that she had "fessed up," she was turning the tables on us.

My brother, her dad, answered first. He related a tale about widespread cheating in his seventh-grade geography class. We all laughed as he recalled an aging teacher more intent on sneaking drinks from the bottle he kept in his desk than on monitoring student behavior. "I used to keep the book open on my lap and look up the answers," my brother admitted. "The only hard part was turning the pages so he didn't see me doing it." The implication of my brother's tale was that cheating was actually the teacher's fault—for not being attentive, for being burned out, for being a drunk. Perhaps that's the rationalization we eventually come to as the years pass.

"I cheated in another class and got caught," he admitted, "and that was awful." As punishment, he and two other culprits had to take their tests in the auditorium. "Just the three of us in this huge place, sitting about 100 seats apart. The only way we could have cheated would have been to yell out the answers."

"That must have been so embarrassing!" his daughter exclaimed. "Did it make you stop cheating?"

She'd asked the most important question of all: What makes students stop cheating? We know that more than six in 10 students cheat in school, while more than nine in 10 surveyed disagreed with the statement, "My parents/guardians would rather I cheat than get bad grades." More than six out of 10 admit to lying to their teachers. And yet, the same Josephson Institute of Ethics survey found that 98 percent of students said it was important to them to "be a person with good character."

"If we keep in mind that liars and cheaters may lie on a survey, it's clear that the reality is even worse than these numbers indicate," Michael Josephson, the Institute's founder, said. And the reality may be worse among high achievers. According to a recent survey by Who's Who Among American High School Students, 80 percent of top students admitted to cheating on an exam, an increase of 10 percentage points in 15 years.

If we're not a nation of unrepentant cheating adults, what happens to put us back on the (relatively) straight and narrow? That is, what makes us stop?

Her question took both of us back in time. Her father smiled ruefully. "I stopped," he said, "because the worst possible thing happened. I got an A on a big test and the teacher assumed that I had cheated." He hadn't been a good student, he told us, and not long after the cheating incident he had a test in Earth science. "I just happened to study the right pages in the book, all the stuff about geology, and I aced it."

A few days later the teacher approached him in class and said he'd done very well on the exam. "I was excited and asked him what I had gotten. He just looked at me, raised an eyebrow, and told me that I had done much better than he had expected. The way he said 'much' told me that he thought I had cheated. I wanted to say, 'I didn't cheat,' but that would have made it worse. From then on, no matter what I did, I knew that he thought I was a cheater. It was so unfair." He paused. "Maybe it wasn't. Maybe that's what I needed, because I never cheated again."

"What about you, Uncle John," my niece asked. "Did you cheat in school?"

"Yes," I admitted. "In junior high school, just like your dad. "I never got caught, but I often wished I had been. I would have been a happier kid."

They looked at me doubtfully as I began my story.

In seventh-grade English class, our teacher had assigned us the task of writing poems, something few boys welcomed. In our house, anyway, poetry was unmistakably feminine: Our mother read books of poetry, could recite dozens of poems from memory and even wrote her own poems. I, however, was 13 and struggling to impress my father, who had shown little appreciation for meter or rhyme. So I put off the assignment until the last minute. Then in desperation I took a book from the very top shelf in our library, one of the poetry books Mom had saved from her own youth. I found a short poem attributed to "Anon." I copied it word for word, gave it a new title, and submitted it as my own.

A few days later our English teacher handed back the poems—to everyone but me. I panicked, assuming that my plagiarism had been discovered and was about to be made public. What happened instead turned out to be worse. The teacher called me to the front of the class and asked me to read my poem aloud. I still recall the opening lines:

Undaunted and fighting relentlessly,
The ship sailed on;
Constantly battling the raging sea,
From dusk to dawn.

There were three or four more verses like that. Red-faced, I read them aloud and then listened as the teacher praised my imagination and my understanding of meter. Did your mother help, she wanted to know? I was able to answer that question honestly. Have you read this to your parents, she asked? Again I could honestly say no. They will be so proud when you show them, she said. I had no intention of doing that, not on a bet. Suppose my mother recognized it? Worse yet, suppose it was one of the poems she'd memorized as a kid? As far as I was concerned, my parents were never going to see this poem.

My teacher, however, had other plans. "Johnny, your poem is going to be in the next issue of our school literary magazine. Aren't you proud?" Far from it—I wanted to disappear. In due time the magazine appeared with "'The Brave Ship' by John Merrow" listed in the table of contents. I held my breath, expecting momentarily to be exposed as a cheat, but nothing happened. Any thoughts I had of confessing vanished, because I was in the clear.

Or so I thought. "I have some great news, class," my English teacher said one day in late spring. "We have a winner in this class in the National Poetry Contest." She reminded us that, as faculty advisor to the literary magazine, she decided what student work would be submitted. She had submitted four or five works this year, she said, but only one seventh-grader had won. "Congratulations, Johnny," she said. My classmates applauded, no doubt mockingly. "You will be receiving a certificate at graduation, and your poem will be published in the National Collection. People everywhere will read it."

Of course my parents learned of my prize. I held my breath as Mom read the poem, relaxed as she gushed with praise. Even Pop was proud as he held the book, but I was paralyzed with fear. Surely some reader somewhere would say, "Hey, I've read that somewhere else." Or maybe "Anon." would stumble across "The Brave Ship" and experience the shock of recognition. Again I was sure that I would be exposed, but on a national scale this time! That night I prayed, asking God for a deal: If He let me get away with this, I would never cheat again.

"Did you cheat again?" my niece asked. "For the rest of junior high I was scared of being exposed as a plagiarist," I told her. That wasn't all. What put me back on the right path was going to a high school that had an honor code, where your word and your reputation meant something. In that environment cheating was something you just didn't do, so I didn't.

When I shared this story with my friend Trish Williams, the dynamic leader of EdSource, she had a story of her own:

> I only cheated once and I'll never forget the experience. In my own family it was my father—a tough Teamsters union leader in the Jimmy Hoffa days—who wrote his own poetry and often read aloud to me the words of famous poets. Self-educated, my father read "The Great Books of the Western World," and that set was the focal point of our small home. Dad also had a very advanced sense—frequently articulated by him—of integrity.
>
> In my senior year of high school, I was in an Advanced Placement English class and doing well. But my family was having some serious problems, making it hard for me to keep my focus on school. At one point in the year I was late with required reading on a novel and was not going to make the deadline for submission of my literary analysis.
>
> I turned to Cliff's Notes.
>
> On the day the papers were returned, my teacher—Madge Gibson, all of five feet tall and called Mighty Madge for her uncompromising standards—called me to the front of the room and sat me down in a chair next to her desk, my back to the class. While my classmates worked on an assignment, Mrs. Gibson spoke to me calmly and quietly. She described my act as "plagiarism," and I grew smaller knowing my father considered it one of the greatest of sins.
>
> Mrs. Gibson then did something else that demonstrated her greatness as a teacher. She told me that she knew from my previous work how talented and insightful I was—and that she was looking forward to reading my analysis when I submitted a paper of my own writing. And, recognizing my troubles at home, she gave me a bit of extra time.

> My father never found out. And I was so grateful to be spared that shame, grateful for Mrs. Gibson's confidence in me, and grateful for the second chance—that I never cheated or cut corners again. And I have never forgotten Madge Gibson.

I believe that several conditions are necessary to minimize cheating—and improve education at the same time. Of course, schools must have safeguards and sanctions; that is, adults have to be watching, and cheaters must be punished. However, cops and cameras and harsh penalties are never enough, and ultimately are counterproductive. Kids will find ways to defeat an oppressive atmosphere, and learning always suffers when schools resemble prisons.

And so teachers cannot be assigned to instruct huge numbers of kids, because that makes it impossible to get to know their work. And work has to develop over time, by which I mean that papers have to be written and rewritten and rewritten again, so teachers can see the work develop.

Lately, there's been a real focus on the high-tech methods (Internet, cell phones, etc.) that kids use these days to cheat. In February 2010, Michael Josephson responded, in part:

> This drives me crazy because the more we focus on all the clever ways youngsters can cheat, the more likely we are to ignore the fact that the biggest single factor in escalating academic dishonesty is the failure of parents and teachers to diligently teach, enforce, advocate, and model personal integrity. It's the adults, not the kids, who have the greatest responsibility to create an ethical culture that nurtures the virtues of honor, honesty, and fairness....The truth is, we will never solve the cheating problem until those who have the opportunity to instill values and shape attitudes of young people engage in thoughtful, systematic, and comprehensive efforts to promote integrity and prevent cheating.[262]

When schools and the adults in them show respect for students and for learning itself, it's possible to develop "a moral atmosphere," a climate where students themselves enforce the code by the way they conduct themselves. When student leaders and older students say "We don't do that here" about cheating, bullying and other harmful behaviors, their disapproval of bad behavior and modeling of good behavior create positive social pressure.

Perhaps cheating can't be eliminated entirely, but it doesn't have to be a constant concern.

Chapter 28
GEOGRAPHY IS DESTINY

I vividly remember a physician friend of mine, Karen Hein, saying that for AIDS, asthma and other health problems, geography was destiny. She meant that poverty and the problems associated with it were key determinants of health. Poor people got the short end of the stick: less access to preventive care, more diseases and fewer resources to help them recover.

Now a report sponsored by the Knight Foundation suggests that geography is also destiny for our democracy. The report, "Informing Communities: Sustaining Democracy in the Digital Age,"[263] indicates that we now have what it calls "second-class information citizenship." The study grew out of the Foundation's awareness that "people with digital access have a new attitude toward information. Instead of passively receiving it, digital users expect to own the information, actively engaging with it, responding and connecting. In sum, they expect to be able to act on and with it in an instant." What, the Knight Foundation wondered, was going on in places where access was limited?

They found out. Many of us suffer from information overload, but some communities—geography again—have a very different problem: not enough information and insufficient skills to separate the wheat from the chaff.

In an era when many[264] are embracing Twitter, Facebook and other "virtual communities," we may think that walls are breaking down everywhere; but this report tells us that real (geographic) communities matter more than virtual ones. Technology itself is inherently democratic. A computer doesn't know (or care) whether you're rich or poor; able-bodied or not; black, white or brown— but access to technology is a different kettle of fish.

Who has access to technology[265] is crucial, and access often comes down to geography. Some have more access to better information, meaning they're better equipped to participate in the digital revolution we're in right now. Others are being left behind, and it may be based on geography.[266]

Marissa Mayer, a vice president at Google and co-chair of the Knight Commission, told the San Jose Mercury News that geographic communities are critical, regardless of income. People spend 70 percent of their money within five miles of their homes, she said. And even if you spend hours on Twitter, MySpace and Facebook, you live in the real world, meaning that, when you need someone to fix the sink, repair your car or educate your children, you find these things near your home. Moreover, we elect officials to govern us by geography and pay taxes based on geography.

"In the end, our democracy is structured geographically," Mayer said. "People don't realize how much they're centered around their home."

Maybe so, but the economically advantaged use technology to leave their geographical boundaries behind, while the poor don't.[267] As the Knight report notes in a powerful parenthesis: "In a world where entry level job applications at McDonald's or Wal-Mart must be made online, denial of digital access equals denial of opportunity."

Here I hold the schools[268] responsible, because it's not just a matter of who has broadband and who doesn't. The report points out a huge gap in the skills and experience needed to take advantage of the benefits of digital communications. That's where the attitude of the adults in schools is crucial. In my experience as a reporter, even when schools in poor areas do have access to modern technology, the technology is generally used to control kids.[269] That is, technology is done *to* poor kids: They go to computer labs to do vocabulary and math drills on the computer. Meanwhile, the affluent are allowed and encouraged to use the technology to create, to cross boundaries and to grow. They're making videos with footage from partners in schools all over the world. They're comparing rates of precipitation in a dozen countries. And so on.

Technology doesn't recognize walls, but people do. Kids in the nastiest places imaginable can be connected to youth in Scarsdale, Palo Alto and prosperous communities in India, Japan and the United Kingdom. Unfortunately, often the adults in charge accept limits and abide by borders. When they do that, they are making certain that geography is digital destiny, and that's unfair, immoral and counterproductive.

One reason I am so proud of Listen Up!—our project that trains less-advantaged kids in media—is its unwavering commitment to access. We believe that everyone has something to say, but we recognize that less-advantaged youth may need help in articulating their ideas and in using modern tools to craft their message. Listen Up! has been doing this work for 11 years in about 160 communities worldwide.[270]

In an ideal world, schools recognize their obligation to be digital enablers. When will that be?

Chapter 29
FAILING AT PRESCHOOL

Every American 4-year-old should have the opportunity to attend a high-quality, free preschool. Whether they go or not would be up to their parents or guardians, of course, but the opportunity should be there. We now know that most brain growth occurs before a child reaches kindergarten age. It is a fact that most American parents are working outside the home. Our economic competitors are already providing this opportunity for their 4-year-olds (and often their 3-year-olds), a fact that has implications for our economic health.

It's not that we haven't made a stab at creating preschool programs. Lyndon Johnson's "War on Poverty" created Head Start back in 1965, but I would say (tongue firmly in cheek) that Head Start is a "failure." The federal preschool program for 4-year-olds was supposed to level the playing field for poor children, and it has not done that.

Educationally and linguistically, poor children are behind from the beginning. Parents with professional jobs speak about 2,100 words an hour to toddlers, while those in poverty about 600, according to a study by Betty Hart and Todd Risley. The study also reported that "between professional and welfare parents, there was a difference of almost 1,500 words spoken per hour. Extrapolating this verbal interaction to a year, a child in a professional family would hear 11 million words while a child in a welfare family would hear just 3 million. Or put another way, a child from a welfare family could start kindergarten having heard 32 million fewer words than their wealthier classmates."[271]

One reason for Head Start's "failure" was the misguided practice at some of its centers, where teaching the alphabet was actually banned in favor of teaching social skills. But the dominant reason for the persistent gap is the fervor with which middle-class and upper-middle-class parents have embraced preschool.

These parents enroll their own children in preschool because they know that 3- and 4-year-olds are ready and eager to learn. The National Center for Education Statistics reports that in 2005, 47 percent of 3- to 5-year-old children below the poverty line were enrolled in some form of "center-based early childhood care and education program," compared with 60 percent of those at or above the poverty level. The real disparity is seen, however, in terms of the mother's highest level of education: Just 35 percent of children whose mother had not earned a high school diploma were enrolled in a center-based program, compared with 73 percent of children whose mothers had a bachelor's degree or higher. And it doesn't take much to imagine some pretty big differences between the programs that these two different groups attend.[272]

Fewer than half of the children whose families fall below the poverty line attend preschool, not because their parents don't want them to but because we haven't created enough Head Start programs. To serve all the eligible children we'd need twice as many programs as we have. Once again, we're talking the talk when it comes to helping poor children, but not walking the walk.

We ought to be embarrassed about our approach to preschool. Most industrialized countries provide free, high-quality preschool for 3-, 4- and 5-year-olds, regardless of family income. Almost all 4-year-olds in England, Luxembourg and the Netherlands go to public school; recent reports also indicate that 70 percent of German, Danish and Greek 4-year-olds go to public school, and over 90 percent of 4- and 5-year-olds in Italy and Spain are in public school.

We're the opposite: a patchwork non-system with weakly trained, poorly paid staff. The quality ranges from excellent to abysmal, the tuition from $15,000 to zero, the teachers' salaries from $45,000 a year with benefits to $8 or $9 per hour.

I spent seven weeks in 2002 driving around Europe, visiting lots of small towns and villages. Every small town I visited in France had a sign, prominently placed, pointing the way to the local *école maternelle,* the town's preschool. Had I stopped to look, I would have found every 3- and 4-year-old from the village at the school.

A few months before that driving trip, I had visited three *écoles maternelles* in very different neighborhoods in Paris. The school serving poor children was virtually identical to those serving middle-class and upper-middle-class children. All three schools were staffed with well-trained, well-paid teachers because, as I learned at the time, all *école maternelle* teachers must have master's degrees, and all are paid at the same rate as elementary school teachers. Today in France, nearly 100 percent of children ages 3 through 5 attend preschool, most in public programs.

In the United States, preschool is a seller's market, and even well-to-do parents have to endure "preschool panic," because there's not enough quality to go around. One of the families in "The Promise of Preschool," our PBS documentary,[273] moved from New York City to France while we were filming. The parents were forced to choose between career opportunities for themselves and a decent preschool for their sons. Today, while both parents are struggling to develop their careers, their children are in sound educational programs.

When New York, California and Oklahoma and a few other states announced their intention to create universal preschool several years ago, I offered some tongue-in-cheek advice: First visit Rome, Athens, Berlin, Cairo, Vienna, Bethlehem, Oxford, Scotland and Geneva.

I left Paris off the list for two reasons: Although the French *école maternelle* system is arguably the best in the world, it's well beyond our reach. After all, France's national early education system of more than a century is closely regulated with a well-thought-out curriculum, skilled teachers with advanced degrees who earn decent salaries, excellent facilities and a fiscal system that devotes more resources to the poorest children. It's free for those who want to take advantage of the opportunity, and nearly all of the country's 3- and 4-year-olds are enrolled.

A second reason for not visiting France: It's expensive. But instead of spending thousands of dollars to fly to Paris, you can touch down at an airport near Vienna, Cairo and Bethlehem for a just a few hundred bucks. With the dollar down against the Euro, staying in France will empty your wallet *tout suite*, while it's only about $450 to rent a full-size car for the 10 days you'll need to tour scenic Rome, Geneva, Scotland and the rest of the places on my list.

Did I mention that you won't need to dust off your passport for this field trip? That's because Rome, Scotland, Bethlehem, Athens, Vienna and the rest are actually in Georgia, right here in the good old USA.

And it's Georgia, not France, that most states could learn lessons (good and bad) from. Except for Oklahoma, which offers free childhood education to all 4-year-olds (and 70 percent of the state's 4-year-olds attended in 2005-2006, ranking Oklahoma first in the nation on access), American states have a patchwork non-system with too many weakly trained, poorly paid workers. Some preschool programs here are run for profit, some are staffed with trained, well-paid teachers, some are storefront operations where a TV set is the caregiver, and so on. Some Head Start programs are excellent, but others are woeful.

That's where Georgia was in 1993 when Governor (later Senator) Zell Miller created a lottery that would pay for the first universal preschool system in any state. Miller explained his reasoning: "We don't say we're just going to educate kids in the first grade who are low-income. It's universal. This ought to be universal." He added, "Preschool is more important than the 12th grade in high school."

In 1995, Georgia became the first state to provide a free preschool education program for 4-year-old children, based on parental choice and regardless of income level. Participation in Georgia's "Bright from the Start" program is voluntary for families, public schools and all providers, whether for-profit, nonprofit, sectarian or non-sectarian. The system currently serves more than 82,000 children, approximately 58 percent of the state's 4-year-olds. In the 2009-2010 school year, the program was offered in 4,100 classrooms, which covers 162 of 182 of Georgia's school districts and all 159 of the state's counties. Georgia goes a step further for children considered "at risk," who receive additional free services, including before- and after-school care and meals. Another first in the nation, Georgia's pre-K program recently celebrated serving its millionth child.

Georgia requires districts to offer pre-kindergarten and pays the hefty bill with money from its lottery revenues and with federal Head Start funds; state funds are not used for the pre-K program. On average, the state spends just under $4,000 per child.

Preschool in Georgia may be free, but it can also be uneven in quality. Savvy parents very quickly figure out how to get their children into the best preschools. In some places Georgia parents have camped out overnight to enroll their 4-year-olds in programs they know to be good. Parent Daphne Johnson explained why she spent the night outside Hawthorne Elementary School: "The teachers at the day care center were nice; they cared for the children. But teachers at Hawthorne are certified, and those weren't."

Georgia preschool classes are offered in private child care centers, elementary schools, career/vocational high schools, technical colleges and on military bases. Many classes are in day care centers, where workers (most often parents) had been making the minimum wage. Overnight, they became teachers, paid at least $19,000 a year and, when I visited in 2004, enrolled in college with the state picking up the tab. Two of them explained at the time how they taught reading to 4-year-olds:

"We cut out cereal boxes with the names on it. That's a reading thing we use," said Teacher One.

"Or a McDonalds sign," said Teacher Two. "Like you know, the parents will say, 'OK, where are we going?' and the kids, even though they can't read, recognize the letters."

"Or a Wal-Mart sign," added Teacher One. "That's reading."

No, it's not, and no parent should be forced to send a child to be taught that way. That exchange took place when I visited a number of preschools in Georgia in 2004. But currently, according to a March 2010 e-mail from the Georgia Department of Early Care and Learning "Bright from the Start" staff:

Georgia's state pre-K initiative is implemented using strict statewide standards that are likely to mean the program is more homogeneous across classrooms than programs in many other states. Pre-K classes must meet for 6.5 hours per day, 5 days per week. All classrooms must follow the Bright from the Start Pre-K Operating Guidelines and use Georgia's Pre-K Content Standards to guide instruction. The state requires all pre-K teachers to have at least an associate's degree in early childhood education, or a Montessori diploma. Class sizes are capped at 20 children, with a 1:10 staff-child ratio in place. Several types of comprehensive and family support services are offered, and regular monitoring is conducted by the state.

In the most recent NIEER (National Institute for Early Education Research) State of Preschool study that looked at Pre-K programs nationwide for 2007-08, Georgia ranked 3rd in the nation for access to four-year-olds and met 8 out of 10 quality standards. For the 2009-2010 school year, Georgia met 9 out of 10 quality standards and will meet all 10 standards by 2010-2011. Currently, the program is piloting a Georgia Pre-K classroom model incorporating instruction in English, Mandarin and Spanish.

Georgia has preschool standards, even if they do sometimes seem to be honored in the breach, and Miller remains insistent on learning. "Pre-K is school," he said. "It's not day care; it's not babysitting. I insisted that there be classes where you learned something. That it not be something where they just go there and fingerpaint." Or, he might have added, be taught by unqualified adults.

Even then Georgia was having difficulty finding qualified teachers. As Robert Lawrence of Georgia's Office of School Readiness noted at the time, "Attracting the best and the brightest to teach in preschool programs is a challenge in any state, whether it's Georgia or California or Kentucky, because, in all honesty, teaching preschool in our society is not a job that has a whole lot of social prestige and status and is not a well-paid position."

Other problems continue. Not all Georgia's profit-makers are participating fully, and other places still provide little more than day care. Private, faith-based providers still take state money reluctantly and worry that state regulators may try to force them to diminish their religious focus and curriculum.

It's good that increasing numbers of Americans seem to be embarrassed about our approach to preschool. Our economic competitors provide free, high-quality preschool for 3-, 4- and 5-year-olds, regardless of family income, as noted earlier.

It won't be easy for any state to create a quality preschool system. I believe the effort will fail unless the goal is to create a system that's good enough for those with money, but make it available to everyone. As Ed Zigler, the founder of Head Start has said, "Programs for poor people are poor programs."

So we have to design preschool systems the way we built our interstate highway system. President Eisenhower didn't create separate highways for rich and poor. Instead, we built an interstate system that was good enough for people behind the wheel of a Cadillac or a Lexus, a Corvette or a Mercedes. There haven't been complaints from those driving a Chevy, a Kia or a Ford. If states follow that road map, the journey will be long, but we will get there.

Today, preschool is on the agendas of at least 40 states. However that phrase encompasses everything from legislative proposals to real programs. According to Jason Hustedt, an assistant research professor at the National Institute for Early Education Research, Oklahoma, Florida and Georgia rank at the top in terms of access, while other states—including Illinois, Iowa, New York and West Virginia—are making great strides. Thirty-eight states currently offer at least some form of active state-funded pre-K programs, but, according to Hustedt, 12 states still do not. (Although two of those states, Rhode Island and Alaska, have started pilot programs.)

Creating high-quality programs is proving to be difficult. No state is starting from scratch, of course, which means that any new program must be grafted onto what exists. And what exists is a hodgepodge of programs. And while some Head Start programs are excellent, others are woeful. One evaluation of Head Start found that some children began knowing just one letter of the alphabet, "A," and left nine months later without having learned "B."

During his presidency, George W. Bush said he wanted to change that, but he did it on the cheap. To improve literacy skills, he gave 2,500 Head Start teachers four days of training in early-literacy instructional techniques, after which they were supposed to pass on what they learned to the other 47,000 Head Start teachers. How absurd is it to believe that one can create reading specialists among Head Start teachers with just four days of training?

Moreover, President Bush's budgets did not allow Head Start to grow, even though the program has never had room for even half of eligible children. At the October 15, 2008, presidential debate at Hofstra University, candidate Barack Obama said: "Early childhood education closes the achievement gap so that every child is prepared for school; every dollar we invest in that, we end up getting huge benefits with improved reading scores, reduced dropout rates, reduced delinquency rates." The early education community cheered. He was telling a television audience of millions of Americans what he had been saying on the campaign trail for years: that preschool and early education matter.

Further evidence that President Obama understands the importance of early education is in his language. In his speeches he has acknowledged that 85 percent of the core structure of the brain develops in the first three years of life, yet only 5 percent of public investments in children occur during these early years. He seems to understand that learning starts at birth, and therefore less-advantaged children begin to fall behind almost immediately.

The president selected as his secretary of education a man who, as a child, went to the preschool his mother ran before he was actually eligible to attend. There Arne Duncan saw the difference that quality early programs make in young lives, and so he came to Washington as a strong supporter of preschool and early education. Secretary Duncan told the NewsHour, "America cannot afford to wait until children are 5 or 6, because too many lives are being lost."

Duncan comes from Chicago, a national leader in the early education movement, thanks in large part to Irving Harris, a strong and successful advocate. Mr. Harris said, "There is no excuse for our society's not putting this scientific knowledge into practical use...we must remember—the first few months of life are not a rehearsal. This is the real show."[274]

Today the science is clear: Children living in poverty who have access to high-quality care and education during their first five years are more likely to develop the skills necessary to succeed in school and in life.

As president, Mr. Obama has spoken forcefully about the need for comprehensive programs that provide services for children from birth, that is, long before the age of preschool. Whether this will come to pass in these difficult economic times will be one of the most interesting and important stories of the next decade.

Creating universal, free, high-quality early childhood education will be difficult, complicated and costly: By one estimate, it would cost $30 billion a year to run programs just for those 3- and 4-year-olds from families making less than $30,000 a year. For all 3- and 4-year-olds, "The cost could easily be $100 billion," Ron Haskins of the Brookings Institute told me more than a half dozen years ago, and the price tag must be a lot steeper now. However, we know that good preschools have long-term benefits for children, and we ought to recognize that as a nation.

It took 50 years for the United States to be able to compete as a peer in soccer's World Cup with Italy, Mexico, Portugal, France, Germany, Sweden and other long-established powers. We cannot afford to take that long to catch up in the world of early childhood education.

Chapter 30
ENDING (AGE) SEGREGATION

Standing tall, up against the kitchen wall, was a ritual when my sisters and I were kids. First we'd take off our shoes, and then either Mom or Pop would mark our height and write the date next to the mark. We'd do this every six months or so, and that let us see if we were getting taller. When our little brothers got big enough to be included, we used the kitchen doorframe. I'm sure lots of families still do that.

Education is embracing that concept. Naturally, educators have given it a fancy name: "The Growth Model." In education it means testing a student at the beginning of the year and then again at the end, to see how much the student has learned.

This education growth model could become the *latest* "best idea ever" because it has supporters among both liberals and conservatives. Many liberals think No Child Left Behind placed too much emphasis on a single end-of-the-year test, like the "before and after" approach of the growth model. Some conservatives are excited about finally being able to measure *teacher* effectiveness.

The family growth model works because, even if the family moves from New York to Oregon, the measure—that yardstick—remains the same. Just copy the numbers and put them on the wall of the new kitchen, and keep on taking measurements.

Education's growth model is problematic in two important ways. It is unlikely to work in most urban schools, where the student turnover rate often exceeds 50 percent (that is, by late spring more than half of the kids who started at one school in September are now going to other schools). If that many students who began in one class go elsewhere during the year, who's accountable for learning?

It's true that tests can be given at the beginning and end of the year no matter how many schools a kid attends, but for the test results to have any genuine meaning, the curriculums must fit and the two tests must be connected. That rarely happens.

In other words, given the high rate of mobility, to have a valid growth model we need a common yardstick and a generally agreed-upon curriculum. We need to debate what belongs in the curriculum and figure out what sorts of performance measures make sense, before we put our children up against the wall, educationally speaking.

But until recently, we haven't been willing to make those tough choices. Instead, in response to the failure of students to achieve academic goals (like learning to read), educators and politicians swing back and forth between two failed policies: social promotion and retention. Despite clear evidence that neither works, the counterproductive fiasco continues. What if instead we ended the artificial separation of young children into grades—a segregation that makes life easier for adults but has little basis in child development?

When New York City mayor Michael Bloomberg drew a line in the sand in the spring of 2004 and announced, "No more social promotion in our schools," one could argue that he was doing what leaders are supposed to do: Set clear policy. But he apparently did more. He gave his chancellor, Joel Klein, marching orders to provide extra services to help those being retained. And it seems to have worked, according to "Ending Social Promotion Without Leaving Children Behind,"[275] a study by the Rand Corporation released in October 2009. That report found that students who were kept in the fifth grade for an extra year made significant improvement in standardized tests for the next three years, compared with low-performing students before the policy went into effect. The key, I would suggest, is that Chancellor Klein required schools to provide additional help for students who were lagging behind, and the Rand study found positive effects for that intervention.[276]

Retention and social promotion are the educational equivalent of Dr. Dolittle's two-headed creature, "Pushmi-pullyu"—going nowhere and wasting a lot of energy in the process. Neither one works. Both do more harm than good (particularly to very young children). And yet school districts can't seem to resist either.

Retention is a popular tool. A 1996 study by the National Center for Education Statistics found that 16.8 percent of high school seniors had repeated at least one grade since kindergarten, which is consistent with the National Association of School Psychologists' 1998 finding of about 15 percent. The grades most frequently repeated were kindergarten, first and second.[277] That seems to be changing, probably because of NCLB's accountability demands. According to a study by Boston College, the rate at which ninth-grade students aren't promoted to 10th grade tripled recently in the space of 30 years.

You can probably guess who's most likely to be retained: poor, minority and inner-city kids. Boys are much more likely than girls to be retained.

Augusta Kappner, the very savvy former president of Bank Street College (and the only member of the mayor's education panel who voted against him and still managed to keep her appointment), notes that many schools eagerly embraced retention in the 1930s, 1950s and 1980s, but each time swung back to social promotion. Lorrie Shepard of the University of Colorado says there's a seven- or eight-year cycle, swinging between retention and social promotion. "Now politicians are seeing retention as the remedy. Once they feel the negative side effects, they'll back off," she told the Harvard Education Letter.

Retention has a negative effect on school budgets, and it may be the *cost* of retention—as much as $5,000 more per student, per year—that will lead to its abandonment. In his autobiography, "Romances with Schools," John Goodlad calls it *economic* promotion. A study done around the beginning of the 20th century, he writes, "alerted the leaders of large urban school districts to the added costs of retaining pupils in grades and thus increasing the time and costs of their completing elementary schooling. Almost immediately, the call to principals was to keep moving the children along."[278]

Actually, New York City has "gotten tough" on failing students before. It embraced retention in the 1980s but found that, despite pumping in additional resources for summer school and smaller classes, achievement levels remained low. After three years New York abandoned the "get tough" policy, probably because those extra years of schooling were costing the city millions and not improving matters.

Most school districts, including Chicago and Philadelphia, have publicly rejected social promotion and embraced retention at one time or another, but without much prolonged success. It was Chicago's *apparent* early success that prompted President Clinton to propose in his 1999 State of the Union address that social promotion be banned nationwide. Later studies indicated that retention didn't work in Chicago, either.

Politicians love to take potshots at social promotion. It's an easy target. Former Florida governor Jeb Bush put himself firmly on the record: "Social promotion doesn't do a child any favors. Work gets harder in the higher grades and students that have not yet mastered the basics have much less chance of learning new, advanced material."

And when Jeb's brother was governor of Texas, he too condemned social promotion in his 1999 State of the State address, although he didn't mention it in his State of the Union messages as president. A number of states and districts have already banned social promotion, and emotions on the subject run high. In February 2010 for instance, Robert Bobb, the emergency financial manager for Detroit Public Schools, signed an executive order immediately banning teachers from passing students, preschool through high school, who are not proficient at their grade level to the next grade. This prompted outrage on the part of the school board and worries about increasing numbers of students being held back, along with the associated costs of doing so.

There's ample evidence of retention's negative side effects, which include higher dropout rates, poor attendance, increased behavior problems and lowered self-esteem. Professor Shepard found that kids who had been retained were 20 to 30 percent more

284

likely to drop out of school. Most research indicates that kids who are held back do not do better academically.

Unfortunately, social promotion doesn't work either. Research confirms that social promotion, just like retention, increases drop-out rates. It does nothing to increase student achievement. After all, the socially promoted students haven't mastered last year's material, which means that eventually social promotion creates graduates who lack the necessary skills for employment. Not a pretty picture.

I had my own direct experience with social promotion when my colleagues Valerie Visconti and Jane Renaud and I filmed in an alternative school for what educators call "overage students," which is their benign term for kids who have fallen three, four or five grade levels behind. Being "overage" means you're 16 or 17 years old and are testing at a sixth- or seventh-grade level. Your peers are in high school, but you are going to middle school.

How does that happen? How does a kid who hasn't learned enough to be promoted get moved up anyway? Here's what we discovered happened in New Orleans. Louisiana administers a state test called LEAP in the fourth and eighth grades, which students must pass to move into fifth grade and ninth grade, respectively. The teenagers at Booker T. Washington Accelerated Academy passed the fourth-grade LEAP—that much we know.

But what happened next? Somehow they were socially promoted *three* times by their teachers and their schools. It might have happened a *fourth* time if the state hadn't checked up again in eighth grade. Only then was someone held accountable.

And guess who was held accountable. The students, not the adults who had let the kids fall through the cracks. The students were told that they were deficient and could not move on to high school.

Are some of these young people angry? Wouldn't you be?

To her credit, Principal Rosemary Martin—in her first year there at the time I interviewed her—was candid. "We understand that somewhere along the road someone dropped the ball," she told me. She said that she tells students it's not their fault and urges them to focus on the future. "I tell them, 'We know that some things happen. But we want to take you to where you need to be. Allow us an opportunity to take you where you should be at, at this point.' And most of them will say, 'Okay.'"

I pushed her. "Are you willing to acknowledge that these kids got screwed?"

She didn't hesitate. "Yes, we have to acknowledge that. That's the first step, acknowledgement."

I am not a fan of cheap bubble tests, but when you hear stories like this one, how could anyone argue against LEAP or tests like it? If some adults in our schools are going to find excuses for promoting students whose skill levels are inadequate, then we need more tests like LEAP, not fewer.

The arguments in favor of social promotion are familiar: Kids need to be with their age group; their self-esteem suffers when they are with kids who are four, five and six years younger; and the younger kids can be victimized by the older youth. Some teachers are under so much pressure with overcrowded classes and such that they end up having to triage. Or perhaps they decide to promote a kid when they realize the alternative is to have him in their class again the following year. Whatever the reasons, I think that "retention versus social promotion" is a false dilemma. Neither option is a good one.

The only viable option is to track progress carefully and intervene right away when kids start falling behind. We need regular testing, we need to trust teachers and their evaluations, and we need to provide the resources those teachers need. It shouldn't take a state-mandated test to "prove" that some kids need help.

And finally, the adults who let this happen must be accountable for their failure. They should not be allowed to collect a paycheck for mediocre work.

For what it's worth, I approve of what Paul Vallas and his team are trying to do for these "overage" youth. Booker T. Washington Accelerated Academy seems to have become de facto "ungraded," in that no one reminds the students that they are still in, say, sixth grade rather than eighth. Rather, the kids know that they must pass the LEAP test, and that when they do, they'll move on to high school.

The school has what amounts to an anger management class, which it needs. In our report viewers saw a terrific young teacher using a so-called "smart board" to make basic grammar, spelling and punctuation a fun game.

But I walked away wondering why school systems create alternatives only after years of failing at the same old stuff. Talk about being "overage" learners!

I believe the answer to the retention/social promotion dilemma can be found in a 2007 study by McKinsey & Company of 25 of the world's most successful school systems. McKinsey found that the American favorites—like small classes, higher pay, small schools, values education, community service, abstinence education and so forth—were *not* the keys to success.

Instead, McKinsey identified characteristics common to the most successful systems, which I will summarize:

- Hire the best possible people and train them before putting them in charge of their own classrooms.
- Make it difficult to become a teacher.
- Make expectations of accomplishment clear to teachers, and then give them the tools and opportunities to reach those goals. That is, tell them where they're supposed to go, give them the tools and hold them accountable.
- And, most critical for this discussion, provide immediate help for any student who appears to be falling behind. Don't wait six months or more for the results from some standardized bubble test; instead, trust teachers and their teacher-made tests. Imagine that—trusting the teachers! Imagine hiring only people who believe that if their students are not learning, then they have to try something new because the approaches they're using aren't working. "If my students aren't learning, then I am not teaching well."

John Merrow

Imagine having a serious national conversation about the purposes and ends of schooling, so we could tell our teachers where we'd like our children to end up, what we want them to be capable of doing and being! That's probably the first order of business if we want to end our national decline.

Educators who know that neither retention nor social promotion works have tried middle-of-the-road alternatives like tutoring, smaller classes for struggling students, longer class periods, caring relationships, "looping" (in which a teacher stays with a class of children for two or more grade levels), and grouping children of different ages in a single classroom.

While this last suggestion comes closest to a solution, it still does not address the flawed design of early education: segregation by age. This remains the only segregation that's completely acceptable and legal.

Who benefits from age segregation? That's obvious. Schools separate children by age because it's convenient for the adults, not because 6-year-olds are that developmentally different from 5-year-olds or 7-year-olds.[279]

What actually makes developmental sense is grouping all the children who normally would be in pre-K, K, first and second grades. Let those teachers work together with the common goal of getting everyone to the agreed-upon "second grade" level, at a minimum.

I believe that teachers would be motivated to do whatever it took to see that every child succeeded. (After all, they would have the same kids for more than one year, which would be reason enough to want them to be successful.) Some young kids would be reading early and therefore would be in groups with older children. Those same children might be with their age-peers in arithmetic. The point is that no one would pay much attention, because everyone would be focused on achieving.

But would this be a return to "ability grouping," something seen as undemocratic? On the contrary, it would reward accomplishment over ability, although teachers would have to monitor progress regularly to ensure mobility within clusters of children.

288

Eliminated entirely would be the phony and harmful concepts of "social promotion" and "retention in grade," which, as noted earlier, are most common in kindergarten, first grade and second grade. It's beyond idiotic to stigmatize 5-year-olds as failures!

The next group would consist of the 8-, 9-, and 10-year-olds, the kids we think of as third-, fourth- and fifth-graders. The next group would have sixth- and seventh-graders together, after which the single grade structure could be retained—especially because by then, most kids would have learned what they needed to know to be successful.

Until we figure out how to provide immediate assistance for kids falling through the cracks, retention will probably remain an option in the higher grades. By that time, students should be expected to take a great deal of responsibility for their learning.

Ending age segregation would be going back to schooling's roots (thus making it "radical" in the original sense). Today we have a clearer idea of standards[280] and know more about measuring learning. We should be using our knowledge to maximize learning, not to make schooling easier for adults, to play "gotcha" and to stigmatize children.[281]

Social promotion and retention by themselves are failed policies that should be abandoned. They're the equivalent of a coin flip, in which both sides lose.

Chapter 31
PRACTICING DEMOCRACY

Two-thirds of Americans know at least one of the judges on Fox's "American Idol," but fewer than one in 10 can name the Chief Justice of the U.S. Supreme Court.

That depressing news spurred former Supreme Court Justice Sandra Day O'Connor to support Web-based civics education. We must not forget, she told a Games for Change conference in 2008, that "the primary purpose of public schools in America has always been to help produce citizens who have the knowledge and the skills and the values to sustain our republic as a nation, our democratic form of government."

While it's a cliché that democracy is not a spectator sport, the unfortunate reality is that our schools are not preparing students to be actively engaged, responsible citizens.[282] Education has a public purpose: to enable citizens to use their full intellectual and emotional potential to live as productive, interactive members of a community. Shouldn't schools prepare students for the deliberative processes that democracy requires, including collaborative, informed action? It can't just be about jobs and getting ahead.

"Of all the civil rights for which the world has struggled and fought for 5000 years," wrote the great educator W.E.B DuBois in 1949, "the right to learn is undoubtedly the most fundamental... The freedom to learn...has been bought by bitter sacrifice. And whatever we may think of the curtailment of other civil rights, we should fight to the last ditch to keep open the right to learn, the right to have examined in our schools not only what we believe, but what we do not believe; not only what our leaders say, but what the leaders of other groups and nations, and the leaders of other centuries have said."

DuBois recognized the fundamental importance of learning to question. What would DuBois write today, one wonders, about No Child Left Behind or our national obsession with machine-scored multiple-choice tests?

Perhaps it would be something along the lines of Justice O'Connor's criticism of NCLB: "One unintended effect of the act is that it has effectively squeezed out civics education because there is no testing for that anymore and no funding for that." She added, "at least half the states no longer make the teaching of civics and government a requirement for high school graduation."

Linda Darling-Hammond, a professor at Stanford and a principal author of "Democracy at Risk," says the challenge is not just a matter of improving the way academic content is taught in failing schools. "Repairing the torn social fabric that increasingly arrays one group against another will require creating an inclusive social dialogue in which individuals can come to understand diverse experiences and points of view," she said. "This suggests not only education for democracy, in the sense that we think of students needing to learn trades and good citizenship, but education *as* democracy—education that gives students access to social understanding developed as they actually participate in pluralistic community, talking together, making decisions and coming to understand multiple views."[283]

Justice O'Connor said that a Web-based civics curriculum will help turn the tide. "We'll have [students] arguing real issues, real legal issues, against the computer and against each other," she told the Games for Change audience. She concluded, "I believe that when we learn something...which you can do by that medium of a computer, and you...make an argument and you learn, 'Oh yes, that's an argument that prevails,' you learn by doing."

But will *simulated* democratic processes take root in the fundamentally undemocratic world of public schools? Can *pretend democracy* thrive in a situation that does not practice true democracy? Will Web-based democracy give students such a powerful taste of civic engagement that they will be empowered to change schools?[284]

Even when educators agree that preparing for life in a democratic society requires learning about, debating and making decisions about controversial issues, they often cannot actually follow through in classrooms because of an unstated public "understanding" that schools should avoid controversy. This behavior flies in the face of the technological reality surrounding schools. Young people everywhere can connect to controversial topics immediately and on a daily basis, often discovering attractively and authoritatively presented material. By denying this reality, schools make themselves irrelevant at precisely the time that youth need guidance.

For a host of reasons, schools and teachers have not made the connections between teaching democratic citizenship and the new technological universe. They tend instead to be reactive, preferring to avoid controversy and possible litigation. Where the "safe road" eventually leads ought to be of concern to everyone.

It's often said that teachers "teach the way they were taught, not the way they were told to teach." What if young people grow up to practice citizenship the way they are treated in schools, which are both hierarchical and authoritarian? Schools deliver an overtly knowledge-based curriculum, but the "hidden curriculum" prizes control and order over inquiry and learning. Stated simply, schools and teachers do not typically like to pose questions they don't already know the answers to—and what kind of preparation is that for effective citizenship in a democracy?

Notions of citizenship based on inquiry and active learning will not take root just because some new technologies are available. But what these new technologies do, much more readily than our schools as they're currently organized, is lend themselves to inquiry. Why? Because nearly any question can be answered—or at least explored in depth—through technological inquiry. In other words, the new technologies are a threat to the status quo (and should therefore be encouraged by all who want to see our youth engaged in the larger society).

Schools are trying to bring civic values, teaching and technology together by harnessing technology to extend classroom lessons. But who benefits from their efforts? A few years ago the schools in Stafford County, Va., proclaimed, "We recognize the importance of teaching children appropriate ways in which to work with others in classrooms, workplace and community." Stafford schools created a citizenship-building "Word of the Month," which it posted on the district's website. This was Stafford's message on the subject of patience:

> At home, as well as at school, exercising patience is a good way to avoid conflicts with brothers, sisters, and classmates. Sometimes self-control is a key ingredient of patience, for example, "holding your tongue" when someone says something you think is "dumb." Waiting your turn is another way of showing patience, whether you are standing in line at the water fountain, raising your hand to speak in class, or waiting your turn to receive dessert at the dinner table at home.

There is, however, no mention of the value of occasionally being impatient—with cruelty and intolerance, for example. And conflict, the passage suggests, is inherently bad. Am I the only one who reads Stafford's deeper message as an endorsement of docility? And that docility is the real value being preached here?

The power and ubiquity of technology are in direct conflict with the *structure* of schools and the *training* of teachers. In most schools, students are rarely encouraged to explore controversy or to question conventional wisdom.

When ninth-graders in upscale Hanover High School, N.H., wanted to start a debate team a few years ago, for example, not one teacher was willing to serve as faculty advisor. When the kids finally did persuade a teacher to serve and debates began, they all found themselves in big trouble—because the students were debating abortion rights, drug abuse and other controversial topics. The adults in charge were apparently so frightened by the idea of students talking openly about complex concepts such as these that they shut down the organized discussion. Perhaps they hoped that if ignored, complexity would just go away.

I asked a tenured high school veteran teacher what he does when a student tries to talk with him about a potentially controversial issue. Does he always try to avoid tough issues?

"I won't say I always succeed, but I try to," he said, laughing nervously. He agreed that he was teaching a value lesson right there but defended his position. "I have to be very, very careful because I could be sued. A parent could take me to task on this. I try not to interfere with what the parent is trying to pass on to their children, and I don't find that cowardly at all."

Fear of ideas, fear of conflict, and blind obedience—that's one a heck of a lesson to teach students. But don't be too quick to blame the teacher, who's only behaving sensibly, given everyone's fear these days of inflaming passions.

Unfortunately, children who are taught to be afraid of ideas stand a good chance of growing up to be ignorant, easily led adults. What's more, older students recognize the "retreat from controversy" approach to education for what it is—and they hold it in contempt.

Of course, teacher training may also be at fault. In a thoughtful essay in The Wilson Quarterly,[285] Charles Glenn placed the blame for teachers' widespread confusion over values squarely upon those who train them: the teacher educators. These professors instruct neophyte teachers to be "evenhanded" and "value-free." Above all, they admonish, don't "impose your values" on your students. "But good teaching," Glenn wrote, "is all about urging those we teach to accept what we believe to be true and worthy of their acceptance. Bad teaching imposes values, too, and schools that are incoherent are not neutral or 'value free.' Cynicism, indifference to truth, disinclination to carry out tasks thoroughly, and disrespect for others—all of these can be learned in school." If they are the lessons learned, then our democracy will not survive.

As Paul Gagnon wrote, "A democracy has a right to ask every student to master a civic core, and students have the right as citizens *not* to be allowed to avoid it."

Given that so many schools shrink from controversial ideas, it's not surprising that our young do not seem to grasp the fundamentals of American democracy. The National Assessment of Educational Progress found in 2006 that only 17 percent of eighth-graders, and just 13 percent of 12th-graders, scored at "advanced" or "proficient" levels in U.S. history.[286] In "Educating Democracy," Paul Gagnon reported that only one-third of high school seniors knew what the Progressive Era was, and many were not sure whom we fought in World War II.

However, idealism, which may be youth's natural state, is hard to extinguish. According to Harvard's Institute of Politics, 69 percent of college students were doing volunteer community service in 2006. Indicating the political-engagement potential of new technologies, a September 2009 report from the Pew Internet & American Life Project said: "Some 37% of internet users aged 18-29 use blogs or social networking sites as a venue for political or civic involvement, compared to 17% of online 30-49 year olds, 12% of 50-64 year olds and 10% of internet users over 65. It is difficult to measure socio-economic status for the youngest adults, those under 25, because many of them are still students." The report went on to say, "The internet is now part of the fabric of everyday civic life. Half of those who are involved in a political or community group communicate with other group members using digital tools such as email or group websites."[287] At least the success of the American Democracy Project,[288] which seems to be adopted by a dozen more campuses every week, augurs well for the future.

Deep democratic principles—particularly the belief that given the proper tools individuals will shoulder the responsibility of democratic citizenship—may have been the bedrock of American education for over two centuries. But nothing, including the survival of public education, is guaranteed. Today, public education is clearly in transition. From the first days of public schools, a tension has risen between the social value of the enterprise and the private nature of education.

Education today seems to be less a social investment and public good, and more a commodity presumed to benefit the individual. Evidence of this trend abounds, whether it's the privatizing of entire schools; the rise of charter schools; a federal law allowing public funds to be spent on private tutoring; or the approval of voucher systems in Cleveland, Milwaukee, the District of Columbia and other places. Critics on the right routinely refer to public schools by the pejorative "government schools."

This growing mistrust of government institutions has been accompanied by increasing central control of education—first by conservative Republicans and now by centrist Democrats. Under No Child Left Behind, the focus of schooling narrowed to emphasize skills that can be measured by machine-scored multiple-choice tests. And cheap ones at that.

The American Dream is private in nature, but public schools have always played a prominent part and have been accepted (until recently) as a main road to achieving that idea. In effect, families entered into a bargain with educators: "We'll send you our children, and you make sure they learn what they need to know to be successful." But there's a growing mistrust of the "road" that schools provide. It's increasingly seen as bumpy, unlit and full of potholes—a road to nowhere.

Media can be part of the solution. In its many forms, it can provide an alternate source of democracy and be a democratizing influence. If embraced by proactive public educators, media (particularly the Internet) can be a "walled garden," allowing students to embark on educational journeys that could not even have been imagined 15 years ago—even as responsible adults are protecting the young from the very real dangers of unlimited access. Many home-schooling parents know this and take full advantage of the Internet.

If schools are to benefit from the opportunities that media and technology provide, significant changes must first occur. Schools, and the adults in them, must become less reactive and controlling, and more open to learning and changing. They must embrace media in its many forms, for, to truly advance student learning and form the democratic habits of thoughtfulness and reflection, they must first become learners.

Whether public schools, long accustomed to a largely custodial role and now under harsh attack, can make these changes is questionable. Our future as a healthy democracy may hang in the balance.

There's ample reason to applaud our youth, considering that media stereotyping and unimaginative or wrong-headed use of technology in schools have put many hurdles in their path to becoming successful, productive citizens in a stronger democracy. Children and adolescents need and want adult guidance, support and companionship. As the number of children increases from 70 million at the turn of the century to a projected 77.6 million in 2020, we cannot disinvest in them, turn our backs on them, use technology to manipulate them, and then dismiss them as "dangerous" or worse. Such policies and practices are more than a self-fulfilling prophecy. They are ingredients in a recipe for democratic failure.

When the Constitutional Convention ended in 1787, and as our founding fathers exited Independence Hall with the Constitution they had worked so long and hard to draft, a woman named Mrs. Powell approached Benjamin Franklin.

"Well, Doctor," she asked, "what have we got—a republic or a monarchy?"

"A republic," Mr. Franklin replied, "if you can keep it."

Can we keep it? With the public school education our children are receiving today, can we have enough well-informed, engaged, civic-minded citizens to actively and intelligently participate in our democracy and keep it strong and vital? I hope we can. And I think we may find out sooner than we expect.

Section Five
AFTER HIGH SCHOOL

Chapter 32
GUESS WHO MADE THE HONOR ROLL![289]

Just about everyone! Even though he studied only eight hours for his four semester exams, Matt Mindrum, a sophomore at Indiana University, made the dean's list with a 3.75 GPA. Then again, it seems as if nearly everyone in college is receiving A's, making the dean's list or graduating with honors—even though college students in general are spending fewer hours studying, while taking more remedial courses and fewer courses in mathematics, history, English and foreign language.

In a study for the American Academy of Arts and Sciences, former Harvard dean Henry Rosovsky found that in 1950 about 15 percent of Harvard students got a B+ or better. In 2003 it was nearly 70 percent. In 2002, half the grades at Harvard were either A or A-, up from 22 percent in 1966, and 91 percent of seniors graduated with honors. (Harvard refused to release the current numbers, saying it wasn't their policy to give that information out; draw your own conclusions.)[290]

If today's college students were smarter or better prepared, that would explain the higher grades—but that doesn't seem to be the case. For more than 30 years SAT scores of entering students have declined, and fully one-third of entering freshmen are enrolled in at least one remedial reading, writing or mathematics course (the highest enrollment being in math). According to Lynn Arthur Steen, a mathematics professor at St. Olaf College, more than two-thirds of all student work in college math is remedial.

If they're not smarter or better prepared, perhaps they're working harder? Not! The assumption behind most college courses is that students will spend two hours studying for every hour they spend in class, but that is rarely the case. The 2009 National

Survey of Student Engagement (NSSE) revealed that, assuming 12 to 15 course hours per week for the average student, not even 15 percent of students come close to this ideal.

George Kuh, founding director of NSSE,[291] says that students get higher grades for less effort because of an unspoken agreement between professors and their students: "If you don't hassle me, I won't ask too much of you." Kuh is sympathetic to the plight of many college instructors, who are often responsible for teaching hundreds of students. "College teachers have too many students and not enough time, so it's easier to give good or at least pretty good grades rather than have to explain to an angry student how a grade was arrived at," he said. We saw this first-hand in 2005 while filming "Declining by Degrees" for PBS on college and university campuses.

So how do students get all those A's without working particularly hard? Easy: They go where the A's are. And they're not enrolling in classes that once were considered essential to good citizenship. A few years ago a U.S. Department of Education study of student transcripts revealed that 26 percent of undergraduates took no history courses, 30 percent took no math, 39 percent took no English or American literature, and 59 percent took no foreign language.

And where are the easy A's? Valen Johnson, biostatistics department deputy chair and professor at University of Texas M.D. Anderson Cancer Center, is author of "Grade Inflation: A Crisis in College Education." He studied 42,000 grade reports and concluded that the easier grades were to be found in the "soft" sciences such as music, cultural anthropology, sociology, psychology, communications and other so-called "practical arts" courses. The hardest A's to earn, he determined, were in the natural sciences such as physics and in advanced math courses. Johnson found a difference of nearly one letter grade between the "easiest" department (music, with a mean grade of 3.69) and the "toughest" (math, with a mean of 2.91).

Harvard also seemed to recognize the problem. In 2004—for the first time in 30 years—Harvard reviewed its undergraduate curriculum and made broad recommendations for change; in 2005, it began limiting the number of students graduating with honors to 50 percent of the class. Skeptics suggest that's more likely to lead to lawsuits from angry seniors who fall just under that arbitrary cutoff point than it is to put the issue to rest.

Princeton saw the light in 2004 as well, when nearly 50 percent of all grades were in the A range. In 2009, the number of A-range grades dropped below 40 percent, causing a campus uproar. Students feared they would lose their chances at good jobs to graduates from institutions that hadn't attempted to rein in grade inflation. The Daily Princetonian editorialized, "too many harmful consequences that outweigh the good intentions behind the system."[292]

Ending grade inflation isn't a magic bullet, but colleges and universities have an obligation to defend intellectual integrity. At the same time, someone ought to tell students how *unimportant* good grades are in life after graduation.

Grade-obsessed students probably assume that high marks lead to better jobs and more money, which seem to be the things they really care about. In 1993, 57 percent of students cited increased earning power as the chief benefit of a college education, and that number is rising. In one study, 37 percent of students said they'd drop out of college if they didn't think it was helping their job chances.

What's *actually* correlated with success is engagement: genuine involvement in courses and campus activities. Engagement leads to what's called "deep learning," or learning for understanding. That's very different from just memorizing stuff for the exam and then forgetting it. As Russ Edgerton, former director of the Pew Forum on Undergraduate Learning, told me: "What counts most is what students DO in college, not who they are, or where they go to college, or what their grades are."

In his thoughtful January 2010 op-ed, "How I Aced College—and Why I Now Regret It," Kevin Carey looked back over his college experience and concluded that his degree was "something of a sham"; instead of delving into the wealth of educational opportunities that lay before him at the time, he (like so many undergrads) just skated on the surface, taking shortcuts, choosing easy classes and having a great time. There's a lot to be said for having fun in college—don't get me wrong—but the regret Kevin expresses is so poignant:

> Who's to blame for this? First and foremost, I am. I was an adult at the time, technically, and I could have chosen to work much harder. Plenty of other students did, and do. As time goes by, my squandered undergraduate education stands as one of my bigger life regrets. The more the demands of career and family build, the more wistful I become when I look at the pile of unread volumes on my nightstand and linger in the philosophy and literature sections of my favorite bookstore—knowing with more certainty each year that you can read only so much in life, and that some of my chances to experience great artistic and intellectual beauty are simply gone and won't return.[293]

By the way, Matt Mindrum, the Indiana sophomore, certainly appeared to absorb the lesson about engagement. He carried a double major (business administration and music theory), performed in multiple opera productions, sang in the church choir, worked nearly full time as a customer relations specialist at the IU Auditorium, and still managed to find some time for his girlfriend.

Chapter 33
MY COLLEGE EDUCATION
294

In a well-known fable, several blind men are asked to describe an elephant. One touches the ear and says, "An elephant is flat, like a pancake." Another, holding the trunk, says it's "like a big snake." Each description is accurate but limited, based on whichever part of the animal the speaker happens to be describing—the ear, the trunk and so forth. America's "system" of higher education resembles an elephant: huge, lumbering and difficult to describe, even for a journalist who's spent more than 35 years reporting primarily on schools. At times I've grabbed hold of a part of higher education, reporting on student debt, profit-making institutions, part-time "freeway-flyer" faculty, and teacher education. But like much of America, I've paid a disproportionate amount of attention to elite colleges—I reported on Dartmouth admissions for NPR in the '70s, Williams for "The MacNeil/Lehrer NewsHour" in the '80s, Middlebury for PBS in the '90s, and Amherst in the 2000s. In other words, I have at various times grabbed hold of an ear or a trunk, but never thought much about the entire enterprise.

So what did we learn from making "Declining by Degrees," our documentary attempt to survey the whole elephant? Full disclosure: Going in, the list of things I did *not* know about higher education was long. I did not know, for instance, that about half of all college students go to community colleges. Or that supposedly publicly funded institutions do not receive most of their support from state legislatures. I was not aware that most colleges and universities accept 80 percent or more of those who apply. Or that most new hires on most campuses are either adjunct or part-time. (Graduate instructors and part-time faculty teach more than half of all undergraduate courses at public colleges and universities, according to a January 2009 study from the American Federation of

Teachers, and 46 percent of U.S. faculty are part-time; the national average for part-time faculty at community colleges is about 70 percent.) Or that few colleges or universities make an effort to systematically measure what (or whether) their students are learning. Or that most college teachers have had no training in teaching.

Once my colleagues and I knew these facts, and once we realized that higher education was not a "system" in the generally understood sense of the term, we began looking for themes that spanned the spectrum of institutions, from community colleges to elite universities.

We spent much of an entire academic year on four campuses that we felt represented most of higher education: Amherst, an elite institution in western Massachusetts; Community College of Denver, a forward-looking two-year institution; the University of Arizona, representing giant land-grant research institutions; and Western Kentucky University, our choice to represent mid-level, mid-size public institutions.

We attended classes, interviewed professors and other faculty members, sat in on the admissions process at Amherst and Arizona, went to athletic events and into locker rooms, dined with college presidents, commuted with part-time faculty and hung out with students.

Five themes emerged from our yearlong odyssey:

1.   Teaching and learning are declining in importance relative to getting a degree, because many students view higher education primarily as a commodity to purchase and financially profit from.[295] We found that institutions "sold" education as the key to making more money—as much as $1 million more over a lifetime than a high school graduate would earn.[296]

2.   Presidents and admissions offices expend a great deal of energy chasing money or prestige, or both. And the general public is growing skeptical about the "business" of higher education, suspecting that the institutions care more about money than about their students.[297]

3. Many instructors and students have reached the equivalent of a non-aggression pact: "Don't expect too much of my time because I have research to do, and I won't ask much of you but will see that you get a decent grade."[298]
4. Binge drinking is a serious issue and may be a consequence of #3.[299]
5. As a nation, we are reneging on our commitment to "access for all." When it comes to higher education today, an individual's *economic* status is the best predictor of his or her *educational* destiny.

Lesson one: "It's the diploma, Stupid!"

Today's message to would-be college students is unambiguously anti-intellectual: You go to college to get a degree and consequently a good job. It's all about the money. This shift in student and faculty expectations began around the time that America realized that college graduates made more money than high school graduates—as much as a million dollars more over their working lives. While filming in Kentucky, we saw billboards around the state proclaiming, "Education Pays"—basically encouraging kids to go to college to nail down that good job.

And so the mantra became, "Since having a degree means you'll make a lot more money, then you will pay for it." We learned that, in this waggish formulation, state-*supported* institutions are now more accurately described as state-*located*, because legislatures everywhere are cutting support, forcing institutions to raise tuition. What we're witnessing, as Peter Likins (then president of the University of Arizona) told us in 2003, is a gradual slide toward privatization; this still holds true. Arizona, one of the four institutions where we filmed, was receiving about 30 percent of its budget from the legislature at the time, and that percentage has dropped.[300]

The message that education pays in ways other than a larger paycheck is being obscured. Many kids arrive on campus determined to major in business, and remain impervious to professors' efforts to introduce new ideas and ways of thinking. Our student financial aid system reinforces the "college-as-investment" message by making less money available in the form of grants and more in the form of loans. The message is that college students are consumers and customers. And if they want to "purchase" a degree that means little in terms of educational achievement, it's their right. In such an environment, professors, colleges and universities are apt to give the customers what they want, not necessarily what they believe students need to know in order to live meaningful lives.

Lesson two: "Show me the money."

Here's a quiz for you. Name the presidents of any three of America's 4,000-plus colleges and universities.

Readers of Change magazine or The Chronicle of Higher Education can probably pass that quiz, but odds are that most citizens would flunk it. Still, it wouldn't be fair to take points off anyone's grade. How could the public be expected to know the names of higher education leaders who remain largely silent on the great issues of the day? Today's presidents get their names splashed across the front page by saying something outrageous (e.g., former Harvard president Lawrence Summers' politically inept comments about women and science), living too lavishly (former American University president Benjamin Ladner) or making millions (former Lynn University president Donald Ross). They're not featured, as they once were, for taking stands on important intellectual issues.

For example, only three university presidents (Cornell, University of Idaho and University of Kansas) spoke out in 2005 against treating intelligent design as science. Maybe Cornell's interim president Rawlings felt he could speak out publicly because he wasn't worried about being fired, didn't want the job on a permanent basis and probably didn't have to spend most of his time raising money. The two other presidents made their views known in a less public way, in letters to their employees. Granted, even speaking out by letter was courageous in Kansas, where in 2005 the State Board of Education mandated including intelligent design in its science curriculum. (In February 2007, the Board overturned that mandate with a 6 to 4 vote.)

It hasn't always been this way. Father Theodore Hesburgh, who led Notre Dame for 35 years, declared, "Anyone who refuses to speak out off campus does not deserve to be listened to on campus." Many 20th-century university presidents were public intellectuals who also served as ambassadors and heads of major national commissions: Clark Kerr of the University of California, James Bryant Conant of Harvard, Jill Ker Conway of Smith, Kingman Brewster Jr. of Yale, and Robert Hutchins and Edward Levi of the University of Chicago. Reporters knew they could call them for opinions on burning issues of the day—and knew they would not get a waffling response or "No comment."

Perhaps today's college presidents are not educating the rest of us on what matters to our national future, due to their preoccupation with dollars. The Chronicle of Higher Education's survey of university presidents has regularly confirmed our observation that they devote much—perhaps most—of their time to seeking money from legislatures and private donors. The top five issues that presidents considered most pressing had to do with money.

I believe that the silence of higher education's leaders on critical issues is contributing to higher education's declining prestige. Nevertheless, they are paid handsomely. President Obama earns $400,000 a year, less than the median salary for the leader of a public university ($436,111, according to The Chronicle of Higher Education's most recent survey of 185 institutions). Leading the pack was E. Gordon Gee, chancellor of Ohio State University, with a compensation package valued at nearly $1.6 million. By contrast, Robert Hutchins earned $45,000 for leading one of the world's pre-eminent institutions, the University of Chicago, in 1945.

Since college presidents need money, they cut corners and save dollars by relying on part-time faculty and teaching assistants. Today about half of all U.S. faculty are part-time; when we filmed our documentary at the Community College of Denver, about 75 percent of the teachers there were part-timers. We introduced the nation to one such professor, Bob Gibson, who was teaching nine courses on four campuses, but has taught as many as 11 in a single semester.

"Today I make somewhere around \$29,000, \$30,000 a year," Mr. Gibson told us at the time, "which is about the same amount I was making 20 years ago as a full-time college professor." Part-timers rarely receive benefits or participate in institutional retirement plans. Mr. Gibson, then in his mid-60s, said he fully expected to teach "up to the end" because he could not afford to retire. He is still teaching today.

Christine Johnson, the former president of the college (and Mr. Gibson's boss at the time), said she was unhappy with the practice of over-using part-timers but was forced into it. "It's a way of both managing costs and discontinuing low-enrollment programs," she said. "If we offer something and there isn't much demand and it was a part-time person, then we just say, 'We don't need you next semester.'"

Institutions are saving money by hiring day laborers. But at what cost? And to whom? George Kuh says students suffer because part-time teachers just aren't around: "The time that one might spend in quiet solitude or talking with students in an advising capacity just isn't there. They don't expect students to do as much of the activities as full-time faculty do that would contribute to deep learning. In other words, they don't necessarily ask students in assignments to draw from diverse perspectives, from different points of view, from different courses."

Bob Gibson, a dynamic and dedicated teacher, said he knew his students were losing out. About his own teaching he had this to say: "I am pretty much an assembly-line kind of a guy. I wish I could tailor-make my delivery—can't do it. Too many students, too many classes."

What do institutions spend the savings on? The presidents I met were caught up in an amenities arms race that had nothing to do with education. They felt they needed to build dormitories with Wi-Fi, athletic facilities with climbing walls, and stadiums with luxury boxes to attract students. They also try to buy prestige. They aggressively recruit students who will raise their rankings in the U.S. News & World Report by offering scholarships to those with high standardized test scores (predominantly white and middle-class or upper-middle-class kids, of course). "Merit aid" is the innocent-sounding term for what others call bribery. We met kids who had done well enough on the PSAT to qualify as National Merit Finalists or Semifinalists and had consequently been offered significant scholarships by universities they hadn't even applied to.

States, too, have merit-aid plans: scholarships to high school students with high averages, regardless of their financial need. Some educators maintain, with a straight face, that increasing merit aid does not reduce the amount of money available to those who need financial assistance. Contradicting that are some hard numbers: several hundred thousand students who could not afford to go to a four-year institution last year alone. Some of these qualified students are in community colleges; no doubt others are in Iraq and Afghanistan or on the street. I don't know how to measure the costs of denying opportunity to hundreds of thousands of citizens, but it has to be significant.

Lesson three: "Let's make a deal."

Teaching runs the gamut on American campuses. One professor gave all of his students "touch pads" so he could quiz them during lectures to find out whether he was getting through. If they weren't getting the concept, he found new ways to make his points clear.

But a colleague at that same university admitted that she was teaching to only 25 of the 250 students in her class because most of them didn't do the reading. Elsewhere, another lecturer droned on, reading from old notes while many of his students slept, exchanged instant messages and read newspapers.

The vacuum created by this kind of sterile atmosphere will inevitably be filled, as any vacuum must be, and too often alcohol is the diversion of choice on campuses.

Like many other students, Keith Caywood—whom I met while filming at the University of Arizona—equated a college diploma with a higher salary. "You go to college because you don't want middle- and lower-class jobs, because you don't want to sit there making $20,000 to $40,000 a year," he told me at the time. "You want to start off at $60,000 and later be at $85,000 and then $120,000." That, he said, necessitates "that piece of paper."

And so, when students came to the Trident, a wood-paneled bar papered with Wildcat memorabilia and photographs, he was sure that some of them looked down on him. Mr. Caywood expected to be on the other side of the bar, ordering drinks instead of mixing them, when he arrived at the university in fall 2000 from Enid, Okla. If things had worked out as planned, he would have graduated in spring 2006. Instead, spring 2005 found him managing a bar just north of the campus—a college dropout.

Mr. Caywood remembers how overwhelmed he felt when he arrived on the Arizona campus, the "classic nerd" with a map and no idea where Old Main was. Course offerings were dizzying. "You didn't have someone, you know, leading you by the hand. No one actually sat there and grabbed me, and said, 'Hey, you know, this is a scary place. Come with me, and we'll talk this through.' I went ahead and just kind of jumped in, grabbed a schedule, and took what I thought was needed." He ended up dropping out during his second semester.

It's not a well-kept secret that many teachers and students expect little from each other. We saw evidence of this everywhere, but particularly on large campuses, in lecture halls where the professors seemed not to care whether their students were attentive.[301]

So, how bad was it? One man lecturing about the politics of redistricting put up a 5-year-old slide of a distant city's voting districts and explained that the city council had redrawn the lines to isolate minority voters. If any students were interested, we couldn't identify them. Had this man been concerned about engaging his students, he could have, for example, "redistricted" the class to make his point. He could have asked all the left-handed students to stand up, and then informed them that from now on they were all residents of Voting District One, and so on. This would make the point about artificial voting lines—and it would have kept the students awake.

A political science class that we observed provided another powerful example of the deal in action. We found the professor to be openly critical, even contemptuous of most of her students. We filmed her walking around the lecture hall returning corrected quizzes. "How could you get that wrong?" she demanded of one student. "You don't know that?" she exclaimed to another. She was, she admitted, teaching only about 10 percent of the class; the rest didn't care about the material, and she didn't care about them.

And the students upheld their end of the devil's bargain. I took over that political science professor's discussion class one spring morning and quickly learned that only three of the 20 or so students had bothered to do the reading (two pages!) to prepare for class. "How come?" I asked. No one raised a hand, so I resorted to the old trick of staring at a particular student until she answered. She hadn't done the work, she said, because the semester was "almost over." I was incredulous. "It's early April," I sputtered. "The semester has five weeks to go!" She nodded in agreement, as if I'd corroborated her observation. With five weeks to go, her semester *was* almost over! Here's the rub: 80 percent of the students in that class received a grade of B or better.

We also spent time in stimulating classes, where teachers challenged their students—and vice versa. I was particularly impressed by Professor Tom Fleming, an associate astronomer at the University of Arizona. He gave his students, who had enrolled to satisfy Arizona's general education requirements, radio transponders to use during lectures. He would explain a basic concept, pose a multiple-choice problem and receive instant feedback as the students' answers (via transponders) lit up a screen at the front of the room. The results determined his next step. If everyone got it, he moved on. If results were mixed, indicating that students were struggling, he asked students to talk with those around them, to try to change minds and votes. When he asked for new answers, the results were usually much improved and Mr. Fleming would move on. Said Lee

Shulman, former president of the Carnegie Foundation for the Advancement of Teaching, "Tom turned a large lecture class into a small one."

But didn't Mr. Fleming cover less material with that approach? He acknowledged that he could only cover about 80 percent of the information that a straight lecture format would allow, but said "that's a reasonable trade off, because the students retain the material." Mr. Shulman laughed when I mentioned this. "It would be a good deal if he covered only half the material," he said, "because when he teaches that way, students learn, and that's the whole point."

I admired Mr. Fleming's credo: "If they aren't learning, then I'm not teaching." And it was heartening to learn that one of the best professors we saw during the three years of filming, Austin Sarat of Amherst, contacted Mr. Fleming after viewing our documentary to learn more about using radio transponders. Let's hope that others do likewise.

We also discovered what most in higher education already know: The pursuit of tenure often gets in the way of effective teaching. Before we began filming at Western Kentucky University, we asked the provost and others to lead us to some outstanding instructors. They introduced us to Brian Strow, a young economics professor then in his fifth year on the tenure track. He was brutally candid about the effects of pursuing that lifetime appointment: He didn't require homework or a term paper, didn't use a textbook and gave only multiple-choice and fill-in-the-blank tests. "As an economist, I understand the concept of 'scarce resources,'" he said, adding that his colleagues advised him to focus on his own writing, not on reading student essays. "I won't get a raise here based on my teaching. If I want a raise, I have to get my research published," he said. Mr. Strow also compromised on grades, so that a grade of 50 (out of 100) became a C. "The name of the game here is retention," he admitted, and his president, Gary Ransdell, agreed.

"If he wants to get paid, he better retain students," Mr. Ransdell said.

Mr. Strow gained tenure, but his students—at least the ones I spoke with—felt shortchanged. They admitted to doing very little work for their high grades (usually an hour a night or less) and told me they expected more. One sophomore in Mr. Strow's class boasted that he was maintaining a 3.4 GPA despite studying less than an hour a night, but then wondered aloud: "It's not supposed to be this easy, is it? Shouldn't college be challenging?"

Lesson four: "Alphonse and Gaston"

We spent two years on college campuses and what we saw continues to disturb. The future does not look bright. The country needs a renewed social contract so that anyone with talent and determination can go to college, and colleges need to pay more attention to teaching and learning. We don't have much time, because while American higher education is declining, much of the industrialized world is moving up fast.

But what's to be done, and what comes first: more support or proof of better performance? Back in the 19th century an Ohio town along busy rail lines was concerned about train safety, so according to legend the town council passed an ordinance: When two trains approached each other, both had to come to a complete stop and neither could start up again until the other had gone. That recipe for a guaranteed stalemate seems to describe the relationship between higher education and government. Higher education argues for more money so it can get better, while government says, in effect, no more money until you get better.

Most control over higher education lodges in the states, but could the federal government do a better job? Let's look at the track record. Federal efforts to police schools of education by requiring them to publish (and raise) competency exam scores of their graduates have been a farce. Last time I looked, education school competency rates hovered around 100 percent, but does anyone believe that the new graduates of education schools are now brilliant?[302]

John Merrow

With or without forceful national leadership, higher education will have to improve, one campus at a time. Happily, this improvement is already underway on some campuses. Efforts like the National Survey of Student Engagement and the Collegiate Learning Assessment provide tools for campus self-assessment. Many universities are creating small learning communities on their campuses—a proven method that makes a huge, impersonal campus feel like a small college. We found that Arizona and many other colleges and universities were offering free teacher training for instructors, sometimes sweetening the pot with free laptops and other inducements.

However, absent forceful academic leadership on many campuses, no one should be surprised if the federal government, state government, politicians, rich trustees and religious leaders attempt to fill the vacuum.

We need national and state leadership that recognizes the societal value of education. It's offensive and immoral when the best educational opportunities go to those with the most money, but that's how it works today. Society is paying a high price because so many graduates leave campus laden not with learning but with debt, and that debt prevents them from becoming teachers, social workers and nurses.

Undergraduate education is paradoxically both suffering from—and simultaneously causing—serious student *underachievement*. Students arrive at college less intellectually and emotionally prepared than ever before, candidates for remediation. In response, higher education has lowered its expectations and changed its priorities. The Academy seems to have constructed a new social contract with too many students: "If you don't bother us, we won't bother you." The end result, it seems to me, is that many students are leaving college with "degrees of mediocrity." American colleges and universities are essentially cheating their undergraduates, failing them educationally. This has clear implications for America's civic and economic future.

The decline in the quality of American undergraduate education has not yet become a major public issue, but that day is fast approaching. According to the "Squeeze Play 2010" report (for more information, see this chapter's endnotes), 60 percent of Americans agree with this statement: "Colleges today are like most businesses and care mainly about the bottom line." That's an 8-point jump in just two years. They also believe college budgets have a lot of "fat" and that most institutions could accept more students without sacrificing quality. Luckily for higher education, their skepticism does not extend to the value of going to college. Over time, the belief that college is an absolute necessity for success has jumped dramatically, from 31 percent in 2000 to 55 percent in 2008 and 2009.

Many students—and the public as a whole—assume without question that the subjects they choose to study in college don't really matter because they will learn what they need to know for today's competitive and complex environment. They accept, apparently unthinkingly, the existence of a 1:1 relationship between college and work, as if the entire purpose of going to college was to enable graduates to "get a good job." It's as if they somehow believe they will be working 24 hours a day.

The result of this mentality (I am resisting the temptation to label it "mental illness") is graduates who are narrowly educated—and often are "trained" for work in fields that will have changed before the ink on their diplomas is dry. These graduates have scant understanding of civic responsibilities or of the possibilities of life beyond work. Accumulating a sufficient number of courses and credit hours to earn a college degree is, in the public mind, synonymous with being educated. But having a diploma bears little resemblance to being educated. "Higher" education has been lowered.[303]

What about for students? Are there secrets to succeeding in college? We learned a couple. First and foremost, students should find out who the best, most interesting and most challenging teachers are and enroll in their classes, regardless of subject. We heard that time and again. And Britney Schmidt, then a senior at the University of Arizona, shared what she had learned. "I wish more students would come in with an open mind," she said. "Get out of your comfort zone. You learn so much more when you have to

317

change what you're doing, than if you just came in and said, 'Well, this is me and I'm always going to be like this and I'm always going to study this.' If you think that way, then you never stop to question whether that's what really you're supposed to do. Relax. You haven't lived 20 percent of your life. What's the rush?"[304]

Bob Seger's "Against the Wind" has a wonderfully enigmatic line: "I wish I didn't know now what I didn't know then." I feel that way about American higher education.[305]

So did we accurately describe the elephant that is American higher education? Or did we spend too much time *behind* the elephant, as a few have suggested? In our effort to describe the beast, we were impressed by students who squeeze as much as they can from their college experience and by teachers who dedicate their energies to seeing students succeed. Too much is left to chance, however, and too many lives are blighted by our national indifference to what happens on our campuses during the years between admission and graduation.

Chapter 34
IF THIS IS BOOZEDAY, THIS MUST BE COLLEGE[306]

You may remember hearing how a 21-year-old Kennesaw State University nursing student named Dorian Varcianna died on a Sunday morning in January 2010 after reportedly drinking until he passed out at a fraternity party the night before. According to news reports, his younger brother took the unconscious Dorian home from the party and, because he and two friends couldn't carry him into the house, put him to bed on a love seat in the garage. Dorian appeared to be sleeping early Sunday morning when his brother went out to check on him; a few hours later, his brother told the police, Dorian "was not breathing."[307]

I ache for this young man's family, and it makes me sad and upset that after all these years of education efforts and programs about the dangers of excessive drinking, it's still so common to see stories like this in the news. Hearing this latest tragedy put me in mind of a student we interviewed at the University of Arizona in fall 2006, who seemed to speak for so many other young people on college campuses across the country.

On many campuses, as you may already know, students have special names for certain days: Tuesday is Boozeday, Thursday is Thirsty. At 9 p.m. on a Boozeday in fall 2006, Robin Bhalla, 22, and friends were downing shots of vodka at his off-campus apartment. "We save money that way," he explained.[308] "Get a buzz on at home, then go barhopping."

Sufficiently buzzed, the University of Arizona[309] students drove to a popular campus bar, where they chugged beer and downed more shots. "I like to get drunk," said Mr. Bhalla. "Not blackout drunk, but I like to get drunk. You're able to talk to girls a lot more. And I like girls." By 1 a.m. he was "Fubar," which politely translated means "fouled up beyond all recognition," and was asked to leave the bar. He spotted a student who he was sure had insulted him earlier that evening, and rushed him, intent on fighting. His friends pulled him away, and Mr. Bhalla reeled around the parking lot, cursing.

Late the next morning, Mr. Bhalla woke up on the floor of an empty frat house. "I was so depressed and I looked at my face and my hands," he said. "I was just like, 'What am I doing with my life?'" But that moment of reflection soon passed. "If I sat there for days like that, what good's going to come out of it?" Mr. Bhalla professed not to remember the previous evening's altercation.

Sitting in a dormitory lounge for an interview, Mr. Bhalla reflected on the purpose of college. "You go so you can get a job and make money when you're older. But at the same time you get life experiences that are priceless, like networking," he said, adding that he expected this to pay off. "I've made so many connections I never would have been able to make without it. And these are all my friends and people that I know from the bars and from classes and, you know, people that I've hung out with that later in life I'm going to be able to call on and be like, 'I know you have a job with this company. Do you know if they're hiring, or can you get me an application, can I use you as a reference?'"

Mr. Bhalla, who majored in psychology with a minor in business (2.85 GPA), said he stopped going to most of his classes after sophomore year, drinking excessively four nights a week: usually Friday, Saturday, Tuesday and Thursday. ("Wednesday is boring at the bars.")

Still, he made the spring dean's list. "I was still able to manage to get my school stuff taken care of during the day," he said. "I wouldn't be just messing around, watching TV or hanging out with friends all day." His approach: "Toward the end of the semester I just start scanning, browsing the readings or looking at my notes to see what the teacher said was important, and I'd usually be fine. And lots of teachers give out, like, study guides that make it easier."

Mr. Bhalla, who grew up in the Los Angeles suburb of Oak Park, chose Arizona to get away from the ground rules of home. "My parents always needed to know where I was, what I was doing. 'You can't do this, you can't do that.' And they'd always be hounding me to do my homework. So I always had someone to tell me what to do." He admits he went "a little crazy" with his giddy new independence. "My parents are, you know, 1,000 miles away, 500 miles away. Other than phone calls, they can't really watch me or see what I'm doing."

Chuck Tatum, former dean of Arizona's College of Humanities, understands how tough it can be to make the transition from the rigid structure of high school to college life. "In high school there are direct consequences for not doing your homework," he said. "You lose points on your final mark. In high school there's instant feedback. You're in a class of maybe 25 or 30. Here you walk into classes where suddenly you're not expected to show the teacher on a daily basis you've done your homework. You're told, 'There's going to be a midterm, and maybe a paper and then a final exam. Go forth and make the best of it.' You'd better believe that certain students can't handle that."

Like a lot of college students, Robin Bhalla found it easy to be anonymous. "Here it's, 'We're not going to watch you. Turn it in if you want; if you don't turn it in, we don't care.'" He said he rarely dedicated more than an hour a night for all his courses. "Teachers say, 'For every class you should do a certain amount of reading,' but I never do that. Now that I look back on it, it's not really hard work. I think anybody, if they really sat down and tried to do the work, could do it."

And he said he was not alone. "A lot of people just try and coast by, and don't do the readings. They try and cheat off the homework, copy their friend's. When they go to the test, they just try and wing it or cheat."

Mr. Bhalla is probably right. Ask 50 students—we did—in an upper-division course in macroeconomics at another university how many hours they study on a typical day, and you discover that more than half of them spend an hour or less getting ready for all their classes. "We do what we have to do," one said. And these students say they have grade point averages well over 3.0.

George Kuh, founding director of NSSE, described students like Mr. Bhalla as "maze smart"—they've figured out what they have to do to get through. "All they need to do is to buy the book and then figure out what's going to be on the exam," he said. "They'll pick large classes. They'll go through the distribution of grades in different majors and pick the easiest one. Then they tend to hang together."

Kuh believes these students miss the point of college. "These are people with enormous potential and talent," he said. "We just need to identify them." He finds it "inexcusable" that colleges can't find a way to get these students to change their behavior. While NSSE's 2009 survey of 360,000 students from 617 U.S. institutions shows steady improvement in the quality of undergraduate education, based on student involvement in effective education practices, it also indicates a contingent of students who do not sample the curriculum, take part in cultural events on campus or put much energy into their own studies.

Richard Hersh, former president of Trinity College and Hobart and William Smith Colleges, says that many professors view teaching as a requirement they have to fulfill in order to do what they prefer, which is their research. "So the professor goes into class and doesn't ask much of students, who in return don't ask much of the professor," said Hersh. "The professor gives out reasonably high grades as a way of camouflaging that this bargain's been struck, his evaluations will be satisfactory, and students don't complain about grades or about whether they've learned much." The criticism recalls grade inflation hand-wringing at Harvard and Princeton.

In the view of Mr. Hersh, a chief player in efforts to assess student learning, students must be held accountable for their own behavior. But he is critical of the low standards that allow them to coast through with minimum effort and still do relatively well. "That's the real disgrace," he said.

Is it possible to get through a major university with so little effort? "As much as I would like to say 'Absolutely not!' yes, it is possible," said Melissa Vito, Arizona's vice president for student affairs. "We have a lot of students whose motivation for coming here is to get a good job. They think, 'How do I get the grades?' instead of trying to learn."

As for drinking, Ms. Vito said that problems often start before college: "We know now that most of our students started drinking in high school, some even earlier than that. Students come here with more habits than they used to." More than cocaine and marijuana, alcohol is the substance of choice, she said. "It's what causes students to make those bad decisions."

Recent studies bear this out. According to the American Medical Association, boys typically take their first alcoholic drink at age 11, while the average American girl first tries alcohol at age 13. Currently, about 11 million kids under age 21 drink alcohol, with nearly half of those drinking excessively ("five or more drinks in a row, one or more times in a two week period").[310]

Binge drinking—typically defined as at least five standard alcoholic drinks for a man, and four for a woman, within a two-hour period, and often done with the mindset of "drinking to get drunk"—is statistically tracked in children as young as 12 to 13 (1.5 percent); percentages rise with age, peaking at 46 percent of Americans aged 21 to 25 being classified in 2008 as binge drinkers.[311]

In terms of "bad decisions," alcohol-related injuries are the main cause of death for young people under 21 (about 5,000 deaths a year, with about 1,900 involving motor vehicle crashes, about 1,600 homicides, and about 300 suicides).[312] Up to two-thirds of all teen and college student sexual assaults and date rapes are linked to alcohol abuse, according to the AMA, and heavy drinking also contributes to unintended/unsafe sex (increasing the chances of unplanned pregnancies or HIV and other STDs).[313] Additionally, alcohol abuse in teens and college students is often associated with illicit drug and tobacco use, academic failure, physical assaults and behaviors that endanger others. "About 45 percent of deaths involving a drinking driver under the age of 21 are people other

John Merrow

than the driver," according to "The Surgeon General's Call to Action to Prevent and Reduce Underage Drinking 2007."[314]

These are the kinds of hard statistics that fill reports, journals and media stories. But what about the results that aren't so easy to see? According to the American Psychological Association, several reports on binge drinking in young people indicate that:

> Contrary to the notion that the brain is fully developed by age 16 or 17, the new studies have found that significant development happens until the age of 21 and heavy drinking by teen-agers may inhibit that development. The recent research suggests that teens who binge drink may do damage to their memory and learning abilities by severely hampering the development of the hippocampus....These studies indicate that teen binge drinking can lead to poor performance in school, difficulty in simple math or the inability to read a map. They also dispel the notion that a person could sustain heavy drinking for several years before causing neurological damage. Adolescent alcohol abuse and dependence may prove to be more damaging than alcoholism in adulthood by killing brain cells in the hippocampus, blocking brain receptors that form memories and causing protracted neurological impairments, the researchers say.[315]

F. Scott Fitzgerald once wrote, "First you take a drink, then the drink takes a drink, then the drink takes you." Drinking games like Beer Pong; the "21 at 21" ritual (a common "rite of passage" in which the one turning 21 consumes 21 or more alcoholic drinks to kick off "adulthood"); and binge drinking, fraternity and sorority hazing, and heavy partying on college campuses are nothing new, but stories of college student deaths due to alcohol poisoning and excessive drinking seem to be on the rise.[316]

- In 2009, a Utah State University fraternity and sorority were charged with felony hazing for the alcohol-poisoning death of Michael Starks, who was bound with duct tape and given enough vodka to raise his Blood Alcohol Content to over 0.35 percent (about four times over the

324

legal limit). In a letter posted on Michael's memorial website, his father wrote, "When it came time to save Michael's life, everyone deferred; the threat of legal consequences of underage drinking was far too intimidating."

- Bradley McCue, a Michigan State junior, died of alcohol poisoning on his 21st birthday; he consumed 24 shots of alcohol in one-and-a-half hours (wanting to break his friend's record of 23 shots), passed out and, after his friends put him to bed, his BAC continued to rise to a lethal 0.44 percent.

- Lynn Gordon Bailey Jr. ("Gordie")—age 18 and just weeks into his freshman year at the University of Colorado, Boulder—was blindfolded with 26 other Chi Psi fraternity pledges and led to the Arapaho Roosevelt National Forest where, according to The Gordie Foundation website, "they were 'encouraged' to drink four handles (1.75 liter bottles) of whiskey and six (1.5 liter) bottles of wine around a bonfire in 30 minutes. They were told, 'no one is leaving here until these are gone.'... Gordie was left to 'sleep it off' for 10 hours before he was found dead the next morning, face down on the floor. No one had called for help."[317]

And in case you're thinking this is mostly a boy's problem, think again. Recent studies suggest that teen- and college-age girls are closing the gender gap in terms of alcohol abuse, and that the sweet, fruit-flavored "alcopops" or "malternatives" that the AMA says "come in colorful, child-oriented packaging" may contribute to this trend. Statistics suggest that alcopops seem to be heavily marketed toward this demographic; in 2002 the AMA reported that "Girls saw a staggering 95 percent more magazine advertising for low-alcohol refreshers than legal-age women on a per capita basis," even though the products were supposedly directed at women between 21 and 34. The AMA added, "Exposure of underage youth to alcohol advertising in magazines declined between 2001 and 2002 in every category except low-alcohol refreshers, for which exposure to girls grew by a staggering 216 percent."[318]

Samantha Spady, 19, is one of many teen- and college-age young women who has died as a result of alcohol poisoning; she drank 30 to 40 beers and shots in an 11-hour period while attending Colorado State University. Spady's parents, joining the ranks of other grieving families hoping to prevent future tragedies, worked with two journalists to create the documentary "Death by Alcohol: The Sam Spady Story" and created a website to educate about the dangers of excessive drinking, in their daughter's memory.[319]

And, tragically, alcohol poisoning is just one of many causes of death due to excessive drinking. Mindy Somers at Virginia Tech, for instance, fell asleep in her bed after a night of drinking that raised her BAC to 0.21 percent; her bed was pushed up against her open window, on the eighth floor of her dormitory building, and during the night she fell from her bed to the ground below.[320]

So what can be done? Parents, educators, concerned citizens and numerous organizations and groups across the country have been working for a long time now to try to figure that out. They implement a variety of tactics—some of which work, some of which don't—hoping to decrease alcohol abuse in children, teenagers and college students.

I wish I had the answers, but it seems to me—as a journalist who's worked for a long time in the communications field—that awareness and honest conversation are the way to start. Comprehensive websites[321] like College Drinking: Changing the Culture, Stop Underage Drinking and many of the educational sites created by families who have lost a child to alcohol abuse offer information and links to resources, as well as some personal stories that may resonate more than statistics do. Keeping up on media stories about the latest trends in teen and college drinking may also be helpful. A great variety of prevention programs exist, some with innovative approaches like the use of new social media to reach kids where they like to hang out online. There's even an organized debate called the Amethyst Initiative, created in 2008 by a group of university/college chancellors and professors, to discuss whether lowering the current legal drinking age of 21 might have a positive impact (you can imagine how hotly contested *that* proposal is).

In a Q&A session with Inside Higher Ed's Scott Jaschik, George Dowdall—professor of sociology at Saint Joseph's University and author of "College Drinking: Reframing a Social Problem"—said: "The most important task of colleges is to place this issue much higher on their own agendas. Colleges ought to look critically and realistically at what they now do; assess, using fresh research, what effect they're having; and engage in serious strategic planning about what to do next. Just pulling a promising program or today's trendy intervention off the shelf and directing it at a small fraction of students probably won't work too well."[322]

When it comes right down to it, perhaps the most effective methods of all for reducing excessive drinking in college are those that take place before kids ever get to campus. Talking openly and honestly—early and often—with children about the use and abuse of alcohol, and your feelings about it; sharing factual information; and helping them understand how to deal with alcohol-related situations they may encounter on their own—all these things can make a positive difference in the decisions kids make later in life.

It's not possible to make their decisions for them. It's not possible to see the future and prevent every tragedy, as parents wish they could. And sometimes, even when you do everything right, the wrong thing still happens. But open, honest communication is a good start. And it's something we can start right away.

There is some good news. According to the 2008 National Survey on Drug Use and Health, current alcohol-use rates in some underage populations declined significantly from 2007 (from 14.7 to 13.1 percent in 14- to 15-year-olds and from 29.0 to 26.2 percent in 16- to 17-year-olds); binge drinking also went down in 16- to 17-year-olds (19.4 to 17.2 percent).[323] The National Institute on Drug Abuse's 2009 Monitoring the Futures survey also observed declines in "lifetime, past year, past month, and binge use" of alcohol in eighth-, 10th-, and 12th-graders, from 2004 to 2009, and a reduction of people driving under the influence of alcohol.[324]

So someone out there is doing something right. But let's not get too comfortable; the numbers are still very high, and MTF also reported a "softening of attitudes in some alcohol measures. Fewer 10th-graders, for instance, viewed weekend binge drinking (five or more drinks on one occasion in the past 30 days) as harmful, and fewer high school seniors disapproved of having one or two drinks every day. Although alcohol use has decreased in the past 5 years among 8th, 10th, and 12th graders, these softened attitudes warrant concern among the underage drinking prevention community."[325]

And what of Robin Bhalla, the University of Arizona student we met in 2006? At one point, Mr. Bhalla's drinking caught the university's attention. He was sent to an alcohol education class after being caught driving under the influence during his sophomore year, and was put on probation for a semester. He did not get caught again.

At the end of a three-hour interview, Mr. Bhalla was asked if he regretted anything he had done at Arizona. "These are the years that I'm not going to have back," he said. "And I don't want to be 30, 50, looking back and wishing I'd partied then because I can't do it now."[326]

In the aftermath of Dorian Varcianna's death at Kennesaw State University, Dean of Students Michael Sanseviro turned his campus focus to grief counseling for students. He said he plans to launch an education campaign highlighting student responsibility. "We have to be responsible for our personal choices," he told 11Alive News in Atlanta, Ga. "But, particularly with young people, they need to look out for each other. And I think if a young person finds a friend of theirs engaging in behaviors that may not be wise, that they need to step in and try to intervene."[327]

I think that's a good start. And I think it's time for all of us to step in and intervene where we can.

Chapter 35
UNSUNG HEROES³²⁸

PLEASE ANSWER THE FOLLOWING QUESTIONS:

1. Joe Morgan grew up idolizing Jackie Robinson, and today both star second-basemen are members of Major League Baseball's Hall of Fame. But that's not their only connection. Name another.
2. Actor Edward James Olmos and the late high school math teacher Jaime Escalante are forever linked, because the actor was nominated for an Oscar for his portrayal of the teacher in "Stand and Deliver." What else do they have in common?
3. What (besides Texas) connects Jim Lehrer, H. Ross Perot and pitcher Roger Clemens?

AND FOR EXTRA CREDIT:

4. What connects California Democratic Congressman George Miller and California Republican Governor Arnold Schwarzenegger?

The correct answer to all of these questions is: They're community college alumni.

And the list of prominent alumni doesn't stop there. Henry Louis Gates, Venus Williams, Calvin Klein, Diane Keaton, Queen Latifah, Sylvester Stallone, Tom Hanks, Clint Eastwood, George Lucas, John Mellencamp, James Belushi, Rita Mae Brown, Amy Tan and Nobel Prize-winner R. Bruce Merrifield all graduated from community colleges. These institutions educate about half of all degree-seeking American undergraduates, plus another five million students who are taking a non-credit course or two.

In the nearly two years that my colleagues and I spent on community college campuses in California, New York, Illinois and Colorado starting in 2006, we met hundreds of dedicated but often frustrated teachers and administrators. We got to know students and their dreams, and we watched some of those dreams flourish while others withered and died.

When you're down and out...

The people who repair your furnace, tune up your car and keep your office IT system running probably studied at a community college. "They prepare people for computer repair jobs, for auto mechanic positions, for construction, for culinary arts, for apparel design and manufacturing, plumbing and electrical work, and even cosmetology," noted Jack Kyser, founding economist of the Kyser Center for Economic Research at the Los Angeles County Economic Development Corporation. "These people make the economy go."

Community colleges, which admit virtually everyone who applies, may be the one place that doesn't turn away those in desperate need of career help. Thirty-year-old José Sosa was a good case in point. A high school dropout with a wife and three young children, Sosa had just lost his job as a clerk in the shipping department of a textile company when we met him in 2007. It was the latest in a string of a dozen or so dead-end jobs he'd held since dropping out of high school. He'd also worked as a food runner at the Olive Garden and the Macaroni Grill restaurants, a janitor at three different factories and a kitchen assistant at a Marriott hotel.

When he lost his job as a shipping clerk, Sosa, his wife and their three children were living in a small one-story house, which they rented for $1,200 a month. His first despairing reaction was to feel "like I let my family down. It was like, 'This can't be happening, not again.'"

But with his wife's support, Sosa enrolled in Los Angeles Trade-Technical College's four-semester culinary arts program. He had long dreamed of making a living as a cook, but now he had free time. "Now I can say, 'Fortunately I got laid off,' because before I never could fit school into my work schedule, and now I could."

At first Sosa struggled to master what his teachers called "culinary mathematics." Said teacher and chef James Lisanti, "They need to be able to buy the right amount of food and set prices for entrées if they want to make it in this business." Added Lisanti, who was working with missionary zeal, "We're giving them a chance to change their lives. We're giving them a chance to get out of the ghetto. We're giving them a chance to get respect."

Sosa made the most of the opportunity, enduring a daily four-hour commute and a housing crisis along the way. As the months wore on, he often thought about quitting. "Every night I am afraid that the next day I'll just get up and not go to school, but if I start that routine, I'd never go back," he told us. "Still, it's hard to get that initial foot out the door in the morning. Easy to quit school, hard to stay in it."

Kay McClenney, director of the Community College Survey of Student Engagement, understands. "When we do surveys of students, 95 percent say they came close to quitting, usually more than once," she told me at the time.

Why didn't Sosa quit? "It would have been worthless to have gone this far and thrown it away," he said. "It would be like what I did in high school, and what's the point? This time it's mine. I deserve this. I'm taking it." He graduated in June 2006 with a job at a prominent Santa Monica beach club. When the club's restaurant shut down for the winter, Sosa found a job at another Santa Monica restaurant where, he reported, he was earning nearly twice as much as he had been a year earlier.

Community colleges enroll hundreds of thousands of students like Sosa, men and women who are one paycheck, one sick child or one small disaster away from collapse. In fact, in a 2009 report by the Pew Hispanic Center, "nearly three-quarters (74 percent) of all 16- to 25-year-old survey respondents who cut their education short during or right after high school say they did so because they had to support their family."[329] Michael Kirst, an emeritus professor of education and business administration at Stanford, noted that most community college students fall into the high-risk category: "They're often the first in their family to go to college, and their own parents may not be high school graduates. If they're going part time, they probably can't get financial aid. They may have to work very long hours to support a family. These are shoes that most of us have not walked in."

Without that community college, José Sosa might still be going from one dead-end job to another. Instead he has done well and a former boss, Chef Whitney Werner of the Beach Club in Santa Monica, said, "Within five years, I could see him running a corporate restaurant, and possibly in 10 years be an executive chef somewhere on his own." And some years from now, perhaps he'll be part of another trivia question: "What do actor Rosie Perez, former United States Treasurer Rosario Marin, and Chef José Sosa have in common besides their Hispanic heritage?"

Dropping the remedial ball

A huge percentage of incoming community college freshmen have to take at least one "developmental" class in math or English, based on their performance on a placement test.

"It's a crisis," said Nancy Shulock—professor and executive director for the Institute for Higher Education Leadership and Policy at California State University in Sacramento—who studies community colleges. "Nobody has the exact numbers, but 60, 70 or 80 percent of incoming students into the community colleges need remedial education."

McClenney calls remedial education "Job One" for community colleges, but remedial classes are most often assigned to new or part-time faculty with no training for the job. We spoke with Aric Eidadu, who was teaching remedial English at four Los Angeles area community colleges in 2007, including Los Angeles Trade-Technical College. "I might get in trouble for saying this," Eidadu said, "but a lot of times these are the classes that are very challenging, and a lot of people who are kind of higher up won't necessarily

332

take these classes." So newer instructors get the courses that more experienced faculty members don't want to struggle with.

During visits to some three dozen remedial classes around the country, we found students wearing headphones, reading non-class materials and leaving after the break. For two hours one afternoon, we watched an instructor at Joliet Junior College lecture on algebra as many students worked on other assignments, text messaged or read. Whenever he asked the class if there were any questions, he received no response. At one point he assumed the role of auctioneer: "Any questions on this problem? Going once, going twice, gone!" Greeted by silence, he directed the class to turn to another page of problems.

Afterwards, when we mentioned that many students were otherwise occupied, he said, "They're adults, and if they don't want to pay attention, that's their choice." The instructor, a biology major in college, worked full time as the college's Web master. Asked why he had been teaching remedial algebra for 15 years, he said, "It's an extra-pay contract—it's money, but I also enjoy teaching and working with students."

Situations like these do not surprise Shulock. The colleges, she said, "are trying to do remediation on the cheap because they don't have the money, and they don't have the money because society thinks that it is cheap. It's a circular logic that's not going to get us out of this box."

Students in the class mentioned above were required to pass it and two other remedial classes before being allowed to enroll in college-level mathematics. In the space of two years, only 45 percent of students taught by the instructor described above did well enough to move to the next level of remediation. When we were there in 2006, the pass rate for all remedial classes at Joliet was around 50 percent.

The most successful remedial teachers we saw were two women who worked to involve themselves in the lives of their students. If someone missed two classes in a row, an instructor phoned to check in. These teachers didn't stay behind the lectern; they moved around, joking and talking and helping (and, incidentally, making sure their students weren't text messaging).

But because so many community college students are under-educated, poor and facing tough family and financial challenges, those circumstances have become a convenient excuse for failure, McClenney said. "With that truth as our shield, we have been able to defend ourselves against the massive reality that we simply don't get enough of our students through to successful outcomes."

Another student we met along the way, Krystal, was as close to being a typical community college student as one is likely to find. "I'm a full-time parent, I have a full-time job and I go to school full time," she said. She also was close to the edge financially, sharing a small two-bedroom apartment with her parents, her boyfriend, her 4-year-old daughter, a gerbil and a cat. And she was behind academically. When we met her, she was taking remedial math for the fourth time.

She was typical in another way: She did not make it. Her 16-hour days left no time to study or to see her professor for help. She flunked and dropped out of LaGuardia Community College, even though the college would have allowed her to try again—and again and again. Like most community colleges, LaGuardia places no limit on how many times a student may enroll in reme-dial classes.

McClenney took the long view of Krystal's educational fail-ure. "I emphatically do not blame Krystal," she said. "We know that Krystal is not ready for college, but what is also evident is that the college wasn't ready for Krystal." After Krystal failed the same course twice, McClenney said, LaGuardia might have brought her in for counseling and perhaps tried a different approach. "It's the classic definition of insanity: sticking with methods that have failed in the past and expecting different results."

George Boggs, president and CEO of the American Asso-ciation of Community Colleges and a former community college president, agreed that intervention was in order: "If a student is taking the same class for the fourth time, we probably aren't doing the student a favor. I think that student could benefit from some career counseling."

Kirst believes community colleges need to be held accountable for their students' success. "We don't know exactly how many students they take who could have succeeded with better teaching," he said, but some community colleges practice what economists call the "churn" model, in which success is irrelevant. "As long as the number of students coming in the front equals the number of students dropping out the back door and side door, their enrollment and full-time equivalence is the same, whether they're advancing and graduating or flunking out." Because demand is high, he said, "There is really no incentive to spend a lot of money to serve these students with special counselors and trained teachers."

Shulock agreed. "All the incentives are on the wrong end of a student's career," she said. "They're all for getting students in the door. Colleges are not funded or rewarded for getting students out."

Some critics of the community college approach to remediation say that potential community college students should be tested while they're still in high school so they know whether they will have to take remedial classes. (Perhaps this would also motivate them to work harder in high school, while they still have the chance.) Shulock said that community colleges just aren't sending the right message to high school students. "They need to say, 'We have standards of college readiness, and you're going to have a really tough time here if you don't meet them.'"

Kirst also questioned the process by which students are placed in remedial classes. "Those placement exams are fairly difficult, and the majority of students fail them, which means they may have to take as many as three remedial courses before they're allowed to take a regular college course." He suggested giving students the incentive to learn on their own by offering them opportunities to opt out of remediation along the way, when they think they're ready for credit-bearing work.

John Merrow

"Many of these students—even recent high school graduates—have been away from classroom math for some time," said
Rose Asera of the Carnegie Foundation for the Advancement of
Teaching, "so of course they do badly on the placement test. We
need to find ways to intensify and accelerate instruction. Pasadena
City College, for example, organized a two-week summer 'math
jam' that involved students in hands-on math problems and projects. When they retook the placement exam, more than half of the
students moved up at least one course level."

To me, it seems that remedial classes are organized largely for
the convenience of administrators. If educators know what knowledge and skills students must have, then why not make that the
constant and let time be the variable? Why not tell students exactly
what they must be able to do and then let them prove their competence whenever they feel they're ready, the way the DMV licenses
drivers? And if educators know how much mathematics someone
needs to be successful in his or her chosen field, why not embed
that material into the core courses, the way LA Trade-Tech has
done with "culinary math" for those seeking to become chefs?

"Community colleges are underprepared to teach the underprepared," Shulock admitted. "But who is doing it better?"

The glass is a quarter full

"I didn't want to go to a two-year school because I didn't see
it as really being college, and right now I'm focused on getting out
of here," said 19-year-old Jennica in 2007, as she sat in an art classroom at her community college. "I thought of community college
as being like, 'Well, I'm not good enough to get into a four-year
school.'"

In high school in Modesto, Calif., Jennica had set her sights
on UC Santa Cruz but learned that it was beyond her reach financially. She saw herself as a classic victim of "middle-class squeeze."
Both of her parents worked: her father as a high school science
teacher and her mother "in computers" for the telephone company. They didn't earn enough to pay for her schooling, she said, but

336

made too much for her to qualify for financial aid. Even attending a community college where tuition and fees are less than a quarter of those charged at public four-year institutions, she was working 35 hours a week at a local art supply store to make ends meet. "I eat a lot of peanut butter sandwiches," she said with a smile.

She reluctantly enrolled at San Diego City College, but what she found there surprised her. "You get more one-on-one attention in small classes," she said. "I think I would feel overwhelmed if I had to walk into a class with 300 students." She developed relationships with several teachers in her major, which was art. One of her favorite teachers was Wayne Hulgin, her instructor in painting, drawing and art history. "I'm not only their teacher," he said. "I'm also a mentor, a best friend, a counselor—many things besides an educator."

Instructors like Hulgin are not unusual, according to Shulock. "The faculty at community colleges are teaching faculty," she said, so unlike many university professors, "they don't have split loyalties to their research and teaching. Not that they aren't scholars and not that they may not do research, but they're not there to be researchers. They're there to teach."

McClenney compared community colleges to small liberal arts colleges. "Typically, you're going to find those smaller class sizes and courses that are taught by faculty members and not graduate assistants. Typically you're going to find that there's a higher degree of personalization at community colleges." At the same time, community colleges have a well-deserved reputation for scheduling classes at times and in places that are convenient to students—such as evening classes off campus—even if that inconveniences the instructors.

Figuring it out

Reshma Tharami may represent a new breed of community college student: savvy about her future, knowledgeable about the ways of the system and determined to save money on her education. Ms. Tharami graduated from New York University in May

2008 with a degree in early education, fully qualified to teach special education or any of the elementary grades. NYU is one of the nation's most expensive colleges (tuition, registration, room and board approach $50,000 a year), but she left owing only "a few" thousand dollars in student loans.

Her secret? Two years at Nassau Community College on Long Island, where she took all her required courses. Instead of paying $50,000 a year, Ms. Tharami lived at home and paid less than $2,000 per semester.

"I knew I would be going to a four-year college," she said. "But I wasn't sure which one, so I decided to go to community college and take care of my prerequisites and get my first degree."

She took some classes in the summers and during her winter breaks to complete her requirements and took "some psychology and math classes I was really interested in," she said. She worked part time at several jobs, including a stint as a telemarketer. Ms. Tharami's parents came to the United States from India about 40 years ago. They met and married here and opened a wholesale clothing business. Her younger brother enrolled at Boston College.

Shulock said that Ms. Tharami fits the description of more and more community college students. "As the tuition has been going up more steeply in four-year institutions, community colleges are an increasingly attractive alternative for savvy kids who want to save money."

These students, she said, "know what they need, know how to get it and don't need a lot of the student services that community colleges are struggling to provide students. They can get through in two or three years and transfer."

Ms. Tharami made it work. She saw an academic counselor regularly. ("There were lines, but I always managed to see the same woman.") She took only courses that her Nassau counselor said NYU would accept for credit, but, just to be sure, she double-checked with a counselor at NYU. NYU offers the Community

College Transfer Opportunity Program, which makes transferring easier for students at 13 area community colleges, including Nassau.

Other universities have similar programs. The University of Florida's Transfer Opportunity Program and Services (TOPS), for instance, seeks to increase the enrollment of African-American students from six urban high schools, by offering qualified applicants who go on to attend a Florida community college the opportunity to work directly with a UF advisor for all four years of their college education (including those spent at the community college); the program also offers scholarships.

Doing well academically at Nassau made Ms. Tharami an especially attractive candidate. Her overall 3.6 GPA meant graduating *cum laude* and an invitation to join Phi Theta Kappa, the community college honor society. In her second year at Nassau, a favorite professor suggested that she apply for a scholarship for prospective elementary school teachers. She won that award, worth $20,000 a year for her junior and senior years at NYU.

A number of prestigious private institutions like NYU seem to encourage community college transfers. Richard Shaw, the dean of admission and financial aid at Stanford, said that community college transfers are "attractive and interesting" often non-traditional candidates who have "stopped out" or raised families. While "Stanford does not have a formal agreement with community colleges the way many public universities do," according to Shaw, he recalled that when he was admissions director at Yale, community college transfer applicants "got first priority," adding that Yale accepts only about 25 new students into its junior class each year.

Amherst College is aggressive about recruiting community college transfer students, according to Thomas Parker, dean of admissions and financial aid. He cited the Jack Kent Cooke Foundation's program that provides scholarships worth up to $30,000 a year to deserving community college transfer students. The foundation also made sizable grants to colleges ($585,000 to Amherst) to enable them to reach out to high-achieving community college students. Other colleges and universities participating in this program are Cornell, UC Berkeley, Mount Holyoke, Bucknell, the University of Southern California, University of Michigan at Ann Arbor, and University of North Carolina at Chapel Hill.

Stanford's Mr. Shaw also served as associate director of admissions and records at UC Berkeley from 1983 to 1988. "We had an articulation agreement with community colleges, which basically means that we accept the candidate's credits if we accept the candidate," he said.

Changing careers

"I've been medicating people for 26 years, and now I'll finally get to do it the right way," Brian Bullas told me with a grin in 2007. He was behind the bar at the Marine Room, the exclusive La Jolla restaurant where he'd been mixing drinks for the past 21 years.

Today Mr. Bullas, now in his mid-50s and a 2007 graduate of SDCC's nursing education program, is practicing as an RN at Scripps Memorial Hospital in San Diego. And graduates like him are in great demand, because California—like most states—desperately needs nurses. U.S. hospitals have more than 135,000 vacant nursing positions now, according to the American Association of the Colleges of Nursing. This shortage of registered nurses is predicted to increase to 260,000 by 2025, according to Peter Buerhaus. (And California alone currently faces a shortage of over 30,000 nurses, if current employment levels and nurse-to-patient ratios are not considered adequate, according to a September 2009 forecast of the state's registered nurse work force conducted for the California Board of Registered Nursing).[330]

One reason the college-educated Mr. Bullas wanted a new career involved his family, particularly his teenage son Ryan. "When my little boy was young, I enjoyed having days off to be with him, but now that he's in school, I want to be home at night when he needs me."

From his vantage point behind the bar in 2007, Mr. Bullas looked out during our interview through floor-to-ceiling windows over the Pacific Ocean. "I probably see 300 sunsets a year out these windows. This is the best view in San Diego, better than any doctor's or lawyer's office," he said. But the genial Mr. Bullas didn't see much future in bartending. "Bartending has been great to me, but as good as it's been, it's been a pretty stagnant job," he told me at the time. "I think I can give more to myself and to my family and to society by trying a new career that I think I'm going to be good at."

AACC's George Boggs wrote in a March 2010 e-mail that his best "guesstimate" is that about 35 percent of all community college students are enrolled in hopes of making a career change. "I suspect that it varies widely by region and by college," he said. "For example, I suspect that the number is very high in Michigan right now. It also varies by the economic cycle. Since unemployment is so high right now, and community college enrollments are surging (up 17% in two years across the country), I expect the number of students preparing for career change is near an all-time high."

Dave Rynders worked as a carpenter and builder all his adult life. It's a trade he began learning when he was just 12, working with his father. But at age 30, after a serious back injury, he was ready for a career change. Like Brian, he decided to study nursing. "I think it's going to be the greatest, to put down the hammer, take out the stethoscope and start helping people," he said. "I honestly can't wait."

More than 1,000 of our country's community colleges train 60 percent of U.S. nurses that enter the profession, and yet Mr. Bullas said he felt like he "won the lottery" when he learned that he would be able to begin nursing classes at his local community college. In a sense, he did get lucky: Three out of every four successful applicants to the nursing program were *immediately* put on the waiting list at the time. More recently, according to SDCC's dean of student development and matriculation Julianna Barnes, every qualified applicant to the nursing program was immediately put on the waitlist through January 6, 2010; the waitlist closed on January 6, 2010, and a new application procedure using a multi-criteria screening process is now in place. Nationally, the application acceptance rate for nursing programs was just 45 percent in 2007, when Mr. Rynders was applying. "They're qualified, we tell them

341

they're qualified, but then they have to go off and flip burgers or tend bar or do whatever, until their number comes up," said Terry Burgess, president of San Diego City College.

But Mr. Rynders did not "win the lottery." Even though he'd already begun taking his nursing prerequisites, he was placed on the waiting list where, he was told, he might remain for at least a year. "My two-year nursing education is going to take me about six years to complete," he said with a sigh. "With all my prereqs, and then my waiting period, and then finally the so-called accelerated two-year nursing program, ah, it's kind of ridiculous."

Too many qualified applicants and not enough room: That's a problem in many nursing programs, according to Mr. Burgess. "It's not uncommon up and down the state to have wait lists that go two and three years out." He added wryly, "We refer to it as our 'five-year-plan.'"

Mr. Burgess said at the time that he could not offer more nursing classes because they are a losing proposition. Classes must be small—by law, a faculty member must not supervise more than 10 students in a hospital setting in California—and expensive equipment is required for student clinical practice (long-lasting equipment, as well as disposables like IV fluids, needles and tubing); in other words, nursing classes cost about three times as much as a regular "chalk and talk" class. But, Mr. Burgess noted in 2007: "The state pays us for what I like to refer to as 'butts in the seats.' We're paid literally by the contact hours and reimbursed at the same rate. So I could have a psychology lecture with one professor and 100 or 150 students or I could have a nursing clinical with 10 students and one professor, and the state reimburses me the same rate." Losing money on nursing and trying to make it up on large classes is a catch-22, Mr. Burgess said, particularly when the state needs nurses.

"We have not increased enrollment in the nursing program, since 2007, but we have not decreased enrollment either," Ms. Barnes added in a March 2010 e-mail. "Many classes and student services at City College have had to be cut with the decrease in funding but Nursing has been allowed to maintain their enrollment showing City's commitment to Nursing and Health Care in California."

As a nursing student, Mr. Bullas said the solution is obvious, a "no-brainer": "The problem isn't going to fix itself, so the population is growing and we need more nurses. They are going to have to come up with the money, and if that means cutting something else out, then so be it."

But Mr. Bullas wasn't arguing for raising tuition when I spoke with him, although the low cost was not the only reason he chose to attend a community college. "It's the fastest way to get to be a nurse, and I already have a degree from a four-year university, from many years ago."

He's a typical career-changer in a couple of ways: juggling responsibilities, trying to give 100 percent to several aspects of his life. In a typical week, he told me in 2007, "I spend eight hours two days a week at the hospital clinic and two days in the classroom on campus. I work four or five nights, seven to eight hours a night, at the Marine Room. I have a couple of days where I carpool kids to school, do the shopping and help out with homework when I can with my son."

He told me that he couldn't make this work without his wife Claire, whom he called "a saint." "She works full time managing a health club, and if it wasn't for her, I couldn't be doing what I'm doing," he said in 2007. "She has a good but stressful job that pays well, which makes it a lot easier for us." He laughed. "I do keep in contact with her to let her know where I am and what I'm doing."

Flexibility is essential, he added. "They let you know that you should have a book in your car at all times," he said. "There's times where I've studied in a parking lot, waiting for Ryan to get done with baseball or basketball or water polo. There's times at work when I'll read and take notes in the bar, when it's slow."

Community college leaders pride themselves on their ability to respond to the needs of career-changers and employers alike. Christine Johnson, then president of the Community College of Denver, told us that she met regularly with local business leaders. "Some industries are laying off workers, while others are hiring and even giving signing bonuses," she noted in 2007, "but then people need training for the new jobs." Both those in need of training and the needy employers often turn to community colleges. When the airline industry laid off lots of workers in the Denver area, she recalled, many might have remained unemployed and added to the city's budget woes, but two other occupations—nursing and industrial security—were desperate to hire qualified people. Her community college set up or ramped up programs for both, she said.

Training workers—many of whom, like Brian Bullas, are changing careers—is the community college's most important function, according to economist Jack Kyser. "The economy would grind to a halt without them," he said.

Dave Rynders acknowledged during our interview that he would not have the opportunity to contribute for some time. But his day would come, he noted with a wry laugh. "Eventually I'll see all the legislators; me or someone like me will see these legislators in my hospital. And then I can tell them what I think as they're receiving low-level care because they didn't fund the programs."

I've since received good news about Mr. Rynders. He is now completing his final requirements for SDCC's nursing program and is scheduled to graduate this year. And what's more, he's class president!

As for Mr. Bullas, he's living his dreams of practicing as an RN. "We're taught that the doctors are our peers, but the bottom line is, when you go into that room, the nurse is the one responsible," he told me in 2007. "When I go in there for the first time on my own, I know I'm going to have support, but I also know that the patient's life is in my hands, and I also want to be sure that I've done my homework."

Border crossing

Personal attention, small classes, convenience and low tuition—what's not to like? Here's one thing: Millions of community college students enroll with the hope and expectation that they will transfer to a four-year institution. But few do. Thomas Bailey, a professor of economics and education and director of the Community College Research Center at Teachers College, Columbia University, said that only about 18 percent of students (tracked in a NELS study that followed them starting in eighth grade in 1988) who started in community colleges, and went on to earn a bachelor's degree after eight years, managed to transfer after six years at a community college; an additional 11 percent transferred but did not earn a degree. The number is somewhat higher in California.

Shulock said this may be the case because many students in California already have been admitted to state colleges and universities and are at a community college to save money.

There are significant obstacles to transferring. Kirst blamed what he called the "mission creep" of the 1970s, when community colleges became market driven. Most were run on a shoestring, receiving about half of what their state provides to four-year institutions, and so "they offered whatever would bring in money" and that meant "adult-education enrichment classes." Kirst recalled former California governor Jerry Brown's devastating comment: "Johnny can't read, and Mom is studying macramé at the community college."

Today many community colleges can't afford to offer enough of the classes that would-be transfer students need, as Jennica discovered. "I wanted to take art history because that's my major, but I couldn't get in. So I took humanities instead. So I had two semesters of humanities that don't really count for anything, but they're there." Matters got desperate one particular semester, she recalled. "I found myself taking the same classes, just the second semester of them. And if I didn't like the first semester, why would I like the second semester?"

An equally serious problem is a shortage of counselors and advisors on community college campuses to help students negotiate the path to the four-year college or university. At SDCC the ratio is over 1,500 students per full-time counselor. "If every student wanted an hour of advising," SDCC counselor Edwin Heil told me in 2007 with a wry smile, "we'd never go home."

"I don't think that sort of ratio is an anomaly," added McClenney. That's a great concern, she said, because "students tell us year after year that the most important service is academic planning and advising."

The road map that good counseling provides is especially important to students who are the first in their families to attend college. "We have students who really don't know why they're here," said Shulock. "That is not to say that they shouldn't be there and couldn't succeed, but they need help in figuring out why they're there, what options are open for them, laying out a clear pathway for them to follow."

Like many community colleges, SDCC has a number of part-time counselors, some of whom also counsel students at other colleges. Said Anne Marthis (now Anne Nelson), who was working at four campuses at the time: "Policies here are different from other community colleges, four-year colleges may have different rules too, and it's easy to get confused. Sometimes I get confused myself." (Today there are 11 full-time counselors and five part-timers at SDCC).

When confusion reigns, students pay the price, as Jennica discovered when she went to see an advisor. "I went in there and picked out classes, and I asked them, 'Are they transferable?' And they told me they were." But when she began filling out forms for transferring, she discovered that she was "two classes short because classes they said were transferable to a UC campus were only transferable to state colleges." In addition to losing time, she said, "that's money out of my pocket that I lost on textbooks and the credits themselves."

In the end, she persevered. Despite spending more than she planned, taking some unnecessary courses and staying a semester longer than she had intended, she transferred to UC Santa Cruz in January 2007. And she was grateful to SDCC. "I don't know where I would be without it," she said. "Maybe in the military."

To better assist students, said Barnes, "We have embarked upon many in-service trainings/workshops for both full-time and part-time counselors over the years to facilitate professional growth and knowledge of counseling-specific subject matter."

The dismal transfer rates are now improving, but not because community colleges are doing a better job. The reason behind the increase is simple: Increasing numbers of college-qualified students are saving money by spending their first two years at a community college and then transferring. Reasonably savvy when they enroll, they don't need the counseling and advising; they go about their business, save thousands and transfer.

So graduation and transfer rates improve, and everybody's happy—except perhaps the less-qualified students, who are being pushed to the back of the line.

What should be done?

Based on what we saw over the two years we spent making our documentary, I have five recommendations for community colleges:

1. Create a public relations campaign based on the quiz I used to begin this essay to let the world, especially high school students and their parents, know about the accomplishments of community college graduates.
2. Give placement tests in the 11th (and possibly the 10th) grade to let students know that, despite open admissions and their commitment to help all students succeed, community colleges have standards.
3. Make remediation "Job One," as Kay McClenney said. That means teaching basic skills in a career context wherever possible instead of making remedial classes separate and distinct. It also means getting the best teachers involved, making skills the constant and time the variable, and giving students incentives and opportunities to "test out" early and often.
4. Make transfer "Job Two," ensuring that students have the help and encouragement they need to navigate the tricky terrain between two- and four-year colleges.

John Merrow

5. Make a concerted effort to connect with students, instead
of creating a distance. As Willy Loman's wife, Linda, says in
"Death of a Salesman," "Attention must be paid." The kinds
of at-risk students who turn to community colleges especially
need to know that they matter. Caring is not enough to get
students over the many hurdles they face, but when they know
that someone will try to move mountains for them, they're
much less likely to just disappear.

It's easy to identify the shortcomings of community colleges;
too many failures in remediation and not enough successful transfers are two of the most obvious. A graduation/completion rate
below 50 percent means that the famous "open door" is for many
a revolving door. There are other flaws, as well: Many community
colleges fail to connect with local high schools, and others waste
time and resources on trivial courses like "Great Western Movies,"
"Significant Conversations" and "Understanding Tennis."

But let's maintain perspective. Most community colleges
are shamefully underfunded. They're higher education's second
cousins, slighted by nearly everyone, including former secretary of
education Margaret Spellings. Her Commission on the Future of
Higher Education included just one community college represen-
tative among the 19 members.

When President Obama's education secretary, Arne Duncan,
selected community college president Martha Kanter to be his
number-two person in the department, it sent a strong message
throughout higher education: Community colleges matter!

Community colleges offer many students what may be their
only shot at the brass ring. Perhaps the best way to see that is to
attend a graduation. In spring 2007, I spoke at the graduation ceremonies at Paul Smith's College in upstate New York. At least half
the graduates received two-year degrees, and they all seemed to
have a sizeable posse with them. The joy was palpable and wonderful to behold. I learned that most of the graduates were first in
their family to attend college and, because their tuition was low,
chances were good that they were not weighted down with debt.

For them, the American Dream is now closer to reality, and a
community college made it all possible.

Chapter 36
GRADUATION SYMBOLS

The long line of college graduates grows longer. In 2006-2007, about 1.5 million men and women received college diplomas, a number expected to be higher at the close of 2010. It's a vast, anonymous sea in which individuals are virtually indistinguishable. Who among us hasn't searched for the one graduate we came to applaud, only to be frustrated by an endless sea of flowing robes?

The long (normally black) gown worn by today's graduating seniors dates back to the 12th or 13th century and is the mark of a cleric. Medieval buildings were unheated, and scholars may have worn those long gowns to keep warm. Unadorned by tradition, the gowns produced an unintended effect: One graduate looks like every other. (Colors, signifying fields of study, are generally reserved for advanced degrees: red for theology, gold for science, green for medicine and white for arts and letters.)

It's unfortunate that graduates are virtually indistinguishable as they march, because the educations they have received are vastly different. I have a proposal that would make their educational experiences more transparent. After spending a good part of three years immersed in higher education while working on a documentary, I am convinced that anonymity is no longer appropriate. Instead, those black gowns should provide clear messages about the degree the student is about to be handed, by affixing one of three symbols: a smiley face, a ball and chain, or a life jacket.

About one-third of graduation gowns should be adorned with large yellow smiley faces to signify that the graduates have gotten financial aid they probably did not need. "Merit aid"—basically free money to students who may not need it, but who receive it based on previous academic performance—has increased dramatically in the last decade. States and institutions now give out $13 billion[331] a year, and nobody knows how much more comes from other organizations like the local Lions Clubs, churches and so forth.

Colleges aggressively recruit students who've done well enough on the PSAT to qualify as National Merit Finalists and Semifinalists, often offering full scholarships. While the National Merit Scholarship Program and the College Board won't release information about the economic status of students earning the designation, it's a good bet that the majority of the 259 National Merit winners "persuaded" to attend the University of Florida in 2005, for example, could have paid their own way, because standardized test scores are highly correlated with family income.

Kara Monsen of Washington state, for example, ended up enrolling at the University of Arizona in Tucson—an institution she'd never even thought of applying to until she got their letter offering a scholarship. She accepted an invitation to visit the campus, and, only after the university offered her a four-year scholarship worth $78,000, did she apply for admission. Her family could have paid for her education, she said. Arizona offers merit aid, said Director of Strategic Initiatives Lori Goldman, because "we're competing for a student that's just above a level of student that we don't have." She added, "If we had a whole class of applicants that looked like Harvard's, we probably wouldn't offer merit aid."

"Merit aid" is not the only term used to describe the sea change in financial aid. Pat Callan, president of the National Center for Public Policy and Higher Education, supplied the options: "One could use the jargon and call it enrollment management, or one could call it incentives, to use the neutral word." He paused and laughed. "Or one could use the most indelicate expression and call it a bribe."

So, 450,000 smiley faces on the graduation robes of seniors who, Callan said, had received merit aid, a number that seems certain to increase because merit aid is politically popular.

Many more graduation gowns should carry a "ball and chain" logo, signifying that these graduates are leaving owing big bucks.

The price of college is rising because public support is declining, and colleges have to get the money somewhere. The natural place to look is, of course, to students and their families. When Kentucky's legislature cut its per-student appropriation, Western Kentucky University in Bowling Green raised tuition to balance the budget. Tuition increases meant that students like Ceylon Hollis, a 20-year-old sophomore at the time, had to work more hours. Which she did: as many as 48 hours a week on the night shift, assembling auto filters.[332]

Western Kentucky's president, Gary Ransdell, acknowledged that students like Ceylon were in a no-win situation. "If they work and earn some money, they may not qualify for federal financial aid. If they don't work, they do qualify for the financial aid, but that's not quite enough money." What's more, Ransdell added, all that work means they don't really experience college. By working, they miss out on the extracurricular and social activities that enrich the college experience. Four years ago, the average senior graduating from Western Kentucky owed $10,000; today, it's around $20,000, which is about the national average.[333] And that number keeps growing.

Lara Couturier of the Futures Project at Brown University worries about this trend. "We're moving toward a system where the only people who will have access to a college education are those who can pay for it," she said.

My third logo is a brilliant-orange life jacket. These should be embossed on the graduation robes of about 20 percent of those marching to receive diplomas. The life jacket signifies that they've basically wasted four years. Savvy observers of higher education say that one out of five students spends four years treading water (or alcohol?) all that time—and is now about to float out into the real world, diploma in hand.

The old notion that students will either sink or swim is outdated, because many students have discovered that they can get by with minimal effort. That is, they can tread water. These students are "maze smart," according to George Kuh. "Many students go to large universities to be anonymous," he said. They even choose majors that grade leniently, he added. "And they tend then to hang together, so you've got this mass of people sleepwalking through college."

Is it possible to get through college without much effort? "As much as I would like to say 'Absolutely not!' yes, it is possible," said Melissa Vito, vice president of student affairs at Arizona. "We have a lot of students whose motivation for coming here is to get a good job. They think, 'How do I get the grades?' instead of trying to learn."

Aiding and abetting the water-treaders are professors who don't ask much of their students. Richard Hersh, a former college president, describes a "non-aggression pact" that exists in some classrooms. "It's an unspoken agreement," Hersh told me, "in which the professor doesn't expect much from students as long as he gets to do his research, and students don't ask any questions as long as they get decent grades."[334]

Kuh calls this higher education's dirty little secret. "If you want to point to a tragedy in American higher education, it's that these folks are getting through college and being handed the same degree other students have."

If George Kuh is correct, then life jacket decals belong on about 270,000 graduation robes.

There is some good news: Universities are fighting back, by giving "swimming lessons." The University of Arizona, for example, outraged traditionalists when it dug a hole in the middle of campus to create a multimillion-dollar "Integrated Learning Center," where freshmen could get advice and tutoring, go online and just hang out. The logic is appealing: Help students develop academic habits, and they just might get something out of their time on campus.

And institutions often wrap their arms around students to increase their chances of succeeding. Western Kentucky and other institutions establish what are called "Living Learning communities," in which freshmen share a dorm, attend the same classes, study together and often share an academic advisor. The goal, according to Nathan Phelps of Western Kentucky (which has about 20,000 students) is to bring the large institution down to size, to make it small. "We're creating a sense of family," he told me.

Come to think of it, there's a fourth logo. This belongs on the robes of graduates who benefited because the adults in charge did their part to fulfill the promise of higher education. These students found their way to brilliant professors; did not have to work 25 hours a week and thus had time to explore new ideas; and were focused enough to resist the temptations created by low academic standards, easy availability of alcohol and other drugs, and the anti-intellectualism that dominates many campuses.

But what logo is appropriate for these fortunate graduates? Clasped hands representing gratitude that their prayers have been answered, or a pair of dice, representing just how fortunate they are?

Chapter 37
"FOUR MORE YEARS"335

"Four more years" is chanted across the country when an incumbent president runs for re-election. The phrase takes on a chilling new meaning, however, when delivered by a recent college graduate. It's what my daughter Kelsey said to me just one year after graduating from college; I told her I didn't understand.

"Four more years," she repeated. "I need to go to college all over again."

"Don't you mean graduate school?" I asked hopefully.

"No," she said. "I need to start over. I want to be a singer. I should have majored in music."

Some background is in order here. Kelsey had recently graduated in theater arts from Brown University, spent semesters in theater programs in London and New London, Conn., and interned in Williamstown, Mass., in the summers. Several professors at Brown had encouraged her to study music. "Develop that instrument," one strongly advised, after discovering her remarkably pure three-octave range. But Kelsey had chosen to stick with theater.

After the shock of Kelsey's declaration wore off, I asked two professional singers for advice. Both suggested she take voice lessons and study on her own. I passed that idea along, but Kelsey insisted that she wanted to learn to read, write and arrange music, and to do that she needed to take classes. "I don't want to be someone who just sings whatever's put in front of her," she said.

As far as financial support, I told her she should consider me a "one-term parent." But that didn't dissuade her. She researched New York area music schools and applied to the one reputed to have the best vocal jazz program. When the New School University (annual cost at the time: $23,000) accepted her, she was ecstatic. She visited the financial aid office, told them she was on her own and asked for help. That night at dinner she was beaming. "They've offered me a $13,000 package."

"How much in grants and how much in loans?" I asked gently. It turned out that most was in loans. Suddenly, the meal I'd prepared didn't taste so good.

Things took a turn for the worse. Having already graduated from college, she was not eligible for a federal Pell grant. She would have to pay back just about every dollar in the "aid" package, and borrow more. "Four more years" was going to cost over 100,000 more dollars—a large sum for anyone and a staggering amount for an aspiring singer.

But Kelsey was determined. She spent the summer tutoring, babysitting, braiding manes at horse shows and substitute teaching. She cared for her cousin's baby in exchange for a place to live, her introduction to the barter economy. In any spare time she could find, Kelsey pulled musicians together to rehearse and then perform in any venue that would have them. By the start of her "re-freshman year," in September 2002, she was singing regularly and knew what she was in school for. "Dad, this is the best thing I've ever done," she enthused.

At my college reunion that spring, friends were sympathetic. "Remember how we used to beat ourselves up for not paying attention in college?" they asked. "We wished we could go back again. Your daughter's actually doing it!"

Fortunately, I've never found myself saying to Kelsey, "Why didn't you...when you had the chance?" Like almost everyone who's gone to college, I have plenty of regrets about opportunities I missed.

Kelsey is the cutting edge of a trend, a statistically inclined friend told me. "Many college students take six to eight years to finish their four years," he said, "so she's just pushing the envelope."

Another friend observed that only about half of all students who start college actually earn diplomas. "Your daughter's going to do it twice and improve the national average," he said.

Soon Kelsey had dark circles under her eyes, because her new study/rehearse/perform/go-to-class routine left little time for sleep. The summer before her second freshman year, she knew six songs. Eighteen months later, she could read, write and arrange music, and her extensive repertoire included many jazz standards that my parents had grown up with. She and her group recorded a CD and then she hand-delivered copies to about 100 clubs and restaurants, in search of gigs.

It was exciting to watch Kelsey become a professional, developing a stage presence that now soars over conversations, bustling waiters and other distractions. She's also developing a thick skin—the requisite armor for performing in public. Although I had my doubts in the beginning, I've come to admire my daughter for having the courage to go down a difficult path to achieve her dream. No doubt, the fact that she'll end up paying for most of the trip herself made every moment all the more valuable.

Her quintet performs regularly now, has cut several CDs of jazz standards with Kelsey's unique spin and (thanks to her brother) has a great website[336] where you can see her schedule and hear a few songs.

She's hardly cavalier about what she managed to do. "I wish I had known at Brown that I could get so much out of a college experience," she told me. "If I had only known from the start what I was there for...but I didn't."

One night, I discovered that Kelsey Gillette Merrow had transformed into Kelsey Jillette. "Everyone kept spelling it 'Marrow,'" she explained, "and pronouncing 'Gillette' with a hard 'G.' They get it right when they see the 'J.'"

She never changed her tune about her need for those "four more years," though. She graduated in 2008, skilled, happy and flat broke (about $50,000 in debt, in fact). In September of that same year, she married another talented musician, Tom Abbott, whom she might never have met if she'd stayed on a more traditional track. They're living in Brooklyn now, working hard and enjoying the life they've chosen.

Incidentally, if you go to hear Kelsey perform some night (and I hope you will), that is *not* a "tip jar" on the piano. It's a "tuition loan repayment jar" for Kelsey Jillette. Please give "jenerously."

Conclusion
A "12-STEP PROGRAM" TO FIX AMERICAN EDUCATION

In this book I have argued that it is necessary to "think outside the box." I have tried to provide examples of men, women, children and schools doing just that. I hope I have persuaded you that age segregation is counterproductive and that educators ought to be held to at least the same standards as swimming coaches and music teachers.

Critics of public education often disparage schools, calling them factories—grim places in which students are mere objects moving along an assembly line, as teachers attempt to pour knowledge into them—but I believe we'd be better off if schools were *more* like modern factories.

This familiar "school as factory" metaphor assumes that factories are the antithesis of quality. However, in many cases, the opposite is true, and public schools could do far worse than emulate today's most modern factories, which are efficient, clean, productive and accountable for outcomes.

Productivity, a fair measure of efficiency among American workers, is higher than it's ever been. Yet studies of schools reveal that only about 60 percent of the school day is devoted to actual instruction. Industry has discovered that workers in a clean, safe, modern factory are more productive. But the average public school is about 45 years old, and most were built either before World War II or immediately thereafter. A 2001 study by the National Education Association estimated that it would cost $268 billion to repair our schools. It put the price tag for New York State alone at $51 billion.

Modern factories stress accuracy. For example, Motorola rejects products that deviate as little as .00001 from specifications.

John Merrow

Schools have trouble measuring student progress accurately and have a long history of promoting students based on their age and "seat time," instead of academic accomplishments.

Unlike schools, modern factories stress teamwork. Employees are trained in team-building, because cooperation isn't taught in school. As everyone remembers, when students "cooperate" in class, they're cheating. Teachers rarely cooperate. They generally work alone, isolated from other adults; and their teaching is almost never seen by their peers, despite convincing evidence in both the MetLife and the Scholastic/Gates Foundation surveys (cited earlier) that collaboration is something most teachers desperately want.

Efficient modern factories practice accountability. When a team member spots a problem, he or she must take action, and team members hold each other accountable. The goal is a failure rate of zero. By contrast, teachers and administrators are rarely held accountable. In a practice known cynically as "passing the trash," some teachers pass failing students, secure in the knowledge that they will be some other teacher's problem next year.

Here's another difference: Factories actually make things, but many schools can't make that claim. Instead, they're more like old-fashioned egg-grading plants: places that exist to sort, classify and reject, but without taking responsibility for the rejects.

Our old-fashioned schools looked and acted that way by design. They were set up to sort children into "winners" and "losers" at a time when an industrial-age economy needed an efficient way of differentiating between those who would dig ditches or work in the fields and those who would get to sit behind desks and give orders. The sorting continues, with standardized tests intended to make the decisions appear to be "objective."

However, our 21st-century economy cannot afford "winners" and "losers." It needs an ever-increasing number of workers who can access and process information, work in teams, communicate easily with others and learn new skills. Unfortunately, the ongoing national effort to raise educational standards focuses largely on test scores, not on these necessary skills.

That's why the shortest route to better schools would be to emulate the modern factory, but with two key differences.

Factories use the same materials and the same processes to produce identical, interchangeable parts, because the aim of the modern factory is uniformity. Of course, that's not what we want for our children. Instead, schools should emulate the modern factory's reliance on clear standards and its low tolerance for failure—but not its concern for uniformity.

What's being produced? I think schools must be "knowledge factories," in which students are the workers, and knowledge is the factory's product. Students would be actively learning and constantly evaluating their work with the help and supervision of teachers, the "factory foremen." The job of the supervisors is to see that each worker achieves to the best of his or her ability and to maximize the factory's output.

Like modern factories, schools should be held responsible for outcomes, and that requires clear goals and standards. When a chip production plant fails to achieve its goals, it doesn't blame the chips. It doesn't run for more hours or more days, the way some education reformers push for more schooling. Instead, the factory examines its own procedures and makes necessary corrections.

Our economy can no longer afford schools that pick winners and losers. What we need is to produce highly educated, well-rounded students based on the standards and approaches used by modern factories.

The growing national or common standards[337] movement shows great promise, but I worry that those who develop them do not get that today's young people operate in a different world, one in which collaboration is second nature. They are used to change, speed, innovation and freedom. The emerging standards will, I hope, stress the verities—reading, writing clearly, computation—but also include data-gathering and assessment, as well as the ability to communicate with others and to work with a diverse group.

In the preface to this book, I asked whether schools were obsolete. I think that's a possibility, unless we think outside the box.

Schools aren't just for safety, custodial care, basic skills and socialization.

We know they aren't the only place to go for knowledge because today knowledge is everywhere, thanks to technology and the Internet. So why should kids go to school?

Children used to go to school to socialize and be socialized, but today there's even an app for that. Kids have Facebook, FarmVille, MySpace, Twitter and other powerful social media, so why should kids go to school?

In the future (just like today) effective schools will teach kids how to evaluate knowledge, how to separate the wheat from the chaff—and how to choose the wheat. Yes, schools must teach values!

To reiterate an important point, the effective teacher will be like a music conductor, but the music isn't classical. It's jazz, full of riffs and tangents, changing from performance to performance. Teaching will be tougher but infinitely more rewarding in such schools, if we are smart enough to build them.

I don't want anyone finishing this book thinking that I am against testing. Testing is not evil, not even a necessary evil. A primary purpose of school is academic learning, and we must know whether, and how much, students are learning. Well-made tests are an excellent way to measure learning and detect weaknesses. Excellent teachers create good tests, grade them carefully and get them back to their students in a matter of days.

Excellence in testing and assessment begins with *transparency*, that is, the policy is open for inspection by all who are interested. It is understandable and defensible. It is connected to the curriculum and the goals of the school.

Excellent teachers have such policies. They explain in advance to students just what is expected, how they will be assessed and why.

Excellent schools do not attempt to evaluate, promote or hold back students on the basis of a single test, particularly a machine-scored multiple-choice exam. That is, they reject high-stakes testing insofar as it is possible.

I believe that teacher-made tests, constructed by excellent teachers, remain the best means of assessing student progress and weakness. Holding schools or (especially) students accountable almost solely on the basis of student scores on machine-scored tests establishes a "whips and chains" system. When we do that, we're using tests as a weapon, nothing more.

And we are either forgetting or ignoring the wisdom of social scientist Donald Campbell, expressed in what is known as Campbell's Law: "The more any quantitative social indicator is used for social decision-making, the more subject it will be to corruption pressures and the more apt it will be to distort and corrupt the social processes it is intended to monitor." Pay attention to those verbs "distort" and "corrupt," because that's been happening, perhaps under your very nose. Stories of surprising jumps in test scores come first, and later we learn that answer sheets had a "surprising" number of erasures. The news dribbles out: Adults gave students some extra (illegal) help, the rise is illusory and public confidence is further weakened.

The common defense of high-stakes tests goes something like this: "We give students many chances to take the test." That's true, of course. Some states let students take the graduation exam as early as 10th grade and let those who fail try again and again. But because these tests do not describe what the student doesn't know, and because most schools do not have the staff to provide diagnosis and treatment, this is akin to taking a sick person's temperature over and over again. OK, so we know he's got a fever. Now what? Multiple testing may actually be worse, because if the nurse tells me every hour that I'm running a temperature, it does not make my condition worse. Failing a test over and over, however, has to be harmful to one's health.

"Multiple opportunities" is basically the driver's test model. The Department of Motor Vehicles allows applicants for a license to take the test again and again. If you don't pass, try again. The machine that scores your test will tell you which questions you got wrong, allowing you to go look up the right answers before trying again. The logic—that it's your own fault if you continue to fail—is inescapable and perfectly reasonable.

This thinking is illogical in education, which should be holding teachers accountable for their teaching, just as students are expected to learn. If I am teaching algebra and none of my students can pass a test, I have failed just as much as they have—perhaps more. The logic behind "multiple opportunities" lets adults off the hook and puts the onus entirely on kids.

"Multiple opportunities" is flawed thinking in a different way. To give a diploma to a student who fails the high-stakes test eight or nine times before finally passing contradicts all that we know about test reliability.[338] If the test is at all reliable, then those multiple failures are a more accurate picture of that student's knowledge. Isn't awarding him a diploma in some way irresponsible?

As we proceed to develop sensible high academic standards for all kids, we need to rely on multiple *measures*, not provide multiple opportunities to be measured in the same way. We cannot do that unless we're willing to trust teachers. A more rational approach is a broad-based assessment consisting of teacher-made tests, teacher evaluations, student demonstrations and standardized, machine-scored tests—all over an extended period of time. We should also measure teacher attendance and retention, because they affect student learning. If some teachers aren't faithful about coming to school, or if many leave after a few months or years, then kids are not competing on a level playing field. Measuring can be the first step in the direction of change.

Relying on a *single* measure to determine whether students pass, get promoted, graduate or earn scholarships and other awards is bad policy. Providing "multiple opportunities" to take the *same* test is not a sensible substitute, just more bad policy.

To save our schools and our democracy, I recommend a 12-step program. I mean no disrespect to recovering addicts or to those who work with them. I intend the parallel as a compliment, and the analogy strikes me as apt. Public education and our democracy are in serious trouble, and recovery cannot begin until we admit we have a problem *and* resolve to solve it. Merely identifying what's wrong is not enough. Action is needed. Moreover, as in cases of addiction, "recovery" is an ongoing process, a journey rather than a destination.

The 12 steps as I see them are:

1. "Own the problem." That is, admit that our public schools are a major problem and then take responsibility for finding solutions. Reach out and involve more than the 20 to 30 percent or so of households with school-age children, because public education has a public purpose.
2. Debate the purposes of school, which means ongoing conversations and arguments about what we want for our children. Remember that "education" and "school" are not synonymous—not by a long shot.[339]
3. Stop obsessing about the "achievement gap" and face up to the fact that our society has multiple gaps in opportunity, expectations, affection and outcomes (not to mention gaps in access to health care and technology).
4. No Child Left Behind, founded on a premise that inadvertently encourages and rewards minimum performance, must be replaced with legislation whose premise is "Every Child Moving Ahead."[340]
5. Strengthen school leadership, which means taking power and money away from the upper echelons. It may also require a new brand of school leader, one not steeped only in education but possessing skills forged in the world beyond schools.
6. Improve the professional lives of teachers. This will require better training, professional working conditions, higher standards, a ban on out-of-field teaching and a revolution in teacher training. Once that is well underway, eliminate seniority privileges and reform tenure.
7. Embrace technology's vast potential. Young people may still go to a building called "school," but there is absolutely no excuse for not working with students and others all across the nation and the world. Sure, kids will go to websites that we don't want them to, but that means adults must be on their

toes. We can't ban the modern world and shouldn't try. And to create this future, as one report notes, "All aspects of brick-and-mortar schools should be on the block: schedules, school day, classroom structure, administration, counseling, parent involvement, co-curricular activities, school year, teacher compensation, tenure, community connections, curriculum, standards, assessment and even lunch."[341]

8.   Burst the "bubble test" bubble by spending decent money on good tests—all part of the move toward national standards.[342] And don't forget the Campbell's Law corollary: "Achievement tests may well be valuable indicators of general school achievement under conditions of normal teaching aimed at general competence. But when test scores become the goal of the teaching process, they both lose their value as indicators of educational status and distort the educational process in undesirable ways."[343]

9.   Elevate art, music, physical education and science in the curriculum.

10. Create high-quality, universal, free preschool for those 3- and 4-year-olds whose parents wish to enroll them.

11. Challenge the "seat time" approach to education. Make it possible for capable students to earn college credit while in high school, or even graduate early by passing demanding examinations to demonstrate their competence.[344] Eliminate retention and social promotion in the early grades by ending age segregation.

12. Practice democracy. It requires diligence and work, but the old saw "Use it or lose it" applies here.

ABOUT THE AUTHOR

John Merrow began his career as an education reporter with National Public Radio in 1974 with the weekly series, "Options in Education," for which he received the George Polk Award in 1982. He is currently president of Learning Matters. Since 1985, he has worked in public television as education correspondent for the "PBS NewsHour" and as host of his own documentaries. His work has been recognized with Peabody Awards in 2000 and 2006, Emmy nominations in 1984, 2005 and 2007, four CINE Golden Eagles and other reporting awards. A frequent contributor to USA Today, The New York Times, The Washington Post, the Los Angeles Times and Education Week, he is the author of "Choosing Excellence" (2001) and co-editor of "Declining by Degrees" (2005).

Merrow earned an A.B. from Dartmouth College, an M.A. in American Studies from Indiana University and a doctorate in education and social policy from the Harvard Graduate School of Education. He received the James L. Fisher Award for Distinguished Service to Education from the Council for the Advancement and Support of Education in 2000 and the HGSE Alumni Council Award for Outstanding Contributions to Education in 2006. He was a visiting scholar for many years at the Carnegie Foundation for the Advancement of Teaching and currently serves as a trustee of Teachers College, Columbia University.

He blogs regularly at Taking Note: Thoughts on Education.

Endnotes

1   The NPR series that grew out of that experience, "Juvenile Crime, Juvenile Justice," won the George Polk Award in 1982.

2   "Children in Mental Institutions" got my program thrown off the air in parts of Texas because of its harsh language, but it also caught the ear of Fred Rogers, who wrote me a complimentary letter about it. Fred and I became friends, and my children spent many hours in Mr. Rogers' neighborhood.

3   Albert Shanker of the American Federation of Teachers won these debates so convincingly that the National Education Association dropped out after three years.

4   Please don't be overly concerned if you come across occasional contradictions. This has been a journey of twists and turns. While I'm not Walt Whitman, "I am large. I contain multitudes," too.

5   It's a film noir parody, with me in the role of the down-on-his-luck detective. A beautiful blonde hires the Sleuth to find an excellent school. In the course of solving the case, the Sleuth gets roughed up by a thug hired by the status quo. (And he falls for the blonde, of course.) My long-time colleague John Tulenko did a brilliant job of producing and directing.

6   The National Commission on Excellence in Education, "An Open Letter to the American People," *A Nation at Risk: The Imperative for Educational Reform* (The National Commission on Excellence in Education, April 1983), http://www2.ed.gov/pubs/NatAtRisk/title.html.

7   The water imagery comes easily because I spent my adolescence on the water, lived on Nantucket for two years while writing my doctoral dissertation and now spend as much time as possible on Martha's Vineyard.

John Merrow

8   Perhaps the most important opportunity, and the one that's in shortest supply in most classrooms, is the *opportunity to fail* and then learn from that experience. Schools just don't get it, but that's how most genuine learning occurs. We are curious from birth, always experimenting and modifying our behavior based on what we learn by doing. I don't know why I put this in an endnote; it deserves an entire chapter!

9   A reliable source of information on ESEA and other federal education issues is the Center on Education Policy in Washington, D.C. www.cep-dc.org.

10   I remind readers again that an essential component of every opportunity to learn is the *opportunity to fail*, learn from that experience and try again.

11   Congress also rejected the Clinton administration's efforts to establish national testing.

12   The name ripped off the Children's Defense Fund's slogan: "Leave No Child Behind." However, CDF uses the active voice, implying its commitment to make sure that children are taken care of. The Bush administration adopted the passive voice, implying that it's someone else's responsibility.

13   In February 2010 Mitchell Chester, the Massachusetts commissioner of education, told an audience at Teachers College, Columbia University, that half of his state's schools would fail to make Adequate Yearly Progress under NCLB's rules. That's patently absurd, but it's the law. Massachusetts is, in effect, being punished for setting its own standards high.

14   Which happened this year in Rhode Island, incidentally, with support from President Obama and Secretary of Education Duncan—and outrage from the school and its teachers. The story is still unfolding—stay tuned.

15   NCLB lets states set their own standards, decide on their own rate of progress toward that "100 percent by 2014" goal, choose their own tests, set passing scores, and even change the passing scores in midstream. These little-known and rarely discussed "loopholes" are buried in the fine print of the law. Using sports analogies from track and field, our News-

Hour report, "Gaming the System," explained four statistical techniques that allow schools to artificially boost performance and avoid federal penalties for low achievement. By taking advantage of these (perfectly legal) loopholes, states can add points to a school's score, thereby converting a failing performance into an apparent success. It aired August 14, 2007. You can view it at www.learningmatters.tv under its new name: "No Child Left Behind: Part 1—The Race."

16 President George W. Bush famously asked, "Is our children learning?" Bad grammar, worse question.

17 I am indebted to Tony Wagner for reminding me of Einstein's observation. See Wagner's "The Global Achievement Gap," (New York: Basic Books, 2008).

18 Will the federal government's Race to the Top make an appreciable difference? To its credit, the Obama administration is trying to change the rules by making states compete for dollars ($4.35 billion of them). It's also running competitions to create common standards and develop better tests.

19 In the 2009 PDK/Gallup Poll, 74 percent of respondents gave their oldest child's school an A or B, which is the same percentage that gave a C or D to public schools nationally. William J. Bushaw and John A. McNee, "The 41st Annual Phi Delta Kappa/Gallup Poll of the Public's Attitudes Toward the Public Schools, Americans Speak Out: Are Educators and Policy Makers Listening?" *Phi Delta Kappan* 91, no. 1 (September 2009): 11, http://www.pdkintl.org/kappan/M-Polldocs/2009Report.pdf.

20 See Sam Dillon's "Obama Calls for Major Change in Education Law," *The New York Times, March 13, 2010,* http://www.nytimes.com/2010/03/14/education/14child.html?th&emc=th. The president sent a message earlier in March when he supported the mass firing of teachers and staff at a failing high school in Rhode Island. His involvement produced outrage from teachers there and elsewhere. See also Michael A. Fletcher and Nick Anderson, "Obama Angers Union Officials with Remarks in Support of R.I. Teach-

er Firings," *The Washington Post,* March 2, 2010, http://www.washingtonpost.com/wp-dyn/content/article/2010/03/01/AR2010030103560.html?wprss=rss_education.

21 During the winter of 2009, observers were predicting that NCLB would not be rewritten and reauthorized until 2012, although the secretary of education has the authority to grant waivers and exemptions to states as he sees fit. The Obama administration's proposal prompted immediate outcries from union leadership, charging that this version put all the blame on teachers. Stay tuned.

22 The draft standards were made public in March 2010 and were promptly adopted by Kentucky. See the National Governors Association Center for Best Practices and Council of Chief State School Officers' "Common Core State Standards Initiative" at http://www.corestandards.org/.

23 However, the U.S. Department of Education published a recalculated figure in October 2009—the NAEP percentage as it would have been if the 2007 test had been scored using the 2005 standard—which turned out to be just 56.1 percent. "State assessment reported results are not comparable," the DOE noted in "Mapping State Proficiency Standards Onto NAEP Scales: 2005-2007," adding that "Almost one-half of the states changed aspects of their assessment policies or the assessment itself between 2005 and 2007 in ways that prevented their reading or mathematics test results from being comparable across these two years. Either explicitly or implicitly, such states have adopted new performance standards." Victor Bandeira de Mello, Charles Blankenship, and Don McLaughlin, *Mapping State Proficiency Standards Onto NAEP Scales: 2005-2007* [NCES 2010-456] (Washington, D.C.: National Center for Education Statistics, Institute of Education Sciences, U.S. Department of Education, 2009), C-5, 47, http://nces.ed.gov/nationsreportcard/pdf/studies/2010456.pdf.

24 I am not the only one saying this, not by a long shot. "We have to stop lying to our children." U.S. Secretary of Education Arne Duncan delivered this message to a crowd of several

thousand educators on March 5, 2010, at Channel 13's Celebration of Teaching and Learning in New York City.

25 The National Commission on Excellence in Education, "An Open Letter to the American People," *A Nation at Risk: The Imperative for Educational Reform* (The National Commission on Excellence in Education, April 1983), http://www2.ed.gov/pubs/NatAtRisk/title.html.

26 Ibid.

27 The Education Trust, "Statement on the 2009 NAEP Mathematics Results," news release, October 14, 2009, http://www.edtrust.org/dc/press-room/press-release/statement-on-the-2009-naep-mathematics-results.

28 The National Center for Public Policy and Higher Education, *Measuring Up 2008: The National Report Card on Education* (San Jose: NCPPHE, 2008), 7, http://measuringup2008.higher education.org/print/NCPPHEMUNationalRpt.pdf.

29 And if you want a breakdown of those averages, the graduation rate was 91.4 percent for Asian/Pacific Islander students, 80.3 percent for white/non-Hispanic students, 62.3 percent for Hispanic students, 61.3 percent for American Indian/Alaska Native students and 60.3 percent for black/non-Hispanic students. U.S. Department of Education Institute of Education Sciences, Public School Graduates and Dropouts From the Common Core of Data: School Year 2006-07, First Look, [NCES 2010-313], October 2009, http://nces.ed.gov/pubs2010/2010313/findings.asp. In other words, the national high school dropout rate in 2006-2007 was over 25 percent. (And if you'd like a breakdown for *that* percentage, in states and districts reporting dropout rates by race/ethnicity, only 2.6 percent of Asian/Pacific Islander students dropped out, compared with 3 percent of white/non-Hispanic, 6.5 percent of Hispanic, 6.8 percent of black, non-Hispanic, and 7.6 percent of American Indian/Alaska Native students.) Ibid.

30 Christopher B. Swanson, *Cities in Crisis 2009: Closing the Graduation Gap* (Bethesda: Editorial Projects in Education,

2009), 16, http://www.americaspromise.org/~/media/Files/Resources/CiC09.ashx.

Just 70 percent or so of students graduate with a regular high school diploma, according to the U.S. Committee on Education and Labor, and the situation is much worse in certain school districts. Out of America's 50 largest cities, Detroit ranked lowest in terms of graduation rates several years ago. However, Detroit, along with some other cities and states, has since been trying to improve the situation by making changes and holding summits as part of the America's Promise Alliance "Dropout Prevention" campaign. Detroit "set a 10-year goal to graduate 80 percent of its youth from the 35 high schools with significant dropout rates," noted America's Promise Alliance. "To support this effort, the local United Way announced the creation of The Greater Detroit Venture Fund, a $10 million fund to assist these schools and improve ACT scores so students are better prepared for college. Since this summit, the city has shuttered, reconstituted, or clustered together 11 of those 35 schools as part of a comprehensive turnaround process." America's Promise Alliance, "High School Graduation Rates Rise in Some Major U.S. Cities, But Significant Work Remains to Curb Dropout Crisis," news release, April 22, 2009, http://www.americaspromise.org/About-the-Alliance/Press-Room/Press-Releases/2009/2009-April-22-High-School-Graduation-Rates-Rise.aspx.

31   U.S. Committee on Education and Labor, "High School Dropout Crisis Threatens U.S. Economic Growth and Competitiveness, Witnesses Tell House Panel," news release, May 12, 2009, http://edlabor.house.gov/newsroom/2009/05/high-school-dropout-crisis-thr.shtml.

32   Lumina Foundation for Education, "Our Work: Student Preparedness," http://www.luminafoundation.org/our_work/student_preparedness/student_preparedness.html.

33   Organisation for Economic Co-operation and Development, *PISA 2006: Science Competencies for Tomorrow's World, Executive*

Summary (Paris: OECD Publishing, 2007), 3, 20, 51, http://www.pisa.oecd.org/dataoecd/15/13/39725224.pdf.

34 McKinsey & Company, Social Sector Office, *The Economic Impact of the Achievement Gap in America's Schools* (McKinsey & Company, April 2009), 9, http://www.mckinsey.com/App_Media/Images/Page_Images/Offices/SocialSector/PDF/achievement_gap_report.pdf.

35 See "Disappearing Dropouts," the Emmy-nominated report that John Tulenko and I did for the NewsHour in 2005, to understand how districts got rid of low-performing students.

36 Apple, "Challenge Based Learning: Take Action and Make a Difference," http://ali.apple.com/cbl/.

37 Organisation for Economic Co-operation and Development, "Education at a Glance 2009: OECD Indicators," Indicator B4: What Is the Total Public Expenditure on Education? Table B4.1: Total Public Expenditure on Education (1995, 2000, 2006), http://www.oecd.org/document/24/0,3343,en_2649_39263238_43586328_1_1_1_1,00.html. (Additionally, in the early 1980s, 28 percent of total government spending went for education. In 2001, that figure was 15 percent.)

38 But before I'd endorse spending more money, I'd want schools to spend what they have in better ways. Mediocrity shouldn't pay as well as it does now!

39 Catherine Rampell, "Teacher Pay Around the World," *The New York Times*, September 9, 2009, http://economix.blogs.nytimes.com/2009/09/09/teacher-pay-around-the-world/.

40 See Chapter 2, "Testing Flea Powder."

41 Just how narrow the curriculum has become as a result of NCLB was documented in a study by the Center on Education Policy in 2006. CEP found that 71 percent of the nation's 15,000 school districts had reduced the hours spent on history, music and other subjects in order to devote more time to reading and math. "Narrowing the curriculum has clearly become a nationwide pattern," said Jack Jennings, president of the D.C.-based organization. We documented this phe-

375

nomenon in a number of pieces for the NewsHour, available on our website at www.learningmatters.tv.

42 Alliance for Excellent Education, "How Does the United States Stack Up? International Comparisons of Academic Achievement," fact sheet, March 2008, 1, http://www.all4ed. org/files/IntlComp_FactSheet.pdf.

43 In March 2010 the Obama administration revealed plans for a new version of the law. It would replace the "all students achieving satisfactorily by 2014" provision with a requirement that all students graduate ready for higher education or work. When might the new law emerge? The ranking Democrat, George Miller of California, told Secretary Duncan that he wanted it done this year, to which Duncan replied, "That is absolutely the goal. There is so much we can do to fix the current law."

44 And he's off to a good start, with many public appearances in support of Race to the Top and the state-level changes it seems to be producing.

45 According to America's Promise Alliance (founded by General Colin Powell), "High School Graduation Rates Rise in Some Major U.S. Cities but Significant Work Remains to Curb Dropout Crisis," news release, April 22, 2009, http:// www.americaspromise.org/About-the-Alliance/Press-Room/ Press-Releases/2009/2009-April-22-High-School-Graduation-Rates-Rise.aspx.

46 U.S. Committee on Education and Labor, "High School Dropout Crisis Threatens U.S. Economic Growth and Competitiveness, Witnesses Tell House Panel," news release, May 12, 2009, http://edlabor.house.gov/newsroom/2009/05/high-school-dropout-crisis-thr.shtml.

47 Barack Obama, "Remarks of President Barack Obama—As Prepared for Delivery, Address to Joint Session of Congress, Tuesday, February 24th, 2009," The White House Briefing Room, Speeches & Remarks, http://www.whitehouse.gov/ the_press_office/remarks-of-president-barack-obama-address-to-joint-session-of-congress/.

48   Patrick M. Callan, "The 2008 National Report Card: Modest Improvements, Persistent Disparities, Eroding Global Competitiveness," in *Measuring Up 2008: The National Report Card on Higher Education*, The National Center for Public Policy and Higher Education (San Jose: NCPPHE, 2008), 5, http://measuringup2008.highereducation.org/print/NCPPHEMU-NationalRpt.pdf.

49   U.S. Committee on Education and Labor, "High School Dropout Crisis Threatens U.S. Economic Growth and Competitiveness, Witnesses Tell House Panel," news release, May 12, 2009, http://edlabor.house.gov/newsroom/2009/05/high-school-dropout-crisis-thr.shtml.

50   Thomas Toch, *Margins of Error: The Testing Industry in the No Child Left Behind Era* (Washington, D.C.: Education Sector, 2006), http://www.educationsector.org/research/research_show.htm?doc_id=346734. Some of the report recommendations seem to have been adopted. It called for more than doubling federal spending on testing, which is happening under the Obama administration, and it urged that more states work together to develop common tests. Largely spurred by the Race to the Top competition, at least six consortia have been formed.

51   My friend Arnold Packer, the distinguished economist, is worried that the people in charge are developing a "one size fits all" model. He wrote in an e-mail in March 2010, "Every study of employer needs made over the last twenty years— from the Secretary's Commission for Achieving Necessary Skills (SCANS) in 1992 to the recent 'Are They Really Ready to Work?' by the Conference Board and the non-profit Corporate Voices for Working Families—has come up with the same set of answers. Successful workers communicate effectively orally and in writing and have social and behavioral skills that make them responsible and good at teamwork. They are creative and techno-savvy. They have a good command of fractions and basic statistics and can apply relatively

simple math to real world problems like financial or health literacy. Employers never mention polynomial factoring."

52　How severe is the shortage? Back in 2006 the competition for people with the required skill set led to salaries of $200,000 plus perks. The New York Times reported that states and districts couldn't find the experts they needed to oversee testing and make effective use of data because—irony alert—they had been hired away by the testing companies, which can afford higher salaries because of their contracts with states and districts. David M. Herszenhorn, "As Test-Taking Grows, Test-Makers Grow Rarer," *The New York Times*, May 5, 2006, 1, http://www.nytimes.com/2006/05/05/education/05testers.h tml?ex=1304481600&en=bec6ba0fec0c3772&ei=5090&partn er=rssuserland&emc=rss.

53　Clay Christensen, e-mail message to author, October 2008.

54　Christopher B. Swanson, *Cities in Crisis: A Special Analytic Report on High School Graduation* (Bethesda: Editorial Projects in Education Research Center, April 2008), 9.

55　The National Commission on Excellence in Education, "An Open Letter to the American People," *A Nation at Risk: The Imperative for Educational Reform* (The National Commission on Excellence in Education, April 1983), http://www2.ed.gov/ pubs/NatAtRisk/title.html.

56　Ibid.

57　For the complete podcast, go to www.learningmatters.tv. A portion of the interview also appeared on the NewsHour on July 23, 2008.

58　Most people call them charter schools, of course, but I like Ted Kolderie's term. After all, they are literally "chartered." Kolderie was present at the creation of this particular reform, along with Joe Nathan, Ember Reichgott Junge, Al Shanker, Sy Fliegel and a handful of others interested in school reform. The seminal meeting took place in Itasca, Minn., in the fall of 1988, and I served as "ringmaster" for a weekend of intense discussions. I didn't realize at the time that we were making history.

59 Our report, "End of the Line," appeared on the NewsHour on August 15, 2007. Three podcasts accompanied the broadcast and are also available online at www.learningmatters.tv.

60 Alas, we didn't win the Emmy.

61 My eight-part NPR series, "Juvenile Crime, Juvenile Justice," was broadcast in 1981.

62 Opponents of widespread use of machine-scored bubble tests often resort to ridicule to make their case. They ask, rhetorically and scornfully, "Does taking a patient's temperature over and over help a sick person get healthy?" Of course it doesn't, but that process has a real beneficiary: the company selling disposable thermometers. Public education needs to be analyzed from that perspective: Who benefits, and what are they being rewarded for?

63 It's difficult to be precise here because estimates sometimes factor in labor costs, and sometimes do not. This website, for instance, compares a "high" 1990s estimate of over $22 billion with a CRESST mid-range estimate of $1,320 per child in the same era, http://www.education-consumers.com/briefs/phelps2.shtm, while this 2001 Ed Week piece http://www.edweek.org/ew/articles/2001/03/14/26cost.h20.html says that states spend half a billion on tests each year. Safe to say it's an awful lot of time and money. As must be clear, I favor fewer but better tests, and I tend to trust teacher-made tests because they can provide instant feedback, allowing teachers to change their instruction.

64 Alan Bersin, e-mail message to author, April 8, 2009.

65 "Teacher Shortage: False Alarm?" We reported that the nation is producing more than enough teachers, but is failing to retain them for a host of reasons, including inadequate training. The program can be seen at www.learningmatters.tv.

66 NCATE defends teacher education vigorously. See, for example, "It's Not Your Mother's Teacher Education (discussing *Spotlight on Schools of Education)* by Antoinette Mitchell, NCATE

vice president, in the organization's spring 2006 newsletter, http://www.ncate.org/public/archivedNCATENews.asp.

67   We spent a fair amount of time looking into California's approach to public education for "First to Worst," a history of public schooling in that state. Go to www.learningmatters. tv to see that one-hour program and its sequel, "California Schools, America's Future."

68   In 2007, total spending on special education approached $100 billion. And, according to the DOE, under the ARRA additional "IDEA funds are provided under three authorities: $11.3 billion is available under Part B Grants to States; $400 million is available under Part B Preschool Grants; and $500 million is available under Part C Grants for Infants and Families." U.S. Department of Education, "American Recovery and Reinvestment Act of 2009: IDEA Recovery Funds for Services to Children and Youths with Disabilities," ED.gov, April 1, 2009, http://www2.ed.gov/policy/gen/leg/recovery/factsheet/idea.html.

69   That's the same Miriam Kurtzig Freedman who is an attorney in Boston, a visiting fellow at Stanford, a consultant, speaker, author and co-founder of Special Education Day. Her latest book, published in 2009, is "Fixing Special Education: 12 Steps to Transform a Broken System."

70   NAEP is our gold standard, while most state results are difficult to trust. If a state's results align with NAEP, as they do in Massachusetts, one can assume that the state has high standards. For many states, the gap is large. In 2007, for instance, the scoring gap between NAEP and Oklahoma's state results for eighth-grade proficiency was 52 percent in reading and 55 percent in math. (See Alliance for Excellent Education, "Oklahoma High Schools," fact sheet, August 2009, http://www.all4ed.org/files/Oklahoma.pdf.) Reviewers also reported that Oklahoma's 2007 science assessment standards were "generally unaligned with the NAEP," with 82 percent of NAEP content statements for fourth grade "unaddressed by Oklahoma," 53 percent "unaddressed" in eighth grade, and

80 percent "unaddressed" in 12th grade. Michael Timms, Steven Schneider, Cindy Lee, and Eric Rolfhus, *Aligning Science Assessment Standards: Oklahoma and the 2009 National Assessment of Educational Progress (NAEP)*, Issues & Answers Report, REL 2007–No. 022, (Washington, D.C.: U.S. Department of Education, Institute of Education Sciences, National Center for Education Evaluation and Regional Assistance, Regional Educational Laboratory Southwest, 2007), iii, http://ies. ed.gov/ncee/edlabs.

71   I am personally sympathetic to an argument I first heard in graduate school: that systems tolerate a small amount of reform in order to keep the peace. It's a safety valve and not much more. Frederick Hess advanced that argument in "Spinning Wheels: The Politics of Urban School Reform" (Washington, D.C.: Brookings Institution Press, 1998). Paul Hill made the case in "Putting Learning First," a white paper from the Progressive Policy Institute, February 2006. As he put it, "Today's public school system tolerates new ideas only on a small scale and it does so largely to reduce pressure for broader change."

72   Joshua S. Wyner, John M. Bridgeland, and John J. DiIulio Jr., *Achievement Trap: How America Is Failing Millions of High-Achieving Students from Lower-Income Families*, a report by the Jack Kent Cooke Foundation & Civic Enterprises with original research by Westat, (2007), www.jkcf.org/assets/ files/0000/0084/Achievement_Trap.pdf.

73   Online learning may be a viable option. Stanford University's EPGY Online High School may be the oldest online learning program around. For a comprehensive profile, see Mitchell Landsberg's "More Clicks Than Cliques," *Los Angeles Times*, June 17, 2007, http://articles.latimes.com/2007/jun/17/local/ me-online17 or visit http://epgy.stanford.edu/.

74   The program title had a question mark at the end, forced upon us by SCETV and PBS, both of which were concerned about lawsuits. We objected, feeling that we had made the case that A.D.D. is often—but not always—a dubious diag-

nosis, but they prevailed. No one ever sued, although I did receive a number of threatening letters and phone calls from irate parents who felt we were saying that their children did not have A.D.D. Because of delays caused by PBS's excessive caution, ABC scooped us on the story, an outcome that still rankles.

75 I wrote about this in 1995; see "Reading, Writing and Ritalin," *The New York Times*, October 21, 1995, http://www.nytimes. com/1995/10/21/opinion/reading-writing-and-ritalin. html?sec=health.

76 Gardiner Harris, "Proof Is Scant on Psychiatric Drug Mix for Young," *The New York Times*, November 23, 2006, A28, http:// www.nytimes.com/2006/11/23/health/23kids.html?ex=1321 938000&en=f1766195258101f2&ei=5088&partner=rssnyt&e mc=rss. There may be other risks. "In a small but startling preliminary new study, Texas researchers have found that after just three months, every one of a dozen children treated for attention deficit/hyperactivity disorder (ADHD) with the drug methylphenidate experienced a threefold increase in levels of chromosome abnormalities-occurrences associated with increased risks of cancer and other adverse health effects." See Medical News Today, "Study Shows Methylphenidate Linked to Chromosomal Changes," February 28, 2005, http://www.medicalnewstoday.com/articles/20433.php. See also the original study, R.A. El-Zein et al., "Cytogenetic Effects in Children Treated with Methylphenidate," December 18, 2005, The University of Texas M.D. Anderson Cancer Center, posted on PubMed.gov, U.S. National Library of Medicine, National Institutes of Health, http://www.ncbi. nlm.nih.gov/pubmed/16297714. However, another study indicates no genetic damage: http://www.sciencedaily.com/ releases/2008/11/081119120143.htm.

And a 2003 study indicated a greater risk of cancer for children taking methylphenidate (Ritalin) http://www.prevent-cancer.com/patients/children/ritalin.htm.

77 Duff Williams, "Poor Children Likelier to Get Antipsychotics," *The New York Times,* December 11, 2009, http://www.nytimes. com/2009/12/12/health/12medicaid.html?_r=1&hp.

78 Tragically, that hasn't changed. In February 2010, The New York Times reported that New York State does not have even one full-time staff psychiatrist to oversee treatment for the 800 or so young people who are in state facilities. The treatment of choice becomes psychotropic medications, just as it was when I did my reporting in the '70s. February 11, 2010, 1.

79 It also led to a lifelong friendship with Fred Rogers of *Mister Rogers' Neighborhood,* who happened to hear the program and wrote me a lovely letter about it.

80 We found that African-American parents were generally not inclined to accept a diagnosis that required medicating their children, whether the diagnosis came from a teacher or a counselor. As one parent told us, "We have enough drugs in our community. I don't believe that more drugs are a solution."

81 The drug is now manufactured by Novartis Pharmaceuticals, a unit of Novartis AG.

82 Which became "Children and Adults with Attention Deficit/ Hyperactivity Disorder." The organization apparently saw an opportunity to expand its reach. In fact, Harvey Parker, the smooth-talking man behind CHADD, had a ready explanation for the disproportionate number of boys labeled A.D.D. Girls have it, he said, but the level of awareness isn't there yet.

83 The full and seamy story is told in "A.D.D: A Dubious Diagnosis?" This program in "The Merrow Report" series appeared on PBS in fall 1995 and won awards for investigative reporting. Both CHADD and Ciba-Geigy attempted to prevent its broadcast, even going so far as to threaten lawsuits against me, PBS, our funders and South Carolina ETV, our presenting station. The program was broadcast as scheduled, and neither CHADD nor Ciba-Geigy sued.

84 Adderall is also commonly prescribed.

85 George Dewey, a veteran educator, provides critical analysis from another vantage point. He wrote on my blog: "The problem with overly-medicated persons is that this hides the real causes for bizarre behaviors (stresses from over-crowding, provocative media blasts, nearly continual stimulation by junk foods, trendy music and lyrics, non-stop schedules in and out of school) and convinces many of us that the problem has gone away. It has, rather, gone underground, and we do not seem to yet have any long-term longitudinal studies of the resulting effects upon adult behavioral problems like depression and addictions."

86 When I blogged about this in January 2009, a woman wrote: "For what it's worth, I'd like to add that the various uses for Ritalin are not lost on its users. I graduated high school in 1995 and saw a lot of Ritalin abuse during my high school, and later, college years. It was traded, sold and shared, and then either swallowed or snorted in combination with alcohol. Kids would say, 'Oh, I only take it when I really need to focus. The rest I share with my friends.' I tried it once in a recording studio, at 19, on the recommendation of a 28-year-old who told me that a line of Ritalin and some whiskey gave him the relaxation and focus to work at his best. I'm sure there are legit Ritalin users out there, but personally, I've only seen it as a super easy-to-get recreational drug."

87 New name: Attention Deficit Hyperactivity Disorder. Maybe to cast a wider net?

88 Jeffrey Zaslow, "What If Einstein Had Taken Ritalin? ADHD's Impact on Creativity," *The Wall Street Journal*, February 3, 2005, http://online.wsj.com/article/SB110738397416844127.html.

89 But still very much with us, if this film, "The War on Kids," is accurate: *The War on Kids*, DVD, directed by Cevin Soling, (Spectacle Films: 2009), http://www.thewaronkids.com/MAIN.html.

90 Large classes *can* work, especially in high school, if the course is organized around projects with the students working in teams, but the projects have to be meaningful—publishing

a magazine, producing videos or working on environmental studies, for example—and the teams have to be selected by the teacher, not by kids, because the kids will be tempted to self-select into cliques.

91 Not to mention the fact that for years millions of American children have lacked basic health insurance—another indicator of an epidemic of the new A.D.D. That may have changed in March 2010 with the passage of health insurance reform.

92 Yes, I ask a lot of softball questions like that. So sue me!

93 After our piece appeared on the NewsHour, I realized that Nancy Welsh is much like a mirror. That is, my liberal friends told me that they were sure she was anti-war; my conservative friends reached the opposite conclusion. She wrote me in February 2010 to say that she was leaving teaching in June, taking early retirement. What a loss!

94 Gary Wieland e-mailed me in March 2010: "I retired from the military on July 31, 1994 and was in my classroom on August 15th of the same year. So I was actually retired for two whole weeks. I like to say that when I left the Special Operations community in the Army and went to an elementary classroom that I went from one hazardous duty to another."

95 Wieland actually hasn't always gotten the dollar back because sometimes returning soldiers are sent to another base. But all but one of the deployed parents from McNair have returned safely, which is the issue. With wry wit, Wieland noted in a March 2010 e-mail that he doesn't mind if parents who come back safely don't return his dollar because, "I have made two major career decisions in my life, I was a soldier, and now I am a teacher, so I am able to spare those dollars from my great accumulation of wealth."

96 Imagine the schools we'd have if we put highway engineers in charge. After all, they want drivers to get to the destination, which means they design highways with this in mind. In highway design, time of arrival is a *variable*, unlike schools, in which time is the constant. Conversely, if educators designed highways, they would have narrow lanes that penalized the

slightest mistake, one speed for all, and so on. That's because most schools are set up to catch errors; it's a "gotcha" game that sorts winners and losers. Kids are branded early—often by the end of third grade—as "A kids," "C kids" and so on. Highway engineers design lanes to be wider than necessary, so a driver can go slightly off-course without crashing. Highways have more than one lane, in order to accommodate different speeds, and so on. The destinations vary. For more on this, see Chapter 13, "A Modest Proposal for New School Leadership."

97   It's invariably defined narrowly. Here's how it's defined in Ann Arbor, Mich., according to a reporter there: "The achievement gap is commonly talked about in terms of a gap between black and white students. In Ann Arbor, the gap shows up in disparities in test scores, failure rates, graduation rates, suspension rates and participation in both remedial and advanced classes." David Jesse, "Achievement Gap Tackled in New Policy: Board Works on Narrowing Performance Disparities," *The Ann Arbor News*, March 26, 2009, http://www.mlive.com/news/annarbornews/index.ssf?/base/news-31/1238078448142920.xml&coll=2.

98   For more about Lincoln, see Chapter 16, "Picturing Superman."

99   Adriana Colindres, "Harcourt Agrees to Pay $1.6 Million for ISAT Foul-Up: Texas Company's Role in School Tests to Change," *The State Journal-Register*, May 19, 2006, in *Higher Ed News Weekly* (Illinois Board of Higher Education, May 19, 2006), 31, http://www.ibhe.state.il.us/NewsDigest/NewsWeekly/051906.pdf.

100   Connecticut challenged NCLB in court in 2005, claiming that the law forced it to abandon a complex testing approach that required essay tests and, in science, the design and execution of a lab experiment. Connecticut was administering these tests, which are expensive to create, every other year, but NCLB requires annual testing. When she was secretary of education, Margaret Spellings advised the state to switch

to multiple-choice questions and eliminate the essay, to cut costs. Connecticut said that regardless of other states' support (or lack thereof), it would pursue the lawsuit. "If there's a bully on the playground, it often takes one brave soul to step forward and stand up to the bully," said Andrew Fleischmann, chairman of the legislature's education committee at the time. Associated Press, "Connecticut Lawsuit Says 'No Child Left Behind' is Illegal," *Los Angeles Times*, August 23, 2005, http://articles.latimes.com/2005/aug/23/nation/nanochild23.

101 Ohio Department of Education, *A Guide to the Ohio Graduation Tests for Students and Families* (Columbus: Ohio Department of Education, 2009), 17, http://www.unioto.k12.oh.us/OGTFamilyGuide.pdf.

102 On its website, Toledo Public Schools states that "Ohio's ninth-grade proficiency test is being replaced by the Ohio Graduation Test (OGT). By law, even students who have earned all required class units will not receive a diploma until all five areas of the tests are passed. Therefore, a student who has not passed all five areas should retake the appropriate area test(s) at every opportunity. Ninth-Grade Proficiency Tests are offered in October, March, May (for seniors), and July. Ohio Graduation Tests are offered in March and July. To qualify for the July test administration, a student must complete a minimum of 10 summer instruction hours in the area to be tested. These 10 hours may consist of summer school or tutoring by an Ohio-certified/licensed teacher." http://www.tps.org/ohio-achievement-testing-information.html.

103 High-stakes tests create intense pressures on teachers and administrators, and unfortunate decisions are being made as pressure for "accountability" overwhelms common sense. Here's an example from my daughter Elise's teaching experience in a New York City middle school. As the mandated state exams drew near in the spring of 2000, her principal directed her to spend 15 minutes of each class period practicing answering multiple-choice questions, particularly in math. "But,

sir," she said, "I teach Italian and English, not math." That did not matter to her school leader. She did what she was told. It did not work, of course, although her students did learn several (unintended) lessons from the experience.

The *first lesson* was that neither Italian nor English really mattered. The *second lesson*, after seeing their teacher treated this way by her boss, was that Ms. Merrow was not in control of her own life and therefore probably not deserving of their respect.

The *third lesson* was that the state test, and only the state test, mattered. That lesson her eighth graders learned well…so well, in fact, that immediately after taking the test about one-third of them stopped attending school, even though there were still five weeks to go in the school year. Although most of these kids did not expect to do well on the state exam, they recognized that the test meant everything…and therefore that nothing else mattered, including coming to school. In the end, most eighth-graders in New York City (including her students) did poorly on the test.

104   Here's more: "Only one state—South Carolina for grade 8—sets its reading standard at NAEP's proficiency level"; "For mathematics, seven states set grade 4 proficiency standards below NAEP's basic performance level, and eight states are below for grade 8"; and "Only two states—Massachusetts for grades 4 and 8 and South Carolina for grade 8—set their standard above NAEP's proficiency level." And "States regularly report the percentage of their students who have scored proficient or above on state tests. But the study found that most of the variation between states, about 70 percent, reflects differences in the difficulty of state standards.…States sometimes change their assessments, and the AIR study took those changes into account. Eight states showed significant differences between 2005 and 2007, the years studied, on grade 4 reading assessments, with half of those lowering their standards compared to the NAEP scale. All seven states that had significant changes in their grade 8 standards lowered

them." American Institutes for Research, "State Education Standards Vary Widely: Study Shows Big Differences in Evaluation of Students," news release, October 29, 2009, http://www.air.org/news/pr/educationStandards.aspx.

105 See http://www.americanprogress.org/publications/archive.html for dozens of valuable reports on public education.

106 This is an intriguing notion: young people growing up swimming in a world of technology will be teachers in 10 years or so. Imagine if schools have NOT changed significantly but expect "The Net Generation" to teach in the old ways. Talk about a collision course!

107 "First to Worst," which we updated in 2007 with "California Schools, America's Future."

108 Children Now, *California Report Card 2010: Setting the Agenda for Children* (Oakland: Children Now, 2010), 29, http://www.childrennow.org/uploads/documents/reportcard_2010.pdf.

109 The California Association of School Counselors, "Student to Counselor Ratios Remain High," In the News, February 2010, http://casc.timberlankepublishing.com/content.asp?pl-14&sl=72&contentid=72.

110 California Department of Education, "State Schools Chief Jack O'Connell Responds to *Quality Counts 2009* Report," news release, January 7, 2009, http://www.cde.ca.gov/nr/ne/yr09/yr09rel2.asp.

111 And he's now a top official at the Bill & Melinda Gates Foundation.

112 See Institute for Research on Education Policy and Practice, "Getting Down to Facts: A Research Project Examining California's School Governance and Finance Systems," http://irepp.stanford.edu/projects/cafinance.htm.

113 There was more to the press statement. "...and watched the Governor sign and place the bond on the November ballot. AB127 is the Strategic Growth Plan education proposal which authorizes the placement of a $10.4 billion general obligation bond to fund K-12 and Higher Education on the November 2006 ballot." Boyle Heights Learning Collabora-

tive, "Schwarzenegger, Villaraigosa and Nunez visit Breed St Elementary," news release, May 20, 2006, http://www.bhlc. net/news/civic_engagement/Schwarzenegger_Villaraigosa_ and_Nunez_visit_Breed_St_Elementary_.php.

114 According to the Boyle Heights Learning Collaborative's website, today the SOS program is in place in five elementary schools, with one as far away as Atlanta, Ga. I recommend that you visit their website—it's inspiring to see how much they've achieved. http://www.bhlc.net/news/student_leader-ship/sos_history.php.

115 And in December 2009, William Ouchi said: "I am very hope-ful that the school board now in place at the L.A Unified School District is very forward-looking and very much com-mitted to the idea of empowering principals of schools. The superintendent is leading the way. The board has asked me to serve on the Governance Committee of the Board of Edu-cation, and the superintendent has asked me to serve on an advisory committee to advise him and the staff in the im-plementation of decentralization. There are many, many is-sues for them to think about, many problems to solve, and lots of analysis to do. They are working their way through that. Meanwhile, they have already launched their first pilot group of 33 autonomously managed schools this year." Paul Feinberg, "10 Questions for William Ouchi, Public Education Expert," *UCLA Today,* December 14, 2009, http://www.today. ucla.edu/portal/ut/10-questions-for-william-ouchi-149940. aspx.

116 California Department of Education, "Budget Crisis Report Card: Report to the Education Community and the Public About the Impact of the State Budget on Public Education," news release of speech by Jack O'Connell, May 21, 2009, http://www.cde.ca.gov/nr/re/ht/bcrc.asp.

117 But words mean less than deeds. The California Teachers As-sociation used its muscle to keep the legislature from amend-ing the state education code so California can qualify for Race to the Top money. The sticking point: tying teacher evalua-

tion and pay to student performance. The union doesn't want that sort of accountability. The law that eventually passed may not be sufficient to persuade Washington that California is serious about reform. And, tellingly, California was not among the 16 finalists in the first round of the Race to the Top competition.

118   California Department of Education, "Budget Crisis Report Card: Report to the Education Community and the Public About the Impact of the State Budget on Public Education," news release of speech by Jack O'Connell, May 21, 2009, http://www.cde.ca.gov/nr/re/ht/bcrc.asp.

119   Jack O'Connell is urging the California legislature to lower the parcel tax approval threshold from a two-thirds vote to a 55 percent vote; for more information on this bill—SCA 6, authored by State Senator Joe Simitian—see http://www.leginfo.ca.gov/cgi-bin/postquery?bill_number=sca_6&sess=CUR&house=B&author=simitian. Proposition 13 capped property taxes and made it very difficult to raise funds for schools and other services. Intended to protect homeowners against rising property taxes, it may have had the unintended consequence of allowing businesses to avoid paying their fair share of taxes. For a detailed description of research done by Jennifer Bestor, a Menlo Park resident with an MBA, see Renee Batti, "Menlo Mom Wonders: Who Wins with Prop. 13?" *Palo Alto Weekly*, March 19, 2010, 7.

120   And being demanded! In early March 2010 a series of coordinated protests led by students and teachers from all levels of California education, elementary through university, took place in Sacramento, Oakland, Los Angeles, Santa Cruz and other cities around the state. It was billed as a "strike and a day of action to defend public education." The governor called the system-wide cuts "terrible" and agreed the system needs more money, but no one seems to know where that money might come from.

121   I have some experience in doing this. For three school years, 1992-1995, we videotaped Diana Porter's efforts to persuade

the faculty and staff at Woodward High School (Cincinnati) to adopt Ted Sizer's Coalition of Essential Schools principles. The documentary, "The Fifty Million Dollar Gamble," is a compelling story of two-steps-forward, two-steps-back school reform, in which the status quo eventually triumphs.

And between 1994 and 2000, I followed David Hornbeck's efforts in Philadelphia, where he tried to implement a 10-part plan he called "Children Achieving." He ran into the buzz saw known as the Philadelphia Federation of Teachers, a union renowned for its rigidity and resistance to change. The resulting documentary, "Toughest Job in America," is still used in college courses for its object lessons in social change, teacher unionism and more. Not only that, it's a well-told tale. If you haven't seen it, please take a look. I bet you'll get hooked and will want to know "what happens next."

122 Jim Lehrer, Linda Winslow and others at the NewsHour were no doubt thinking of "Making the Grade," our seven-part serial that followed five rookie teachers in Brooklyn during school year 2000-2001. I think that may be the most popular extended coverage ever on the NewsHour, as viewers got invested in the trials and tribulations of Jack, Renee and the others. Jim jokingly referred to it as "the PBS version of Survivor."

123 Cat McGrath and Jane Renaud have worked on the Washington story from day one. Valerie Visconti has worked with at least three other producers on the New Orleans story. David Wald has assisted throughout.

124 Eleven episodes from each city at this writing, with at least one more planned about each.

125 A shout-out to Richard Laine and Lucas Held at Wallace, Marie Groark at Gates, and Karen Denne at Broad!

126 Rhee told The Washington Post, "It was a zoo every day..." but she vowed not "to let 8-year-olds run me out of town." According to The Washington Post, "She discovered learning improved when everyone sat in a big U-pattern with her in the middle and she made quick marks on the blackboard

for good and bad behavior without ever stopping the lesson. She spent an entire summer making lesson plans and teaching materials, with the help of indulgent aunts visiting from Korea. She found unconventional but effective ways to teach reading and math. She set written goals for each child and enlisted parents in her plans. Students became calm and engaged. Test scores soared." No one has been able to document those gains, leading her opponents to accuse her of deception. Apparently no records were kept; but her colleagues from those days recall her determination and hard work. See Jay Mathews' "Baptism by Fire Vulcanized Rhee, 'Brat Pack' Peers," *The Washington Post,* October 27, 2008, http://www.washingtonpost.com/wpdyn/content/article/2008/10/26/AR2008102601972.html.

127 Rhee has always given Mayor Fenty credit, praising him to the skies for his leadership. The rest of the world hasn't been so understanding. At the Democratic Convention in Denver, a Newsweek editor told me they were thinking of putting Rhee on the cover and asked what I thought. Bad idea, I said, because to be accurate you have to put Mayor Fenty on the cover with her. Without him, she's toast, I said, and she knows it. "We won't do that," the editor said. "It won't sell magazines." Later, of course, Time put the chancellor on its cover, all by herself.

128 And she's been in the glare for quite some time. Political junkies will recall that both Barack Obama and John McCain praised her during the debates. Did they agree on anything else?

129 Nearly half of which were already charter schools, meaning that Vallas had little influence over their day-to-day operations.

130 When he signed his contract, he told State Superintendent Paul Pastorek that he would be going home to Chicago after two years, anyway. He promised to improve the system and to train his successor.

131 Why the train instead of a much shorter trip on a plane? Vallas hates to fly. He often drove to Chicago to see his family, meaning that he'd spend most of his long weekend in the car.

132 Vallas, a member of the Greek Orthodox Church, is right at home among people of faith. Part of what drives him, he said, is his conviction that one must use his talents for good. To do otherwise is a sin, he believes.

133 The actual line in the movie is "Build it and he will come," but everyone and his brother rewrites the line, and so do I.

134 She did more. By the end of the school year, she'd removed 36 principals, 22 assistant principals and 121 employees in her central office.

135 She initially pegged the number at 80 percent in our interview, but then asked us not to use that figure, saying she'd been overstating the problem.

136 Randi Weingarten, president of the American Federation of Teachers, refers to Rhee and New York Chancellor Joel Klein as the leaders of the "Blame Teachers First" movement.

137 Rhee was also losing students, of course, but she professed not to be concerned. As long as kids were in a good school, she said on numerous occasions, she didn't care if it was one of hers.

138 Initially, the money for the higher salaries was to come from foundations. Down the road, Rhee said, she would find the money by cutting costs elsewhere. But before long, the economy collapsed, jeopardizing everything. Rhee's proposal would have made her "green path" teachers the highest paid in the nation. A new contract was announced in early April 2010, subject to ratification by union members. Details had not been released as this book went to press.

139 Teachers told us that Rhee blamed Time for using that particular photo. One said, "What she said was that she actually took several pictures. They didn't display the pictures of her sitting around with several kids or her sitting in a classroom. Of course they're going to pick the actual picture that's go-

ing to get all the teachers all stirred up." But Rhee could have declined to pose with the broom in the first place.

140 However, the other (larger) teachers union doesn't agree. Early in March 2010, I interviewed the president of the National Education Association. I began by asking Dennis Van Roekel, who taught high school math for 25 years, if a teacher could be judged in part based on how his or her students perform. He said no.

Van Roekel: For example, in a class, you never know which part of a geometry lesson a class isn't going to get. If based on my assessments, a quiz or whatever, they didn't get my unit on slope, then what (administrators) should be watching for is what did I do as a result once I realized that they didn't know it? Did I adjust my teaching? Did I find a new way of doing it? That's what I should be judged on.

Me: *And if you didn't?*

Van Roekel: If I didn't, I think that's part of the evaluation system.

Me: *So it's the practice, not the test score?*

Van Roekel: Yes

Me: *But the test scores are the measure of the practice.*

Van Roekel: I don't believe that.

141 He's trying. He thought he had found the perfect person, but then St. Louis hired him to run their schools.

142 Perhaps someone should write a history of education's pursuit of panaceas. The list would include subject matter specialization in math and science, the open classroom, busing, parental choice, learning styles and differentiated learning, computer-assisted teaching and learning, competency-based education, assessment-driven improvement strategies, charter initiatives, small schools and turnaround specialists. I think it could be a dynamite musical!

143 The approach has its detractors to be sure, including Ted Kolderie of Education Evolving. He writes: "Once again our national government is setting out to get America better schools and better learning. Once again, however, its effort

starts inside the traditional 'givens' of school and learning. So again it will probably disappoint. The need today is for policymaking instead to open to *non*-traditional concepts of school and learning—and to find a theory of action that can accommodate this radical change." For more, see http://education evolving.org.

144 "The School Turnaround Specialist Program entails a close working relationship between district personnel charged with supporting school turnaround efforts—referred to as the district shepherd—and the principals who have been identified to participate in School Turnaround Specialist Program and initiate the school turnaround." Also, "In the spring of 2004, the Virginia Department of Education contracted with the Darden/Curry Partnership for Leaders in Education to design and implement the Virginia School Turnaround Specialist Program." The first program was small-scale, nine days in the summer, another few days during the year and some consultant visits. Today it's a two-year program. See http://www.darden.virginia.edu/html/standard.aspx?menu id=626&id=19294&styleid=3.

145 "The University of Virginia School Turnaround Specialist Program includes coursework, case studies, and discussions to share information and practical experience in proven business and education turnaround strategies....School Turnaround Specialist Program participants also study business management strategies, organizational behavior and communication, and restructuring and renewal of troubled organizations," according to their website, http://www.darden.virginia.edu/html/standard.aspx?menu id=626&id=19294&styleid=3. Oh, and everyone read Jim Collins' book, "Good to Great."

146 The program also adopted another business concept: financial incentives. Each principal in the first cadre got a $5,000 bonus upon completion of the training and development of their plans and—if test scores hit the turnaround targets— bonuses of $8,000 the first year and up to $15,000 the next two years. The state also agreed to provide participating prin-

cipals $50 per pupil for critical items that contributed to the turnaround process.

147 Louisiana is a case in point. Here's part of what its website says about its two-year turnaround specialist program: "The Louisiana School Turnaround Specialist (LSTS) Program is an 8(g) funded leadership development program designed to recruit, groom and build a cadre of school leaders prepared to turnaround chronically underperforming schools. Schools with an Academically Unacceptable Status (AUS) or Academic Assistance Status (AA) are eligible to participate in the program; with increased priority given to schools at the AUS1, AUS2 and AA levels and districts with a higher percentage of labeled schools. The LSTS Program utilizes best practices from education and business to strengthen the organizational and instructional leadership skills of currently certified and experienced principals through rigorous selection criteria, significant integrated field-based experiences, relevant coursework, and strong coordination with local schools and districts." http://www.leadlouisiana.net/la_state_turnaround_specialist_program.asp.

148 See www.learningmatters.tv. Doing this story was not my idea. In fact, I had to be talked into it by my colleagues John Tulenko and David Wald. My reaction to the program was beyond skeptical, but they felt it was worth pursuing. They went to the summer training and videotaped interviews with six participants, including Parker Land. Once I watched the interviews and some of the case-study classes, I signed on, and we asked Land if we could follow him throughout the year. I'm glad we did, although he came to regret letting us into his life.

149 He left that school in 2008 and was reported to have resigned "for health reasons."

150 With substantial funding from Carnegie Corporation of New York and the Bill & Melinda Gates Foundation.

151 Have children's lives become so structured and over-scheduled that they may now need "recess coaches" to stimulate their imagination and help them relax? For that chilling view,

John Merrow

see "Playtime Is Over," by David Elkind, *The New York Times*, March 27, 2010, A17.

152 He's also an author and president of an education consulting company.

153 See our report that appeared on the NewsHour, "Turning Around St. Louis Schools," August 17, 2004.

154 See *Education Week*, June 23, 2004.

155 Ibid.

156 The Broad Foundation also provided the funds to pay for the Council of the Great City Schools analysis of St. Louis.

157 Education Week, January 12, 2005.

158 Bill Roberti wrote to me in an e-mail on February 19, 2010: "We had two contracts. The first contract was with Orleans Parish School Board and was for total management and oversight; it had a Memorandum of Understanding with the state and I reported to an oversight committee. That was originally $16.7 million and was revised and extended several times. The second contract was post storm with the state to open schools and oversee all the claims and insurance management as well as oversight of construction. That was for $29.1 million."

159 Jeff Archer, "State Vows to Fix Finances in New Orleans," *Education Week*, March 9, 2005, http://www.edweek.org/login. html?soutce=http://www.edweek.org/ew/articles/2005/03/0 9/26orleans.h24.html&destination=http://www.edweek.org/ ew/articles/2005/03/09/26orleans.h24.html&levelId=2100.

160 Featured on the NewsHour, November 1, 2005. See the related podcast, "Rebuilding New Orleans," at www.learningmatters. tv.

161 The Elementary and Secondary Education Act of 1965 (ESEA) and Title I.

162 Lowell Milken's TAP: The System for Teacher and Student Advancement program is a good model to look at. Paul Vallas in New Orleans is one of a number of superintendents endorsing and adopting it. Vallas told me he likes it because it bypasses the "pay for performance" debate by paying some

teachers more for their leadership and other contributions, not their students' academic achievement.

163   How bizarre can things get? How far will educators go to keep control? Try this, from the Associated Press on February 20, 2010: "A suburban Philadelphia school district accused in a lawsuit of secretly switching on laptop computer webcams inside students' homes says one of its administrators has been 'unfairly portrayed and unjustly attacked.' The Lower Merion School District has acknowledged remotely activating webcams 42 times to try to find missing, lost or stolen computers, which would include a loaner computer taken off campus against regulations. One family alleges a school official mistook a piece of candy in a webcam photo for a pill and thought the youth was selling drugs. The district says in a statement Saturday that the official was trying 'to be supportive' and denies that the photo was being used to discipline the student. Officials say the system has now been 'completely disabled.'"

164   Nobody attempts to ban all books and magazines when a teenage boy is caught with Hustler or Penthouse. Why the double standard?

165   Lately, however, I've been told that many school technology directors fear for their jobs, assuming that they will get fired if kids are found on controversial websites. One protection against that is having kids work in teams—teams created by the teacher and not self-selected. The work has to be challenging and reasonably complex, so that the teacher has opportunities to see it develop and improve.

166   Elyse Eidman-Aadahl of the National Writing Project also participated in that Google conference. She cautions about the casual use of the word *technology*: "I am reminded of an old commercial. The announcer comes out on stage to say, 'Bayer is the answer.' Then a voice from the audience asks, 'What's the question?' The differences among various technologies and their uses—the problems they are solutions for—are significant. Are people who are talking about digital delivery

399

of learning objects and associated micro-assessment talking about the same thing as people interested in unleashing the power of, say, Twitter or mobile devices in their classroom, or the people who are interested in whiteboards? Until we can get beyond the glitter of the tools to talk about pedagogy and purpose in equal measure, we will miss much of what we need to see to thoughtfully exploit the learning potential of technology—in schools, after school, or in the family market. We all need to be as critical and reflective about the technology as we are about schooling."

167　It's not hard to find people writing—often enthusiastically—about teachers and students using cell phones in their classrooms for learning purposes. I'm a bit of a skeptic on that one.

168　For more, see "Mandatory Testing and News in the Schools: Implications for Civic Education," a January 2007 report from the Carnegie-Knight Task Force on the Future of Journalism Education at Harvard, issued by the Joan Shorenstein Center on the Press, Politics and Public Policy and funded by the John S. and James L. Knight Foundation and Carnegie Corporation of New York. http://www.knightfoundation.org/dotAsset/221294.pdf.

169　See Debra Viadero, "N.Y.C. Charters Found to Close Gaps," *Education Week*, September 22, 2009, http://www.edweek.org/ew/articles/2009/09/22/05charter.h29.html?tkn=OLYFq33N%2BFjk147jbm6389Vaz1MIIRVGJAba.

170　See analysis by Stanford Professor Sean Reardon in his review of "How New York City's Charter Schools Affect Achievement," (Boulder and Tempe: Education and the Public Interest Center & Education Policy Research Unit, 2009), http://epicpolicy.org/thinktank/review-How-New-York-City-Charter.

171　The thoughtful reformer Deborah Meier sounds a cautionary note about the public purpose of public schools. She wrote in part: "The question is who is accountable for the whole—every last child. That's the purpose of public schools. Alas, the way charters have evolved it no longer seems to me that they accept that commitment, that definition of publicness. They more and more resemble the 'system' they were organized to disrupt—but without the same responsibility. We are not talking about innovative mom&pop stores, but large national companies, licensed by the state to operate with public money and very little public oversight or responsibility.

"Charters could have become more like the 'pilots' in Boston had we moved carefully together without using them for other purposes—such as busting a large public union, lowering the wages of teachers, ending 'governmental' monopolies, dividing the public into competing 'publics' etc. The immediate constituents of the school make fewer and fewer on-site decisions, and are less and less accountable to each other than under the mindless system that I assumed charters were intended to change.

"What next? Fire departments? Police? We've already begun to privatize prisons—maybe we'll call them charter prisons?

"Schools can be the centers of a revived public life—or another symptom of a disintegrating common purpose." She posted this comment on my blog, Taking Note.

172   Are they truly accountable? According to Julie Woestehoff, Parents United for Responsible Education did a study in 2008 of accountability in Chicago's Renaissance 2010 schools, which are predominantly charter schools; see Julie Woestehoff, *Public Accountability and Renaissance 2010* (Parents United for Responsible Education, November 2008), http://pureparents.org/data/files/FOIAreport11-16-08.pdf. She wrote in an e-mail: "Fifty-seven schools or charter networks were sent Freedom of Information Act requests for board minutes, membership lists, and by-laws. Even after follow-up letters from the Illinois Attorney General's Office, more than two-thirds failed to respond to our FOIA requests. We concluded that these schools have no governing bodies, which violates the law and Chicago Public Schools policy. Within the smaller set of 18 responding schools/networks, we found, among other things, that only 7 of the 152 board

members of the responding charter schools are parents, or less than 5%. The by-laws of most of the schools were in violation of the Open Meetings Act. Our research certainly does not support the claim that charter schools are 'more accountable' to the public."

She does not explain why she believes boards are the key. After all, parents who are dissatisfied can vote with their feet, an option that's usually not available in regular public schools.

173 Nancy Haas, "Scholarly Investments," *The New York Times*, December 6, 2009, Sunday Styles section, 11.

174 Nelson Smith of the National Alliance for Public Charter Schools weighed in on that issue, writing in part on my blog: "On the quality issue, there's been a considerable shift toward 'tough love' among the leadership of the charter movement in the past few years, and it's just beginning to show up in numbers. NACSA (the authorizers' group) points to a dramatic drop in the percentage of new approvals between 2003 and 2008—it's getting a lot tougher to get a charter in the first place—as well as a striking increase in closures (either revocation or non-renewal) as well as a shift toward non-renewals for purely academic reasons. In Ohio this year, about 16 charters will shut down as a direct result of legislation that Ohio and national charter leaders asked for in 2006 (and yes, it takes time to compile the record on which to take action). The National Alliance for Public Charter Schools has committed to increase overall quality both by encouraging replication of high-performing models and by working with states and authorizers to get more aggressive in closing low-performers.

"But you can't just wave a magic wand. One of the reasons the National Alliance created a new model state charter law is that in many states, the rules for intervention are opaque—and some authorizers don't take action because they fear they'll get sued. So states have got to hold these authorizers harmless if they do their job right.

I'm no fan of 'mediocre' charters either—but we need to distinguish between malingerers and schools that are struggling through startup, or that are pinched for classroom resources because they're paying 20 percent of income for facilities in a state that provides nothing. The preponderance of charters are in the mid-range of performance, and they need equitable funding and technical support to keep on an upward trajectory. It's a serious mistake to think that only a small group of charters are succeeding."

175 For evidence of school board hostility, see our NewsHour report about San Diego, where the school board battled long and hard—and ultimately unsuccessfully to keep two schools from becoming charter schools. Superintendent Alan Bersin lost his job because he defied his board. (See "End of the Line," August 15, 2007, at www.learningmatters.tv.) Or see the San Jose Mercury News editorial, "Despite School Closing, Alum Rock Provides Good Choices," December 30, 2009, A15, http://www.mercurynews.com/opinion/ci_14088331, about the value of competition between charter schools and traditional ones in the Alum Rock school district. It concludes, "The district should work with charter schools as partners and embrace the changes that are coming." Let's hope!

176 Monty Neill of FairTest took strong exception to this analogy. He wrote on my blog: "The example of a restaurant is terrible. Schools are (still, most of them) public spaces, part of our (endangered) social commons. Restaurants are private. Public schools serve the common good through common ownership and decision making. That is one of its great contributions to society and to democracy, the other being the education of citizens. Both are often not done well. Both, but particularly the latter, become arguments for charters. However, the evidence is that charters are on average worse, based on test scores.

"But the first issue pertains to democracy and the role of common spaces such as schools in maintaining a democracy, and in part to how to exercise that well in face of often problematic school boards, low voter participation, etc. But that discussion is rarely raised, drowned out by proposals to eliminate or greatly curtail the power of school boards, or to the effective replacement by corporations (charters).

"It seems that as schools are increasingly defined in only instrumentalist and economic terms (I just read a truly awful 'vision statement' for MA's schools). The ideas of schooling for democracy heads toward disappearance. The marketization of control over education is the parallel phenomenon leading to the elimination of schooling as democracy. There are those (e.g., Fred Hess) who pretty much equate the market with society and thus marketization with democracy. I find him quite unpersuasive, in part because "free market election day" is about dollars not one person one vote. (Yes, I know money greatly impacts elections.)

"In sum, we need to look at both the educational quality of charters and whether they produce real improvement (they don't, as a whole). Even if they did, that would still not address the question of the privatization of effective control of public space. Even if one is willing to trade better outcomes for loss of democratic control, how much better (by what measures) should they be to give up what sort of democratic control? That is not a way to frame it I would support, since I am not supportive of further erosion to democracy, but framing it that way might lead to further questioning of the role of charters in a nominally democratic society.

"A final note—I agree there are excellent and truly innovative charters. A few pose no harm to democracy and could spur innovation, something that has not been built into the system."

177 He told me that he would actually make more money if he retired!

178 He's also recently recruited Vincent Riccitelli, a professional drummer for Micky Dolenz (of the Monkees) for several years on the road, who Albano says is "very big into music technology, and Fred Motley, the jazz band leader at St. John's

University and pep squad leader at Hofstra University who, according to Albano, "instills in our children the value of the arts, which could possibly be parlayed into scholarships at institutions of higher education."

The arts are part of the recipe, and Lincoln is suffused with them. "Art and music programs are alive and well at Lincoln, and are an integral part of our success story," said Albano. Cultural arts assemblies at Lincoln include McDonald's Corporation African-American history featuring the music of Ray Charles, Aretha Franklin and Ella Fitzgerald (this was donated to the school), music concerts by world-famous classical pianist Katya Grineva at Lincoln School, a trip to Carnegie Hall, and school-wide trips that network with other schools to see, for example, Grineva in a solo performance at Carnegie Hall. Albano has also networked with Broadway producer Pat Addiss to offer Lincoln's students a command performance of the Broadway show "39 Steps," including the opportunity for the children to meet with the cast and talk about performance logistics. These incredible experiences are an integral part of the Lincoln success story.

179 Ms. Bhatnager has since married and moved to Colorado. Her sister Geeta (also a featured performer at Carnegie Hall) was a regular substitute art teacher at Lincoln when she lived in New York City; she is currently project leader and ambassador for the West Coast chapter of Sing for Hope which, according to Nobel Prize-winner Muhammad Yunus, "maintains a roster of compassionate, world-class artists who donate time and talent to the humanitarian causes that inspire them."

180 And matters seem to be deteriorating for Mr. Albano. He wrote in an e-mail in early 2010 about his situation: "After 40 years of serving the children of Mount Vernon, I firmly believe the current administration in Central Office is more concerned with political patronage, vendors, and inundating teachers with ridiculous assessment mandates that strictly prep for state tests. I have resisted the directives from the leadership which has resulted in me receiving a negative

evaluation this year, for the first time in 40 years.... What a shame that locally people resent the Lincoln success story, and in fact the current Superintendent has visited once in three years to read a book to a fifth grade class for five minutes, that was two years below grade level. What a Joke!!!"

181 National Center for Education Statistics, "Participation in Education: Preprimary Education," Indicator 2 (2008): Early Education and Childcare Arrangements, *The Condition of Education 2008,* http://nces.ed.gov/programs/coe/2008/section1/indicator02.asp.

182 I am indebted to John Simmons of Strategic Learning Initiatives in Chicago for these insights. John's book, "Breaking Through: Transforming Urban School Districts," contains additional valuable insights.

183 National Assessment of Educational Progress, 2007.

184 It now has a beautiful, colorful playground for the kids because of the national nonprofit community-building organization KaBOOM! which, according to its website, "envisions a great place to play within walking distance of every child in America." http://kaboom.org/about_kaboom.

185 C. Juel, "Learning to Read and Write: A Longitudinal Study of 54 Children from First through Fourth Grades." *Educational Psychology* 4 (2008): 437-447.
C. Juel, P.L. Griffith, and P.B. Gough, "Acquisition of Literacy: A Longitudinal Study of Children in First and Second Grade," *Journal of Educational Psychology* 78, no. 4 (1986).

186 We documented this in "Early Learning" on PBS. When it aired nationally, the principal was shocked (although many wondered why she hadn't seen it happening during the year). She arranged for her teachers to take summer classes in reading instruction, and she put all the children from the young woman's class into Johnny Brinson's class for the next year— where they learned to read!

187 Across the country in Salinas, Calif., just a block away from John Steinbeck's historic home and minutes from the museum dedicated to his literary life and work, veteran teacher

Sue Quetin uses a variety of creative and innovative methods to get her first-graders at Roosevelt Elementary School excited about reading. Roosevelt is a pre-K-6 school of predominantly English language learners, with about 500 students. It's a school that is struggling to meet the demands of No Child Left Behind, but Roosevelt has seen improvement in test scores. In March 2010, Ms. Quetin said:

"There are a lot of children at my school who don't have access to books and magazines at home. They have access to TV and video games, but not books. They don't see their parents reading, and that's very sad to me—when you don't have that parental example. So, I know I'm going to lose books, but one of the things I do in my first-grade class is put books in my kids' hands and send them home with them. It's one of the best things I can do for my kids. And the kids and I make a big deal out of it when we get a new book in class, or check one out from the library. We 'ooh' and 'ahh' over the books, we smell the books—you know how wonderful it is to open a book and really breathe in the pages—we really experience them. And I tell my students how much I love books. I really want to share with them what I feel about reading.

"You use all sorts of different methods in teaching. You may have a standard textbook for language arts, but you have to find a way to present the material to children so they're truly engaged. We all learn in different ways; there's not just one style that works with all children. Some kids are physical, some are visual, some can hear the language and really get it. But you can't wait until first grade to start reading to kids. Reading is important to every child—they need the experience of having someone read to them, starting from the time they're babies. I think it's the rhymes, the cadence of the voice. Babies don't understand the words, but they're still hearing the language, the lilting of the voice, the melody. Words are beautiful. And I almost think words create even more of a feeling in the little ones.

"We have a tendency to want to do the 'band-aid' approach later on, as kids get older. To try to fix things and put more money and resources into a system that's already so broken. But the earlier, the better, especially when it comes to reading. It's much, much easier to address issues early on, rather than trying to fix things after they're broken. I think we tend to do it backwards; it's such a shame that we tend not to realize the importance of that good, solid beginning."

188　The program has had three names during my time there: "The MacNeil/Lehrer NewsHour," "The NewsHour with Jim Lehrer" and (as of December 2009) "PBS NewsHour." Older viewers still call it "The MacNeil/Lehrer Report," its name when it was only 30 minutes long.

189　Mr. Porter may actually have said, "Turn up the lights," but Mr. Sullivan presented the quote as a paradox, which made it intriguing fun to wrestle with.

190　Many years later I was attacked in a blog by someone, apparently a former student, for not having served in Vietnam. (I was ineligible because of my spinal fusion and major knee surgery.) That blogger asserted that I had introduced the war poetry section by having some students carry me into my classroom in a closed coffin, whereupon I opened the top and sat up, waving an American flag. Now *that* I am sure I would remember doing, if I had done it!

191　I watched Barack Obama take his oath of office in an auditorium with about 425 students, grades 6-12, and their joy and optimism were both palpable and contagious. Hope springs eternal!

192　See "The Real World of Teach For America: The Series" on our website at www.learningmatters.tv.

193　See Steven Farr and Teach For America, *Teaching as Leadership: The Highly Effective Teacher's Guide to Closing the Achievement Gap* (San Francisco: Jossey-Bass, 2010).

194　Amanda Ripley, "What Makes a Great Teacher?" *The Atlantic*, January-February, 2010, http://www.theatlantic.com/magazine/archive/2010/01/what-makes-a-great-teacher/7841/. This is one of those articles that is truly exciting to read, one you wish would never end.

195 Another "must read" about teachers and their training is Elizabeth Green's "Building a Better Teacher," *The New York Times Magazine*, March 7, 2010, 30, http://www.nytimes.com/2010/03/07/magazine/07Teachers-t.html. Green shows how serious, thoughtful on-the-job training can help most teachers do a better job. It's a thoughtful answer to those whose solution is wholesale firing.

196 With few exceptions, TFA's press coverage is largely uncritical. See, for example: Amanda Ripley, "What Makes a Great Teacher?" *The Atlantic*, January-February 2010, http://www.theatlantic.com/doc/201001/good-teaching.

197 At their formal pinning ceremonies, nursing students typically recite the Nightingale Pledge. Different versions of the pledge exist, but this particular rendition has two lines that strike me as also applicable to education: "I will do all in my power to maintain and elevate the standard of my profession…and devote myself to the welfare of those committed to my care." "Nightingale Pledge," http://www.registered-nurse-canada.com/nightingale_pledge.html.

198 In the original version of this essay, which appeared in The Washington Post in 2008, I gave TFA just two cheers. The more I see, the more I see to like.

199 Dennis Van Roekel, interview for the NewsHour, March 5, 2010.

200 According to "Primary Sources," the Scholastic/Gates Foundation survey of teachers, 36 percent of teachers say that paying for performance is not at all important and 25 percent say it is "absolutely essential or very important in retaining good teachers." Scholastic and the Bill & Melinda Gates Foundation, *Primary Sources: America's Teachers on America's Schools* (Scholastic Inc., 2010), 41, http://www.scholastic.com/primarysources/pdfs/100646_ScholasticGates.pdf.

201 Many teacher unions across the country declined to support their state's application to the federal Race to the Top pro-

gram, reportedly because of that program's insistence on tying salaries to student performance. In Florida, for example, only 14 percent of unions signed a memorandum of agreement supporting the application.

202 Randi Weingarten, president of the American Federation of Teachers, has accepted this. She said as much in a January 2009 speech—and that speech will guarantee her a seat at the table as the rules are hammered out.

203 This battle is just being joined and will heat up as reauthorization of ESEA moves ahead. The Education Equality Project is pushing hard for connecting student performance and teacher evaluation. See its strongly worded March 2010 "Open Letter to the President" at http://www.edequality.com/press/archive/open_letter_to_the_president/.

204 Quoted in Elaine McArdle, "Right on the Money," *Ed.Magazine: The Magazine of the Harvard Graduate School of Education*, Winter 2010, 18.

205 See National Council on Teacher Quality, *2009 State Teacher Policy Yearbook: National Summary* (Washington, D.C.: National Council on Teacher Quality, 2009), 174, http://www.nctq.org/stpy09/reports/stpy_national.pdf.

206 According to the NCTQ's *2009 State Teacher Policy Yearbook*, "Figure 70: How Long Before a Teacher Earns Tenure?" 175, http://www.nctq.org/stpy09/.

207 Daniel Weisberg et al., *The Widget Effect: Our National Failure to Acknowledge and Act on Differences in Teacher Effectiveness* (Brooklyn: New Teacher Project, 2009), 4, http://widgeteffect.org/.

208 Ibid. 5.

209 He also thought we'd been discussing "Hamlet"!

210 Scholastic and the Bill & Melinda Gates Foundation, *Primary Sources: America's Teachers on America's Schools* (Scholastic Inc., 2010), http://www.scholastic.com/primarysources/pdfs/100646_ScholasticGates.pdf. While it's not a scientific study, 40,000 teachers did respond to the blind questionnaire, perhaps motivated by the offer of a gift certificate for

completing the survey. The process also included 12 focus groups and follow-up questions.

211 Harris Interactive and MetLife, *The MetLife Survey of the American Teacher: Collaborating for Student Success,* (New York: MetLife, 2009). They may not get to observe each other teaching, but they say they collaborate a lot. "*Nearly all teachers engage in some type of collaborative activity with other educators at their school each week.* On average, teachers spend 2.7 hours per week in structured collaboration with other teachers and school leaders. Elementary school and secondary school teachers spend a similar amount of time each week in collaboration with others at their school, but the ways that they collaborate are different. At the elementary school level, collaboration among teachers is more common within grade level (87% of elementary school teachers vs. 57% of secondary school teachers). At the secondary school level, collaboration among teachers is more common across grade levels, but within subject area (74% of secondary school teachers vs. 59% of elementary school teachers)." The reports for the entire series are now available online at www.metlife.com/teachersurvey.

212 Tragically, Mr. Betts was murdered in his home in Silver Spring, Md., on April 14, 2010, by an unknown assailant or assailants. They stole his car, which was later found in downtown Washington.

213 "Quality Counts" is an annual publication of Editorial Projects in Education and a wonderful source of comprehensive data on a wide range of issues.

214 These numbers are downright scary. A 2006 University of Chicago study noted that only about 54 percent of inner-city ninth-graders eventually graduate, one-fifth of them with a D average. Less than one-fifth of those who start ninth grade go on to a four-year or a two-year college, and only one-third of those earn diplomas. To make that perfectly clear, that means that fewer than seven out of every 100 inner-city ninth-graders get a post-secondary degree. Among African-Americans, not even three out of 100 will make it.

215 The 2009 PDK/Gallup Poll shows that nearly two-thirds of Americans support charters, up from 51 percent last year. An August 2008 poll of Washington, D.C., parents indicated that only 22 percent of parents would willingly choose a regular public school for their children.

216 And Weingarten, now president of the national union (the American Federation of Teachers), said in a December 2009 speech that her union was prepared to accept the use of test scores to evaluate teachers, provided adequate safeguards were in place. For more on Weingarten's views, refer back to Chapter 20, "Evaluating Teachers."

217 If you have ever heard me speak in public, you may have seen the video clip of the young man going through the spelling words for the day, including "strenous." It's beyond disrespectful to the profession to force teachers to go out-of-field, and it's criminal to treat students that way, because they don't get a do-over when they have an unqualified teacher.

218 Richard Ingersoll and David Perda, *How High Is Teacher Turnover and Is It a Problem?* (Philadelphia: Consortium for Policy Research in Education, University of Pennsylvania, 2010).

219 Consortium on Chicago School Research at the University of Chicago Urban Education Institute, "More Than Half of CPS Teachers Leave Their Schools Within Five Years; African-American Schools Hit Hardest," news release, June 29, 2009, http://ccsr.uchicago.edu/news_docs/8898teacher%20mobilityreleasefinal.pdf.

220 For a comprehensive and mostly optimistic view of the future, see Barnett Berry and the Center for Teaching Quality, *The Teachers of 2030: Creating a Student-Centered Profession for the 21st Century* (Center for Teaching Quality, October 2009), http://catalog.proemags.com/publication/1e41a2a8#/1e41a2a8/1.

221 For more about this, see Arthur Levine's report, *Educating School Teachers*, (Washington, D.C.: The Education Schools Project, 2006), www.edschools.org.

222 The National Commission on Teaching and America's Future, "Policy Brief: The High Cost of Teacher Turnover," June 2007, http://nctaf.org.

223 An estimated 1,300 to 1,400 institutions prepare teachers; 632 belong to the National Council for Accreditation of Teacher Education, the membership organization that accredits teacher education programs. Another 100 institutions have applied for membership.

224 NCATE distributes a list of "red flags," including degrees that can be earned in less time than at a traditional college, addresses that are box numbers or suites, and names that are similar to well-known, reputable universities.

225 See http://www.siemens-foundation.org/en/competition.htm.

226 Which remains in force until Congress amends it.

227 See www.jasonproject.org.

228 Kristen Garabedian contributed a significant amount of important new material to this chapter, an earlier version of which appeared in "Choosing Excellence."

229 Not their real names, of course.

230 In the words of Blanche DuBois, from Tennessee Williams' "A Streetcar Named Desire."

231 Excerpts from "Cry of the Hunters" & "The Sound of the Shell," from LORD OF THE FLIES by William Golding, copyright 1954, renewed (c) 1982 by William Gerald Golding. Used by permission of G.P. Putnam's Sons, a division of Penguin Group (USA) Inc.

232 Ibid.

233 If you haven't read "Lord of the Flies" lately, I recommend that you pick up a copy; it's a great book and a good reminder of what, metaphorically, many kids are going through every day on their own "islands" across the country.

234 Jean Sunde Peterson and Karen Ray, "Bullying and the Gifted: Victims, Perpetrators, Prevalence, and Effects," *Gifted Child Quarterly* 50, no. 2 (2006), http://www.nagc.org/uploadedFiles/GCQ/GCQ_Articles/Bullying%20-%20Spring%202006.pdf.

John Merrow

Also see http://www.consumeraffairs.com/news04/2006/04/bullies.html.

235 Rana Sampson, "Bullying in Schools," *Problem-Oriented Guides for Police, Problem-Specific Guide Series, No. 12*, (Washington, D.C.: Center for Problem-Oriented Policing, Office of Community-Oriented Policing Services, U.S. Department of Justice, 2009), 4, http://www.cops.usdoj.gov/files/RIC/Publications/e07063414-guide.pdf.

236 Jean Sunde Peterson and Karen Ray, "Bullying and the Gifted: Victims, Perpetrators, Prevalence, and Effects," Abstract, *Gifted Child Quarterly* 50, no. 2 (2006), http://gcq.sagepub.com/cgi/content/abstract/50/2/148.

237 Thomas Tarshis and Lynne Huffman, "Psychometric Properties of the Peer Interactions in Primary School (PIPS) Questionnaire," *Journal of Developmental & Behavioral Pediatrics* 28, no. 2 (2007): 125-132, http://journals.lww.com/jrnldbp/Abstract/2007/04000/Psychometric_Properties_of_the_Peer_Interactions.8.aspx.

238 U.S. Department of Education, "Lead & Manage My School: Exploring the Nature and Prevention of Bullying," ED.gov, http://www2.ed.gov/admins/lead/safety/training/bullying/bullying_pg14.html.

239 Susan Limber and Maury Nation, "Bullying Among Children and Youth," *Juvenile Justice Bulletin* (Office of Juvenile Justice and Delinquency Prevention, April 1998), http://ojjdp.ncjrs.gov/jjbulletin/9804/contents.html. Also, page 9 of the U.S. Department of Justice's "Bullying in Schools" discusses the vicious cycle and intergenerational aspects of this issue:
"The belief that bullies 'are insecure, deep down' is probably incorrect. Bullies do not appear to have much empathy for their victims. Young bullies tend to remain bullies, without appropriate intervention. 'Adolescent bullies tend to become adult bullies, and then tend to have children who are bullies.' In one study in which researchers followed bullies as they grew up, they found that youth who were bullies at 14 tended to have children who were bullies at 32, suggesting an intergenerational link. They also found that '[b]ullies have some

similarities with other types of offenders. Bullies tend to be drawn disproportionately from lower socioeconomic-status families with poor child-rearing techniques, tend to be impulsive, and tend to be unsuccessful in school.' In Australia, research shows that bullies have low empathy levels, are generally uncooperative, and, based on self-reports, come from dysfunctional families low on love. Their parents tend to frequently criticize them and strictly control them. Dutch (and other) researchers have found a correlation between harsh physical punishments such as beatings, strict disciplinarian parents and bullying. In U.S. studies, researchers have found higher bullying rates among boys whose parents use physical punishment or violence against them."

240 Jean Decety et al., "Atypical Empathic Responses in Adolescents with Aggressive Conduct Disorder: A Functional MRI Investigation," *Biological Psychology* 80, no. 2 (2009): 203-211.

241 John Roach, "Bullies' Brains Light Up with Pleasure as People Squirm," *National Geographic News*, November 7, 2008, http://news.nationalgeographic.com/news/2008/11/081107-bully-brain.html.

242 This is more than a polemic against irresponsible leadership. It's also an argument in favor of school choice.

243 Susan Donaldson James, "Immigrant Teen Taunted by Cyberbullies Hangs Herself," ABC News, January 26, 2010, http://abcnews.go.com/Health/cyber-bullying-factor-suicide-massachusetts-teen-irish-immigrant/story?id=9660938.

244 Melissa Newton, "Police: Texas 9-year-old Boy Hanged Self at School," CBS News, January 22, 2010, http://cbs4denver.com/national/Boy.Hanged.Self.2.1442854.html.

245 Transcript of Interview with Leticia and Chris Montelongo, "Bullying a National Problem?" *Anderson Cooper 360 Degrees*, CNN, interview aired April 1, 2010, http://transcripts.cnn.com/TRANSCRIPTS/1004/01/acd.01.html.

246 Rick Hampson, "A 'Watershed' Case in School Bullying?" *USA Today*, April 5, 2010, http://www.usatoday.com.

247 Phoebe Prince's mother also reportedly complained to school staff that her daughter was being bullied.

248 Mike Plaisance and Patrick Johnson, Michael Brault, "Mom Says Springfield Boy, 11, Who Committed Suicide Was Repeatedly Bullied at School," *The Republican*, April 9, 2009, www.masslive.com/news/index.ssf/2009/04/mom_says_springfield_boy_11_wh.html.

249 Kate Nocera and Helen Kennedy, "Mom of Boy Who Killed Himself Near Where Suicide Teen Phoebe Prince Lived Blames the Schools," *Daily News*, March 31, 2010, www.nydailynews.com.

250 Harris Interactive and GLSEN, *From Teasing to Torment: School Climate in America, A Survey of Students and Teachers* (New York: GLSEN, 2005).

251 Rana Sampson, "Bullying in Schools," *Problem-Oriented Guides for Police, Problem-Specific Guide Series, No. 12,* (Washington, D.C.: Center for Problem-Oriented Policing, Office of Community-Oriented Policing Services, U.S. Department of Justice, 2009), 14, http://www.cops.usdoj.gov/files/RIC/Publications/e07063414-guide.pdf.

252 Here's a suggestion: Teach the First Amendment! "Congress shall make no law respecting an establishment of religion, or prohibiting the free exercise thereof; or abridging the freedom of speech, or of the press; or the right of the people peaceably to assemble, and to petition the Government for a redress of grievances." This is, arguably, the most important sentence in any of our essential documents and in our lives. For more on this, see Sam Chaltain's book, "American Schools: The Art of Creating a Democratic Learning Community."

253 Although it is highly unlikely that schools will become primary targets of terrorist attacks, every school should have a contingency plan in the event that another surprise attack brings normal routines to a temporary halt. One school I'm familiar with has stocked food, water, blankets and first-aid equipment in sufficient quantity to keep students on campus

for three days, just in case. Its routine includes two major disaster drills. One empties the school to a certain place for a head count; the other requires everyone to remain indoors, with doors locked and shades down.

Is this overreacting? Unfortunately not. We are at war with a new enemy, and we need to be prepared. But precautions alone could make matters worse. The first essential step is to create an environment that is physically, emotionally and intellectually safe, to be supportive and forthcoming in discussions with students, both now and in the future. It's a tall order. I am hopeful that our schools are up to the task.

254   Rana Sampson, "Bullying in Schools," *Problem-Oriented Guides for Police, Problem-Specific Guide Series, No. 12,* (Washington, D.C.: Center for Problem-Oriented Policing, Office of Community-Oriented Policing Services, U.S. Department of Justice, 2009), 11, http://www.cops.usdoj.gov/files/RIC/Publications/e07063414-guide.pdf.

255   Bulleted information from the National Crime Prevention Council, "What Is Cyberbullying?" Circle of Respect, http://www.ncpc.org/programs/circle-of-respect/understanding-bullying-and-cyberbullying/cyberbullying/what-is-cyberbullying/?searchterm=bully.

256   Emily Bazelon, "Could Anyone Have Saved Phoebe Prince? She Was Tormented by Bullies at School and Online. Here's What We Can Learn from Her Suicide." *Slate,* February 8, 2010, http://www.slate.com/id/2244057/pagenum/all.

257   Rick Hampson, "A 'Watershed' Case in School Bullying?" *USA Today,* April 5, 2010, http://www.usatoday.com.

258   Most schools segregate students by age (and sometimes by sex or by academic performance). Schools "pay" in letter grades and are set up for mass production, not for individual attention. When technology is used imaginatively, students experience the thrill of discovery and the joy that comes with accomplishment—the kind of "pay" adults hope to get in their work. And the students probably receive high grades as a by-product, a bonus.

259 "Hi, Mom" is the bane of our existence, because it immediately destroys the illusion that we are trying to create—that we're not there!

260 Everything is digital today, but we'd still run out of time and patience.

261 Michael Josephson, "Cheating Isn't the Problem 657.2," Commentary by Michael Josephson, February 8, 2010, http://character counts.org/michael/2010/02/cheating_isnt_the_problem. html.

262 Knight Commission on the Information Needs of Communities in a Democracy, *Informing Communities: Sustaining Democracy in the Digital Age*, (Washington, D.C.: The Aspen Institute, October 2009), www.knightfoundation.org/dotAsset/355770. pdf.

263 The Kaiser Family Foundation reported in January 2010 that children 8-18 spend more than seven-and-a-half hours a day using a smart phone, computer, television or some other electronic device, compared to less than six-and-a-half hours five years ago. 76 percent own an MP3 player, and 66 percent own a cell phone. Only 29 percent have a laptop.

264 You may be thinking of computers, but hand-held devices, including cell phones, seem to be the wave of the future. See Victoria Rideout, Ulla Foehr, and Donald Roberts, *Generation M2: Media in the Lives of 8- to 18-Year-Olds* (The Henry J. Kaiser Family Foundation, January 2010), 11, http://www.kff.org/ entmedia/upload/8010.pdf.

265 Hillary Kolos, a former colleague at Learning Matters who is now at MIT's New Media Literacies Project sharpens the point: "I've seen way too many classrooms with broken computers lining the walls or software so old or slow that students might as well do their work with pencil and paper. On the other hand, even when there is up-to-date hardware and software, teachers aren't sure where to start with it or it's so restricted that students are shut off from incredible resources that will help them develop the 21st-century learning skills they need to succeed in the future."

266 A professor from Connecticut suggests that technology is not used all that effectively in most schools. John Bennett noted that open-ended inquiry would be enhanced by open access to technology in gifted and talented classrooms, but said that's not happening widely either. He wrote in part, "If school activities that promoted creativity and motivation were made so much richer with technology, more effective learning [and improved mastery test scores by the way] would happen as a matter of course."

267 I am leery of my own generalization here, because many schools are leading the way. Consider San Francisco's City Arts and Technology High School, known as CAT, a charter school with 350 students in a blue-collar part of the city. Technology is a big part of the curriculum, but so are project learning and teachers who say, "We keep track of each kid. We don't just let kids fail." Technology is an enabler, something I would call necessary but certainly not sufficient.

268 I am happy to include a dissenting note from John Lavine, the dean of the Medill School of Journalism at Northwestern (and my high school classmate). John writes: "I don't know anything about schools who don't want their students to use computers or who act in the ways you describe. I know they exist, but from the inner city to the universities I regularly deal with, they are the exception. Whether it is faculty who are our age or those who are just starting out, the ones who care would not cripple their students like that."

269 And our youth producers at Listen Up! received broadcasting's highest honor, the George Foster Peabody Award, in 2007 for "Beyond Borders."

270 Brookes Publishing, "Simply 'Talking' Can Ensure No Child Is Left Behind," news release, October 8, 2002, describing Betty Hart and Todd R. Risley, *Meaningful Differences in the Everyday Experience of Young American Children*, (Baltimore: Brookes Publishing, 1995).

271 U.S. Department of Education, National Center for Education Statistics, "Fast Facts," citing source material from *The*

John Merrow

Condition of Education 2007 (NCES 2007–064), Indicator 2: Percentage of Prekindergarten Children Ages 3–5 Who Were Enrolled in Center-based Early Childhood Care and Education Programs, by Child and Family Characteristics: Selected Years, 1991–2005, http://nces.ed.gov/fastfacts/display.asp?id=78.

272 You can find it on our website, www.learningmatters.tv.

273 I first met Mr. Harris in the late '70s in Chicago when I interviewed him for my weekly "Options in Education" program for NPR.

274 See Jennifer Sloan McCombs, Sheila Nataraj Kirby, and Louis Mariano, ed., *Ending Social Promotion Without Leaving Children Behind: The Case of New York City* (Santa Monica: Rand Corporation, 2009), http://www.rand.org/pubs/monographs/MG894/.

275 Jennifer Medina, "Students Held Back Did Better," *The New York Times*, October 15, 2009, http://www.nytimes.com/2009/10/16/education/16promotion.html?_r=1.

276 Flunking first-graders! What insanity! Could there possibly be a stronger argument for grouping the first-, second- and third-graders together? Then the adults in charge could at least work together to see that they all reached the "end of third grade" standard. Of course, we'd have to agree on the goals, and we seem to be moving in that direction.

277 John I. Goodlad, *Romances with Schools: A Life of Education* (McGraw-Hill, 2004).

278 Booker T. Washington Accelerated Academy basically eliminated age segregation because it had no other option. Its students are as many as six years below grade level—picture a 16-year-old who reads and computes at a fifth-grade level. What's to be gained by telling that youth that he's a sixth-grader? Instead, the educators tell the students that they have to reach a certain standard (the ninth-grade level), and then they can move on to high school. It's just common sense. No, actually, it's *uncommon* sense. Would that it were common sense!

279 The proposed national or common standards were released in March 2010 for comment and (probable) revision. However, Kentucky immediately adopted them. Two states, Texas and Alaska, have declined to consider adopting them, but everyone else is moving forward. If the standards are challenging and relevant, we could be in for interesting times.

280 The New York Times published a thoughtful op-ed, "Playing to Learn," by Susan Engel of Williams College on February 2, 2010, page A27, arguing that our current educational approach and the testing driving it are at odds with how children learn and develop during the elementary school years. You'll find it at http://www.nytimes.com/2010/02/02/opinion/02engel.html.

281 Many people—count me in—are concerned that Americans don't understand or value the First Amendment. Virginia's State Board of Education banned "The Diary of Anne Frank" based on one parent's complaint, and it took about a year for reason to prevail. The Knight Foundation is addressing our First Amendment "knowledge deficit"—see http://www.teachfirstamendment.org/.

282 Americans don't hold a monopoly on such views. The distinguished South African educator John Samuel told a Rhodes University audience that "Schools are not social institutions existing in splendid isolation—the walls of schools are not impervious, and the world outside looms large on a daily basis....Democratic societies are meant to shape, strengthen and support the development of democratic education and public schools are the critical vehicle to realising this vision. And as part of this dynamic interplay, democratic schools then become the arena in which the democratic education agenda is given shape and content."

283 Legal scholar Thomas Ehrlich, former president of Indiana University and co-creator of the American Democracy Project, said, "In the first half of the 20th century, many high school civics classes were models of activist education." Then academicians took over and it became a "science," he added,

his tone indicating that he really meant "pseudo-science." Ehrlich believes that a huge reservoir of youthful idealism and energy is just waiting to be tapped. He's writing a book, "What You Can Do for Your Country," in which he points out that Stanford freshmen in the 1920s and 1930s took a year-long required course called "Problems of Citizenship," because university founders Jane and Leland Stanford considered education for civic leadership to be a primary goal of undergraduate education. Faculty members representing 10 departments gave weekly lectures, and students also met three times a week in small groups with an instructor.

"Citizenship is the second calling of every man and woman," said Professor Edgar Eugene Robinson in the 1928 opening lecture, adding that 60 other colleges and universities had already developed courses like Stanford's and more were sure to follow.

So what happened? Why did education for civic leadership and citizenship disappear from the curriculum? "In the immediate post-World War II years, disinterested, disengaged analysis became the dominant mode of academic inquiry, and quantitative methods became the primary tools of that analysis," Ehrlich writes. "What was previously called government or politics became Political Science, with a stress on positivism. Students were no longer encouraged to become politically engaged. They were to be *observers*, not participants.... Learning *about* government was substituted for participating *in* it."

284 Charles Glenn, "The Teachers' Muddle," *The Wilson Quarterly* 23, no. 4 (1999): 52-59, http://public.clunet.edu/~mccamb/glenn.htm.

285 U.S. Department of Education, National Center for Education Statistics, National Assessment of Educational Progress (NAEP), 2001 and 2006 U.S. History Assessments, "Table 126: Percentage of Students Attaining U.S. History Achievement Levels, by Grade Level and Selected Student Characteristics: 2001 and 2006," *Digest of Education Statistics*, table prepared

May 2007, http://nces.ed.gov/programs/digest/d08/tables/dt08_126.asp.

286 Aaron Smith, "Civic Engagement Online: Politics as Usual," Pew Internet & American Life Project, September 1, 2009, http://pewresearch.org/pubs/1328/online-political-civic-engagement-activity.

287 The American Democracy Project, a collaboration between AASCU and The New York Times, is, according to its website, a "multi-campus initiative to create intellectual and experiential understandings of civic engagement for undergraduates enrolled at institutions that are members of the American Association of State Colleges and Universities." To learn more, see http://www.aascu.org/programs/adp/about.htm.

288 An earlier version of this piece appeared in USA Today on February 4, 2003.

289 For additional information see Catherine Rampell's "Want a Higher G.P.A.? Go to a Private College," *The New York Times*, April 18, 2010, Education Life section, 8, and http://education-portal.com/articles/Grade_Inflation_at_US_Colleges_and_Universities.html.

290 Alex McCormick is NSSE's current director.

291 Lisa Foderaro, "Type-A-Plus Students Chafe at Grade Deflation," *The New York Times*, January 31, 2010, 30, http://www.nytimes.com/2010/01/31/education/31princeton.html.

292 Kevin Carey, "How I Aced College—And Why I Now Regret It," Education Sector, January 31, 2010, http://www.educationsector.org/analysis/analysis_show.htm?doc_id=1154846.

293 Portions of this chapter appeared in The New York Times, "Survival of the Fittest," April 24, 2005.

294 They may have arrived on campus hoping for something different, however. George Kuh observed that most students start with high expectations that are rarely met. "They expect to read more, write more, spend more time with faculty and study more," he said. "They expect to be writing three, four or five papers, but students, particularly at large institutions,

can get through their first year of college without ever having written a paper at all."

295 That turns out to be a gross exaggeration, but we saw the billboards alongside highways in Kentucky, for example. Mark Schneider of the American Institutes for Research calls this "a million dollar misunderstanding." He calculates that the real difference in lifetime earning between a college graduate and someone with only a high school diploma is about $280,000. Sandy Baum, a retired economics professor, says the difference in earnings is more like $450,000. Both are a far cry from a million bucks! For more information, see Mary Pilon, "What's a Degree Really Worth?" *The Wall Street Journal*, February 2, 2010, D6, http://online.wsj.com/article/SB20001 4240527487038224045750190828199966538.html.

296 This was confirmed in 2010 with the release of "Squeeze Play 2010: Continued Public Anxiety on Cost, Harsher Judgments on How Colleges Are Run," a report by Public Agenda and the National Center on Public Policy and Higher Education, http://www.highereducation.org/reports/reports_center.shtml.

297 Perhaps that's why the graduation rate is so low. Much of American higher education has trouble holding onto students. The year we did our documentary, SUNY Buffalo and the University of Kentucky lost 22 percent of their freshmen. In the same year, Eastern Michigan University lost 28 percent, and three University of Massachusetts campuses lost at least 24 percent of their freshmen. After six years, only 57 percent of the Arizona freshman class had earned degrees.

298 See Chapter 34, "If This Is Boozeday, This Must Be College."

299 In 2009, the Arizona legislature approved a fiscal year budget that reduced by $50 million the amount given to the Arizona system from the state's general fund. Under the regents' distribution plan, the university had to cut its budget by $19.6 million. The rest of the money comes primarily from tuition, donations and research grants.

300 My colleagues and I joked about creating a video reel for insomniacs: images of sleeping students with droning profes-

sors as a voiceover. Our advertising motto would be, "Safer than Ambien, more effective than Melatonin!"

301   At a national policy level, it's easy to conjure up a three-step scenario in which:

1.   A higher education commission issues a blue-ribbon report recommending improved graduation rates and other external measures of "quality."

2.   Congress and state legislatures pass laws requiring improvement.

3.   Graduation rates go up almost immediately. Victory is declared.

    Should that happen, I promise you it won't be long before another pesky documentary filmmaker (maybe even us!) demonstrates that the government-mandated improvements are illusory.

302   Pat Callan of the National Center for Public Policy and Higher Education told me that colleges have responded to the financial crisis by raising tuition and fees, increasing enrollment, building more classrooms and increasing some class sizes, cutting expensive programs, seeking more grants and contracts, stepping up fundraising and hiring more adjuncts to cut labor costs. What they could do but haven't so far, he told me, is ask faculty to teach more classes, increase and improve distance learning, and adjust the course schedules so that more classes are available at night and on weekends.

303   But it wasn't all bad. It was gratifying to see how young people responded to serious questions about college and its purposes. I came away feeling that most were fully capable of habits of inquiry that they should have developed earlier in their schooling. I salute those college professors and instructors who labor to reverse the poor study habits and low expectations of so many students, even though their efforts are often neither appreciated by students nor rewarded by their institutions. And I was heartened by those who believe so truly that education has the power transform their lives—like the first-generation American I met who, denied the opportunity

to attend a four-year university, determined to do so well in community college that the university that had spurned her would ask her to transfer. I think of the All-American basketball player who refused to isolate himself in the cocoon his coaches offered, and instead became part of the larger campus. I won't easily forget the 29-year-old woman, a mother at 14 and a high school dropout, who now feels she has a free pass to learn anything and everything. She and the people at her community college who opened those doors for her—and held them open when she stumbled—are the heart and soul of the enterprise.

304 Kristen Garabedian contributed a significant amount of new material to this essay, part of which originally appeared in "Survival of the Fittest," *The New York Times*, April 24, 2005.

305 Toxicology reports were pending as I was writing this, but it appears that this young man, a recent transfer to KSU who had just rushed Delta Tau Delta fraternity, may have died as a result of binge drinking. See Marcus Garner, "KSU Student Dies After Passing Out at Party," *The Atlanta-Journal Constitution*, February 2, 2010, http://www.ajc.com/news/cobb/ksu-student-dies-after-289516.html.

306 My colleague David Wald spent a lot of time with Robin and his friends, including one late-night binge that ended with Robin nearly getting into a fight outside a bar at about 2 a.m. David watched and videotaped but did not participate; nor did he pay for any of the liquor.

307 Like most large research universities, the University of Arizona is a virtual city: 38,000 students and more than 14,500 employees on a sprawling campus. The home of the Wildcats has 185 buildings and over 18,000 parking spaces. And also like most of the country's colleges and universities, it is not particularly selective. The university admits the majority of students who apply.

308 American Medical Association, "Facts About Youth and Alcohol," Alcohol and Other Drug Use, AMA website, http://www.ama-assn.org/ama/pub/physician-resources/public-health/

promoting-healthy-lifestyles/alcohol-other-drug-abuse/facts-about-youth-alcohol.shtml.

309 U.S. Department of Health and Human Services, Substance Abuse and Mental Health Services Administration, Office of Applied Studies, "Results from the 2008 National Survey on Drug Use and Health: National Findings, SAMHSA website, http://www.oas.samhsa.gov/NSDUH/2k8NSDUH/2k8results.cfm#3.1.

310 Department of Health and Human Services, *The Surgeon General's Call to Action to Prevent and Reduce Underage Drinking* (Washington, D.C.: U.S. Department of Health and Human Services, Office of the Surgeon General, 2007), http://www.surgeongeneral.gov/topics/underagedrinking/calltoaction.pdf.

311 American Medical Association, "Facts About Youth and Alcohol," Alcohol and Other Drug Use, AMA website, http://www.ama-assn.org/ama/pub/physician-resources/public-health/promoting-healthy-lifestyles/alcohol-other-drug-abuse/facts-about-youth-alcohol.shtml.

312 Department of Health and Human Services, *The Surgeon General's Call to Action to Prevent and Reduce Underage Drinking* (Washington, D.C.: U.S. Department of Health and Human Services, Office of the Surgeon General, 2007), http://www.surgeongeneral.gov/topics/underagedrinking/calltoaction.pdf.

313 R. Ballie, "Teen Drinking More Dangerous Than Previously Thought," In Brief, *Monitor on Psychology* 32, no. 6 (2001), http://www.apa.org/monitor/jun01/teendrink.aspx.

314 "A Letter from Michael's Father," MichaelStarks.org, http://www.michaelstarks.org/index.html.

315 The Gordie Foundation, "Gordie's Story," www.thegordiefoundation.org.

316 David Jernigan et al. (Courtesy of CAMY), "Sex Differences in Adolescent Exposure to Alcohol Advertising in Magazines," Archives of *Pediatric & Adolescent Medicine*, July 2004, http://archpedi.ama-assn.org/cgi/reprint/158/7/629.pdf and Amer-

ican Medical Association, "Alcopops and Girls: Fact Sheet," http://www.alcoholpolicymd.com/pdf/alcopops_factsheet-4. pdf.

317 The SAM Spady Foundation, http://www.samspadyfoundation. org/.

318 Sabrina Rubin, "Binge Drinking on Campus: The Hidden Epidemic of Social Drinking at Campuses Across the Country," *Reader's Digest,* November 1998, http://www.rd.com/living-healthy/binge-drinking-on-campus/article15309.html.

319 National Institute on Alcohol Abuse and Alcoholism, College Drinking: Changing the Culture, http://www.collegedrinking prevention.gov and Stop Underage Drinking: Portal of Federal Resources, http://www.stopalcoholabuse.gov.

320 Scott Jaschik, "College Drinking: Reframing a Social Problem," *Inside Higher Ed,* February 26, 2009, http://www.insidehighered. com/news/2009/02/26/drinking.

321 U.S. Department of Health and Human Services, Substance Abuse and Mental Health Services Administration, Office of Applied Studies, "Results from the 2008 National Survey on Drug Use and Health: National Findings," http://www.oas. samhsa.gov/nsduh/2k8nsduh/2k8Results.cfm#3.1.

322 National Institute on Drug Abuse, "Monitoring the Future Survey, 2009," http://www.nida.nih.gov/newsroom/09/MTF09 overview.html.

323 Stop Underage Drinking: Portal of Federal Resources, http:// www.stopalcoholabuse.gov/.

324 Mr. Bhalla graduated after four-and-a-half years and moved to Miami, where he went to work for a pharmaceutical sales company. That last statement—about partying hard now so he won't have regrets later—never fails to shock adults who have children. It strikes many as the epitome of upside-down values.

325 Jon Shirek, "Binge Drinking Possible Cause of Kennesaw State Student's Death," 11Alive.com, http://www.11alive.com/ rss/rss_story.aspx?storyid=140443.

326 Portions of this chapter appeared in Change, November-December 2007, and in "Dream Catchers," *The New York Times,* April 22, 2007.

327 Mark Hugo Lopez, "Latinos and Education: Explaining the Attainment Gap," Pew Hispanic Center, October 7, 2009, http://pewhispanic.org/reports/report.php?ReportID=115.

328 Joanne Spetz, *Forecasts of the Registered Nurse Workforce in California,* Conducted for the California Board of Registered Nursing, September 29, 2009, http://www.rn.ca.gov/pdfs/forms/forecasts2009.pdf.

329 Gary Stern, "Why Do So Many Students Overlook Advice on Obtaining Merit Aid?" *The Hispanic Outlook in Higher Education,* January 26, 2009, http://findarticles.com/p/articles/mi_hb3184/is_200901/ai_n32204293/.

330 Until the stress became too great, and she dropped out without earning a diploma.

331 According to Edie Irons, communications director for the Project on Student Debt, the national debt averages for graduating seniors in 2008 who borrowed are: $20,200 for public colleges, $27,650 for private nonprofits, and $33,050 for for-profit schools. Jacques Steinberg, "Putting That $23,200 Average Student Debt Figure in Context," The Choice: Demystifying College Admissions and Aid, *The New York Times,* December 3, 2009, http://thechoice.blogs.nytimes.com/2009/12/03/debt-context/.

332 To see this for yourself, watch "Declining by Degrees."

333 An earlier version of this essay appeared in The New York Times, January 18, 2004.

334 www.kelseyjillettte.com

335 This time a diverse group is developing the standards. Last time each interest group created a wish list. With nothing holding the music folks back, for example, they set these nine goals for all students:

1. Singing, alone and with others, a varied repertoire of music.

2. Performing on instruments, alone and with others, a varied repertoire of music.

3. Improvising melodies, variations and accompaniments.

4. Composing and arranging music within specified guidelines.

5. Reading and notating music.

6. Listening to, analyzing and describing music.

7. Evaluating music and music performances.

8. Understanding relationships between music, the other arts and disciplines outside the arts.

9. Understanding music in relation to history and culture.

That's enough to fill out the entire day and school year, with no room for English, etc. Not to be outdone, the arts people set 90 goals for dance, visual arts, theatre and music! The National Association of Music Education, "National Standards for Music Education," http://www.menc.org/resources/view/national-standards-for-music-education.

336 Reliable tests can be trusted to come out the same way again and again. This matters in medicine, for example, where there's heightened awareness of what are called *false positives.* A test for HIV that regularly produced false positive results (i.e., it reported that you were HIV-positive when you weren't) would be denounced and abandoned. However, according to David Rogosa of Stanford University, the widely used SAT-9 standardized test of reading can report negative growth 25 percent of the time. That is, a student who has actually improved her reading from the 50th to the 60th percentile has a one-in-four chance of producing a test result showing a loss of reading ability. What high-stakes decision should be made based on that unreliable test?

337 Tony Wagner's book, "The Global Achievement Gap," (Basic Books, 2008) makes a strong contribution to this debate. He writes persuasively about a new set of seven "survival skills" that he believes our children must have.

338　At this writing, some Democrats in the House were calling it the "All Students Achieving through Reform Act," or ASARA. Easier to say than NCLB for starters. Stay tuned…

339　Barnett Berry and the Center for Teaching Quality, *The Teachers of 2030: Creating a Student-Centered Profession for the 21st Century,* (Center for Teaching Quality, October 2009), http://catalog.proemags.com/publication/1e41a2a8#/1e41a2a8/1.

340　*Endorsing* standards is a lot easier than actually *creating* them. That task involves two types of standards: *content* standards and *performance* standards. Some person or group must decide on content: what, for example, 11th-graders should master in English. Let's say the group agrees that 11th-graders must be able to present a complex argument persuasively and must be familiar with drama, poetry and fiction. Let's go further and say that they also agree that 11th-graders should read and be able to understand a Shakespearean play. Assuming they've gotten that far (and that's a big assumption, considering the cultural climate we live in), that's only halfway home. Now it's time to decide what levels of performance are "satisfactory," "outstanding" and "unsatisfactory." How much of that play does the 11th-grader have to grasp to meet the new standard, and what measures of her knowledge will we trust? These questions are neither trivial nor easy to answer.

We now enter the somewhat arbitrary process of standard setting. Just what performance standards are established depends on who is asked. Each expert will have an idea of what is acceptable, outstanding and insufficient. Are these ideas to be given arbitrary numerical weights and then averaged? Once a number is (somehow) reached, that number takes on magical qualities—it is what a student must achieve to pass, or to be promoted to the next grade or to graduate.

341　Donald T. Campbell, *Assessing the Impact of Planned Social Change* (Hanover, N.H.: The Public Affairs Center at Dartmouth College, 1976), http://www.wmich.edu/evalctr/pubs/ops/ops08.pdf.

342   This is going to happen! At least eight states are introducing a program to allow 10th-graders to test out of high school early. The program is being organized by the National Center on Education and the Economy and is supported by the Bill & Melinda Gates Foundation. For information, see <u>www.ncee.org</u>.

INDEX

John Merrow

John Merrow

CPSIA information can be obtained at www.ICGtesting.com
Printed in the USA
LVOW082103280612

288098LV00018B/61/P

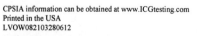

9 781450 503532